CW00545738

WHERE TRUTH ABIDES

WHERE TRUTH ABIDES

EXTRACTS FROM THE DIARIES OF
HENRY PELHAM FIENNES PELHAM-CLINTON
4th DUKE OF NEWCASTLE-UNDER-LYME

Edited by
John Fletcher

With best wishes
John Fletcher
September 2004

Published by:
Country Books
Courtyard Cottage, Little Longstone, Bakewell, Derbyshire DE45 1NN
on behalf of:
The National Trust
Clumber Park, Worksop, Nottinghamshire S80 3AZ

Printed and bound in Great Britain by
Antony Rowe Ltd., Chippenham, Wiltshire

ISBN 1 898941 57 2

© 2001 John Fletcher

The rights of John Fletcher as author of this work have been asserted by him in
accordance with the Copyright, Designs and Patents Act, 1993.

All rights reserved. No part of this publication may be reproduced,
stored in a retrieval system, or transmitted in any form or by any means,
electronic, mechanical, photocopying, recording or otherwise,
without the prior permission of the author and publisher.

British Library in Cataloguing in Publication Data:
a catalogue record for this book is available from the British Library.

Fig. 1 [title page]:
4th Duke of Newcastle

The 4th Duke of Newcastle-under-Lyme wrote his diaries during the period
1822 to 1850.

Primarily, the Selection of Extracts included here were chosen
to better understand the development and maintenance of his country seat
at Clumber Park, Nottinghamshire.

Of the ten 'Dukes of Newcastle-under-Lyme', the 4th Duke had
(after the work of his grandfather in forming the ducal estate)
the most influence in introducing new features
and reshaping the original design.

The fascination of the Diary entries led to a much wider Selection of topics
than had originally been intended.

CONTENTS

THE 'DUKERIES' AREA OF NORTH NOTTINGHAMSHIRE

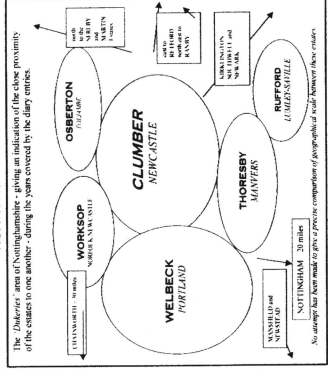

The *Dukeries'* area of Nottinghamshire - giving an indication of the close proximity of the estates to one another - during the years covered by the diary entries.

OSBERTON
FOLJAMBE

CLUMBER
NEWCASTLE

WORKSOP
NORFOLK-NEWCASTLE

WELBECK
PORTLAND

THORESBY
MANVERS

RUFFORD
LUMLEY-SAVILLE

north to the WERE BY and MARTIN Diaries.

east to RETFORD north east to RAMPY

KIRKLINGTON SOUTHWELL and NEWARK

CHATSWORTH - 40 miles

NOTTINGHAM   20 miles

MANSFIELD and NEWSTEAD

No attempt has been made to give a precise comparison of geographical scale between these estates.

A *broad guide to family names/titles used in these 'extracts'.*

Clumber: Newcastle/Lincoln/Clinton/Pelham.
Osberton: Foljambe/Milton.
Rufford: Lumley/Saville/Scarbrough.
Thoresby: Manvers/Newark.
Welbeck: Portland/Bentinck.
Worksop: Norfolk/Surrey.

NOTTINGHAMSHIRE

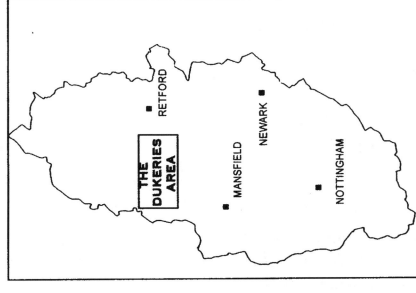

RETFORD

THE DUKERIES AREA

MANSFIELD

NEWARK

NOTTINGHAM

The 'Dukeries' description originally referred to the late-18th century area of the county owned by the Dukes of Kingston (*Thoresby*), Newcastle (*Clumber*), Norfolk (*Worksop*) and Portland (*Welbeck*).

6

INTRODUCTION

Henry Pelham Fiennes Pelham-Clinton, 4th Duke of Newcastle, wrote his 'Journals', in eight bound volumes, during the period May 1822 to May 1850. These documents are now in the custody of the Keeper of Manuscripts and Special Collections, at the Hallward Library, University of Nottingham. Their content is voluminous and these Extracts (estimated at less than one fifth of the whole) are limited, in the main, to those relating to the family and the development of the Clumber Estate – also to those Newcastle properties (such as Worksop and Hafod) that were closely associated with this 'Clumber' duke. His daily records vary in subject content, moving abruptly from international and national matters to the more mundane affairs of his immediate family.

The 2nd Duke formed Clumber Park, Nottinghamshire (as country-seat of the Newcastle-under-Lyme dynasty), between 1760 and 1794, although he only made it his main home from around 1788. Vast amounts of money had been spent on its development and, at the time of his death, the 2nd Duke was in some financial difficulty. The farming project that he had originated had largely failed. In addition, extravagances on his various estates in Lincolnshire, Nottinghamshire and Surrey (together with the loss of income from withdrawn sinecures) had drained his resources.

The 4th Duke was the eldest son of Thomas Pelham-Clinton, the 3rd Duke. Thomas (following a marriage of which his father strongly disapproved) was virtually disinherited, held the title for only one year, and died in 1795. The 2nd Duke's grandson, Henry, was ten years of age when he inherited the title. His inheritance was encumbered by many mortgages. Fortunately, the eleven years of his minority gave opportunities for the Trustees to reduce outgoings and save some of the income. By the time that he came of age in 1806, the financial condition of his estates was considerably improved.

In July 1807 he married a wealthy heiress, Georgiana Elizabeth Mundy, at Lambeth Palace. They had fourteen children, ten of whom lived beyond their early teens. Their eldest daughter, Anna-Maria, died in May 1822, aged fourteen. In September 1822, the Duchess died less than thirty-six hours after giving birth to a stillborn female child and a son, named George. George died on the 7th

October. The Duke's brother and two sisters were dead. His stepfather (Sir Charles Craufurd) had died in 1821 and his mother, the dowager Duchess, lived alone at Ranby Hall. He was left to cope with his large family of young children at Clumber. He never remarried – although not for want of trying!

A deep sense of family and public responsibility shows throughout these diary entries. His creed of 'King, Constitution and Church of England' never wavered ('I stand in the center [*sic*], where truth abides'); neither did his deep religious convictions. An intense desire to stand out from the crowd and proclaim his views is a prominent feature of his writing. However, he had great difficulty expressing himself in public speeches and was agonisingly aware of his deficiencies in this respect.

From the time of his wife's death, the Duke, an awkward, diffident, sensitive and frequently isolated man, found consolation in his diary writing. He regularly recorded his intimate thoughts regarding his devotion to the children and emphasised that he found little happiness outside his immediate family.

The journal entries contrast dramatically with the established view of this '*most hated man in England*', the supposedly powerful, ruthless autocrat and '*enemy of the people*'.

His entries have been extracted with minimal alteration of their grammatical form, or of the spelling. Editorial additions are entered in italics. The Selections are my own, copied at the Manuscripts Department and typed up by me.

In money matters, readers may find that multiplying up, by fifty, makes some of the Duke's financial dealings more relevant to today's prices – and perhaps even more amazing!

John Fletcher
Edwinstowe
May 2001

Fig. 2

THE NEWCASTLE FAMILY
DURING THE PERIOD OF THE DIARIES

The **DUKE** – HENRY PELHAM FIENNES PELHAM-CLINTON Born 1785
The **DUCHESS** – GEORGIANA ELIZABETH (née Mundy)   Born 1789

Their Children –

Anna Maria	Born 1808 Died May 1822
Georgiana	Born 1810
Henry [later 5th Duke]	Born 1811 Married Susan Douglas Hamilton 1832

[As heir to the Dukedom, Henry carried the family's secondary title; Earl of Lincoln.He was commonly known as 'Lincoln', and is referred to as such throughout the Diaries.]

Charlotte	Born 1812
Charles	Born 1813 Married 1848
Thomas (Charles' twin)	Born 1813 Married 1843
William	Born 1815
Edward	Born 1816 Died 1842
John	Born 1817 Died after only 18 hours
Caroline Augusta	Born 1818
Henrietta	Born 1819
Robert Renebald	Born 1820
George [*and stillborn twin sister*]	Born 1822 [*George died after only ten days.*]

The **DOWAGER DUCHESS** – ANNA MARIA (née STANHOPE/HARRINGTON)

The DUKE's brother-in-law – LORD COMBERMERE
[Widower of the Duke's sister – Anna Maria.]

BACKGROUND

The following is a short summary of the Duke's life, prior to the commencement of his 'Journal' writings:

Born on 30 January 1785 – the Duke's mother was Anna Maria Stanhope, youngest daughter of the Earl of Harrington. His father was Thomas Pelham-Clinton, Earl of Lincoln (3ʳᵈ Duke of Newcastle-under-Lyme from 1794). Thomas was an army officer and had served with his relative, Sir Henry Clinton, in the American wars.

During the late 1780's and early 1790's, the family (parents and four children) were living at Kelham Hall in Nottinghamshire, leased to them by the Manners-Sutton family. Henry began his schooling at Eton in 1793. Prior to this he appears to have attended preparatory schooling in Harrogate, together with his brother, Thomas. On the death of his father in 1795, Henry became the 4ᵗʰ Duke of Newcastle-under-Lyme. He continued his studies at Eton until 1802.

In 1802, with his mother and stepfather (they had married in 1800), he went to the South of France. His journal's single reference to this mentions only a *'two year'* period in France (for the *'sake of the health'* of his step-father). However, he appears to have been away from England until 1806. The detention of English citizens in France during the 1803 to 1806 period is well documented elsewhere – but no confirmation that this was the 4ᵗʰ Duke's situation has been noted during the selection of these 'Extracts'. His reference to being apart from his mother whilst 'abroad' (see entry for 25 December 1822) may indicate that they were separated for more than one New Year's Eve. There are no other allusions to time spent away from England during his youth, other than an expression of dislike of foreigners and British Foreign Embassy personnel. Unlike many of his peers, he did not attend university – an omission that he tried hard to remedy in the case of his sons.

His future wife, Georgiana, spent much of her childhood at Kirklington, Nottinghamshire, with her aunt. She and Henry may have first met in that location, as he was living only a few miles away at Kelham. He writes of visiting her there on '*many*' occasions 'as *Miss Mundy*'. An early 1790's letter from a Craufurd (his step-father's family name) at Elvaston may also give a link with the Shipley home of Georgiana's father. These Derbyshire estates were in close proximity of each other. Whatever the circumstances of their first meeting, the couple were married (by special licence) in July 1807, at Lambeth Palace. The honeymoon was at the Barnet home of the Marquis of Sligo. Their move to Clumber commenced immediately following the honeymoon.

Anna Maria, their first child, was born in August 1808. From then, with the exception of 1809, 1814 and 1821, the Duchess was confined each year until her death in 1822, at the age of thirty-three.

In his journals, the Duke mentions the names of family friends with whom they associated during those years. He also recalls houses that they had rented in the London area, presumably whilst he attended his duties in the House of Lords. They purchased a house in Charles Street, Berkeley Square, in 1811.

Although there was a chapel attached to the north west wing of Clumber House, the family also worshipped at Bothamsall village church, just a couple of miles from the gates of the estate. The Duke and Duchess planned to erect a new church at Bothamsall, to serve as parish church and Newcastle family mausoleum.

From the estate accounts, it is clear that there were many improvements made to Clumber House during their married years, both internally and externally. The Duchess had a 'little farm' created, close to the area of the Thoresby gate. She also appears (by 1809) to have sponsored a charity school on the estate.

Around 1814, a substantial sized boat was built for the Clumber Lake (to join the smaller craft, there from his grandfather's day) and a huge flagpole erected at the lakeside. The Duke took a close interest in the farming matters of his bailiff at the Hardwick home farm.

As a major landowner in Nottinghamshire (with smaller holdings in Yorkshire), land purchases were a feature of the Duke's life. The Tuxford estate was added to his enormous land holdings during this period. Income from timber sales and from minerals (e.g. coal) was added to his revenue from estate rents. The Duchess had independent income from her own family.

Appointed as Lord Lieutenant of Nottinghamshire in 1809, the Duke was soon involved in the suppression of the Luddite troubles of the following years. He became a Garter Knight in 1812. Around 1820 he was concerned with the plight of Nottinghamshire frameworkers, whose livelihoods had been threatened by new industrial methods. To alleviate their distress, emigration to the Cape Colony of South Africa was an offered solution – which brought much abuse on the Duke.

By this time, the Duke had established himself, in the political world, as a reactionary to reform.Later, he was proud to claim that he was '*rooted to the center, where truth abides*'. He was reluctant to attach himself to any one party, but was adamant that any scent of liberalism was anathema to him.

His father, brother and both of his sisters had died by 1811. A son born to the Duchess in 1817 (and named John), died after only eighteen hours. The duke's stepfather died in 1821.

Fig. 3

Of the three coronations that took place during his lifetime, the July 1821 ceremony for George IV was the only one attended by the Duke. Here he was awarded the privilege of carrying the blunted sword 'Curtana' (the 'Sword of Mercy'), at this service in Westminster Abbey.

Soon after this event, the Duke was reporting to his neighbour at Welbeck, (the Duke of Portland), that Georgiana, Duchess of Newcastle, was at Scarborough, benefitting from the sea air and the bathing.

LESS THAN ONE YEAR LATER,
THE DUKE BEGAN WRITING HIS JOURNALS.

EXTRACTS
FROM
THE DIARIES
1822 to 1850

Fig. 4 *This sketch (drawn by the Duke) was placed amongst the front pages of his earliest known diary.*
It is of Georgiana Elizabeth, Duchess of Newcastle-under-Lyme.

1822

27 May	On this melancholy day we have lost our dear child, Anna-Maria ... the first born of our children. She was born at Ealing on the 6th August 1808 – How well I remember the first sensations at the birth ... those only who know what it is to have children can tell what it is to lose them ...
28 May	Mr Westmacott the Sculptor has taken a cast of her beautiful serene face – He is to make a bust or statue of it.
1 June	[*Following Anna-Maria's burial at Marylebone Church*] – I propose to remove her remains to Bothamsall when I shall have completed the Church and family vault there.
19 June	My dearest wife taken seriously ill ... frequent bleedings are resorted to ...
16 July	This day we left London ... Slept at Stevenage ...
17 July	Slept at Alconbury Hill.
18 July	Slept at Grantham ... dined at Newark. Mr and Mrs Sutton called upon us.
19 July	Arrived at Clumber, the Duchess certainly much fatigued ... The 4 elder boys are at Ranby ...
AUGUST	[*The Duchess*] has been obliged to give up going out in the garden chair, and has lost strength and flesh very visably ... I have involuntarily gazed upon her sunken cheeks and hollow temples ... Her patience, fortitude, and resignation to all her sufferings, which both of mind and body must be great indeed, are beyond my description – They are worthy of a Christian and such a Christian as she is!
15 September	An alarm of approaching labor – sent for Doctor Falkner – came to nothing.
24 September	A dreadful labour, at last at ¼ past 10 at night a girl was brought forth, still-born – and in 20 minutes afterwards, a boy, who tho' thin appeared hearty. The Duchess – my dearest Georgiana – wonderfully well, I have seldom ... seen her better after her lyings-in ...

1822

26 September   Here all my fondest hopes are crushed, I have this day lost that inestimable treasure which has made the happiness and comfort of my life for 15 years. My beloved and amiable Georgiana, my wife, my companion and my friend died on this day at quarter past 8 in the morning !!! As she has been my guardian angel here, so may she continue to be in heaven!!

At the last moment she seemed to suffer excruciating pain internally, I was rubbing her first in one place then in another, when the dear Soul rapidly seized my hand, made sign to me to rub the pit of her stomach, expressed by her hurried uneasiness that this afforded no relief, exclaimed "Oh! This is too much, I can bear it no longer" and almost instantly with that breath, in my arms, resigned her spotless Soul to the hand of her Creator. I will not attempt to record my feeling – Here am I, one who at 22 married a wife of his choice at 18 – Naturally domestic but made more so by the secluded life I led nearly to the time of my marriage, being married and finding in my wife all that my fondest wishes could desire ... the chief star of the circle was of course that which is now set, how I must deplore such a loss ... I feel a lost creature,

With a life, as it were, to be begun again after 15 years of marriage, accustomed to and regulated by habits which must now be totally unhinged ...

Note – I have written a separate account of all relating to this severe blow ... [*This 'account' does not appear to have survived.*]

... the little infant has been poorly for some days. Today the (6th Oct.) finding him so very ill and weakly, he was baptized by Mr Frederick Mundy. I called him <u>George</u>, in memory of his ever dear Mother.

Fig. 5 *This monument, by Sir Richard Westmacott, was designed and constructed under the watchful eye of the Duke.*

It represents Georgiana Elizabeth, Duchess, together with her stillborn daughter in her right arm and her son, George, in her left. The angelic figure (in high relief) denotes Anna Maria, their fourteen-year-old daughter, who died in May 1822.

The monument, begun in 1825, was placed in the family mausoleum at Markham Clinton, Nottinghamshire in December 1839.

1822

7 October	The dear and beautiful – for such he was – infant died at 25 minutes past 10 at night.
8 October	[*The Funeral day of Duchess Georgiana.*]
10 October	The dear Infant was buried this day – at Bothamsall. When the Funeral took place on the 8th my dear child Anna Maria, whose remains had been brought from London, was at the same time interred, so that nearly at the same period the inestimable Mother and three of her children were laid in the same vault by the side of each other.
19 October	Mr Mundy, my dearest Wife's Father, died this day. He was an excellent man and a perfect pattern of an English gentleman.

———————————

25 December   Christmas Day ... Every thing reminds me of old customs ... went to Chapel and received the Sacrament ...

All this reminds me of what once took place during my former life abroad. My Mother on new year's day sent me a cup of [?] tea (bitter) which she was in the habit of sending accompanied by a few verses wishing that this ought to be the bitterest potion I might drink thro' life ... I answered too prophetically,

Thanks, matchless Mother, for the gift you sent,
It was not bitter, for from you it came,
Wish not that life with me so smoothly went,
For, Virtue then would be an empty name.

The year is ended, I trust I may have profited something by what has passed and that I may be the better fit for the future.

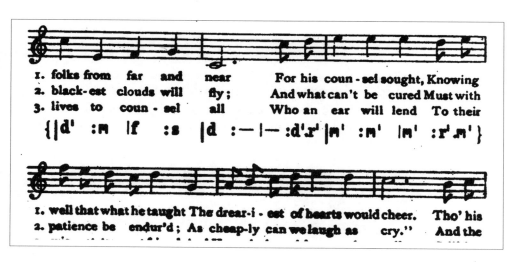

Fig. 6
'AND WHAT CAN'T BE CURED – MUST WITH PATIENCE BE ENDURED'
[*see Diary entry dated 1 July 1823*]

From 'Hope the Hermit' – a 17th century poem by John Oxenford –
from the National Song Book.

1 January ... After making presents to all the dear children and receiving from them their little presents I go to Ranby where I dine and remain till the next day with my Mother, who is not well enough to come here.

12 January A Sunday passed in uninterrupted tranquillity, in the enjoyment of my little circle without any alloy, in the possession of peace of mind, and in the entire thankfulness to Almighty God for such inestimable blessings.

George Mundy is here, he arrived two days ago.

15 January ... How much, how <u>very much</u> I miss my dear companion, it is at such seasons that nothing can supply the want of such a blessing ...

20 January ... One should always live as if one was about to die ... My only failing is not to have been made to be sufficiently punctual.

30 January Today is my birth day ... For the sake of my dear children may [*God*] in his almighty favor continue to me a sound mind and a sound body. May He enable me to conduct myself that I may be to them a kind Parent and just monitor, and be a conspicuous example for them to follow, and may they when they arrive at my time of life have as little to reproach themselves for as I fortunately have – knowing as I do what an inestimable blessing it is to have a clear conscience, how I do earnestly pray and anxiously, most anxiously, strenuously desire that they may inherit it, even, if possible, in a greater degree – Good God! What ineffable joy, contentment and happiness would it bring to my mind if I could hereafter see my ten children, possessed of every virtue, bright examples to the age they live in and securing to themselves that peace of mind which passeth all understanding, and which most assuredly would ensure them a high situation in our heavenly Father's mansion hereafter.

3 February I have written some lines to be inscribed on Sir Thomas Lawrence's portrait of Georgiana ... Collins' little picture is more

1823

like [*her*] ... Hargreaves' miniature [*has features which*] give me painful pleasure ... I can hardly recall a failing in her.

4 February Wrote to the Secretary of State to obtain the King's pardon and the release from imprisonment of my late bailiff, Hardy. He has refunded the £2000, which he embezzled – leniency may be more beneficial than punishment.

10 February Mr Lumley Saville called here today about the exchange of properties between us and other matters ... I gave up to him Maplebeck ... he gives me in exchange, Morton Grange and lands in Tuxford and Willoughby. Saville says this exchange cannot take place immediately.

15 February [*Referring to press attacks on the aristocracy*] ... It is insupportable to be trampled on and systematically set at naught by men who have risen from the dirt.

18 February My dear son Edward is 7 years old today.

21 February Wrote to the Duke of Portland. [*Regarding an exchange of land – Newcastle wished to buy the land between Carburton gateway and the Ollerton/Worksop turnpike road – he received an immediate refusal.*]

1 March Wrote to Portland again – [*this time offering to exchange Newcastle's Brinsley land for Portland's Gringley property*] – his reply said that an exchange of land would cost a lot of money ... the Dutch blood comes out!

I shall offer him Flawborough for Carburton and take all his lands on the Gringley side of the county.

3 March Mr Thompson [*engineer*] is here to erect a water engine here to work by a balance beam.

6 March Rode to the Decoy with Mr Thompson – he was much pleased with it. The Walesby enclosure is already commencing ... I observed the fences were begun.

9 March [*Sunday*] – I rose at 8 – breakfasted, heard Edward [*age 7*] his catechism – went to Chapel – dined with Mr Thompson and the four eldest boys at 1/2 past 1. Walked with them to see the large firs at Osberton ... returned home, dressed.

Had all the children down at 1/2 past 6 ... The youngest, Robert [*age 3*] began going to bed at 20 minutes past 7 and the others successively, Georgiana [*age 13*] being the last, who goes to bed a little before 9 – had my tea. Mr Thompson then came to sit with me till 1/4 before 11, read newspapers, talked over their contents and other matters and went to bed – most of my days have latterly passed in a similar manner – except dining with the boys.

10 March [*Four year old Caroline is giving trouble and anxiety.*]

... marked obstinacy ... undutiful ... a bad disposition.

1823

11 March	[*Caroline*] I was obliged to have recourse to the rod. This had the desired effect.
14 March	My late servant, [*his Valet, Benjamin Candler, arrested in September 1822*] and two others have been tried at Lincoln. Guilty of a horrid and unnatural crime [*of a sexual nature, the offence was said to have been committed by a 'gang of Monsters'*], they are to be executed (hanged) on Friday.
19 March	Admiral Sotheron called here today. [*Previously Frank Frank, the Admiral was from Kirklington Hall, which he had inherited on the death of Mrs Whetham, aunt of the late Duchess. Mrs Whetham had taken custody of her niece Georgiana, almost from her birth.*]
26 March	Rode with Mr Parkinson to see new enclosures at Walesby, Egmanton and Kirton. A surprising improvement – home at 8 o'clock after 7 or 8 hours on horseback.
27 March	At Ranby [*his mother objected to his plan to go to London with all the children – a big argument ensued*] ... she has a high opinion of herself ... perpetually dictating ...
9 April	Have written to Mr Smirke ... to attend here to mark out the site and foundations for the new church. [*Intended, at this stage, to be at Bothamsall.*] I have taken Mr Louth's house at Chiswick. [*Grove House*]
12 April	[*His mother was still very troublesome about the children being taken to London – the Duke expressed his anger over this and wrote that he has no one with whom he could share his frustrations.*] I am without a private friend.
28 April	[*After putting it off for months he had spent much time looking through his late wife's 'things'*] – did not find a Will.
30 April	[*More trouble with his mother*] – If I give her an inch she will take an ell.
2 May	Left at 1/2 past ten to go to London ... travelled with Georgiana and Charlotte ... dined at Grantham..arrived at Wandsford about 1/4 before 7.[*Comments on his two eldest girls*] – Georgiana is mild, amiable, cheerful and serene. Charlotte is quick, lively, playful and droll. Both are feminine, modest, agreeable, beautiful, artless and innocent.
5 May	The younger children [*girls*] have arrived. [*The journey to London had taken them three days.*]
7 May	The boys and Mr Thompson [*their tutor*] arrived. Miss Spencer was also there [*as governess to the girls*]. A dancing teacher was arranged.
22 May	May Lincoln be an ornament and a blessing to his country.

1823

23 May [*Rode into London to the House of Lords to present a petition from Newark about* 'no further concessions to the Roman Catholics'.]

25 May [*Whilst they attended the church, an 'old gentleman' had asked if the children belonged to the Duke of Newcastle – when told that this was so, he said* 'I never saw a finer family in my life'.]

30 May [*Major trouble with the servants – most are threatening to leave.*] A married servant is a peculiar nuisance.

2 June [*At Ealing, he mentions that his first child (Anna Maria) was born there and that the house they lived in had been demolished.*]

4 June [*Mentions a 1822 event when he, the duchess and the two eldest girls travelled from Maidenhead to see the annual* 'Etonians row'] –

I love to cherish your dear memory beloved Mother of my dear children, and to own and feel within me how deeply indebted to you we all are and how grateful eternally so I trust, I am and ever shall remain under any circumstances!!! To you under Heaven I owed all that made my comfort and happiness here and perhaps hereafter!!!

5 June [*An old nurse, 'Marshall', called to see them. He wrote that the children did not recognise her, which surprised him.*]

16 June The four eldest boys visited the dentist – several fillings needed.

17 June [*Still in London*] – the excellent Rowlands got 'Punch' to perform – all the children were highly delighted.

18 June The Archbishop of Canterbury [*Charles Manners-Sutton*] called.

30 June The girls went to the dentist and then to an exhibition.

1 July What cannot be cured must be endured. [*He entered this observation without further clarification. It is similar to a line from a 17th century folk song 'Hope the Hermit' – "And what can't be cured, Must with patience be endur'd."*]

2 July A 'Fun Day' – entirely passed with the children.

3 July [*Mentions that Charlotte was born at Clarence Lodge [Richmond?] and that they had hired the Lodge*] – my ever beloved wife liked it best and it was a great favourite of hers, it cannot therefore be but dear to me.

4 July Robert [*age 3*] has been giving me cause to be displeased with him ... stubborn and obstinate ... the bad effect of spoiling children is but too clearly shewed ... allowing him, with the nursery children, to dine with Miss Spencer ... I must have implicit obedience for the sake of my children ...

6 July I had a letter telling me that the antiques belonging to the late sculptor Nollekens had been bought for me at auction at

1823

Christies – at a low price, almost incredible. The Minerva; Commodus; Mercury head and Faun marble – £899.11.6d for the whole 10 with antique pedestals – Nollekens had asked 1000 guineas for the Minerva alone – I am much pleased with my purchase.

9 July   [*Went to the Lords, having prepared a speech*] – so nervous – I found it perfectly impossible to speak.

10 July   Spoke to the Lord Chancellor of my inward failure.

12 July   My Valet, Wright, came home tipsy yesterday evening. Today I had to lecture him ... They gave him many sorts of wine at the Duke of Devonshire's, which upset him. I believe it was a trick upon him, which he was weak enough to fall into.

14/15 July   Mr Thompson [*tutor*] is ill – Mr Trimmer from Brentford will take his place travelling in each day.

17 July   Ordered my [*newly purchased*] antiques to be packed and sent to Clumber. Called on Mr Smirke, I saw him and settled with him about commencing the new church early in September [*at Bothamsall.*]

18 July   Sir W. Clinton called – I settled my account with Rowlands – I wish I had paid all my bills – still £8000 to £9000 [*outstanding.*]

24 July   Went to London – sat to Sir T. Lawrence for my portrait which he is about to compleat, having had it in hand now about 15 years. Called on Mr Reynolds who is engraving a print of my beloved Georgiana from a picture by Sir Thom. Lawrence.

25 July   I took Georgiana and Charlotte with me to London .

26 July   [*With 6 of his children*] I went to see Sion House – it has an avenue of Lime Trees.

28 July   Sat again for Lawrence – he painted a leg [*having painted the body at the previous sitting*]. I may loan £7000 or £8000 from my bankers to repay all debts to tradesmen. My whole debt to clear everything will be about £22,000. After that I expect to live well within my income.

1 August   Sat again for Lawrence. [*Mentions anecdotes regarding the "filth" of the late Duke of Norfolk who was said to have boasted that he never washed. Also mentions "Newark Tythes lately purchased".*]

5 August   Played a match of cricket today with the boys – Mr Trimmer plus three and I and Lincoln against them. The first game we were beat in one innings. Towards the next game I have gotten 31 and not out.

6 August   Finished our game today, we got 51, they only 8 or 9.

1823

7 August	[*Hoped to buy Cuckney from Lord Bathurst, to add to Pleasley and Langwith with the long-term aim to exchange with the Duke of Portland for Carburton.*]
8 August	Sat again for Sir T. Lawrence – one more will finish it. Called on my bankers and agreed £9000 loan.
10 August	[*SUNDAY*] – Rain – no church [*recalls his childhood attitude to church attendance* – "it was made a drudgery".]
14 August	[*To London with Georgiana and Charlotte, they wanted to buy presents from the Bazaar at Soho.*] – Charlotte had four teeth out today.
15 August	Sat the last sitting to Sir T. Lawrence ... Home late, I have missed seeing the children before going to bed.
20 August	Complete day of sightseeing for the eldest four boys – British Museum – to Portman Square for dinner. Afterwards, the Tower, the Jewel Office, Great Armoury – finished by writing down our names and going over the draw-bridge – then to Exeter Change [*this may have been the Exeter Rooms, on the Strand*] and saw the menagerie. Back to Portman Square, tired, ate a good supper – then back to Chiswick. This has been a very fine day.
21 August	Miss Spencer is on leave, the two eldest girls came to me – we had a little concert when their music master came – he on the violincello, they on the piano forte and I on the violin.
22 August	Called on Mr Westmacott – saw Mr Reynolds and Mr Smirke.
24 August	Took the children on the water for the first time – nearly to Fulham and back.
1 September	[*Reminiscences of his childhood*] – from servants I learnt many bad things very early and it was a great torment to me. I also went very young to school at Eton and there learned everything that I ought not to have known. Frequent were my trials and temptations and often I have been on the point of losing my virtue.
2 September	[*Mention of his 'new Evidence Room at Clumber'*].
	I am about to sell stock to pay off nearly £40,000 of old mortgages. I am surprised to find myself so well off after having added nearly £100,000 worth of land to the old property and bought and fitted up and furnished a house in London.
5 September	Went to London – bought many books of value and interest to add to my Library.
7 September	Went to church and had a delightful day with all the elder children, 6 of whom dined with me – the little ones coming occasionally.

1823

10 September	Mr Smirke was to meet me at Clumber on 1ˢᵗ October to have marked out and commenced the foundation of the new church at Bothamsall ... he has to complete the new Post Office near St Paul's within three months. He will not be able to attend my concern – defer to next spring.
12 September	My Bailiff reports that 300 to 400 acres of corn harvest is in – and is in the best possible condition.
13 September	I have bought some superior books today – very fine editions of the original English Historians and others which will be a valuable addition to my Library.
15 September	[First mention of the Duke of Hamilton – in connection with a parliamentary matter – Lincoln was to marry Hamilton's daughter 9 years later.]
17 September	Made progress on what I call "A speech which ought to have been made on Lord Lansdown's motion to grant the elective franchise to Roman Catholics". If I have the opportunity to finish it, I shall publish it, without a name, in the form of a pamphlet.
20 September	Robert fell and cut his chin. Miss Spencer [governess] asked if I was [generally] displeased with her [lately, she had noticed a change in him] – I assured her this was not so.
21 September	Went to church – an admirable sermon.
22 September	Today I saw Mr Smirke, Mr Reynolds and Mr Westmacott – the latter consult Mr Smirke regarding the Monument [for the late Duchess.]
23 September	Sat to Mr Reynolds – he completed the portrait – it is Kit Kat size [36"x28"] and is admirable
26 September	This is the anniversary of the loss of her who was so truly and [justly?] dear to me ... Beloved spirit of departed worth and [?] goodness, if you are allowed to take any part in the direction of earthly matters, seal my fervent wishes, watch over us, be with us, accompany us in all our steps, be to me still my wife, to our children still their kind, their affectionate, their inestimable mother!!! ... Farewell!
27 September	Lincoln rode with me on his pony for the first time.
1 October	My dear Charlotte's birthday.
2 October	[Prepared to leave Grove Lodge, Chiswick and return to Clumber] – The children left at 9 o'clock. They will dine at Hatfield and sleep at Biggleswade.
3 October	I left with the boys a little after 9 – I greatly fear that in returning to Clumber I am returning to many discomforts, plagues and annoyances, to say nothing of the mournful recollections ...

1823

4 October   Arrived at Clumber at 7 o'clock.

15 October   Purchases at the Fonthill sale – including books, manuscripts and pictures (*'Regent Murray', 'Sir Thomas More' by Holbein and others*). My dear little Robert's birth day – 3 years old.

23 October   Working on the Cascade – it will one day be very pretty.

1 November   Spent about £700 in total at the Fonthill sale.

4 November   Preparing the new 'Evidence Room'. [*Shows his mistrust of lawyers – describing them as* 'scoundrels'.]

6 November   Big trees cut down in the Pleasure gardens – especially a large silver fir to the right of the dial – near the Library window.

7 November   My farmer has bought Highland Scotch oxen at £8 a head ... Edward, who can now read and write, began his grammar today – Caroline stands by and attentively listens, gathering all she can.

12 November   [*Following a dampness problem at the House.*] A man has proposed to me that the House be raised up a Storey!

26 November   Unpacked my pictures from the Fonthill sale – Holbein's 'Sir Thom. More' is very fine, so is the nun [*much more on the individual items*].

28 November   Unpacked my antique marbles [*especially pleased with Nolleken's 'Minerva' – on 1 December, he describes this as* 'the best draped figure I ever saw'.]

Fig. 7 *This statue remained at Clumber until 1937, when it was sold for just £95 in Christie's sales.*

29 November   Dined at Thoresby – the night was so dark that even with lamps it was difficult to keep [*to*] the road.

4 December   Great winds blown down many very fine and valuable trees.

18 December   Yesterday a change of life took place in my dear eldest girl, Georgiana, she is not yet 14 so it is early. Rain and snow – the Cascade under the Bridge is very fine, and the current opposite the house almost like that of the Thames.

26 December   Yesterday brought back many old recollections and deep regrets – we always used to take the sacrament <u>together</u>. My House Steward [*Todd?*] who is a very good man, took the sacrament for the first time.

31 December   The Bank of England is to take all my mortgages at 4 per cent. I shall pay off £40.000 entirely of my mortgages – my affairs will then be in a nutshell.

1 January   Went to Ranby [*his mother's home*] Exchanged our wishes and New Year gifts to the great delight of the children. [*Later, at Clumber*] – we had the poor people to the front of the House and then my eldest girls and I dispersed the different articles of clothing to them, for which they seemed truly thankful.

6 January   Twelfth Night – we had the drawing for King and Queen cake etc. and all the children have been very happy this evening. [*The 'cake' contained monies which, when found, entitled the recipients to take the 'thrones' during the meal.*]

7 January   Considerable progress on my pamphlet.

13 January   I know of no one whom I can make my friend. I am of consequence to none but my children.

18 January   Have been to my kennels today. [*Distemper was affecting the ferrets there.*]

19 January   Commenced my works on the lawn lowering the approach road [*and*] making the terrace etc.

22/24 January   Much occupied with my works ... which will, effect a material alteration in the situation of the house. It will no longer appear flat, low and uninteresting. My pamphlet is complete – I only pretend to ordinary abilities.

27 January   We went to shoot at Bevercotes yesterday ...

28 January   The terrace is forming fast and the excavation of the road on the lawn is a formidable operation.

30 January   I am 39 years old today – 10, 12 or 14 more might be better ...

31 January   Shooting – excellent sport in the wild ground in Budby Corner.

2 February   Pamphlet sent to the printers ...

5 February   John Bowskill, farm labourer of Elkesley, drowned at Gamston whilst taking a message ...

7 February   [*Back at Clumber, from his mother's at Ranby, where he had met the Chesters*] – the eldest Miss Chester is a very superior person in appearance, conduct and intellect – she, along with the

1824

Duchess of Leinster, was very highly thought of by the late Duchess.

12 February   Lincoln shall go to Eton school after Easter ...

15 February   I have too many irons in the fire – I intend to resign from the Command of the Yeomanry ...

Fig. 8 *The church of All Saints, at West Markham – beautifully restored and pictured here in the 1990's.*

25 February   I took Mr Smirke to West Markham where there is a very bad church and I mean to move it to a central position between West Markham; Milnton [*currently known as Milton*] and Bevercotes. Afterwards I shall remove the parsonage house and place it near the church. Mr Smirke approves much of my plan and of the change from Bothamsall to this place.

26 February   Mr Smirke staked out the new church at Markham – he also suggests the enlargement of the terrace here.

1 March   I found a book worm in my books in the Library ...

14 March   I went to view the new line of approach from London, decided Cabin Hill gateway should be removed lower down away from the Inn and the avenue a little turned to meet it. We also traced the whole line to Clumber Bridge which will, I think, be as good as nature and act can make it.

Fig. 9 *A wing of the Drayton Gate near Cabin Hill.*

18 March   This is my dear child Georgiana's birthday. It is utterly impossible that a more perfect creature can exist ...

30 March   Went to Newark [*regarding the planning for a new church*] – returned home via Mr Sutton's at Kelham.

1824

1 April   Went to Nottingham to see [my] Castle – it is in bad repair.

Many foreigners are in Town buying lace, they intend to sell it back to us as French lace – what gulls we are!

5 April   A Woodcock's nest has been found.

9 April   [After putting it off for some time] – Selected [the late Duchess] Georgiana's wardrobe items for her maid.

14 April   [On the way to London] – Stopped at West Markham, fixed the site of the new Church and settled for the commencement of the building.

[Whilst in the London area, they stayed at Grove House, Chiswick and also at the Duke's Portman Square home.]

23 April   ... Mr Peel's plan for reviewing the Yeomanry Cavalry has most amply increased the correspondence of the Lieutenants of the Counties.

24 April   I today weaned Edward from the nursery and had his bed put with his brothers where he is now fast asleep ...

I left Miss Spencer in London – and Mr Thompson went there as soon as I arrived here, so that I have the children with me entirely.

28 April   Mr Thompson went to Eton to arrange and prepare every thing for Lincoln's arrival ... it seems that nothing is found there in private houses, beds, linen and all furniture and utensils to be found by the occupiers.

29 April   The Archbishop of York ... highly approves of my plans for the new Church at Markham ...

1 May   Mr Thompson brought the boys ... to see the chimney sweeps in full dress ...

4 May   Attended the House of Lords on the Unitarian Marriage Bill. I had a great mind to say something but my courage failed me ... I should be sorry to appear ridiculous – my great evil, is my almost <u>total</u> want of memory ... all is chaos, blank and confusion.

Fig. 10 'The First of May.' Illustration by George Cruikshank From 'Sketches by Boz', by Charles Dickens

5 May   Called upon the Archbishop of Canterbury at Lambeth ... I was wet thro' on going to Lambeth on horseback

8 May   ... [Saw] Mr Denison who had much to say about the Troop of Yeomanry which he is about to take the command of ...

1824

11 May   A debate in the H. of Lords ... I took Lincoln down with me to see and hear what was done there to give him an early notion of such things ... afterwards took him to the House of Commons ... he will I am sure make a distinguished figure, perhaps in both houses.

14 May   ... News arrived of the death of Lord Byron, by fever, at Missolonghi, – It is an awful consideration that one so ill prepared should suddenly have to meet his Creator, but for this consideration, it is well for the world to be rid of a being of such powerful talent, profligate, infidel, industriously mischievous.

22 May   ... Went to see Kew gardens – I had never seen them ...

23 May   ... went to the House of Lords ... I was nearly on the point of getting up once and have seldom felt so inclined to speak ... I cannot gain presumption enough to take upon me to make the House listen to my voice.

29 May   Paid some bills yesterday to booksellers for books which compleates my payments to Christmas last. I now owe no bills to tradesmen in Town or country which is a great comfort to me ...

31 May   [*After more distressing arguments with his mother, over her access to and influence over his children*] – [*This*] harrasses me excessively ... O my beloved angel, you may perhaps see with compassion my state of trial ... my sorrow, the deep and perpetual affliction which came upon me thro' the loss of you, and my constancy in maintaining all those principles which were so often the subjects of our conversations. If it may be permitted to you, dearest spirit, lend me your loving aid to smooth my difficulties and console my impaired mind ...

    Mr Bewsher arrived today, I have seen and engaged him as tutor to my youngest boys.

1 June   Consulted with Mr Fynes Clinton on the provisions of Mr Chadwick's will [*uncle of the late duchess*] ... Went to Coutts ... [*and instructed them to*] invest the dividends as they were paid (arising from the money in trust for my dear children under Mr Chadwick's will, which will make an excellent provision). I thus lose £3,700 a year when I begin to want it most – but it will ultimately be greatly for the benefit of the children.

3 June   [*Records that Bewsher, the new tutor, will receive £200 per year.*]

6 June   Rode with Lincoln, which being Sunday, is a very unusual circumstance ... I do not make a rule to forbear using servants or horses on Sundays, and that I ever do so is for examples sake – for neither my servants or horses have such work in the week as to need rest on Sunday ... Matthew, who takes care of the children ... a good and trusty. servant and has been many years with me. I am very glad that he remains.

1824

8 June   Rode almost round London today with Lincoln going along the city road, by Finsbury Square, the Bank and by the India house passed the Monument over London bridge thro' Southwark, over Westminster bridge and by the Vauxhall road and the Park house to Portman Square. Lincoln was much pleased and amused and I must say so was I ...

11 June   Dined with Lord Winchilsea.

15 June   Brought my very dear boy to Eton ... he is never distressed or disturbed by any situation or circumstance ... takes every thing as it comes ... may constitute him a blessing and an ornament to his Country and Mankind ...

The dear boys at Chiswick and his Sisters did not leave him with dry eyes ...

I live alone for them and God has indeed most richly blessed me in such a possession.

19 June   I have been much plagued and annoyed at home by Miss Spencer (my girl's governess) whose hasty temper and jealous dispositions are very difficult to manage – still she has other good qualities ... change might not lead to amelioration.

A Bill has been brought in to allow the D. of Norfolk to exercise the office of Earl Marshall without taking the prescribed oaths – I would ask do his loyalty, his merits, and his will to do harm if he could, entitle him to such favor or distinction – I answer <u>NO</u> ...

22 June   Drew up a Protest this morning against the Earl Marshall's Bill, which I submitted to the Duke of York and received his Royal Highness' high approbation of it ... I presume I shall not be in high favor with my neighbour the D. of Norfolk.

24 June   [*Spoke in the House of Lords debate*] – as well as I could but very imperfectly no doubt, from my total disuse of speaking extemporarily ... it has made public my opinions ...

25 June   Received a very kind and very flattering letter from the Duke of York ...

9 July   [*Records that the Archbishop of Canterbury had congratulated him on his recent contribution to the Lords debate.*]

10 July   ... played amongst the hay with the dear children.

11 July   ... An account of wasps killed this season at Clumber amounts to <u>7995 single wasps</u> before the nests are made [*the wasp hunters received one penny for each wasp*].

13 July   [*Arrived back at Clumber*] ... my presence is wanted greatly – my absence has created a period of idleness for the numerous and varied workmen now employed in and about here ...

1824

14 July   ... Rode to Markham to see the new Church, it is now 4 feet out of the ground and the foundations excellent. I have also been to the new Thoresby lodge – it is very well built, but unfortunately not quite rightly placed to the road.

17 July   [*Returned to London.*]

29 July   ... Met Sir William Clinton and his son ...

31 July   ... remedy for an incipient cold – To put the feet in warm water [*before*] going to bed, and to take a common saline draught of 20 gms Salt Wormwood and table spoonful of syrup of [*Poppirs*?] in it.

2 August   [*Left London for Clumber. Slept at Wansford.*]

3 August   Set out this morning from Wansford at 7 and got in here at 5 o'clock – we breakfasted at Wetham Common and dined at Tuxford. It is a general complaint along this road ... that the steam packets have most materially injured the posting – Even the Duke and Duchess of Northumberland, to my knowledge, returned to Alnwick this year by the steam packet ...

5 August   Mr Smirke called here today - on his way to Lincoln – he is to look at Markham Church ...

7 August   ... Played cricket with the boys.

12 August Walked with Lincoln to see the new lodge at Thoresby gate – on returning I passed down the avenue to the Little Farm – it was planted for my dear partner.

Fig. 11 '
South Lodge' at the Clumber/Thoresby border.

14 August Thoresby lodge is much advanced – the roof putting on and the chimneys above it have been completed.

18 August Began lowering and altering the pavement of the West Front.

25 August [*A dispute with St John's, Cambridge regarding the Manor of West Markham*] – have checked my papers, and between 1790 and 1802, the Court Rolls are in my name or my grandfather's name ...

1824

13 September	Rode out to Welbeck with Lincoln and Mr Thompson, to shew it to the former. Nothing could look more deplorably than all did there, the wretched furniture and the equally wretched care that is taken of the house and place, make the whole a miserable concern. It is indeed disgraceful to a man of the Duke of Portland's situation and fortune to allow things to get into such a state. The pictures, that is, the portraits, are very fine, curious and rare. Some of the old portraits I should consider invaluable.
14 September	Lincoln left me to go to Eton – I accompanied him in my chaise to Tuxford. I afterwards rode home by Markham to see the church. The work is considerably advanced since my last visit.

[From 23 September there are frequent mentions of a plan to lease Nottingham Park for the building of 'good houses'.] |
29 September	Lord Surrey has arrived at Worksop Manor. – *[Lord Surrey, heir to the Duke of Norfolk, had contacted Newcastle to ask about references for a servant.]* – He has written in a vastly foolish way … *[Starting]* 'My Lord Duke' and finishing 'Your Grace'. I meant nothing personal when I opposed our having a Popish Earl Marshall … I merely did my duty as a Protestant legislator.
2 October	A violent storm … a beautiful and large Acacia tree blown down by the water side.
5 October	Miss Spencer *[governess]* went out today for a week's holiday … Georgiana and Charlotte have come to me. I received a letter from the Archbishop of Canterbury offering to come here the day after tomorrow. I have been obliged to request him to postpone his visit for a week.
6 October	Mr Gilpin came today *[William Sawrey Gilpin, eminent authority on garden design]* … he much approves of all that has been done here.
8 October	On this day two years *[ago]*, the funeral of my beloved Georgiana took place … though I may no longer wear the outward symbols of mourning … the inward record will still remain the same.
10 October	Dr. Faulkner M.D. who attends us here is alarmingly ill … he has known all the children from their birth and is an excellent practitioner … I left off black this morning. What a span of time it appears since I first put it on. Out of my house I feel little interest in society. My Country, My Children and the World to Come, are the foundations of most of my thoughts.
11 October	Dr. Faulkner died yesterday … he had known and attended my valued Georgiana *[the late Duchess]* from a child and by that knowledge … he assisted to prolong for several years a precious life very insecurely held.

1824

12 October   Mr Gilpin arrived, so that I hope he may have fair weather for his operations.

13 October   My excellent friend, the Archbishop of Canterbury [*Charles Manners-Sutton*] came today.

16 October   The tradition of this country [*county?*] has it that Robin Hood shot an arrow from Gamston to Apley Head – a pretty good shot with a long bow!

Robin Hood had a nephew by the name of Gamwell and it is thought that Gamston was called after him – [*through* 'Gamwellston']

18 October   My keeper has been to inform me that a gentleman sent by Mr Saville [*of Rufford*], with Mr Saville's keeper, were shooting this morning on my land at Walesby and would not go off. He says he is Lord of the Manor and will shoot there – I will soon and decisively set this at rest. No man, and least of all Mr Saville, shall tell me that he will invade my rights and privileges.

20 October   Busily engaged with Mr Smirke and Mr Gilpin planning the final arrangement of the terrace and a future entrance by the northern front. The former is settled, the latter is very difficult to effect.

22 October   Mr Smirke and Mr Gilpin went away. Their meeting here has brought all my projected improvements. Mr Gilpin has given me some slight sketches of the elevation of the new entrance, which I entirely approve [*without disturbance of existing arrangements*]. I accompanied Mr Smirke to the new church at Markham which is going on satisfactorily.

1 November   Looked over old papers – from Mr Green's office. They were papers belonging to the late Mr [*John Gally?*] Knight relating to my affairs during his guardianship ... My education was sadly neglected and misconducted ... being so much left to myself.

2 November   My mother left me today ... her conduct is greatly altered ...

The Craufurd infection is, I trust, losing its force never to be caught again.

[*Craufurd (with various spellings) being the name of his late step-father. This appears to be the only entry that gives any indication of the Duke's attitude towards him.*]

4 November   Mr Willement is here to settle as to the correct and best arrangement for the heraldic painted glass for the 3 staircase windows.

5 November   [*Mentions*] St George's Chapel, Windsor – my Father was also laid [*there*] in 1795. [*Retford Elections*] – it cost the present members not less than £10,000 each for two elections. This is indeed purity of Election!

1824

10 November	Began today the new alterations to the terraces, which was fixed on when Mr Smirke and Mr Gilpin were here. These will take it down to the water on a second level, the first to about two thirds of the way between the house and water; the present is a great improvement on the former plan.
11 November	I always thought the Retford freemen the worst of their sort, today it has been fully proved ... [*They had reversed their voting intentions.*]
18 November	Every horse in my stable is ill with coughs, colds and sore throats.
20 November	Lincoln has fought a determined battle [*boxing*] at Eton.
	He fought for 3/4 of an hour... [*displayed*] unshaken courage.
28 November	[*Mentions Lincoln Chapel, St George's Chapel, Windsor being used as a* 'lumber room'.] There is no monument to my dear Father who is buried in the vault in Lincoln Chapel. I shall immediately set about raising one in his memory.
3 December	My dear boys, Charles and Thomas, are 11 years today ...
	The ground is covered with snow.
8 December	Saw two candidates to fill Doc. Faulkner's place here ...
9 December	... The gentleman who was acrimoniously in treaty with me about taking Nottingham Park on a building lease, has thought it expedient to consent to my terms, which at first he declared to be most objectionable – he proves to be Mr Chas. Wright, son of the Nottingham banker and has depreciated my property in the true sense of mercantile cunning – however I have fortunately proved a match for him ...
10 December	My dear boy [*Lincoln*] arrived this evening ...
11 December	... the alteration in Lincoln's looks is occasioned by the effects of his battle [*see 20 November above*], his face is still swelled about the eyes and the eye balls are red with blood ...
15 December	Went to Markham to see the new church, it is now in a very considerable state of forwardness.
17 December	... Mr Wright came to settle about taking Nottingham Park, he is to have a certain portion of it on lease for 99 years containing about 126 acres ...
	I think I have done well for my family ... I could have obtained an infinitely higher price if I had chosen to try for it – but enough is as good as a feast.
23 December	[*Displeased with a letter from Mr Wright over the proposed lease*] – this I am decided upon. No one shall touch Nottm. Park until I am sure that it shall be well done to, and for the honor and advantage of the capital of the County.

1824

25 December   This day has brought back ... the same intense bitterness [*over the loss of his wife*] ... Received the Sacrament ... faults no doubt I have in abundance, the lot of man, but my conscience reproaches me with nothing that should cause me to fear meeting my Maker whenever it should please Him to call upon me.

27 December   [*Comments relating to certain of his grandfather's purchases especially mentions the* 'Sigismunda' – *later reported as being placed in the Yellow Room at Clumber House.*]

[*This final entry of the year was written on the inside cover of the first bound volume of his diaries.*]

31 December   With this book, here ends the year 1824 ...

My dearest children are well ... One thing only seems to be wanting, a dear companion who once shared my discomforts and my happiness ... It is doubtless best as it is and I submit to the wisdom of Him who knows what is best for us ...

1825

1 January	[*Referring to his children*] may I never see their dear little brows furrowed by care or grief ... The poor could not come to the House as the smallpox rages very much in the villages.
6 January	[*Whilst out hunting, the Duke saw*] – the little farm which the late Duchess had created – beautifully kept by two old people [*who had*] honestly, faithfully and punctually done their duty unattended to and unseen.
8 January	Went to the boys garden in Hardwick Wood ... [*Worked there all day* ...] am stiff as a post horse.
15 January	Markham [*Mausoleum*] is up to the roof.
17 January	[*My*] children are making their garden by the Engine House.
19 January	Lincoln left for Eton.
20 January	Shooting at Bevercotes – recent enclosures thereabouts. Lately bought an Estate at Wellow ... from Lord Howard, for £15,510 ... it will pay nearly 4% ... a good purchase. I owe £9,000 to Coutts ... Captain Mundy will take this.
21 January	... I cancelled my Codicil this day, wherein I gave to my youngest children a considerable sum, being part of my personalty, which had been expended in the purchase of land. They will now be well provided under the provisions of Mr Chadwick's will [*see 1 June 1824 entry*] – By that will they will be entitled to between 5 and 600£ a year, the sum is now accumulating and will continue to do so until they arrive at age. This is my reason for cancelling the Codicil.
23 January	Admiral Sotheron called ... accompanied us out shooting and staid the night. I am always glad to see him ...
26 January	... It is impossible to describe what pains a naughty child causes to an anxious Parent ...
30 January	Today I have reached my fortieth year ... most of my relations and friends are gone ...

1825

31 January   A very beautiful day. I took my farewell of shooting for the season, the fineness of the day permitted me to shoot partridge in the morning and pheasant in the afternoon. Of the former I killed 6 brace and a snipe in an hour in two turnip fields ...

8 February   The Duke of Wellington has offered to Sir William Clinton [*elder son of General Sir Henry Clinton*] in a very handsome and gratifying manner to appoint him Lt General of the Ordnance, it is an honorable and good appointment which he will accept. I am glad to see a Clinton noticed at last ...

12 February   [*After learning that Lincoln was ill*] – ... I can scarcely think of any thing else – My Mother came today.

20 February   [*Records that Lincoln is now declared* 'convalescent'.]

21/22 February   [*Travelled to London. Slept at Witham Common.*]

23 February   Went to Eton ... I shall take Lincoln to London tomorrow – I am told that they mean to make an embankment by the side of the Thames to keep out the floods – this will be a great improvement ...

25 February   My dear Lincoln is much better today ... nothing can supply a mother's care, I can do much and shall do all in my power, but such an assistant would indeed be valuable.

5 March   Appointed a meeting with Lord Liverpool and went to see him at 1/2 past 1 ... on the matter of very extraordinary nature ... [*the matter was a published letter on 'the R.C. question' – it was alleged that the letter was either written or prompted by the King.*] ... I left the man in great perplexity – I am more than ever convinced that it is the King's handwriting ...

8 March   Called on Mr Peel [*who insisted that the King had no hand in 'the letter'*] ... I must believe it, altho' it almost exceeds belief ...

14 March   Called at Mr Green's house and signed a deed transferring Mr Sissons mortgage of £11,000 to Sir Edmund Antrobus.

Snow today. Lincoln began to learn the violin of Mr More.

16 March   Attended a meeting of the Council of the Royal Society of Literature of which I am a member, for the first time – I was at the same time received as a member in due form ...

18 March   This is my dear Georgiana's birth day – She is now 15, and a more delightful and perfect girl, I am very convinced, does not exist ... No parent was ever blessed with two more distinguished children (*as elder children*) than her and Lincoln, their dispositions strongly resemble each other allowing to each the difference of sex.

23 March   I have busied myself in endeavouring to incite the parishioners of St Mary le bonne to petition Parlt. against the R.C. bill – If it can be obtained it will incite others, and may be of essential service ...

1825

24 March [*Records that the Vestry were 'indisposed towards a petition'.*]

25 March Mr Reynolds ... at last succeeded in bringing out such an entire likeness of her whom I so dearly loved and now more than ever venerate ...

28 March Signed an agreement for Mr [?] to have 20 lots on a lease of 65 years in Thurland paddock, Nottingham at a rent of £56.

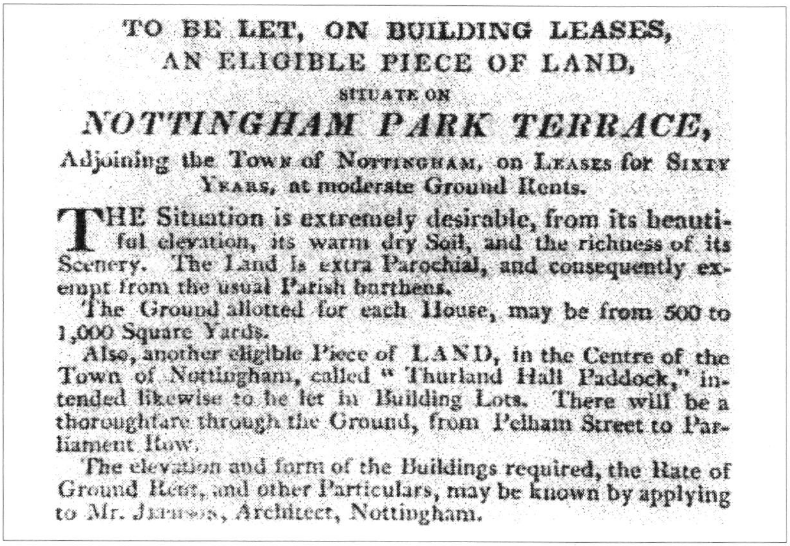

> **TO BE LET, ON BUILDING LEASES,**
> **AN ELIGIBLE PIECE OF LAND,**
> SITUATE ON
> **NOTTINGHAM PARK TERRACE,**
> Adjoining the Town of Nottingham, on Leases for Sixty Years, at moderate Ground Rents.
>
> THE Situation is extremely desirable, from its beautiful elevation, its warm dry Soil, and the richness of its Scenery. The Land is extra Parochial, and consequently exempt from the usual Parish burthens.
> The Ground allotted for each House, may be from 500 to 1,000 Square Yards.
> Also, another eligible Piece of LAND, in the Centre of the Town of Nottingham, called "Thurland Hall Paddock," intended likewise to be let in Building Lots. There will be a thoroughfare through the Ground, from Pelham Street to Parliament Row.
> The elevation and form of the Buildings required, the Rate of Ground Rent, and other Particulars, may be known by applying to Mr. Jarvis, Architect, Nottingham.

Fig. 12 *An advertisement from the 'Nottingham Review'*

31 March ... Dined with a very pleasant party at Lord Westmoreland's [*Lord Privy Seal*], he himself is a queer madcap, but ... entertaining and promotes others being so ...

1 April Good Friday – I took the Sacrament ...

2 April Saw Mr Hakewell, architect, and settled with him to go to Nottingham for the purpose of planning the new town in the Park in the best and most advantageous manner ...

12 April ... For the last three days I have felt unusually low and depressed ... My solitary existence comes home to me on such occasions.

14 April [*In the House of Lords, the Duke presented a petition*] – from Retford against concessions to Roman Catholics – I proved entirely unequal to the task and totally failed ... It is very uncomfortable and vexing to be so headless ... when one would wish to be useful ...

17 April ... a Sunday principally passed with my children – the Godfrey Mundys, their daughter and 2 sons came in the evening.

1825

20 April   Went to the Levee today, the king looked tolerably well in the face, but his legs are shrunk to nothing and he appears to me to have no use in them. H.M. sat on a high stool and almost appeared as if he was standing. He conversed with no one, but appeared satisfied and gracious to all ...

21 April   Presented a petition from Nottingham to the House of Lords ... against the Papists ...

26 April   My Mother arrived in London today. Took Georgiana and Charlotte and Lincoln to the Opera. The first time that they had ever been at a public place ...

27 April   [*He declined an invitation that he be proposed as the leader of the opposition to* 'the present state of affairs'] – I had neither the talents, habit or spirits to qualify me for such an undertaking. This is nothing but truth, I am sensibly conscious of my deficiencies in every necessary qualification but that of rectitude of intention.

28 April   Went to the House of Lords, where I presented 4 petitions, 2 against popery, 2 against any alteration of the Corn laws.

30 April   ... Westmacott has a beautiful group in marble of a Madonna and child which he made thinking I might like it for a monument – but I shall prefer an alto-relievo and I have given him the idea, it is to be my dear child Anna Maria borne on a cloud, ready to receive my beloved and ever lamented wife, who looks towards her having in each arm an infant who are preparing to ascend to Heaven – How seldom and hour passes without being painfully reminded of this irreparable loss ...

           [*A footnote to this day's entries, which may refer to a dinner at the Royal Academy, reads:*] – ... Sat opposite the Duke of Norfolk, I took pains to shew him that I was not personally opposed to him. Took wine with him and other civilities.

3 May   Took Lincoln to see St. Paul's ...

5 May   Left London for Clumber [*Slept at Stevenage.*]

6 May   [*Arrived at Clumber*] – I called at Thoresby in my way and was truly glad to learn that Lady Manvers and their little boy were quite well ...

9 May   ... Mr Clinton F. Clinton called to see me on business, he was married to Miss Welby on this day week ...

10 May   [*Back at Clumber*] Met Smirke at Markham – it wants nothing but the dome – I was highly pleased.

11 May   Busy with Mr Smirke, we have marked out and settled the terrace, it is to be begun upon immediately the building will commence in a week or 10 days. The Library and all concerned it is to be begun upon at the same time.

1825

12 May   Mr Smirke left me this morning.

16/17 May   [*Set off for London, stopped the night at Biggleswade. He was involved in an accident* 'on entering London after passing the first toll bar'. *All four horses fell and the post boy was fortunate to escape serious injury.*]

19 May   I rode with Lord Combermere to see the Tunnel which is commenced, to go under the Thames ...

20 May   ... all the world is at Epsom races.

21 May   Dined with the Duke of York and met there a large Protestant party ...

22 May   This being my dear boy Lincoln's birth day I have brought Georgiana and Charlotte to Salt Hill and have got leave for Lincoln to join us. He is now 14 ... my little party are as happy as can be.

23 May   [*Mr Thompson (tutor to the boys at Eton) discussed his intention to marry.*]

24 May   [*With the children*] ... visiting my old haunts ...

25 May   [*Scarlet fever at Eton*] – I have decided to take Lincoln to London with me tomorrow.

26 May   [*Mentions the death of Mrs Stanhope – his Mother's sister-in-law*] – Miss Spencer has been giving me trouble since my return home ... she is so touchy and suspicious ... every thing gives offence ... how constantly plagued I am ...

29 May   [*Reports that Army and Navy promotions have been announced – amongst them, Lord Combermere has been made a full General and George Mundy was to take command of the Royal Sovereign Yacht.*]

1 June   I took Lincoln to the riding school for the first time ...

7 June   This has been a melancholy day to me, in the evening I dined with Lord and Lady Combermere and then took a painful leave from my oldest and only remaining confidential friend. [*Lord Combermere was being posted to India.*]

8 June   [*Took Lincoln back to Eton.*] Dined with the Lord Mayor at the Mansion House ...

11 June   ... I took my dear girl Georgiana to Lambeth Palace to be confirmed. My excellent and esteemed friend the Archbishop performed the ceremony. To me the scene was peculiarly painful. 18 years since I was present in the same Church and at the same altar for a different purpose, how changed is my state ...

16 June   I have long been made very uncomfortable by Miss Spencer's unpleasant conduct ... [*problems had arisen over his wish to arrange horse riding lessons for Georgiana – as a result, Miss*

1825

Spencer had threatened to resign. The Duke indicates that he would not attempt to dissuade her from leaving.] How eternally am I plagued and harrassed, how miserable my life is!

20 June Lord William Bentinck [*brother of the Duke of Portland*] called upon me this morning – he came to announce his intention of resigning his seat for Nottinghamshire at the next Election ...

24 June My Mother has seen Miss Spencer today ... the result is that she stays. ... Went to see Mr Westmacott to see his model of a monument to my dearest Wife and children ...

26 June ... Mr Nash shewed me the plans for the alterations of Buckingham House ... It is a wretched site and nothing can be made of it – Hyde Park within the Ring is the best place for a Palace.

29 June ... Saw Mr [*Richard A. Freebairn 1797-1826*?] the Sculptor – ordered of him two statues, one a boy and a tiger licking his foot, the other a boy as a Cupid, a companion to Psyche which he made for me. Lincoln came home today.

1 July ... I received today an invitation to the King's party on the 4th the cards have been out for several days, nearly a week; I shall not go and shall excuse myself, if I am not worthy of being invited amongst the first ...

2 July Bought two fine carriage horses 4 years old one at £110 the other £100.

9 July [*He had planned to leave London for Clumber but had been delayed. Charlotte had been very ill for several days and most of his diary entries relate to her progress.* Today he writes of 'her attendant Mary Kerrod' *and, on finding Charlotte somewhat recovered*: 'I could only discharge my feelings by tears of joy and heartfelt thanks'.]

10 July [*Charlotte very ill again – the Duke prepared himself for her death.*] 'To Thy Will O' God I bow, if it should please thee to take from me my dear child, I will not express a wish even, but if it pleases thee to restore her to me, I hope I may know how to conduct myself under such a blessing – To thy protection and mercy O Almighty God, I humbly but confidently resign myself and my beloved children! – all in fact that I hold to on earth, for tho' I live here I have for some time ceased to belong to this world.

16 July ... Charlotte ... out of danger.

21 July ... Charlotte ... [*ate*] the wing of a chicken in some broth ... and with considerable relish ...

22 July ... Yesterday I had the satisfaction of seeing the print [*an engraving by Reynolds*] of my ever beloved Wife completed. Thirty of the first proofs were sent to me for distribution to our friends, the likeness is admirable.

1825

28 July	... Drove out in the curricle this evening, with Lincoln.
29 July	... Went to see a cricket match in Lord's ground between Eton and Harrow school ...
1 August	At least we have left London! ... stopped for the night at Hatfield [*Although offered accommodation at Hatfield House, he declined, and stayed at the Inn.*]
2 August	... went to see Hatfield House [*Lord and Lady Salisbury's*] ... very like Blickling in Norfolk. We arrived at Eaton ... where we sleep.
3 August	Arrived at Witham Common.
4 August	Today we reached Clumber at 6 o'clock ...
5/6 August	Played cricket at Clumber with the boys who were old enough.
12 August	... About 40 red legged partridges which had been hatched here were brought into the pleasure ground today in their coops. I have hitherto been unsuccessful in increasing the breed of these birds here, I am now making another attempt.

Figs. 13 and 14

14 August	Charlotte went to Chapel [*within the House*] – Caroline went to Church for the first time in her life. [*Probably at Bothamsall.*]
18/19 August	... we amuse ourselves pleasantly in various employments and amusements, looking at the works and particularly in forming a grotto near the Engine house, which promises to be a beautiful thing – then comes cricket, feeding the young partridges ...
25 August	... we all went by water ... to the Engine House garden to see the grotto making, staid there some time and returned by water ... [*He and all ten children went in one boat, the Duke and Lincoln 'pulled' and Charles 'steered'.*] Miss Spencer returned this evening.
29/30 August	Turned out some red legged partridges in Bothamsall fields ...
31 August	I have taken the first opportunity since my return of seeing the new Church at Markham – I was fully satisfied with it ...

1825

1 September   Went out shooting, killed 17½ brace of partridges and 8 hares ...

2 September   [*The 'excellent Rowlands' was due to visit Clumber but was unwell – the Duke mentions that Rowlands would have been delighted at the changes made to his* 'Old Master's [*2nd Duke*] favourite place'.]

3 September   Went out shooting ... killed 17 brace of partridges plus 5 hares.

5 September   Went out shooting, killed 20 brace of partridges, 2 hares and 5 rabbits.

7 September   When shall I be at rest? Probably not on this side of the grave! My House-Steward and my Farmer are going, probably my land Steward will follow ... During my absence they have been doing wrong, which I have detected and as much [*sic*] of the heads of departments seem combined and connected – if one suffers all must – Honesty and good conduct seem extinct ...

8 September   Queen Anne's Bounty has been offered to the Curacy of Bothamsall, which has been refused as neither the Incumbent or I wish for it – but the Archbishop of York seems inclined to insist upon its being received, I on the other hand shall persist in refusing it ...[*The 'Bounty' being a fund for augmenting poor livings.*]

11 September   [*Records the death of the sculptor, Richard A. Freebairn*] –

                His 'Pysche' which I possess, will perpetuate his name, his talents and his exquisite taste – It is the only work that he ever executed in marble ...

12 September   This morning the disposition of the lower class was practically illustrated. Some men (8 or 10) who were employed to dig foundations for the new terrace, did not keep their time or work properly when here – the clerk of works spoke to them – when they told him they should work as they pleased – they did not come here to work as they would any where else – He said they must, they then said they would leave the work, they one and all struck and within 5 minutes left the place ...

14 September   Poor old Rowlands arrived today ...

15 September   I have shewn him [*Rowlands*] some of my alterations, which I call improvements, and he is quite delighted with them.

19 September   My farmer and house steward are to stay, it appears that they are less to blame than I thought ...[*See 7th September above.*]

20 September   ... I should record an anecdote of my noble boy Lincoln, among other excellencies, infinitely to his praise – On the morning of his leaving me, I forgot to give him the usual pocket money, but he never hinted at the omission, nor did any expression of his countenance betray his thoughts – So little selfish and mercenary is he, that I really believe his mind never turns towards having the money given to him – Nobody ever knew a finer or more noble boy than he is.

1825

21 September	John Sinclair, my sailor, died this morning ... with me for many years ... been in all the great actions from the beginning of the revolutionary war and was remarkably clever and handy about every thing – He is quite a loss to me.
29 September	Two persons from Retford waited upon me to solicit me to send a candidate to Retford on the true Protestant interest ... I told them that I was afraid to have any concern with such slippery people.
30 September	Sir Wm. Clinton came here this evening from Newark where he had been to dine with the Mayor ...
3 October	Wrote to Portland – soliciting him to give up that part of Carburton lying between the turnpike road and this Park. [*He doubts that Portland will agree.*]
6 October	My farmer has purchased 40 Scotch Bullocks at £8.18.6d each – they will average 34 stones next year.
9 October	Busy with Mr Smirke [*arranging to enter the Library through the 'Marble Room' instead of the western end. He also planned to build an extension to the Library on the eastern end – a long half-octagonal – and make a wide opening so as to join the existing room.*]
11 October	Mr Smirke left me this morning. I went to Nottingham to attend the annual meeting of the Asylum ...
12/13 October	The lake is covered in ice ... I received sufficient confirmation yesterday of the high value of my property at Nottingham. I shall endeavour to profit by it – by ornamenting the town and benefiting myself at the same time.
16 October	My mother is meddling again. [*Over the children's upbringing.*]
18 October	Wrote to Col. Lumley on his own and his mad brother's affair ... I shall deprive him of hunting my coverts.
21 October	A deputation from the True Blue Club came to take my opinion about a candidate for Retford – they are determined to bring in a protestant member. Received from Mr Saville a most abusive and indecent letter – he is a madman ...
22 October	Called on Lord Manvers ... [*he was advised to ignore* 'the pen of a liar and a madman'.]
23 October	They are fitting the Mausoleum inside.
24 October	... Some mischievous and evil spirited people went into the new Grotto yesterday and broke off the shells carrying some away and leaving others on the ground, some of the shells were found by the Retford road side. This tendency to wanton injury has much annoyed me. I never can keep anything from the destruction of the people, if it is exposed to their depredations and unguarded.

1825

25 October ... began cutting the sand rock for the approach thro' the hill on the lawn ... I have made my plan completely and feel sure that I may be able to make it a very beautiful as well as a handsome thing.

26 October The good old Rowlands left us today ... he made all the family happy by his presence.

28 October Except when I was teaching the children – I have been occupied all day in directing the workmen how to form the sand rock. It requires that one should stand over them nearly all the day to prevent their making mistakes and spoiling the scenery.

31 October ... It is lamentable to see what men can get into the Church – the son of Salvin, butcher of Elkesley, merely went to a Mr Brooks, a mischievously Methodistical curate at Retford, he there qualified himself for the Ministry and is now officiating as a country Curate ... it can only produce evil – a correction is loudly called for ...

2 November My Mother came here today ...

6 November ... Very busily engaged always with my workmen at the cut thro' the hill, it requires constant watching to get them to form the rocks as they should be.

12 November ... A sharp frost each of these days, the lake covered with ice today, such an early beginning of winter announces that the winter to come will be mild – and yet the trees of all descriptions are covered with acorns, nuts and berries.

16 November My Mother left today – I do heartily wish that she was less meddling, pryingly anxious and inclined to dictate from thinking that she alone is right. This must always make us uneasy and ill together, notwithstanding her many excellent qualities which I respect as a Son and a man – I have exercised much patience and forbearance during her short stay now and I hope that I may be able to continue to do so, altho' much against my nature, which is not well calculated for concealment.

17 November ... Sir Henry Wilson has offered himself for Retford as an avowed and staunch opposer of Rom Cath. pretensions – he has therefore my fullest support, altho' I believe he is otherwise somewhat queer in character and conduct – Sir Henry called here this evening and thanked me for my support of him.

18 November As the Archbishop of Canterbury could not come here I went today to Kelham to see him ...All my good and kind friends at Kelham received me with that attention and true cordiality which I always experience from them.

19 November Returned to Clumber ...

1825

20 November	Only Henrietta and Robert [*aged 6 and 5*] remain in the Nursery.
22 November	Rode to see how they were proceeding in fitting up the inside of Markham Church – and also to look at the new Lodge at the entrance to the avenue near Drayton – the roof is on and I was greatly pleased with the effect of the new building which I think truly pretty and suitable.
23 November	Nothing new – occupied with inspecting my workmen.
25 November	Mother took the Sacrament with us.
27 November	Came to Ranby on a visit to my Mother for two nights.
28 November	I could not sleep well last night in spite of all reasoning – My Mother has given me for a bedroom, the room where [*my step-father*] Sir Charles Crawford died – the bed is in the same place, and as I thought, the same which he had used – the idea is so unpleasant that it requires many appeals to my reason to get the better of my prejudice – Still I could not so far overcome it as not to pass a sleepless night – My Mother gave me to understand in conversation this morning that the bed is one from another room – however I was glad that I was enabled to gain a victory over weak feelings – for I no longer thought much of the matter.
29 November	... Returned from Ranby – found all my dear children well.
30 November	To Nottingham to meet Mr Robinson [*architect*] and my Steward relative to the new town – busily engaged with them on the ground and with plans.
1 December	After a thorough search of the ground this morning and a very minute inspection of every thing, we have at length matured a very grand, a very beautiful and if ever executed a very useful plan for the town and public –
	My opinion is that the scheme will take well and that it will be highly beneficial and productive to me and eminently ornamental and beneficial to the Town and County – It certainly is a bold and grand scheme.
	Reached Clumber this evening at 7 o'clock.
3 December	... Mr Smirke has sent me a beautiful sketch of a monument to be erected to my Father's memory at Windsor. I have suggested an alteration by substituting two warriors, as Clinton and Pelham, instead of two Angels – I shall derive infinite gratification from discharging this long neglected duty to a kind and excellent Parent.
5 December	My House Steward Todd dangerously ill of a violent inflammatory fever ...
7 December	My very dear boy Lincoln arrived this evening from Eton ...

1825

10 December   Todd died this morning – respected and regretted by the whole house – his end was peaceable and his conduct throughout firm and collected ...

17 December   ... I have had my wood at Morton valued at 42,000£ – I cut down and sell from 10 to 15,000 of it, to assist me in compleating my alterations here.

20 December   Caroline left her nursery and went to Miss Spencer – only Henrietta and Robert remain in the nursery ...

25 December   My Mother came today before Chapel and took the Sacrament here with us – On this day how mournfully is the remembrance of my beloved partner brought to me. In every thing have I missed her this day, first congratulations in the morning, at the altar, and at the fireside.

30 December   I have been unwell with a bowel complaint ...

1 January	... I wish I could think that I had done more good, my lot is to be contented with the negative praise of not having done any positive evil ... I have no taste for the modern life ... My life, except for my family ... is a misery to me.
	We exchanged our gifts with great joy and satisfaction this morning and all the dear children were well and truly happy.
2 January	Today, as yesterday was Sunday, the annual gifts of clothing to the needy poor in my parishes, was distributed to them – they assembled at 11, had their tea, bread, cheese and small bun and then round to the front of the house to have their separate parcels distributed to each.
9 January	... Out shooting today, Captain Mundy, in shooting back at a rabbit, killed a Newfoundland dog led by one of my keepers and wounded the man a good deal in the thigh ...
	[*Very, very upset by his mother's involvement with the children*] ... makes property of them, spoils them, talks nonsense ... and unsettles my mode and plan of education ... she is little to be trusted.
17/18 January	Passed a day at Thoresby and returned this morning.
19 January	My very dear delightful and noble boy [*Lincoln*] left me this morning for Eton ...
30 January	On this day I am 41 years old – a great age to have lived without having achieved extensive usefulness or distinguished service ...
1 February	[*Out shooting but unenthusiastic about the sport*] ... I am quite down, and would gladly have declined ...
2 February	The Ice is not clear lower than opposite the Temple.
4 February	... my present rents are founded upon a price of 56s a quarter of wheat ...
6 February	Came to Shipley on a visit for a few days. I have not been here for several years ...

1826

8 February	Went to see the new jail at Derby ...
10 February	Returned home ...

11 February   On my return home yesterday I found a great pile of letters on my table – many of them were relating to the contest now carrying on at Retford ... they intimated to me that the town of Retford was in a dreadful state, that the mob was rioting from morning till night, that every sort of outrage was committed, that there was no personal safety and that the civil authority was set at naught ... I returned for answer that unless I received a representation from the Magistrates stating that their authority could do nothing and that extensive danger was to apprehend, that I could do nothing ...

I did not write so but I inwardly thought that the popery candidates and their abettors deserved all that had or might happen to them. They will be very mad when they find that all their acts and machinations fail, for what amuses me most is, that these ragamuffins threaten to take away my character.

[*Sir H. Wilson called to inform the Duke of his 'triumphal procession from Tuxford to Retford'. Sir Henry stayed the night at Clumber House.*]

17 February   Engaged for several days past with Mr Gilpin, finishing up the line of water towards the bridge and giving ornamenting touches to all that I have done on the lawn and around the House as well as towards Thoresby Lodge – and the rock gardens.

18 February   [*Mentions the death of Mr J. Manners Sutton of Kelham*] –

His great kindness from childhood to my dearest Georgiana [*late Duchess*] will ever be remembered in grateful affection.

20 February   Mr Gilpin went this morning. I took him to see the new Church at Markham which he admired very much and indeed I think it is well worthy of admiration on account of its architecture, finish and completeness.

10 March   ... I passed by my Girl's garden and stopped there to meet them, they gave me some early flowers and I bid them farewell – I stopped at Markham new Church ... I arrived at Grantham rather late and slept there.

11 March   Arrived in London.

14 March   ... went to see the Lincoln chapel in St. George's Chapel, Windsor, with a view to decide upon the situation for a monument to my father. I found the old monument of the 1st E. of Lincoln in bad condition and wretchedly repaired – I shall have it all made better and put in compleat repair. Soon after we reached London, Miss Spencer and her charge arrived from Clumber, the 3 dear girls were perfectly well ...

1826

16 March [*He records that he has been informed that his family is descended from Rosamond Clifford – commonly known as Fair Rosamond, the most famous mistress of Henry II. Other family associations are noted, such as those with Henry de Lacy, Earl of Lincoln – also with a John Baron Clinton.*]

19 March [*Mentions that he has only recently become aware of the benefits to be gained by regular reading of the Bible*] – I cannot express the gratification which this study conveys.

25 March Miss Spencer [*governess*] ... impertinent, giving trouble and vexation.

29 March Dined with the Duke of York, which is to me always an honor and a pleasure. It was not a large party ... I only wish that he was much younger ...

30 March I wore yesterday for the first time the broach with King William's portrait, given me by Lord Combermere with an injunction to wear it on all Protestant occasions, which I promised to do and shall observe ...

I was for some hours today with Mr Westmacott modelling the head for the figure intended to represent my ever dear wife ...

31 March Again with Mr Westmacott about our work ...

6 April Went with Lincoln to see the Tunnell making under the Thames ...

10 April Took Lincoln to the theatre to hear Matthew's recitation etc ... it was his first time of hearing English acting – he was once at the opera. I shall take him in a few nights time quietly to a play, perhaps Georgiana also – I must begin to take them to these things to teach them what to do and what to avoid.

20 April Mother is matchmaking ... !! ...What could be more ill judged ... She unfortunately considers that she has control over me, as her child – forgetting that I am a rather old child of 41 ...

21 April A model of a monument to my Father was brought to me. I directed some alterations in the figures. I shall feel a great satisfaction when the monument is completed and created.

26 April ... Mr Godfrey has resigned the agency at Newark ... I have appointed Mr Tallents in his place.

1 May ... Dined with Lord Westmoreland and met the Duke of York ...

2 May ... Dined with the Duke of Northumberland with a large party to meet the Duke of York ...

4 May ... I waited on the Duke of York today and invited H.R.H. to dine with me which he kindly accepted.

20 May ... went to see the new London bridge ... We then went to the Tunnel ...

1826

21 May ... I proposed to Mr Murdoch an eminent commercial man to come into parliament which he has declined on account of age ...

22 May This is my dear and noble boy (*Lincoln's*) birth day. He is now 15. May God bless, protect and guide him a long and useful life to his Country and to the cause of every thing that is great good and exemplary.

24 May As a specimen of the state of the lower orders now, I must record what I have heard of a hack cabriolet driver – He was driving a gentleman who told the story and who found the man talk [*sic*] very well and freely and on all subjects, after a little time he said to the gentleman, "do you see that slug, do you know him". No was the answer – He replied "Oh that's the Bishop of – one of the black slugs that eat all the corn up, that's all he's good for". These are the fruits of the march of intellect and the progress of knowledge.

27 May The Duke of York did me the honor to dine with me, we were a large party of all the principal and best people who are supporters of those principles which we cling to and which we believe are necessary for the welfare and political existence of the country ... the whole thing ... went off most satisfactorily ...

28 May ... Yesterday and the day before were most painful days to me. I had to look into stores where various ornaments were laid up, which had actually been packed up by the hands of one so dear to me, thus taking me back several years to very different times. Now all was to be done by myself, recalling most painful recollections. I called too on [*Lord?*] St. Helens, who lived in the very house to which I had often resorted previous to my marriage, and then went to the Statuary's [*Westmacott*], who wished to see me, and there I saw the monument to the memory of several dear objects, and for the first time, the cast taken from my dear child Anna Maria, of whose figure Westmacott had just made a sketch in clay, full size, for my inspection ...

29 May I have been called upon to complete the purchase which I made the year before last of Wellow. I have not the money ... The sum is about £15,000 and all that I can do is to ask the Trustees to allow me to postpone the payment.

31 May ... Several new Peers are made ... it is a prostitution of the Peerage ... several Irish and Scotch Lords are to have English titles ... mere jobbers and higglers who by their craft make themselves useful in a certain way, and then receive a reward to the disparagement of the British peerage ...

1 June [*Heard that Lincoln had scarletina.*]

1826

2 June   ... My Mother was at Frogmore to stay with Princess Augusta and saw the doctor who attends [*Lincoln*].

3 June   My letters today tell me that Lincoln is perfectly well ...

4 June   Georgiana, Charlotte and Caroline were revaccinated today by Mr Macgregor in both arms. So many persons have taken small pox after vaccinated that it is thought prudent to renew it ...

5 June   Plagued out of my seven senses in making settlings and arrangements preparatory to leaving London.

6 June   My daughters went off to Clumber this morning – Mr Thompson has found a nice house for Lincoln at Richmond, where I hope the dear boy will be well and comfortable during his three weeks quarantine ...

7 June   ... reached Biggleswade at 10, where I sleep ..

8 June   Arrived at Clumber at 7 this evening – I left Biggleswade at a little after 6 in the morning. At Newark, I stopped some time with Sir Wm. Clinton and Mr Tallents ...

9 June   Today the Elections will commence in many boroughs. At Retford there has been much disturbance and the soldiers were called in. As far as I can learn, they behaved very improperly and charged the band of Sir H. Wilson's party whilst they were playing God Save the King in the Market Place, many were much hurt and one woman nearly killed ...

10 June   [*Election riots at Newark*] – Yeomanry and Militia staff were called out and order was restored ...

11 June   [*After mention of the Elections at Aldborough and Boroughbridge*] – ... these elections will cost me much money.

22 June   [*Following several days of illness amongst the children*] – ... How one loves the dear little creatures when one sees them suffering with patience, and how God must love them for such obedience and resignation ...

26 June   ... Signed a Bond for £5,000 to Admiral Sotheron, to bear 5 per cent Interest dated June 24 ...

28 June   ... the heat is very great, yesterday on a Northern Wall, the thermometer stood at 90.

29 June   ... 4 sheep killed by lightening – under the larch tree on the eastern side of the Gardens near the Cow Pasture ...

10 July   Lincoln is returned to Eton ...

12 July   ... I began my harvest yesterday – a field of oats near Cabin Hill – perhaps this is the earliest harvest in the memory of any living man.

14 July   Went to the Assizes at Nottingham, dined with the Judge, Lord Chief J. Abbott, and returned home ...

1826

17 July   The hooping cough is going on favorably – but my dear little Robert has it severely, the phlegm chokes him almost ...

18 July   ... Charles was taken alarmingly ill today with choking ...

19 July   ... After dinner Edward was taken ill ... pulse at 120.

21 July   My dear children are better today ...

24 July   Mr Russel, our Doctor, tells me that he is well satisfied in his own mind that we have all (I included) gone through scarletina anginosa ...

25 July   ... Turned out 30 red legged partridges in a wheat field in this Park – out of 12 dozen eggs these are all that I have reared – those which I turned out last year have bred this year.

30 July   ... Tomorrow, I go for a night to my friend [*Henry Gally*] Knight at Firbeck.

1 August   My very dear Lincoln arrived this afternoon ... very much grown ...

3 August   Executed a Bond to Mr Collyer of Park Place – for £3,000 ...

5 August   I have lately been placing my boundary fence in its proper place. The Duke of Portland has inquired whether I have the right to place it where I have placed it – for once, I shall perhaps to be able to gain a point against him, not an easy matter with one so alive to every thing relating to his interests.

9 August   ... Lincoln began to shoot with a gun today for the first time, he shot at some sparrows, but did not kill any, he has a very good notion of shooting and in a few days, will be able to hit his mark with tolerable certainty, I have little doubt – at every thing he is so adroit and intelligent – he is also very obedient to all which I tell him.

15 August   Much of the plain work is prepared for the Terrace – begun the addition to the Library today. In its former state I found the dimensions to be too small so that altho' up to the top of the plinth I determined upon pulling it down and extending it to its present size, it will now form an excellent room of 30 feet clear and give me a better opportunity of ornamenting the exterior.

18 August   Yesterday Charlotte commenced a change in life, she is yet very young, as she is only 14 in Oct. and I should have been glad if this period had been deferred, however she is going on well, thank God, and tho' it will probably stop her growth, yet if she has health, that is the main thing.

Sir H. Wilson who called here today ... [*informs me*] ... that he should found a hospital for 12 decayed freemen at Retford, with a house garden and £10 a year each and that he should leave it to me after his death [*currently known as 'Protestant Place'?*]

1826

19 August	... Lincoln shot 43 little birds today with the new gun I have given him ...
23 August	This is my dear little Caroline's birth day ...
24 August	[*Notes that he had signed a Lease from the Bishop of Lincoln, relating to the 'tythes of Clumber' and mentions three new 'lives' at £1,000 – possibly 'livings'?*] Lincoln killed a partridge flying today ...
29 August	I have had the ill luck to lose a remarkably fine horse which I bought in London for my own riding, at £150 – he died of mercurial physic improperly administered.
30 August	... my excellent and highly valued friend Sutton, died at Kelham this morning ... I find myself bereaved of all old friends and well known and well tried intimates ... alone in the world.
1 September	Lincoln went out shooting with me ... he shot very well for a beginner and killed 4 partridge and 2 hares ... We killed only 21 partridges, 5 hares and a rabbit ...
4 September	... began my fountains on the terrace ...
5 September	Went to Ranby with my children to prepare rooms for them ... for a change of air.
8 September	Mr Westmacott came here to see about a fit situation in the New Church for the monument which he has in hand for me.
10/11 September	The 3 eldest girls and Miss Spencer went to Ranby for a change of air to stay for a week. Went with Mr Westmacott to Markham Church ... all plans changed regarding the Vaults ... remove the present catacombs in the aisles of the transept and placing them under the floor of the body of the church, then to leave the aisles and that part of the building clear as a depository for monuments – the idea is excellent and precisely accordant with my feelings on such a subject – I shall adopt it.
12 September	Mr Westmacott left me today ...
13 September	... A Mr Morison is come here to model my profile in wax, which he is executing for Sir Wm. Clinton.
14 September	My Mother is gone on another visit to Princess Augusta at Frogmore ...
16 September	We went (Lincoln and I) to Ranby to breakfast this morning and arrived at 1/2 past 8 – We afterwards went shooting and arrived at Morton Farm at 1/2 past 10.
17 September	My three girls returned from Ranby to go to Chapel here ...
19 September	[*He commissioned Mr Morison to 'form a likeness' of the late Duchess, using the profile sketch drawn by the Duke and an engraving by Reynolds.*]

1826

20 September | My House Steward (March), has been dreadfully beaten by five men at Worksop ... I am informed that this is a constant practice at that town ... intend to take up the matter ... discover the offenders ... endeavour to break up the gang of scoundrels which abound in the town.

22 September | Lincoln returned to Eton today, I accompanied him as far as Mr Thompson's and then mounted my horse which was waiting for me ... My 3 dear Girls also returned to Ranby, so that I am, as it were, quite solitary, and have full cause to lament the absence of such delightful companions.

26 September | The events of this day 4 years are not forgotten by me – How should they indeed – My life, ever since, has been as it were a mere blank!

1/6 October | .. having a large party in my house, my time has been a good deal occupied in shooting ...

7 October | Looked at the Clumber Park boundaries with Mr Parkinson ... quite evident – it is marked by a bank of earth and a ditch beyond it.

[*Probably along the Carburton Lodge to Worksop 'Truman's' Lodge boundary.*]

9 October | I have seen a letter from an Officer at the Cape of Good Hope (Major Molesworth) who, in answer to enquiries made of him, writes that the Settlers from Nottinghamshire are thriving well in their location, "that there is no such thing as poverty in Albany except amongst those who have brought it upon themselves by drinking and idleness". A wife of one of the party (Dennison formerly a Sergeant and an orderly well conducted man) can earn 30 dollars ... a month as a nurse ...

12/13 October | ... My new addition to the Library is now nearly up and looks very well – it seems to me to enrich the garden front and is of itself a very beautiful specimen, as I think.

14 October | A small Balloon was picked up yesterday in this Park which was seen to descend in the West fields between 5 and 6 o'clock, tied to it there was a note signed Saml. Parr stating that it was started from Bolton in Lancashire Oct 7 1826, it is surprising that it should have remained up so long in the air.

17 October | Came to Nottingham today to be ready for tomorrow morning, the anniversary meeting of the Hospital ...

I am assured too that my building scheme if undertaken would be successful and that I have been cajoled when I have been told that it would fail. Houses are in great demand and cannot be had for money. Such a house as I am letting for £40 a year is let by another for £150.

1826

18 October	Returned home from Nottingham this evening. Lord Manvers accompanied me in my carriage ...
23 October	The Manor of Willoughby and a small estate belonging to Mr Gally Knight was sold today by Auction and I became the purchaser for £4,000 and auction duty £116 – the wood on the Estate to be taken at a valuation, it will pay only 2 per cent but the land is so situated that it was incumbent upon me to purchase it.
30 October	Came here (to Kirklington) on a visit of a few days ... The Admiral and Mrs Sotheron are all kindness to me ... It was here that my ever dear wife was educated from her earliest years, under the parental care of her wise and good Aunt, Mrs Whethem ... I passed many well remembered and interesting days here during my first acquaintance with my future wife as Miss Mundy. [*Georgiana's mother, previously Lady Middleton, had died when Georgiana was born.*]
31 October	We rode to Southwell today to see the recent alterations, or rather the restorations, of the Minster. These are all judiciously and well done and the Minster is now beginning to assume its actual character and the whole is very well and carefully kept.

Fig. 15 *Southwell Minster from Greenwood's map – surveyed in 1826*

1826

This building is perhaps the most curious specimen of Saxon architecture in the kingdom – it was built in the time of John – and is in high preservation, considering its great antiquity. A new library has just been made within the Church by merely erecting bookshelves within the arches of one of the out chapels and making a fireplace – it is a very compleat and comfortable little establishment.

I saw the painted glass windows lately put in, which are beautifully executed and greatly ornament the Church. These windows contain the arms of the lessees of the Chapter, of which mine is one which I have given to the Chapter – It always gives me pleasure to see this Church of which we have justly reason to pride ourselves, both from the interest which it creates by its antique variety, as by the high condition in which it is kept.

1 November   Went to the Southwell House of Correction ... Keeper, Mr Mole ... saw the operation of the tread-mill for the first time. Afterwards went to see the associated Poor House [*Southwell Workhouse*] – which has been erected about two years ... It is too much on the prison system without the necessity for it, and for the aged there are not those comforts and accommodations which one would desire to see given to old age, which is compelled to dwell under this roof. I have mentioned this and it will be rectified. The plan is an excellent one and as a proof of it, out of a population of 14,000, there are not now more than 45 men, women and children in the House, many of these are idiots and those who are not sufficiently insane to send to an asylum.

2 November   ... Returned to Clumber ...

3 November   I have arranged to increase the water engine power from 6480 gallons in 24 hours, to 11,520 gallons in 24 hours. I shall be able to afford a constant supply to the fountains at the Terrace.   Today commenced putting the roof on the new addition to the Library.

6 November   [*Notes that he will only support an applicant for the vacant living at Thorpe, near Newark, provided that he is willing to reside there.*]

11/12 November   Passed a day at Thoresby ...

20 November   ... Today I came to Nottingham with Mr Robinson, to settle what shall be done as to building here ...

21 November   ... in the Spring we shall commence building the first house of a range ... Returned home from Nottingham this evening.

27 November   The Duke of Portland has announced to me, thro' his Agent, that he shall not object to my placing my Park fence where I am now laying it down. He has not given his sanction in a handsome manner, nor should I have expected to have obtained it, unless my claim had been so evident as to bar all dispute.

1826

29 November	... I mean if possible to continue from henceforth to appropriate 2 or 3,000£ a year to alterations, so as to compleat my house to what it ought and I wish it to be – £20,000 would be required to effect my plans and then I should possess as good and as noble a house as the place deserves and my rank requires.
3 December	Charles and Thomas are 13 today ... every promise, thank God, of being a future honor to their family, comfort and blessing to their Parent, and a benefit to their Country.
7 December	My dear Lincoln arrived this afternoon ...
11 December	Lincoln is becoming a very good shot ... 11 pheasants and 3 hares and another day killed 2 woodcocks ...
15 December	... Wrote to the Editor of John Bull, to urge him to use his utmost endeavours to recall the Country from its infatuation ...
21 December	Came to Ranby ...
24 December	I have been engaged today in preparing Georgiana for receiving the Sacrament for the first time tomorrow. I have been delighted and gratified to the greatest degree by the way in which she has conducted herself ...
25 December	This being Christmas day, all my dear little family met together in the morning and exchanged their congratulations. After Chapel, my delightful girl received the Sacrament with me ... My Mother came this afternoon ...
31 December	The last day of a very eventful year. The seeds have been sown of much future evil to England, and I fear that we are doomed to witness some unpleasant times.

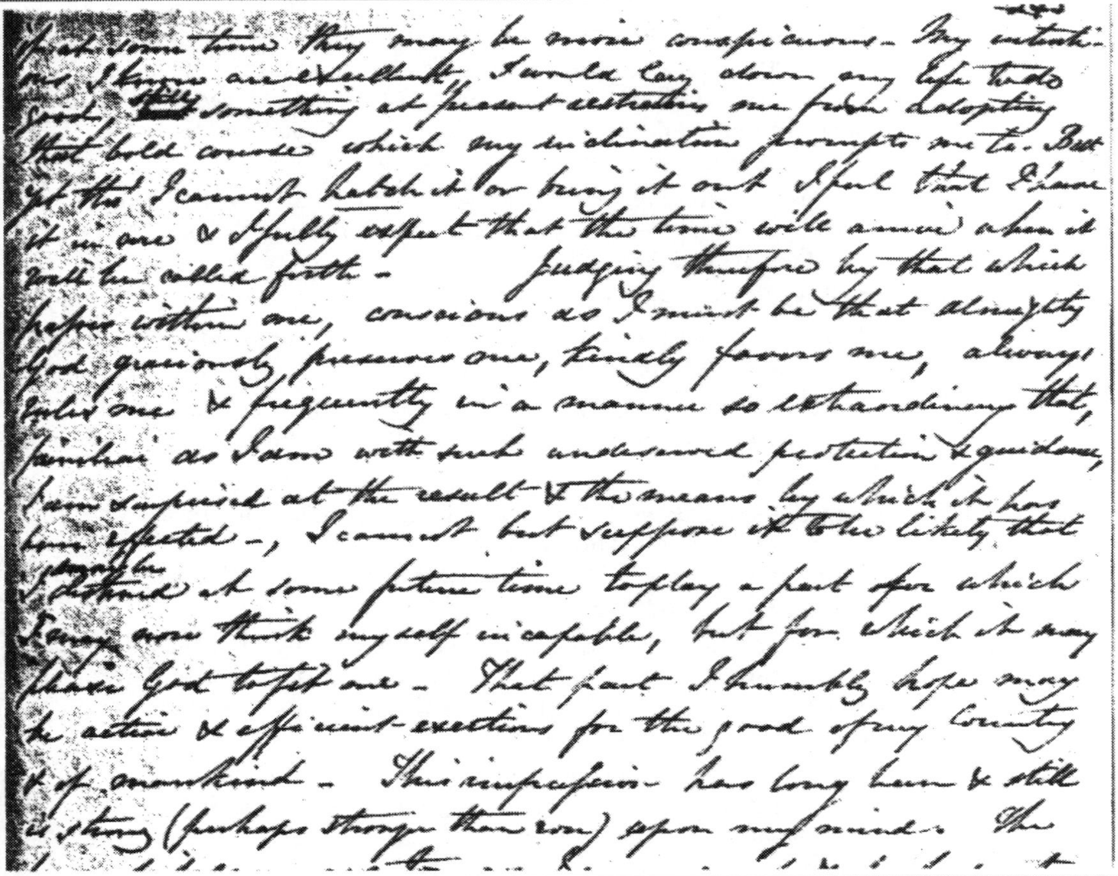

Fig. 16 *Section of a page from the Diaries,*
this one recording the Duke's agonising on 4 June 1827.

1 January   We have passed a most busy and as it has been apparent to all, a very happy day. Our own grand exchange of salutations and presents first took place, which was no small matter! We then distributed clothing to the poor – we dined at 2 o'clock and finished the evening by music and conversation. We gave my mother an agreeable surprise by a trio – Georgiana on the harp, Charlotte on the pianoforte and I on the violin.

6 January   Today being Twelfth Night, we had our cake drawing for King and Queen etc. etc. All the children dressed up in different characters and looked very well ... William [*age 12*] looked an excellent Falstaff. We have never had such a grand Twelfth night.

7 January   The excellent Duke of York is dead ... I fully expect that his death will cause great political changes.

10 January The Duke of Portland came here today to confer about the boundaries of Clumber Park [*on the western side*]. It was agreed that I am to have my fence set within two feet of the ditch on the side of the birches from Worksop Gateway to Carburton Gateway, in rights of deer leap – but from Carburton Gateway to Budby covan, I relinquish the rights of deer leap to the Duke of Portland who, in lieu, gives up to me the clump adjoining the Worksop Gateway.

11 January [*Following a summons from the King that he attend the funeral of the Duke of York as* 'one of the Supporters of the Pall'] – I shall accept the honor with readiness and gratitude ...

12 January My Mother went back to Ranby today.

14 January A violent storm of wind has blown the Old Thorn tree down, near to the House. I painfully regret this loss for it was under this tree that my dearest wife sat to take the air only two days before her death ...

18 January Left Clumber this morning with Lincoln, Charles and Thomas and Mr Thompson – we arrived at Wandsford at 1/2 past 6 and slept there.

61

1827

19 January	Arrived at Portman Square at 7 o'clock.
20 January	Went to Windsor to attend the Funeral of the Duke of York. The Pall bearers besides me were the Dukes of Beaufort, Rutland, Dorset, Northumberland and Wellington – The Duke of Clarence was Chief Mourner ... an extraordinary and to my mind a very indecent part of the proceedings was the appointment of the Duke of Norfolk as Earl Marshall. He looked as insignificant in person as he is in character and the view of him on such an occasion was quite unpleasant to me ...
21 January	... I took Charles and Thomas to Dr Keate and entered them as Etonians and gave them a sight of what the school and schoolboys are.
22 January	... In the evening after dinner and after a suitable admonition to them on launching them into this little world, I parted with infinite regret from my dear and delightful boys ... I think it quite improbable that a more perfect love can subsist between parent and children than subsists between us.
25 January	Received a very pleasant account from Mr Thompson of my dear boys ...
26 January	Left London about 12 and went to see a house at Acton – The Priory – with a view to taking it to put my children into instead of leaving them at Clumber when I am in London – it is a pretty but small place ... Slept at Eaton.
27 January	Arrived at Clumber at 6, after a most dreary and cold journey, the ground covered with snow and very [*severe?*] weather ...
28 January	[*Noting the continuing bad weather*] – as proof of the roads, people were skating <u>up the hill</u> at Norman Cross.
29 January	Lord Newark [*from Thoresby, a young man, just finished his studies*] shot with me at Clumber.
30 January	I have reached 42 this day ... I saw the Hounds at Thoresby ... not done so for 10 or 12 years ...
4 February	Executed duplicates of a Memorandum of an agreement between the Duke of Portland and me arranging the boundaries of Clumber Park – one copy to be kept by the Duke of Portland the other by me.
8 February	I completed a likeness in wax of my dear wife Georgiana [*assisted by the sketch he had made in his 1822 diary.*]
9 February	... Mr Gilpin has been here for some days. I am finishing the Island opposite to the house and touching up various parts by planting single and groups of trees, opening others, finishing the [*banks?*] near the bridge etc.
25/26 February	... left Clumber ... arrived at Biggleswade ...

1827

27 February Arrived in London ... went down to the House of Lords ...

28 February Went to Eton ...

1 March Brought Lincoln with me to London ...

2 March ... Went to the H. of Lords, took the oaths and my seat, – afterwards presented 5 petitions against an alteration of the principle of the Corn Laws ...

[*Notes that Mr Thompson had written to report Lincoln's excellent conduct towards his young brothers at Eton.*]

10 March [*Writes that he is being urged to lead a new parliamentary party – two days later he explains that it was to be called 'The King's friends'.*] – I have been too little used to such affairs to be fit for the purpose ...

12 March ... rode to Wimbledon common to look at a house which I propose to take to have all my children near to me ...

15 March [*Presented a petition in the House of Lords*] – against the Rom. Cath. Pretensions. I took the occasion to make some observations ...

17 March My dear boys ... returned to Eton this evening ...

18 March Georgiana is 17 today ... [*Speculates (and approves of the possibility) that she might marry Mr Cavendish, heir presumptive to the Duke of Devonshire.*]

22 March The plot thickens upon me and upon the country ...

How the world alters and how men and women are merely players having their exits and their entrances! A short time since and I was busied only in my domestic concerns thinking only of my children and my family affairs – Now I am suddenly thrown into a position, as unlooked for as it will be troublesome, of chief of a party and the only one (as they say) whom they can now look up to for supporting those principles with unshaken firmness, which can alone ensure the integrity of our Constitution and the welfare of our Country – I am fully aware that I am utterly unfit for such a post, but there is no one else, such is the dearth of talent, of great and of good men – It happens that thro' God's providence, I have preserved a good character and now in this hour of peril and of difficulty, it has its weight and thus possibly the frequent and most earnest prayer of my heart may be accomplished, that I might be a humble instrument of God and for its highest exultation. If I could see my Country glorious in virtue as it is in arms, arts, science and all the worldly acquirements, if I could see my children the brightest ornaments in such a country, what on earth could surpass the feelings of unbounded bliss which such a consciousness would convey!

1827

24 March   Had an audience with the King [*George IV*] at 2 o'clock.

> [*He then left more than six pages blank in his diary – a most unlikely action for him to take as he usually filled every corner. He wrote a separate report of the interview – which, he felt, included a commitment by the King to 'appoint an undoubted Protestant' as his Prime Minister. This Report is also held at the Manuscripts and Special Collections Department of the University of Nottingham.*]

27 March   [*Disillusioned with many peers who had previously expressed their support*] ... our frothy adherents are frightened out of their wits at taking a decided step in Parliament altho' they can talk very highly in private ... what wretched mortals men are! ...

31 March   Came to a house in Putney heath which I have taken for a few months. My dear little children from Clumber are here today ...

1 April   Returned to London this evening ...

6 April   Went with six of the children and Miss Spencer to see the Palace and new Gardens at what was lately Buckingham House ... Nash the Architect has done wonders ... forms a noble House and grounds and certainly our King will be well lodged altho' inferiorly to most other Kings ... came to Roehampton to dinner where I sleep. Lincoln, Charles and Thomas came with me.

7 April   ... Went to Kenwood on a visit to Lord Mansfield.

8 April   Returned from Kenwood ...

11 April   Lincoln was confirmed today by the Archbishop of Canterbury ... This morning I heard that the King had commissioned Mr Canning to form an administration ... 'on the principles of Lord Liverpool' – these are the King's instructions. How this is to be interpreted I know not. Neither can I conceive how the King can forswear himself so much, as to choose Canning, after solemnly assuring me that he would have none but a most truly Protestant Premier – 'It is better to trust in God than place any confidence in Princes' ...

12 April   ... The Protestant part of the administration have resigned ...

> I came to Roehampton yesterday. Today being Good Friday I went to Church at Putney and took the Sacrament there ...

16 April   Returned to London ...

22 April   I came yesterday to Roehampton.

26 April   Came to London from Roehampton and brought my boys ...

28 April   ... Dined at Lambeth ... the excellent Archbishop seeming well and in good spirits.

1 May   Went to the House of Commons to hear Mr Peel make his statement ...

1827

3 May   Took Charles and Thomas to the play – their first time to a theatre.

5 May   Went with the 3 boys to Roehampton this morning to breakfast and for them to take leave of the little ones – Returned to London at 2 ... the dear boys left me for Eton – they are so delightful that parting from them is always most painful. Dined at Somerset House – Royal Academy dinner. [*During the morning he had also seen Mr Hooke, Editor of 'John Bull', regarding political bias in that publication.*]

6 May   [*Met with the Duke of Wellington*]

9 May   ... Dined at Roehampton ...

10 May   [*Attended the Chapter of Garter Knights – thought the King looked 'shy of me'.*] – Went down to the House of Lords ... took occasion to say a few words expressive of my opinion of Mr Canning and his administration ... almost all power of thought left me for a time and it was with difficulty that I could rally my mind and flounder thro' my few sentences ... until I had performed my hated task ...

11 May   Yesterday a cricket ball broke Charles' nose – only one bone broken although there is a deep gash ...

12 May   Charles' nose was set today by Mr Macgregor ...

13 May   Dined at Mr Peel's – all the principal people of our side were there ...

19 May   ... The Thames tunnel has failed ... the water oozed thro' the roof ... the failure will be the total ruin of many.

20 May   ... dined with the Duke of Wellington ...

22 May   This is my dear Lincoln's birth day, he is 16 today ...

23 May   Attended in the H. of Lords ... I afterwards had a large party at dinner ... about 24 ...

26 May   [*Lavish praise for the talents of the sculptor, Lough.*] – I shall contribute to sending him to Italy ...

27 May   Came to Roehampton ...

28 May   Returned to London and attended a dinner of the Pitt Club. I am not a member ...

2 June   Came to Roehampton for 2 or 3 days ...

3 June   A delightful day with the dear children – besides the younger children – the 3 girls are here and came with me from London.

4 June   ... I have seen no one here and have only been occupied with my dear little children, who are overjoyed to have me amongst them.

1827

There is a peculiarity in my life, to which my attention is frequently drawn and which often strikes me in a forcible point of view – I mean the sort of direction and protection which has always been present to me, from my earliest years until the period in which I now live – My trials, my mortifications, my humiliations, have been numerous, severe and perpetual – Born with an ardent mind and strong passions, I have always been under a certain influence which has, absolutely in spite of me, prevented my indulgences of the one on the other – Often I have been on the hazardous brink, but a power stronger than that of the temptor has preserved me from the impending danger – In adversity I am never cast down by despair, because hope never leaves me, in prosperity I have never been blinded or elated, because I am sincerely grateful to the only giver of all good things. Rarely has prosperity been my lot, but if it has, it has always been attended with so many concomitant evils, that one has been a set off against the other and forced reason to draw the balance, humility never failed to follow, and a leaning upon Him only who can at his pleasure bestow ... good or evil – The present world is a most vicious world, society can hardly be worse, and it so happens that perhaps no one of my rank and situation in the country ever was so little in it. By severe trials, by long preparation, I am arrived at a time when I can with more fortitude enter into the affairs of life; at this juncture I am insensibly called forth – My abilities by long disuse, are become unavailing and almost useless to me and yet I find that they are rather improving, and I should not be surprised if at some time they may be more conspicuous – My intentions I know are excellent, I would lay down my life to do good, still something at present restrains me from adopting that bold course which my inclination prompts me to. But yet tho' I cannot hatch it or bring it out, I feel that I have it in me and I fully expect that the time will arrive when it will be called forth. Judging therefore by that which passes within me, conscious as I must be that Almighty God graciously preserves me, kindly favors me, always rules me and frequently in a manner so extraordinary that, familiar as I am with such undeserved protection and guidance, I am surprised at the result and the means by which it has been effected – I cannot but suppose it to be likely that I may be destined at some future time to play a part for which I may now think myself incapable, but for which it may please God to fit me – That part I humbly hope may be active and efficient exertions for the good of my Country and of mankind – This impression has long been and still is strong (perhaps stronger than ever) upon my mind. The force of it increases too, as I see a great and perhaps tremendous crisis approaching which, when it arrives, may appal the stoutest hearts, but which I really believe will be to me the stimulus to exertion, in the humble but fervent hope that I may be an instrument in helping to prosecute that better state of things, that reign of Virtue, which I calmly but steadily look forward to as a thing which after a severe struggle will ultimately prevail –

With this view of what may, and what I am firmly of opinion certainly will, happen, I endeavour to ascertain by enquiry within myself what I ought to do, and what I suppose that I am permitted to do, this I endeavour to perform to the best of my ability, patiently awaiting the issue.

5 June   Returned to London in the afternoon. Dined with Ld. Shaftsbury ...

6 June   Dined today with the Duke and Duchess of Northumberland to meet the Duke and Duchess of Clarence ...

7 June   [*Expresses his displeasure, following a decision in the House of Lords, that they would not to take a vote on the Corn Laws*] – ... as I like plain dealing and I wish that the country should know who are their friends.

9 June   Dined with the good and great Lord Eldon ... the Duke of Wellington, Duke of Rutland and many others were of the party ...

10 June   Today being Sunday, after going to Church, I called upon my Mother and then rode out to Roehampton where I stay tonight ... [*He then entered a further endorsement on the abilities of the young sculptor, Lough.*]

11 June   Returned to London ...

13 June   ... I gave a large dinner to Mr Peel and our friends ...

16 June   I dined at Ld. Beresford's today ...

17 June   Dined at Ld. Casseles to meet the Duke of Clarence ...

18 June   It was my intention this evening to have asked some questions [*in the House of Lords*] about the intended creation of Peers, to ensure a majority, but my courage failed me ...

21 June   Signed the first agreement for building leases in Nottingham Park to a person of the name Patterson ... I have settled to turn Thurland Hall into an Inn – and the present Inn (Black's Head) into shops.

23 June   Went to see the monument, which is in hand, that I intend [*to*] erect at Windsor to my Father's memory. Mr Nichols the Sculptor has made considerable progress in it, and I think it will make a beautiful monument ...

1827

27 June   ... Bought of Mr Westmacott his statue of Euphrosyne – I think it is a beautiful thing.

[*See also – 3 August 1840.*]

Fig. 17

28 June   ... I signed a petition against the Corn Bill.

30 June   Came to Roehampton – I mean to remain here for a week in order that Miss Spencer may have her holidays and that Mr Brewsher may go to Eton to learn how they proceed there in order that he may be the better qualified for preparing his pupils for the school ... I have been checking my accounts and find a considerable deficiency ... I am too prone to expenditure ... my powers of resistance are weak...£5 or £6,000 would clear my debt to tradesmen ...

1 July   Dined with Ld. Ellenborough at his villa here ...

2 July   I rode into London to attend the H. of Lords ... [*then returned to Roehampton.*]

7 July   ... Returned to London today.

9 July   ... a case arrived today containing two slabs, a present from Combermere [*who was still in India*] whose kind remembrance is constant. The slabs are of marble inlaid with agate and lapis lazuli, of which there is a border all round with an ornament in the centre.

11 July   Mr Brewsher and the children came from Roehampton, I could not get away till afternoon, I go with the first division of two carriages, the two others follow tomorrow – reached Eaton and slept there.

12 July   Started early in the morning ½ past 7 and arrived at Clumber this evening ... found this place in a wretched plight – the grass burnt up and the foliage of the trees worse than last year.

15 July   Wool buyers are offering 29 shillings a todd [*28 lbs*]– I said they could have it for 30 – almost giving it away.

17 July   [*The Mayor of Dublin wrote to inform him that he had been enrolled as a freeman of Dublin.*]

19 July   Today I broke up the nursery – Henrietta went to Miss Spencer and Robert to Mr Brewsher ... I shall now be more at liberty, as having to teach these little dears and attend to them confined me a good deal. It is however of the utmost importance that a

parent should sow the first seeds, and at some day I trust that I may gather a rich harvest – it promises well at present. My delightful children are my only comfort, nothing else interests me, if it was not for them this world would be to me a barren waste. My isolated and lonely life is a cheerless business – and my spirits under a constant cloud and oppression – so that my case seems remediless – I doubt not but that there are good and sufficient reasons for this which in time I shall perceive – In the mean time my trials, difficulties and temptations are great, for when one is wretched, one looks for what can amuse or afford relief, nothing can do this but woman, of this solace I am bereaved and nothing should induce me to put the happiness and welfare of my children to hazard by a new alliance, without a previous certainty of temper and every other suitable quality – such persons are as rare as the finest pearls and it is in vain to hope again to find one.

21 July   ... Thomas has the mumps at Eton.

22 July   No news – went to dine at Thoresby and stay the night..

24 July   One of my maid servants died this morning – this is the third death in one and a half years. I am going with Lord Manvers to the Nottingham Races tomorrow .

25 July   [*Reports that they arrived at the Nottingham races too early and were the only people in the stand – also indicates that he was not a regular there and that he was surprised by the sparcity of spectators.*]

27 July   [*Reports on the departure 'to her own country' of a Princess who he says has behaved 'outrageously' – and declares that 'as the old vulgar adage – its good riddance of bad rubbish'.*]

28 July   I began my harvest today ... indifferent from the extreme drought.

30 July   Went to the new church at Markham – the vaults below are above half done. It is a very good work and will make a most fit and proper cemetery. When I went below and saw the space and accommodation, which I had provided for the family – should it endure for centuries – I could not help reflecting upon the futility of all human arrangements. Nor mindful that my forecast might be useless, for families more numerous than mine have all been swept away even before manhood.

31 July   My three dear boys returned home from Eton today ...

1 August   [*He learnt today that he had been 'ridiculed' in the 'Edinburgh Review'. The June edition of this quarterly magazine had an article referring to the 'Catholic Question' and the opinions of certain un-named 'bigoted Tories' had been quoted.*] – I will not swerve from my principles or yield a jot to this unprincipled and lawless crew.

1827

2 August · Went to Nottingham Assizes – the calendar was not heavy, nor were there any very bad cases except one for the rape of a child 5 years old.

10 August · ... Lincoln and Thomas were taken with mumps yesterday ...

23 August · ... My dear little Caroline completed her ninth year today.

25 August · ... My dear girls gave me a breakfast at their gardens today, it was very prettily done and very well contained. I played them a trick which surprised and amused them very much. I desired my Cook, who plays upon the guitar, to come whilst we were all at breakfast and play some tunes. When he struck up they were all in wonder and still more when they went to look and saw a man with a dark face and shabby dress. They asked him certain questions and he answered like a foreigner and, though they guessed that it was the cook yet cannot make it out, as I carried on the joke and pretended to know nothing about the man.

1 September · ...Lincoln [*aged 16*] shot 15½ brace of partridge & 10 hares today.

3 September · Went to Nottingham with Lincoln to meet Mr Robinson about all the building projects in preparation in the Park. The whole plan is taking well ... I did not reach home until 11 o'clock.

14 September · Went to Bawtry to sleep at the Inn and shoot at my estate at Martin tomorrow.

15 September · A good fine day, very hot ... on our journey back to Clumber, the post boys walked the quarter part of the way, the roads were bad.

24 September · My 3 boys have returned to Eton – I feel quite lonely altho' I have people in the House.

1 October · Went for the first time to see the little Farm – I had crossed it by the road about a year ago when out shooting [*see 6ᵗʰ January 1825 above*], but today I determined to look it over. It was an extraordinary sensation to me to visit a place close to my house which I had not seen for 5 years. To my surprise and infinite gratification, true and faithful to their well loved and well remembered mistress, the excellent farmer and his wife (John and Jane Hutchinson) had most minutely and carefully sustained every thing in the precise order in which it had been left, so that I saw no difference except in the growth of the trees and shrubs. I really felt transferred to old times and at every step and in every bush, flower, walk, seat etc. could trace the hand which had originally arranged the whole and whom I remembered with the tenderest affection. I shall now frequently go and visit this former scene of many a delightful hour, the favourite haunt of Her who created it.

1827

2 October   Came to Kirklington for a few days.

4 October   I rode today to see Newstead Abbey. Col. Wildman has really made it a most beautiful spot ..

Fig. 18 *Newstead Abbey, in the mid-1830's.*

5 October   Returned to Clumber in the evening ...

9 October   ... Shooting today – Mr Gregory had the misfortune to shoot my 3rd best dog ... it died in a quarter of an hour. [*Was it one of the famed Clumber Spaniels?*]

10 October   A white jay was killed by one of my keepers – on the Thoresby side of the Park. The plumage is beautifully white all over.

15 October   This is my dear little Robert's birth day – he is 7 years old today – a remarkably fine boy ...

16 October   My Mother arrived from London ...

17 October   Walked about with my Mother to show her all the alterations, she was much pleased with them. The quarrymen and workmen plague me about the Terrace. [*He was urging them to complete the work before Christmas.*]

19 October   My Mother left me this morning ...

20 October   Came to Shipley on a visit for a few days.

21 October   Went to see the Derby new gaol ...

25 October   Returned to Clumber ...

1827

26 October — Looking at my works, the basins for the fountains are nearly finished and progress has been made towards completing the balustrading of the Terrace.

29 October — I have sold a leasehold estate at Walkeringham for £5,250 held under Trinity College with 13 years unexpired to Mr Neville – they are troublesome properties ... I am in much want of money just now for my various works ...

1 November — [*Went to Nottingham for the Anniversary meeting of the Lunatic Asylum.*]

7 November — Executed mortgage deeds on the security of Wellow and Tuxford to [*Coutts Bank?*] for £14,000. With this sum I pay the Trustees of Lord Howard for the purchase of Wellow.

15 November — Dr Fynes Clinton died quite suddenly at Cromwell ... he was an excellent man ...

20 November — Came to Langwith yesterday [*for two nights*] ... great sport.

22 November — Returned home ...

23 November — – Came to Thoresby for two nights ...

24 November — Went out shooting, more woodcocks than I ever remember, I saw 8 rise in a space that one might have covered with a net.

Fig. 19
Woodcock

27 November — [*To Bawtry for three nights*] – ... 247 pheasants, 147 hares, 24 woodcocks, 124 rabbits, 18 partridges, 1 snipe ...

5 December — To Ranby – mother spoke of buying the house and some land at Ranby.

25 December — ... [*Explaining that his Mother would not be joining them for Christmas*] – My Mother not only does not like to desert her sick servants, but is fearful of taking the complaint into another house ... Lincoln took the sacrament today for the first time – we all dined together at half past 2 o'clock, I and my ten children – and a very happy party we are ...

26 December — The lists for the poor have been given in by the clergymen ... there were never so many – never so much unemployment – many are said to be living only on potatoes and salt ... I fear that something may happen.

28 December — I am now staying at Mr Hildyard's at Flintham – went with him to attend a Ball at Newark ... It is many years since I have attended a Ball in this worthy town ...

31 December — ... Here ends a most eventful and disastrous year ...

1 January   In entering on a new year, I have again to thank God for the great and many blessings which I have received, but above all ... the most perfect welfare of my family ... My mother is here, we all met together in the morning and exchanged our presents, afterwards we attended the giving away things to the poor. Then, as usual, dined together and remained in our family party for the rest of the day.

2 January   ... signed a new lease to Mr Boothby of his new house and land in the [*Nottingham*] Park ...

5 January   [*Sole entry*] Castor Oil applied to the place, destroys ringworm.

7 January   Yesterday being Sunday, we kept Twelfth Day today. In the evening we had a family masquerade, or rather a mummery. Georgiana and Charlotte were Savoyards, looking extremely well and sustaining their part with spirit and identity – Lincoln an excellent clown, very well dressed, very droll and very active – Charles a [*French?*] postboy – Thomas, Paul Pry, a very fair attempt – William and Caroline, Dutch broom women – Edward, an excellent fisherman, capitally dressed – Henrietta, a French milliner and little Robert a very good little chimney sweeper. My Mother, a ballad woman, very good – and I an old clothes man – We made very good fun and passed a very [*amusing?*] evening.

9 January   I have a bad sick headache ... I am not disposed to think or write.

13/15 January   ... Again my Mother and I are at variance, we never can be long together without the arrival of something unpleasant – there are doubtless faults on both sides – but as I have noted before my mother is so injudicious, meddles and interferes so dogmatically, so perpetually, and so unwisely obtrudes her ideas of parental authority that it requires the exercise of all the control which I possess, not to come to an open rupture. [*This*] sort of thing wears me to death and hurts me beyond description.

1828

21 January   My dear boys left me today for Eton ...

28 January   ... Left Clumber at 10 o'clock, at 9 I arrived at Biggleswade, where I slept.

31 January   ... Since I arrived in London I have had much said to me about the Borough of Retford ...

1 February   *[After disagreeing with the Duke of Wellington, Prime Minister, over his selection of new Ministers]* ... Left London at 5 o'clock, reached Eaton where I slept – breakfasted at Alconbury Hall – met Lord and Lady Manvers changing horses at Grantham – dined at Newark and arrived at Clumber at 7 o'clock.

5 February   My terms are being accepted at Nottingham and my property there is progressively improving – at Basford too Mr Chambers writes to me that he has increased the letting of one farm at that place from 338 to £744 a great increase and by no means extortionately obtained.

6 February   *[He notes that a stocking frame had been destroyed at Arnold. He reports a general increase in crime and the filling of the prisons. In particular he mentions that* 'Cold Bath fields' *was* 'scarcely ever known to be in such a crowded state'.]

7 February   *[After hearing of a plan to set up a large Roman Catholic college at Ranby]* – I suspect that the Jesuits of Stoneyhurst have chosen the spot purposely and aimed particularly at me ... I will be a match for them, Jesuits though they are.

10 February   The same person who informed me of the plan for purchasing Ranby for a Jesuit's College wrote the same information to my Mother – with her usual officious zeal she has dashed about to the right and left telling this and that person and taking a leading part in the steps which are to be taken for the suppression of this mischievous scheme – I always object to female politicians, but in this instance I am sure that a temperate prudence is above all things necessary and that my poor Mother is the last person to display this quality, and therefore that she will do as usual more harm where she really means to do good – She writes me word that she has been seeing Ld. Eldon on the subject and is too proud of "not setting with her hands before her when the country and I are in danger".

15 February   Yesterday was one of the most worst days I ever remember, about 8 in the morning the wind got up and blew very hard, then came snow ... the drops that melted from the snow freezing as they fell and making long icicles – the lake froze too notwithstanding the high winds from the S.E. ...

18 February   Dear little Edward's birth day. 12 years of age today – we have celebrated it by a partial holiday and being all together.

1828

22 February   I invited the Archdeacon of Nottingham (Eyre) to rally his clergy and get them to petition against a Jesuit College at Ranby ...

23 February   Another robbery has taken place at Hardwick of 24 fowls and 4 ducks – about a fortnight since a helper's clothes were stolen out of the Stableyard. Theft is most prevalent ...

In digging for stone for the roads at Maplebeck a skeleton of a man has been found ... a spear or battleaxe was laid under him which I now have – it is of brass ...

26 February   Left Clumber at 1/2 past 9. My dear boys were very sorry to lose [*me*] – William especially ... I arrived at Eaton at 1/4 before 9.

28 February   [*In London*] – My 4 girls and their governesses etc. arrived today ...

29 February   Attended in the H. of Lords ...

2 March   My mother told me today that she has bought Ranby as she thinks this [*'joiked' or 'spiked'?*] the Jesuits. She has made a very imprudent purchase and done a thing of which she will in future regret.   Ranby is not a situation which can suit her, she is lonely there and so much too near me as to be in a constant state of fidgety uneasiness, which perpetually harasses us both. I am very sorry for what she has done.

4 March   The Bill for disenfranchising Retford now occupies the H. of Commons – evidence is being heard to prove corruption ...

10 March   In lowering the road into Nottingham Park from Standard Hill a subterranean passage of considerable extent has been discovered, it divides near the opening, one passage leading towards the Leen, the other towards the Castle gate.

11/14 March   [*Visited and stayed at Eton with his sons.*]

18 March   This is Georgiana's birthday, she this day completed her 18th year ...

19 March   [*Mentions Edmund Mundy, an attache at Lisbon.*]

20 March   ... [*my*] boys who are now at Eton [*are*] ornaments to the school and patterns of good conduct.

24 March   ... It was voted by a majority of 36 in the H. of Commons that the borough of Retford should be thrown into the [*Bassetlaw*] hundred ... my name has been freely used in the debates – but no truth that anyone can speak against me – I am as much sans [*peur or peux?*] as sans reproche ...

27 March   Attended the King's Levee ... he spoke to no one, we all passed by making our bow and retiring ...

2 April   Left London for Clumber ... Took my 3 boys with me and reached Wandsford.

3 April   Arrived at Clumber ...

1828

9/11 April ... chiefly occupied in seeing my various works and looking about the place – fishing and shooting with a rifle – we also had a game at cricket ...

My mother has renewed her approaches and her imprudent interference, as I foresaw. She will tease and harrass me to death about Georgiana, who is coming out. I must check it decidedly or it will be intolerable to me and bad for my dear girl.

14 April Left Clumber in the afternoon and slept at Grantham.

15 April Arrived in London ...

18 April ... I have a good deal to do to prepare Georgiana [*who is*] being presented at the Drawing Room on the 25th. This is the commencement of her life and an awful period to me in prospective bad as the world and vile as the morals and conduct now are ...

23 April Today is an important era in my life. I presented at Court my dear daughter Georgiana ... ... I felt ready to vent my feelings in tears. [*Then some 250 words or so in praise of her perfection.*]

24 April I hear today that the town is in admiration at the exquisite behaviour and appearance of my dearest girl Georgiana yesterday. I felt quite sure that she would blaze like a meteor ...

26 April [*The Duke accepted an invitation to dine with the Duchess of Kent but made an excuse for Georgiana, saying that she was ill.*]

I thought it wise not to launch her in society under such formidable circumstances to her ...

I never before saw the Duchess of Kent – I was much pleased with her ... [*the*] little Princess [*Victoria*] is a charming child and is admirably brought up ...

Fig. 20 *Duchess of Kent and Princess Victoria – circa 1821*

3 May By appointment I took Georgiana to Kensington Palace to introduce her to the Duchess of Kent. H.R.H. received her most kindly and admirably, the little princess came in, and we thought her a most promising child both in behaviour and looks. Afterwards, with Charlotte and my three boys we went to the Opera ...

1828

4 May   [*His mother is matchmaking for Georgiana*] – the most disgraceful indignity to which a girl can be subjected.

6 May   [*In the Lords, the Duke voted against the new game law proposals.*]

8 May   ... dined with Lord Bathurst to meet the Duke of Cumberland.

10 May   ... Saw Mr Neale respecting his standing for Retford.

13 May   Went to Eton to take William to school ... had some cricket in the evening ...

14 May   ... accompanied my 4 girls to a morning concert given by their master ... Georgiana is to go to the King's ball, the first she has ever been to – I shall be full of anxiety for ... what may happen to her.

15 May   Georgiana went to the King's Ball in the evening ...

16 May   Signed a lease to Mr Gill for land built on in Nottingham Park ...

17 May   Rode with Colonel Dawkins to the E. India Docks to see a leopard which has been sent to me by his brother who is with Lord Combermere in India.

    The animal was still on board the ship – he is a most handsome creature and remarkably tame, so much so that the men play with it as with a cat – I shall have it removed to Clumber.

18 May   Called on Mr C.F. Clinton and found him at home – had a long conversation with him about Retford – I have endeavored all in my power to make the place more respectable with a view to its preservation but the rascals are so low that they will not allow me to lift them out of the mire.

19 May   I saw my leopard, and am to know tomorrow what will be the best way of sending him to Clumber. [*The animal was kennelled in Clumber Park until 1833. It was then sent to a London zoo.*]

20 May   [*Notes that the House of Commons vote, on the motion to transfer the franchise from Retford to Birmingham, was lost by 18 votes.*]

22 May   This is my very dear Lincoln's birthday, he has completed his 17th year this day ... May God bless him ...

26 May   I went to the King's ball with Georgiana ... [*The King stayed until between 2 and 4 o'clock.*] ...

11 June   Went to St James' Palace with Georgiana to a concert ... by the young performers of the Royal Academy of Music ... On going up to the King, H.M. shook hands with me and congratulated me on the majority of the preceding night [*a vote against the enfranchisement of Roman Catholics*] this he did without disguise and before the Court circle.

1828

13 June My Mother wrote a note which I found on returning home last night saying that she wished to see me ... [*He went to her*] ... She appeared in peculiarly good spirits ... I saw evidently that she wanted to get me into the best humour ... the object was that Georgiana should call upon the Princess Augusta ... I plainly saw what the animus was, namely to get Georgiana away from me and carry her in triumph to the Princess Augusta thus indulging her [*his Mother's*] wish to assume her command on my children and take the credit which belongs to my education of them ... there has been the bone of contention – jealousy and mortified pride are at the bottom of all ... There is no one ... so impossible to live with ... so domineering, so intriguing and so worldly in her objects ... I wish the beginning of wisdom to be the love of God ... my Mother begins at another end ... I do not mean to say that she means ill ...

I replied to my Mother that I did not desire that Georgiana should be a hanger on to the Royal family ... she then demanded that I permit her to have [?] intercourse with my children, usurp the place of a mother ... I would make no reply ... rose to take my leave, wishing her my affectionate farewell and leaving her in perfect forgiveness but in a state of mind the pain of which cannot be described.

14 June [*He received a letter from his Mother*] – my answer was short ... My daughter is universally admired wherever she goes, she goes no where but with me ... [*My Mother*] forgets that she is an old woman and that for the last 30 years she has been living in retirement not seen or heard at Court or in the party going or party giving portion of this town ... here I will terminate this hateful subject, I have not half stated what has taken place, what I feel, what I know my Mother to be doing and how unfair and unjust are the imputations laid to my charge ...

16 June ... received a letter inviting me to become an Orangeman and meet the Duke of Cumberland in Grand Lodge tomorrow.

17 June [*Records that he had decided to temporarily decline the invitation received yesterday.*] ... My Mother has written to me another injudicious letter ... She really causes me more uneasiness than any other person living – ever since the death of my ever to be regretted wife, which of itself cut me to the very heart, she has not ceased to persecute, dictate to and annoy me, by all sorts of interference, ill placed reflections, and the most incipient and extraordinary attempts to exercise over me an authority similar to that of a parent over children of the tenderest age ...

21 June Took my children to see the Zoological gardens in the Regent's Park – Tho' small and only one year old, the thing has been well done ...

1828

22 June   [*MOTHER!*] ... tells me that I am altogether in the wrong ... and she will break with me ... I know not what to do ... I cannot believe myself to be in the wrong.

24 June   I have loaned [*from Coutts*] £15,000 upon the security of my house at Portman Square.

25 June   ... In the evening, went with Georgiana to Almacks, [*social club*] a very brilliant and full meeting, but as hot as Calcutta, we did not get away till between 3 or 4 in the morning ...

26 June   ... Came to Salt Hill ...

27 June   [*At Eton College*]... I proposed to give a prize for the best essay or composition testifying a knowledge of the Christian religion combined with a fundamental knowledge of Greek and Latin ... to found a Scholarship for 3 years of £50 annually ...

28 June   [*He mentions that the girl's governess, Miss Spencer, has behaved 'so impertinently and outrageously' before he left Clumber*] – it must not be overlooked by me.

30 June   Went with Georgiana to a dressed Ball ... magnificent in costumes from all parts of the world ...

4 July   [*Still in London*] – 'The Protestant Club' is formed ... [*the Duke joined*]

9 July   ... I have accomplished today what I never did before in my life, I have paid everything that I owe up to Christmas last ... I have paid away above £80,000 ...

10 July   [*Left London – slept at Stevenage.*]

11 July   [*Back to Clumber.*]

19 July   Sir Patrick Macgregor [*'eminent practitioner'*] is dead. ... I have known him ever since 1802 and for two years knew him intimately as he lived in the house with us in attendance upon Sir Charles Craufurd, when we were in the South of France for the recovery of his health ...

22 July   ... the death of the excellent Archbishop of Canterbury ... my eldest and invariably affectionate friend, he had known me from a boy – but I lament him even more as a public loss ...

2 August   ... the Bishop of London has been appointed Archbishop of Canterbury ...

4 August   [*After several days of illness*] I am weak, low and unhinged.

12 August   My dear boys gave us a very pretty fête and breakfast at their Garden – we went there by water. In the evening we heard that my sailor was missing and that his boat had been found adrift and his oars floating about ... we at last found him, quite dead, stiff and cold. But two hours before we had left the poor man in perfect health.

1828

17 August   I have been busily and earnestly engaged in writing a short commentary on the times ... [*His 'Letter to Lord Kenyon', to be published in the 'Standard'*]

21 August   [*The Duke went to the south coast for the sake of his health. He took all the children. They rented a house at Ramsgate and travelled around the area until early December. Rochester, Canterbury and Broadstairs were amongst the places visited.*]

31 August   ... Lawrence has finished my portrait .. [*After upwards of 21 years.*]

1 September My boys bathed in the sea for the first time today. I accompanied them in the machine in order to give them courage and prevent alarm ...

17 September [*He had been busy over several days, writing a letter to Lord Kenyon. The letter, published in the 'Gazette' – on his usual anti-R.C. theme, was to provoke a considerable response from both sides – See 8 Oct. below*]

29 September I have decided that Lincoln will leave Eton ... [*Comments on Lincoln's 'so manly appearance'.*]

1 October   This is my dear Charlotte's birth day – she has completed her sixteenth year – she is now taller than Georgiana ... She is a beautiful and most charming girl.

8 October   O'Connell is most incensed by what I said of him. [*See 17 Sept. above.*]

20 October   [*Notes that he has been advised that he is a 'marked man'.*]

25 October   [*Mentions that his Mother had a state pension granted to her on the death of the 3rd Duke (in 1795).*]

26 October   [*Mentions that at a celebration party following a parliamentary debate, the assembled group sang 'God Save the King' and 'Oh Dear, what can the matter be?'.*]

3 November   [*Read a limited issue pamphlet, 'Hints on Irish matters to the Duke of Wellington from Windsor Forest'. He believes that this paper had been written by the King, or by someone close to him.*]

11 November Mr Robinson came from London to settle with me every thing relating to the lease to Smith of Thurland Hall for 30 years for an Inn at Nottingham (Black's Head) into shops and dwelling houses ... to begin immediately.

15 November [*Notes that he is not in favour of 'Evangelicals'. He comments on the Rev C. Fynes-Clinton who he had placed in his Cromwell parish. Following an interview with a non-conformist, he wrote*] – I maintained that there was no excuse for dissenting from the Church of England the truest Christian Church in the world.

1828

17 November	Georgiana went out to a dinner for the first time. [*She missed the meal by taking too long over her 'preparations'.*]
6 December	[*Notes that Lord Liverpool had died.*]
9 December	[*Returned to London from Hastings.*]
13 December	[*To Eton, where he discussed the 'Newcastle Scholarships'.*]
15 December	[*He insisted on changes to the Lawrence portrait of himself.*]
22 December	Left London – slept at Eaton.
23 December	Arrived at Clumber ...
24 December	Went out shooting ...
25 December	14 of us at dinner ... [*including his Mother*]
27 December	[*Notes that the Duke of Wellington had taken one of the sinecures previously held by Lord Liverpool. Writes that Wellington is known as 'Gobble', as he 'swallows up every thing that falls'.*]
31 December	... Here ends a year eventful with many nascent events of the utmost consequence. End of 1828.

WHAT WILL THE DUKE OF NEWCASTLE NEXT ATTEMPT?—Will the country believe that to such an extent is the Duke of Newcastle carrying his oppressive power, that he is not satisfied with discharging his tenants who did not vote for him, nor even those who voted half for him; but, *credat Judaeus*, his agent, William Edward Tallents, has sent to those tenants of the Duke who *did* vote and had disobedient *under* tenants, blank discharges for them to fill up? Will this, ought this to be borne?—*Newark Times.*

Fig. 21 *This cutting gives the flavour of many newspaper comments over the eviction of the Duke's tenants, in his attempts to ensure the success of his own candidate.*

His Diary entries dated 29 September and 11 October 1829 refer to this matter, as does the record of his reception at the 'Playhouse' on 18 December 1829.

1 January ... How I miss Her who could so pre-eminently well have guided our dear child [*18 year old Georgiana*] thro' the difficulties and perils which she must have to encounter ... my spirit is prostrated by the loss and absence of the dear and incomparable companion of so many former years ... My dear children continue to give me ever more and more comfort and satisfaction ...

My Mother came here this morning – the day has been lovely and beautiful beyond example and we have passed it very pleasantly ...

[*Due to lack of time*] – I have not been able as usual, to dispense clothing to the poor people ...

[*He enters here his usual retrospective on the past year – on his widowed state – his pleasure in his children – his engagement in promoting and defending the sacred course of Christianity and the moral welfare of the State.*]

5 January The hounds met here today ... a very pretty sight, as it always is on the lawn.

6 January We have just finished our Twelfth Night, and have been really much amused. We all dressed up some character which we endeavoured to maintain and some did them very well – William was Falstaff and very good. Charlotte very really [*sic*] as a Sheffield ware woman, Lincoln, Georgiana and Thomas also acted their parts very well. Edward was Guy Fawkes and had [?] scope for his antics.

12 January As I came here so late in Dec., I had not time to prepare for the distribution of clothing to the poor on New Year's day – It was therefore issued on this, the earliest day ... Mr Mason [*his Chaplain*] ... said a few words to them expressive of the blessings they enjoyed under the British Constitution, to which I added that they should fear God and honor the King. Mr Mason then called upon [*them*] to give 3 cheers for the King and the Constitution and Protestant ascendancy, to which they

1829

replied with a quickness and enthusiasm which quite surprised me – they lost all reserve, and cheered most lustily, many of the old women pulling off their bonnets and waving them in the air. I then called upon them to cry "God save the King" and cheers, and they gave it instantly most heartily, mixing with it "God save the Duke, God bless his Grace" etc. etc – some of the people said "Shall [we] shout 'down with Popery'?" – but we did not require them to do that. I never saw any feeling more unequivocal, which was the more remarkable as it was perfectly genuine and wholly unprepared – I am perfectly convinced that the same feeling prevails from one end of the country to the other. I never saw people more gratified, delighted and self-contained in my life – they all seemed to feel a certain consequence in themselves, at the same time that they openly and warmly testified their gratitude and affection to me – I have never had so good an opinion of them before.

15 January Came to Ranby on a visit to my Mother and brought Georgiana, Lincoln and the three boys with me.

17 January Returned from Ranby after dinner this evening ...

19 January Went to Nottingham to meet Mr Robinson and see the progress that had been made in my works there.

20 January [In Nottingham] ... a great many buildings have been erected and roads formed so as quite to alter the appearance of the Park and the scheme is now a favourite with the Town – so that its success is no longer in doubt. Returned to Clumber and reached home at 12 at night – snow and bitterly cold.

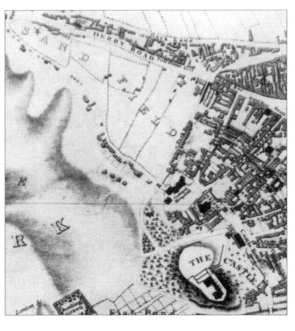

Fig. 22 *Part of Nottingham Park – from Staveley and Wood's Plan – published in 1831.*

1829

21 January   [*Mentions the anti-R.C. meetings in other counties.*] ... Nottinghamshire is now nearly the most disgraced county in England. We have a wretched gentry and I cannot get them to stir.

22 January   Went to attend a ball at Newark ...

26 January   Attended a general meeting of the Lieutenancy ...

30 January   I this day complete my 44th year ...

31 January   Out shooting today for the last time ...

3 February   [*Travelled to London – slept at Grantham.*]

5 February   [*Attempted a speech in the House of Lords*] – ... I made a very poor thing of it ...

13 February   [*Made another short speech – anti government policy – in the Lords and presented petitions*] – ... the Duke of Wellington [*Prime Minister*] was mum and glum ...

22 February   [*Mentions the Newark elections – Mr Sadler will be his man although the electors would prefer a member of his own family*] – this election will cost me a good deal of money ...

25 February   ... Sir William Clinton vacated his seat for Newark the day before yesterday ... [*Sir William had warned that he would resign if Newcastle persisted in opposing the government moves on electoral reform.*]

1 March   ... Sgt. Wilde opposes [*Mr Sadler*] – he is sent by the Government as a piece of spite – worthy of such apostates ...

2 March   [*The Duke made another speech in the Lords – provoking strong opposition.*]

3 March   ... Sgt. Wilde had government people and government to help him at Newark ...

              [*The Duke spoke in a House of Lords debate on electoral petitions, including one from Worksop, which he opposed.*] ... The D. of Norfolk was in the House and doubtless very angry – and must have made a lot of his frightful faces.

7 March   ... Mr Sadler is at last elected for Newark.

8 March   [*Mentions Mr Sadler's 'Yorkshire dialect' as 'rather broad' and 'the only thing against him'.*]

9 March   ... Strange – I have become a people's man at last! ... [*'the mob' had cheered him outside House of Lords – whereas the Duke of Wellington had only received 'groans and hisses'*].

1829

11 March [*Saw the King at Windsor. They had an audience of 1¹/₂ hours. The Duke's report of this event fills almost six pages of his diary.*]

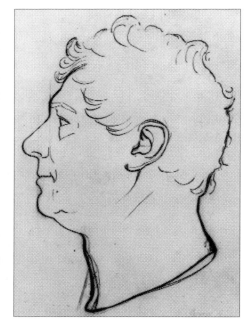

Fig. 23 *King George IV – by Sir Francis Leggatt Chantrey – circa 1821 – reproduced here by courtesy of the National Portrait Gallery.*

15 March [*Travelled home to Clumber, via at Hatfield and Stamford, then detouring into Lincolnshire to visit Sir Jenison Gordon at Haverholme. Travelled on via Sleaford and Leadenham to Newark, where he slept.*]

17 March [*Reports that he was well received by the people of Newark*] – Arrived at Clumber. ...

19 March ... Mr Gilpin came today.

22 March [*He mentions a pistol duel having taken place between Lord Winchilsea and the Duke of Wellington. Neither man had been hurt.*]

25 March Left Clumber at ¹/₂ past 10, breakfasted at Clumber but went to Ranby ... arrived at Alconbury Hill at ¹/₂ past 9 ...

26 March Arrived in London ...

31 March This day the atrocious and revolutionary popish bill came into [*the House of Lords*] ... May God protect us ...

7 April My dear boys came home from Eton today ...

9 April I was told today by the librarian of the House of Lords that yesterday a rat was seen running across the floor of the House whilst the house was sitting, two of the officers gave chase and at length ran him to ground under the Throne – is this not ominous?

10 April [*In the Lords*] ... I was unexpectedly called up to speak and floundered thro' my say as well as I could.

12 April ... The Duke of Cumberland and a large party dined with me today ...

1829

18 April   [*He discussed with friends the establishment of a 'Society for the preservation of Protestantism'.*]

20 April   [*Back to Clumber, having stopped at Biggleswade for the night.*]

22 April   ... This evening I was invited by cards to a concert – started with a pianoforte duet (Charlotte and Henrietta) – then a trio (Georgiana, Charlotte and Lincoln) [*Lincoln sang very well*] – then a duet with Charlotte playing the harp. 2nd Act – a song followed by an instrumental trio (violin played by Lincoln). Finished with 'The Red cup [?] Knight'. Charlotte is uncommonly quick and clever and the most charming girl I ever saw. She is beautiful, amiable, clever, sensible, agreeable and excellent.... My late political blow has overwhelmed me and in addition, my financial prospects are bad ...

1 May   The weather today is milder and I am better ... the lilacs are only now shewing their bloom, buds of about one inch long, almost every other tree at a little distance, looks as brown as in winter.

8 May   [*Mentions East Retford*] – the proposal to transfer the franchise to Birmingham has been defeated. Mr Peel has indicated that he will vote for Retford to be included in the [*Bassetlaw*] hundred.

17 May   The country looks more beautiful than ever, to my deep regret I leave this place tomorrow and leave the peace and comfort of the country for the turmoil and disquietude of London – it is an irksome operation. The Duke of Cumberland writes to me ... tells me that my political friends wish to see me back again. What can I do if I am back again and what is the estimate of my political friends, only how far I may be useful to them, without making me any return, or shewing any regard for me personally. Lord Falmouth, Lord Mansfield and Lord Winchilsea, I can call my friends for they are disinterested and have a regard for me but I can count no others.

18 May   [*To London – stopped at Wandsford.*]

20 May   [*Edward starts at Eton – four of the boys are now there.*]

23 May   [*He informs another peer that he refuses to ally to any place or party at present. Says that he is 'sick of public men and measures.'*]

28 May   [*The Duke took Georgiana to a party at Lady Hertford's house – he says that he did this to annoy the King, who had invited Georgiana to a children's party*] – He deserves to be reminded of his miserable and culpable conduct.

11 June   [*Accepted an invitation for himself and Georgiana to attend the King's Ball at St James's Palace.*] – the King received me very graciously.

1829

14 June   Saw the plate of Turner's engraving of my portrait from Sir Thomas Lawrence's picture.

Fig. 24

15 June   [*Left London for Clumber*] – travelled with Lincoln – stayed at Eaton.

16 June   [*As they approached Clumber, one of the wheels of his carriage caught fire*] – 3 hours delay – the wheel was repaired at North Muskham ...

18 June   I never saw things in such a beautiful state in Clumber Park ...

21 June   [*To London, via Leicester and Nottingham (to check the building progress at the Park development).*]

23 June   [*To Ramsgate for a holiday.*]

2 July   Mr Sadler has done our interests very great good at Newark ...

8 July   [*Reports the engagement of Mr Cavendish, the heir to the Portland title. Expresses regret that Georgiana will not be marrying him. Throughout the Diaries, this appears to be the only time he links Georgiana with a named man.*]

3 August   Caroline is 11 years old today – she is a very fine girl.

29 August   My dear little Henrietta is 10 years old today.

9 September   Georgiana has received a very amiable and kind letter from the Duchess of Kent. [*Over this period he had called on the Duchess and recorded that he was much taken with her character.*]

1829

15 September	[*Left London for Clumber with Georgiana, Lincoln and Robert*] stayed at Wansford overnight.
17 September	Lord Harrington, 'my uncle' [*of his late wife's family*], died yesterday. [*He mentions the 'follies' of that family.*]
29 September	Notices to Quit have been given to those of my tenants at Newark who voted against Mr Sadler at the last election – this has found its way into the London papers which have been very severe on me. What I have done, I will do again and no clamour will turn me from the straight path.
1 October	My dear Charlotte's 17th birthday – a beautiful and in every way a charming girl.
5 October	Lincoln and I came to Bawtry to shoot at Martin tomorrow. [*He mentions that the newspapers have continued their attacks on him.*]
6 October	... I learned today for the first time that there was formerly a considerable Roman station at Martin – it is easily traceable when one looks at the ground with that view. Mr Lemon of Bath, a good antiquarian, went all over it last year and traced the whole of it and made notes upon it – he is since dead and has not published. The camp was on the rising ground between Short's and Cartwright's farms near the pond. The Holt shews many fortifications – in a field near to it was a [*Roman?*] pottery and pots may at any time be found in it – some very good coins were found in the field a short time ago – they are of [*Antoninus?*] and the stones in the camp are all burned probably by the watch fires. The great road went close by and thro' the low grounds belonging to Lord Scarbrough towards Tickhill.
11 October	[*Sent Notices to Quit*] – to two principal tenants at Newark – Gardner and Massey [*who had*] been hostile at the last election. I suppose that I shall hear of this hereafter.
12 October	I went over to Thoresby to settle with Lord Manvers regarding the Hunting arrangements ... I shall restore to Mr Saville all the country to the South of the Poulter and the road from Twyford bridge to East Markham [*He mentions Foljambe as also being involved. He recognises that he is going to upset someone with his proposals.*]
13 October	A white partridge has been seen in a covey on the other side of the lake. A hooper was killed there a few weeks ago.
23 October	[*In Nottingham*] – Went to Church this morning, dined at the Ordinary and went to the Ball in the evening. Whilst in Nottingham ... I went to look at my buildings etc. – they are not every thing that I could wish – but altogether it is a very great improvement not only to my property but to the Park.

1829

2 November   Mr Foljambe called upon me yesterday [*Regarding the hunting arrangements – Foljambe was polite but not happy!*] As Master of the Hounds he intends to speak to the gentlemen of his Hunt.

4 November   [*Mentions* 'steam carriages on a rail road' *and their maximum speeds of* 'less than 30 miles an hour'. *He writes that there is a strong feeling that this method of transport will* 'supplant all others'.]

17 November   Yesterday I heard of a prizefight being held at Elkesley between a man from Nottingham and a man from Sheffield (*or E....?*). People had come from as far as London. A magistrate managed to stop the fight but the mob only moved to Ollerton – about 4000 were present. The Nottingham man was beaten. Warrants were issued against the combatants, their backers and all concerned – they were bailed to the Sessions. There is no Fund and I am obliged to prosecute and bear all the expenses myself.

25 November   Heavy snow has fallen, said to be the worst for twenty-five years.

29 November   Tomorrow Lincoln goes to Oxford to enter himself ... at present he is an admirable and most promising youth.

4 December   Lincoln returned from Oxford ... much pleased ... likely to have Mr Hussey as his tutor.

10 December   My dear boys came home from Eton today ... they are indeed noble boys.

15 December   Sir Henry Clinton died on the 11th ... [*He goes on to praise Sir Henry and to give him credit for the Waterloo victory, saying that the Belgium and English armies had been built up by Sir Henry for a year before the battle. A full obituary follows. He is fierce in his criticism regarding Wellington's attitude to Sir Henry.*]

17 December   Came to Newark to attend the Ball. I am staying with Mr Hildyard at Flintham. Most people are extremely cordial.

18 December   We arrived at the Playhouse [*deliberately late*], there was a large crowd at the door. Inside, there was a disturbance [*allegedly*] *caused by hired demonstrators*] – there was shouting and placards were thrown down from the galleries into the boxes. Other placards were exhibited over the sides of the gallery ... on leaving, the crowd on the door seemed quite friendly.

20 December   [*He notes the continuing snow*] – What will become of the poor under these circumstances?

[*From 24ᵗʰ to 29ᵗʰ December 1829 there are no entries relating to family or estate matters.*]

30 December   As far as I am concerned, I shall do my utmost to give comfort to my poor. On the 1st [*January*] I shall give them [*more*] butter and warmer clothing [*from London*] than I have ever yet

1829

obtained for them ... I am also about to send fuel to all my villages and will endeavour to make all ... privations as little as possible in this inclement season and very disastrous times.

31 December Sir William Clinton came here today ... Here the year 1829 terminates ... here we are ... a prey to the most tormenting uncertainty for the future ... our reliance must be on God alone.

'Everything went off Admirably and
with Flying Colours for
the House of Clumber'.

[See Diary entry 6 August 1830]

1 January   [*Snow since 17 December*] – ... the accustomed exchange of presents took place to the delight of all, and afterwards the poor of the different parishes had the clothing etc. distributed ... they seemed to be particularly grateful, and to feel the kindness which is extended towards them.

6 January   We passed our Twelfth Night as usual. Edward was the King and Charlotte the Queen ... my dear little Edward is to go to sea at Easter.

8 January   [*A major event had occurred, the Duke gave no details saying that it was 'between God and myself'. He did write that it had caused him 'anguish and broken-heartedness'. On the 11th he recorded that 'the cause of bitter anguish has been removed'.*]

10 January   Sir Thomas Lawrence has died.

22 January   My delightful boys left me this morning for Eton ...

30 January   [*At Ranby with his mother and Lincoln*] – This is my birthday ...

2 February   [*To London – slept at Grantham.*]

11 February   [*I have*] arranged today the final completion of the arrangements by which I transfer the mortgages of my estate to my children in Trust, thus taking their money out of the now insecure funds and placing them on land. Around £126,000 involved – leaving £10,000 to £11,000 in the Stocks. This would be about £600 a year to each of them (excluding Lincoln) if taken now.

15 February   [*To Clumber – stopped overnight at Eaton*] – I have laid the foundation of a 'Country Party' ...

16 February   My admirable Lincoln has been to me the personification of everything that can be most amiable and agreeable.

20 February   Today Lincoln was skating, the ice thicker than ever and the ninth week of frost.

24 February   At last the frost has broken up ... I went out today for the first time for nearly a week ... everywhere the sufferings of the poor have been dreadful.

1830

25 February [*News of a petition from Newark*] from certain persons who have been dismissed from their tenancies by me ... There appears to be a regular plot against me and it is breaking all at once. I have no intention to yield an inch and ... I fear not what man can do unto me.

2 March Mr Smirke came here to settle everything for the completion of my different works ... my Library shall be finished in August ... it will be beautiful then.

8 March Began cutting out the Garden of the Terrace, and the ground on the Lawn on the Western side of the Terrace is within three days of completion and my tedious and very difficult works in this way of the ground work are now surely completed.

11 March [*Tripped and hurt his back.*]

15 March Of several farms which have become vacant through failures, I have let the last today. [*He notes that it has become difficult to find good tenants, whereas once there was a general feeling that his farmers could make their fortunes on his land.*]

18 March Georgiana is twenty today ... as near perfection as possible ...

19 March Began to plant the Terrace today ... I am also doing a great deal in the pleasure ground, altering the line of walks that go from each end of the Terraces etc.etc. I never was more busy at this time of year or ever did more work or satisfactorily.

27 March 65 degrees today – we were glad to seek the shade. I yesterday sat for an hour and a half on a bench in the Colonnade with a friend ... and I set my two fountains playing for the first time ... the effect was beautiful. Today the lower terrace was completed as to the flower-beds and plantings.

Fig. 25 *This sketch indicates a development plan for the terraces. The central fountain was added in 1839.*

1830

29 March   67 degrees today – my terrace and pleasure grounds are now a real resource and pleasure to me.

30 March   My dear girls gave me a surprise today. When I went out of the breakfast, I found a very prettily contrived tented seat pitched in the pleasure grounds near the dial, which had been made principally by them as to the contrivance and fitting-up. I found in it a chaise-longue, table writing apparatus etc. and different things to make it gay in decoration within and without. This had been made in order that I might be enabled to sit out of doors and write my letters in the open air and without being cold – and the end was answered perfectly, for a more convenient and agreeable seat could not be contrived and as pretty as it is suitable. They were all delighted to see me like and use it.

31 March   My dear boys arrived about 2 o'clock today ... leaving Eton yesterday morning at 5 o'clock and slept at Wansford.

1 April   A fall of snow.

3 April   It has never ceased snowing since it first began ... extensive and irreparable injury to all my finest evergreens in the Pleasure ground. Some Cedars of Lebanon of above 60 years growth are half stripped of their branches ... the Virginia Cedars ... have shared the same fate.

9 April   Good Friday and we all took the Sacrament.

21 April   Edward planted a cedar tree on the hillside near where the Worksop and Retford road joins the London road on the Lawn. Tomorrow he will plant others, the dear little fellow is anxious to have these memorials of himself.

23 April   Georgiana, Lincoln, Charles, Thomas, William and Edward planted some trees this afternoon by the approach road on the other side of the water, the trees were Dalmation Oaks and Chestnuts raised from seed sent by Sir Bryan Martin, nine in number. Edward planted yesterday on the lawn a Pine.

29 April   My dear boys left me today on their return to Eton. Edward alone did not return as he is going to sea. My dear little fellows were exceedingly affected, and I not less so, at their parting not knowing when they may meet again – it is delightful to witness the affection which they bear to each other.

5 May   [*Left Clumber for London – slept at Wansford.*]

6 May   Arrived in London at 1/2 past 7. Lincoln was already arrived ... I am sleeply [*sic*] and will add no more tonight.

7 May   I go tomorrow to Oxford with Lincoln to see him placed there. I shall be much gratified by personally assisting in his first starting in life, which is always of paramount importance and frequently influences the whole course of future life.

1830

8 May   We arrived at Oxford this evening. Lincoln went up to Christ Church and found that he was a day too late to keep term. The Dean had written that if he were here not later than the 8th that he would be in time but it seems that he was not correct and this disagreeable consequence has ensued – it is very unlucky and makes a bad start.

9 May   This being Sunday, went to Church ... It rained all the morning ... I visited Lincoln's rooms which are wretched things. I do not envy the life of an Oxonian, it may be a necessary evil ...

10 May   ... having settled everything as far as was possible so that Lincoln shall get into his temporary room tonight, I prepared to leave Oxford. Stopped at Salt Hill where I found my three dear Etonians and their tutors, had tea with them.

12 May   ... my dear boy [*Edward*] is now in the navy and will very soon join his ship. [*Sir J. Benton's ship 'Donegal'*.]

25 May   I went with Edward to Sheerness. [*On the 3rd of June there follows a description of the Duke's feelings for his son's personality and character. He includes in the detail of their parting:* 'his dear honest face covered in tears, which fell from his smiling and affectionate eyes'.]

26 June   The King [*George IV*] is dead – he died this morning at ¼ past 3.

28 June   I took the Oaths of Allegiance, Supremacy and Abjuration and signed my name today in the House of Lords.

1 July   My dear Lincoln came home today.

2 July   ... My affliction of the back returned today.

6 July   [*He comments on the new King William IV having appointed a 'Papist' amongst his Privy Counsellors – also 'some R.Caths. Ladies have been appointed to the Queen's household' – he adds 'this is most unwise'.*]

15 July   About 1 o'clock last night ... [*I*] saw a splendid fireball passed thro' the air from West to East – and many falling stars. Lincoln accompanied Lord Combermere to Windsor today to see the funeral procession of the late King.

16 July   I am torn to pieces again by worries and perplexities. My Mother is at me on the old story of want of attention and confidence to her, this annoys me to the greatest degree ... I am really unhappy and, as it were, on the sack. My money affairs are in a bad order in as much as my expenses greatly exceed my receipts ... my children are my only comfort.

19 July   Went to St. James's Palace to be sworn in as Lord Lieutenant [*of Nottinghamshire*] before the King in Council.

22 July   [*After the third reading of the Bill*] – The Retford business is now finally settled.

1830

23 July   By appointment, I waited on the King today at ½ past 2 to have an audience with him. [*It transpired that the King was on his way to prorogue Parliament and was just leaving at the time appointed for the Duke's audience. The King acknowledged the Duke in the waiting area but had no time to talk. The Duke 'bowed low' and left.*] – I am certain that this has been done for one of two things, either to make a fool of me or else to put me off ... I will never submit to be treated in such a manner by any one tho' he may be the King himself, for no one has the right to sport or trifle with the feelings of another because he may possess the superior power or authority.

24 July   I declined an invitation to an audience at ½ past 2 today, which I was not able to keep from the shortness of time. [*This invitation had followed closely on an 'apologetical letter' from the Palace.*] – Then I received an invitation from the Lord Chamberlain to a party at the Palace this evening, after the Chapter of the Garter. This I declined, as I leave London in the morning. Then I received a letter ... telling me it was His Majesty's desire that I should dine with him today at 7 o'clock. This of course I was able to accept.

Fig. 26 *William IV – by Sir Martin Arthur Shee.*

I went to the dinner and to my dismay found the whole Royal party set down to dinner. The King was very good humoured and kind ... The Queen sent her command that I should take my place at the table, which of course I did! After dinner the King took me to his closet to give me the audience ... he made every apology about the matter of yesterday ... I said that I was overwhelmed by his goodness ... and that he had not a more faithful subject in His empire.

26 July   Left London with Lincoln – stopped at Grantham – much [*election*] noise during the night.

27 July   [*Home (Clumber), via Newark and Tuxford*] – My dear boys arrived late this evening from Eton, grown and looking remarkably well.

1830

1 August | [*Receives a letter regarding Edward – praising his abilities*] – he will be an ornament to the profession.

6 August | [*After the Duke's man was victorious at the Newark election and Lincoln had made a speech at the celebratory dinner*] – Everything went off admirably and with flying colours for the House of Clumber.

8 August | [*Regarding the election in Bassetlaw, the constituency which now included Retford*] – the Duke of Portland dealt in humbug and polite incivility, meaning to be very cutting and very [*adverse?*].

[*He mentions good reports of Lincoln's speech at the Newark dinner on the 6th, and writes*] – He is eminently qualified to be a leading character hereafter.

16 August | The bills for the Retford election are collected and will amount to about £3,500, a serious sum.

23 August | This is my dear Caroline's birthday, she has completed her 12th year – clever, gay, so much to say for herself, fine, delightful, a great deal of genius, a mind perhaps more male than female.

26 August | Robert is very unwell today [*full details of his fever etc.*] – I sent for Mr Russel from Blyth.

2 September | [*Robert is*] so much better as to make me quite happy [*an extended section in praise of Robert follows*] – I think him a most superior boy.

22 September | Rather a curious thing happened today – a sparrow hawk pursued its prey so intently that it did not perceive the windows of the conservatory – it dashed thro' the glass and fell dead ... I have sent him to be stuffed and he will figure in my collection of Clumber birds.

Today they began to repair the 'Lincoln', almost every plank is rotten – most of the timbers are good – tomorrow they will haul her up on the slip and on the next take all the rotten out.

Fig. 27 *A later version of the 'Lincoln' frigate, undergoing repairs at the Clumber Lake arm, near Hardwick, in 1911.*

1830

23 September   [*He mentions the Duke of Wellington as having*] – no more feelings than a flint stone ...

27 September   Came to Kirklington for a few days. Georgiana and Lincoln have accompanied me. The coming here of those dear offspring of her who was bred up here, brought back many painful reflections and tender recollections and has clouded me exceedingly.

1 October   This is Charlotte's birthday, she has now completed her 18th year ... I can write it without fear of contradiction that such a family is not to be found in the world besides.

6 October   Came to Bawtry to shoot at Martin tomorrow. Lincoln accompanied me.

8 October   ... made calls on our way home at Dowager Lady Galway's at Serlby, and Blyth.

9 October   At last my pilasters for the Library are arrived [*in England*] from Italy and are now on the road, I shall be able to complete my room.

15 October   Lincoln left me to Oxford today. [*The Duke fears the 'vice' that Lincoln will meet there.*]

16 October   The marble Pilasters and capitals for the Library are arrived here and were unpacked today – fortunately perfectly safe and only a few small pieces broken off ... the capitals. The marble is beautiful and the whole remarkably executed.

23 October   By the Post this evening I received a letter with the Newark post mark on it, upon opening, the smell was horrid. I then perceived that some human excrement was upon the paper, amongst the filth I just caught sight of the words, dirty and yellow, but all my letters were poisoned with the smell, which altogether with the nature of [*the*] act as well as the stink quite turned my stomach.

28 October   The Pilasters are up in their place in the Library, the effect is excellent and the archway will be a splendid feature in the room.

Fig. 28 *The pilasters, capitals and archway. Westmacott's 'Euphrosyne' statue is displayed in the Reading Room of the Clumber Library.*

1830

29 October	[*To London – via Grantham, where he slept – Stamford, where he had breakfast – and Stevenage, where he 'dined'.*]
1 November	I took my seat in the House of Lords today. Who knows if it will be the last time?
2 November	[*The King opens Parliament*] … I shall wait a little longer before I decide upon any steps that I myself shall take, and if after a short time I find that I can do no good here, I shall retire to the country and await events which will not be long in arriving.
4 November	Lincoln has passed his 'little go' and I hope with considerable credit. His Latin composition was highly approved, also his Greek and Latin – his Logic was as good as the rest.
7 November	[*He mentions the need to guard the gasometers from the mobs.*]
10 November	Edward arrived from his ship today.
19 November	[*With Edward*] Visited the Zoological Gardens, the Coliseum and Lambeth Palace …
20 November	Edward left today, by steam-packet from St. Catherine's Docks – to Sheerness.
2 December	[*After learning that the Attorney General had spoken in public of the need to* "extinguish the Boroughmongers and affirmed [*that*] the power which has called forth from a Nobleman that scandalous and wicked interogatory 'Is it not lawful to do what I will with mine own?' ought to be abolished by the law of the land".] – This I saw this morning in the Morning Chronicle.
3 December	[*After speaking in the House of Lords on the matter of the Attorney General's speech – and being disappointed with his own performance*] – a cool, a clever and a practised man would have cut the Attorney to pieces.
4 December	[*Regarding the Reform Riots*] – God's vengeance is upon us …
10 December	Edward has been discharged from the 'Donegal' unexpectedly … [*Edward was awaiting a posting to a new ship*] … by this bad arrangement he will lose three days [*pay*].
11 December	[*Mentions money problems – especially the high cost of recent election expenses* '£2,000'] – added to others … have quite crippled me and I am really so perplexed and disturbed that I am at my wit's end to know what to do to meet the demands upon me.
14 December	[*Left London for Clumber*] … in my carriage for 4 o'clock and reached Eaton at a little before 10 – drank tea and slept there.
15 December	Arrived at Clumber at 20 minutes past 10 [*via Newark*] – found all well, thank God. Georgiana and Charlotte were up – I went and kissed Caroline and Henrietta and Robert in their beds but they did not wake.
16 December	Lincoln arrived with Edward.

1830

24 December   There is some mischief going on in the neighbourhood, two days ago it was currently reported all about that all my farm yard was consumed. I have today heard how this report originated. A man came towards Hardwick in a gig, he got out of it near the stack yard and tied his horse to the rails. He was seen to jump over the stack yard fence into the yard and was going towards the stack, when two of my men went up to him and asked him what he wanted. He made a shuffling reply, and immediately retreated to his gig and rode off – my boobies never thought of stopping the man, nor did they for some time even mention the circumstance to the farmer – the man went to Worksop, and the next day the same man asked some bystanders at Markham Moor if they had heard the news that the whole of the Duke of Newcastle's stacks and farming premises had been burnt down. From several things which I see and hear I much fear that mischief is close to the door.

25 December   My Mother joined our Christmas party today. My eldest children received the Sacrament with me – we all dined together ...

27 December   The weather is very particularly severe for the last four days – [*daytime temperatures 27 to 22; night 18 to 15*]. The river by Markham Moor is frozen over, a thing not known by the inhabitants of the neighbourhood.

31 December   ... We here terminate a most troublesome and most eventful year ... I think more than ever that the consequences of a marvellous kind are very shortly to arise from what is now passing,

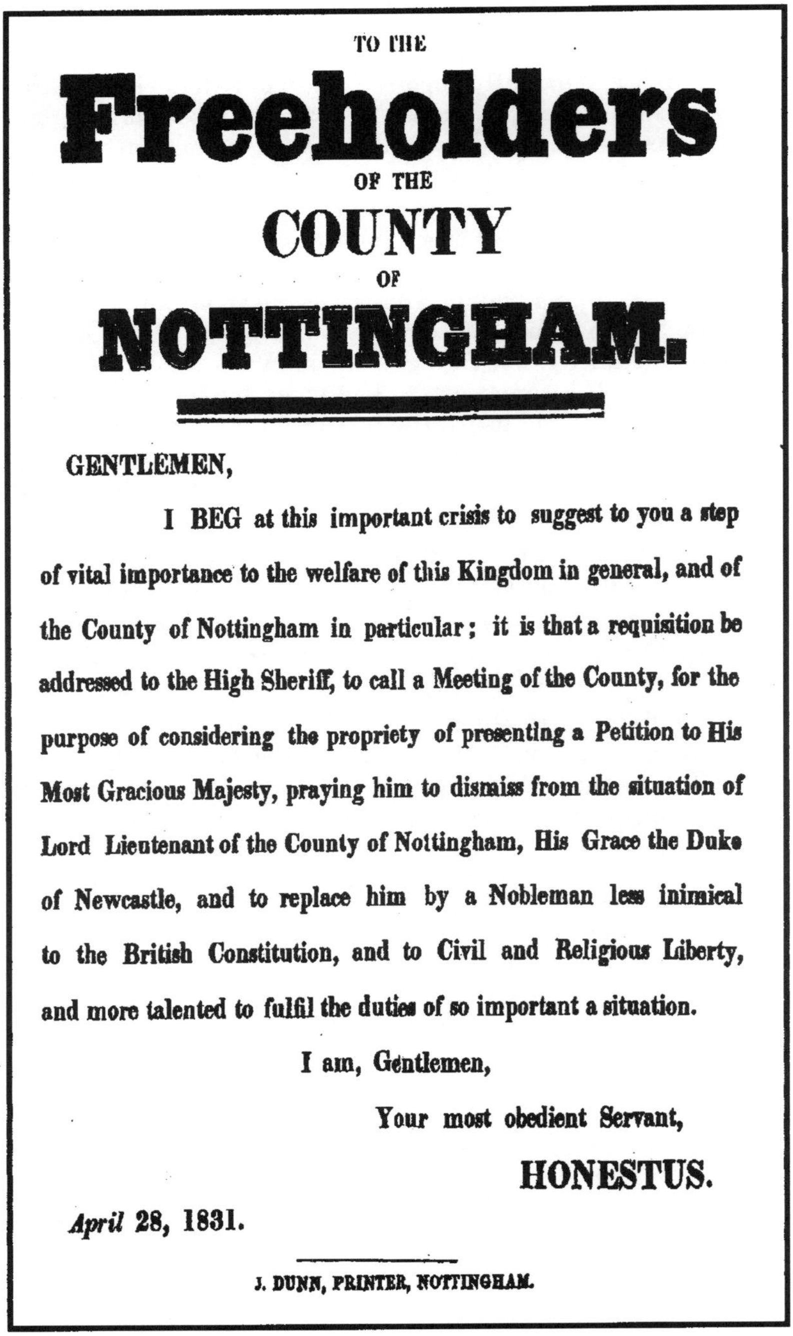

TO THE

Freeholders

OF THE

COUNTY

OF

NOTTINGHAM.

GENTLEMEN,

I BEG at this important crisis to suggest to you a step of vital importance to the welfare of this Kingdom in general, and of the County of Nottingham in particular; it is that a requisition be addressed to the High Sheriff, to call a Meeting of the County, for the purpose of considering the propriety of presenting a Petition to His Most Gracious Majesty, praying him to dismiss from the situation of Lord Lieutenant of the County of Nottingham, His Grace the Duke of Newcastle, and to replace him by a Nobleman less inimical to the British Constitution, and to Civil and Religious Liberty, and more talented to fulfil the duties of so important a situation.

I am, Gentlemen,

Your most obedient Servant,

HONESTUS.

April 28, 1831.

J. DUNN, PRINTER, NOTTINGHAM.

Fig. 29 [*See Diary entry – 4 May 1831*]

1 January   ... We have passed a very happy day ...

4 January   Gave away the things to the poor people today. They appeared particularly grateful ... the people of the county generally are in full work and at good wages (2/- a day).

6 January   Twelfth Day ... Edward was the life and soul of the party ...

7 January   Having to attend a Ball at Newark, Sir Robert Bromley invited me to Stoke, where I came today before dinner – Great pains have been taken to deter me from going to this Ball and the [*low*?] party at Newark gave out that if I came I should not leave the Town alive. However, in the evening I started out from Stoke and was on the road within ¾ of a mile from Newark when a man on horseback came up and asked if I was in the carriage – on being answered 'yes', he said 'I want to speak to His Grace'. I let down the window and the man said that he was sent by the Stewards of the Ball to tell me that there was a riot in the Market place, that the [*rioters were*] insulting every body that came up thinking that I might be in the carriage, that they had been waiting for me a long while on the road where I was, but, thinking that Mr Norton's carriage had been mine they had followed it through the Town and were very tumultuous – that the Stewards, fearing mischief had sent the request that I would consent to relinquish my attendance at the Ball, as they could not tell what might be the consequences – as my appearance would excite the mob and might cause a serious tumult – I was at first staggered by this message for I thought that if any thing serious should happen that it would be chargeable upon me for being so obstinate as to persevere in coming into the Town – however, after asking the man a few questions and then passing the whole matter over in my mind (for I was alone in the carriage, none of the party at Stoke having the zeal to accompany me) I considered that at all risks it would be decidedly preferable to encounter any degree of riot than to incur the disgrace of retreat and to give to the rabble a triumph

1831

– I therefore ordered the post boys to drive on, to be stopped by nothing and to go directly to the Town Hall – When I arrived at the Market place I saw a great many flambeaux and arriving at the Hall steps, the rabble began to shout and to [exult?] at my arrival – as soon as the carriage stopped they crowded round the carriage and seemed very desirous of getting near to me – as soon as the door was opened I got out quickly and as if I was regardless of their hisses, cries and scuffling. Some people standing near, among whom I remarked some [?] servants, aided the constables in clearing a way …in spite of myself, I was impelled forward by a strength so superior to my own that I could not resist it – the man said nothing but pushed me forcibly and strenuously forward … he told me that his name was Bell and that he was the Chief Constable. I said that I was very much obliged to him for his spirited exertions – he came and shook me heartily by the hand and said that he would serve me with his life. I asked him a few questions about what was passing at the door – he said that now I was come that it would soon be all over and I heard afterwards that in the course of a quarter of an hour all the rascals went their way – as far as I could observe there were not more than 50 or 60 people. I learned from my servant that one of them had knocked him down by a blow at the back of the head and that one of them dashed his flambeau at me and covered my cloak with the wax – I then found that the danger had been strangely magnified – that the mob was a most [contemptible?] one and that if I had not persevered in coming to the Town that I should have sacrificed my reputation and done irreparable mischief by giving courage to a set of miscreants who were all hired to do what they did – In short by shewing that their menaces and insults are disregarded this [low?] party is completely fallen, beaten, and overcome, and in future, I think, I may pass thro' Newark without any molestation.

I went into the Ball room where I was most kindly and cordially received by every one, it was really most gratifying to me. I passed a very agreeable evening and staid till nearly 1/2 past 2. On retiring, a large party of gentlemen attended me to the door and it was plain to perceive that my visit had given very great satisfaction.

8 January   Returned to Clumber [via Thoresby] – It is here that I like to be, it is delightful to return home and repose after all the flutter which collusion with public concerns occasions.

13 January   It is my fine and dear boy William's birthday – he has today completed his 16th year.

14 January   Lincoln left me at 6 o'clock this morning for Oxford.

1831

19 January	My expenses have been so great and my means so inadequate that I have been obliged to borrow money. I today executed two Bonds bearing the date 17th of this month each for £5,000 – one to the Rev. Martin of Warsop the other to John Beresford [*Eagle*?] of Ashbourne, Derbyshire. It has been particularly unpleasant to me to do this, but without it I cannot pay the numerous applicants for payment of their bills. The Elections have severely injured my resources. Came to Ranby with 6 of my children.
23 January	Came to Kirklington – I have to attend a general meeting of Lieutenancy tomorrow morning.
24 January	Attended the general meeting ... the Regiment of Militia is to be called out for a months training on the 6th of March.
28 January	Called upon the General of the District, Sir Henry Bouverie, who has just settled at Blyth.
30 January	This is my 46th birthday.
17 February	Charles' name appears in the last Gazette as Cornet and Sub-Lieutenant in the 1st Life Guard.
18 February	This is Edward's birthday. He has completed his 15th year ... a universal favourite.
20 February	... I myself have been visited by a troublesome attack, a sort of inflammation of the bladder and urinary passage ... much pain ... Dover's powder, a preparation of opium, has done wonders for me. [*The Doctor*] tells me that the ailments of this season affect the brain ... a curious proof is that 3 poor women tenants of mine at West Markham, Elkesley and Drayton have destroyed themselves.
21 February	The waters being very low to lay the ways for the launch of the 'Lincoln', I took the opportunity of fishing the end of the lake head. We found nothing but pike and not a great many of them, the mud and weeds were so thick that the net rolled and not a single carp or tench was in the net. There were 232 pike and a few large perch in the net. I put all the former into the [*sleu*?] below the cascade.
23 February	The 'Lincoln' being completed, we launched her today. She went off remarkably well and made a sight. She is greatly improved upon the water – She has been completely rebuilt and is quite a new ship – I hope that she may now with proper care, last for a long time as the work and materials appear to be particularly good.
2 March	[*To London*] Left Clumber at so late an hour that I could only get to Grantham where we slept. Edward and Robert were with me.
3 March	Arrived in London between 9 and 10.

1831

12 March   [*At Kenwood with Georgiana to see Lord and Lady Mansfield.*]

18 March   This is my dear Georgiana's birthday.   She has now completed her 21st year ... an ornament of her sex.   In my family I am most widely blessed. Every one is a prize and not a single blank.

27 March   It has been my duty today to urge to many of those with whom I act, the absolute necessity of acting upon the principle of resisting all reform. I am sure that to act on the opposite principle will be our ruin.

31 March   [*Maundy Thursday*] – Charlotte, William and Edward were confirmed today at the Chapel Royal by the Bishop of London.

1 April   [*Good Friday*] – We all, that is, Georgiana, Charlotte, Lincoln, Charles, Thomas and I took the sacrament, 3 of them for the first time.

9 April   [*At Portsmouth*] – Edward sailed today [*On the 'Belvidere'.*]

13 April   My worthy cousin, Lord Harrington has just married Miss Foote, the Actress, who has lived with many people before and has several children by Col. Berkley – he is 53 – she 33.   Charlotte was to be presented [*to the Queen*] at the Drawing Room tomorrow but she is so unwell with bad and oppressive cold and cough that Doctor Maton says it will be risking too much to venture upon such an undertaking – Georgiana is not well either and Caroline has been extremely unwell – in short 2 thirds of the house are much indisposed with colds of a very peculiar kind.

20 April   Georgiana and I dined at the Duchess of Kent's today ... a very large party ... nearer 40 than 30 I believe – the little Princess [*Victoria*] is a charming child ... I sat next to the Duchess, we had a great deal of conversation on education and conduct in general.

21 April   [*The King agrees to dissolve Parliament*] ... Thus the Revolution begins and here will commence a violent struggle between the good and the bad of the country ... my heart is sick and I cannot write any more on this subject.

23 April   I dined with the King who gave a dinner to the Knights of the Garter. I never dined at so dull a dinner ... I was quite alarmed at the state of his mind.

25 April   A ball at St. James' Palace. Lincoln being invited he came from Oxford and attended it with us. He was in full dress and played his part very well for one so young and totally inexperienced in society, it was the first time in his life that he had ever been to a ball or even an assembly. He is but an imperfect dancer and scarcely knew the figures but he made it out very well on the whole. I was greatly pleased with his whole demeanour. He was presented to the Queen but not to the King.

1831

27 April [*The windows of his London home are smashed as he refused to place a light in them – as ordered by a Proclamation calling for a 'general illumination' – to denote the Dissolution of Parliament. Police protection saved him from worse violence. He wrote that he would not light* 'even a Farthing Candle'!]

28 April I went to the Drawing Room. Charlotte was presented there to the King and Queen – she looked beautifully (*sic*) I never saw any thing more perfect – she and her dear Sister were the handsomest girls at the Drawing Room.

29 April After a few hours sleep I rose at 4 o'clock and was in my carriage at about 20 minutes past 5. Reached Oxford at half past 11, the roads being heavy. Here I took up Lincoln ... off again about 1 o'clock. We could not with all our exertion get farther than Loughborough – we arrived at 11 ... I have travelled nearly 150 miles today.

30 April Reached Clumber about 4 o'clock [*After calling on Mr Rolleston's at Watnall and learning that his chances at the Newark election were hopeless*]

1 May Received a letter from my dear Edward ... off Cadiz.

4 May I have learned today that handbills have been in circulation, calling for the Sheriff to call a county meeting ... petitioning the King to dismiss me from the Lieutenancy of the County ... I wish it may be so – it will at once display the designs of our enemies and will tend to open the eyes of the King ...

5 May I have proposed today to form a King and Constitution Society ...

6 May [*Regarding the King and Constitution Society*] – I mean to include every body, high and low.

9 May Arrived in London – around half past 8. We had an invitation to a ball at St. James', and as Georgiana and Charlotte, with Lincoln, were to go, altho' tired to death, I went and was very happy to find myself at home again before 3 in the morning. This was the first time Charlotte had ever been to a ball or public assembly in the evening – she was rather bewildered, but she behaved in her usual becoming manner and looked truly beautiful.

22 May This is my dear Lincoln's birthday, he has completed his twentieth year. His time of action now fast approaches and he may soon take his part in public affairs, for which I think he is as well prepared as any one.

23 May Robert has been very unwell.

25 May Thomas has just received his commission in the 1st Life Guards.

26 May [*The Duke absented himself from today's Garter Chapter as a protest – he called those who did attend* 'a grovelling set'.] Robert is surprisingly better today. [*After being prescribed quinine.*]

1831

28 May   The King's birthday today ... I staid [*sic*] away, I cannot pay respects where respect is not due.

13 June   I had the pleasure of hearing Paganini at a concert at the Opera House tonight ... his exquisite taste and delicate feeling regulates every thing and forms a performance which will perhaps never again be equalled ... his tones are melodious beyond description ... He never errs by a false note or playing out of tune and in the most difficult and rapid passages never deviates from the utmost correctness ...

4 July   I was to have left ... for Clumber today but Thomas was taken so much more unwell.

5 July   Thomas is no better – and Charles being also ill – defer my journey – I sent all the others, fearing that they might fall ill one after the other.

7 July   My two dear boys being so much recovered, Doctor Maton gave us leave to go ... we started in the afternoon and arrived at Biggleswade where we sleep.

8 July   [*Arrived at Clumber*] This place is looking beautiful, and now that every thing is so much finished and put to rights it is very enjoyable.

26 July   William came home today for the holidays [*the only one of the Duke's sons still at Eton.*]

20 August   Lincoln has been called upon to attend the King at his coronation as one of the train bearers – I wonder why, and I wish that he had not been selected. I should have been glad to be quite clear of the shabby and uninteresting ceremony.

21 August   In the violent and terrific thunder storms which we have had within the last six weeks ... very great mischief has been done – here, a tree at the back of the gardens was stricken, which I went to look at today – it was a small oak situated between and touching two very [*fine?*] fir trees much taller than itself. This therefore appears to have been a curiously capricious selection. In Hardwick Wood also, the lightning struck an old oak in the wood nearly a hundred yards from the outside – the fluid penetrated into the interior of the tree and split it all to pieces, driving large pieces of the tree to a distance of 60 feet from the tree. It is evident that there is no security from such a powerful and destructive assailant, but in God's goodness alone.

23 August   This being my dear Caroline's [*13th*] birthday ... we dined out of doors and the younger ones had their supper out also. [*Glowing praise of Caroline's merits follow.*]

1831

28 August   A very atrocious act has been perpetrated at Wellow early this morning – someone fired a blunderbuss into the windows of Wombwell a farmer at Wellow, a child in bed was slightly wounded by the shot. [*There were early suspicions that the deed was done by Wombwell's brother* 'a noted character'.]... Mansell [*the Duke's Gamekeeper*] only a short time ago lost all his bacon and his ferrets. The farmers all around have had nearly all their poultry stolen ... The population is in a very bad state.

29 August   This is Henrietta's birthday. In the evening she played some duets with Caroline ... [*followed by a* 'large concert' – *harp, violoncello, violin and pianoforte.*]

30 August   Letters from Edward off Cyprus and Malta – the latest dated 30th July.

1 September   Went out shooting ... I never saw fewer birds here ... we killed 53 partridges and some hares.

2 September   I have omitted to mention ... that I was appointed one of the four to hold the Pall over the King at the anointing at the Coronation – Lincoln to be one of the King's train bearers – Both of us have declined. I would not in the first place accept an inferior office after having held a superior. Next I wish to have no part in the coronation of such a king – then, not to be indebted to such an administration for any honour or favor, and above all not to participate in a ceremony conducted by a Popish Earl Marshall.

11 September   Went to sleep at Tuxford with my four sons in order to be early on the ground for shooting the next day.

19 September   Went to Martin to shoot.

26 September   [*The Duke travelled to London, without the children – mob violence was widely reported, over the Reform Act speeches and voting intentions.*]

9 October   [*Whilst riding to the House of Lords*] – the crowds were held back by the police – some fellows made a determined spring forward like bulldogs at me, but were caught and pulled back by the policemen – but for them these fellows seemed determined to injure me and no doubt would not have cared to take my life away. [*Later whilst returning to his home at Portman Square*] ... as I approached this Square, I saw a large mob and it immediately occurred to me that they were waiting for me – I kept out of the light and away from the pavement as much as I could, and on arriving near to my house I saw that it was surrounded by people and that it would be quite imprudent for me to attempt to enter my house – I therefore rode past and on the opposite side of the Square found a large party of Police ... I learned that about 1/2 past 5, the mob had come in large force and in an instant smashed all my windows ... I went to the Head

1831

of the Police – [*requested*] protection of life and property ... returned home at 10 – I found all quiet – but my servant's told me that they had made a most determined attack upon the house, knocked in the shutters and nearly so the entrance door – they had broken nearly every pane of glass.

11 October   Lord Melbourne tells me ... bad news from Notts. that Nottingham was in a shocking state and that the rioters had set fire to Nottingham Castle.

I have heard nothing about it, so I hope that it is not true, but I much fear that it is ...

Fig. 30 *Nottingham Castle ablaze. (Picture by Thomas Allom.)*

... I hope that Clumber is not in their black books.

12 October   Having received authentic information of the destruction of Nottingham Castle by fire by the mob – of the sacking of Colwick, which they stripped of everything and afterwards set fire to – of the audacity of their proceedings and of the entire impunity with which they have perpetrated all their outrages, I have determined to go to Clumber this evening. I went to the Duke of Wellington and had a long consultation with him how I should proceed, the cry of the mob was that they would proceed to Clumber and the opinion of many was that they would go there – but the Duke of Wellington thinks and [*justly?*] that they will never go so far – ... all the shops were shut by orders of the

people as a sign of mourning for the loss of the [*Reform*] bill. A letter arrived from Georgiana telling me that they [*his daughters*] were then all at Mansell's house, whither they have been sent for safety ... [*and that Lincoln had taken every precaution for Clumber's defence.*]

13 October   Started [*for Clumber*] at 4 – a letter from Newark advising me to be cautious and change horses out of the town. Stopped at Mansell's, my dear daughters and William perfectly well. At Mansell's, Miss Spencer, the Swiss governess and their maids were with them so it must have been closely packed. I staid about an hour and then went to Clumber, notwithstanding the wishes of Mansell that I would stay as he thought it very likely that I should be shot at as I went through the woods where several men had been seen for several days lurking about – I learned that the outhouse of the Park cottage had been burned with a cow of Mr Tomlinson's in it.

Mrs Tomlinson had only been brought to bed 3 or 4 days before and was removed although to the danger of her life – such is the villainy of these rascals –

I reached Clumber at about 11 o'clock; having met videttes of Yeomanry [*mounted sentries*] patrolling within two miles of the house – on my arrival at the House, the garrison expressed their rejoicing and welcome by loud and long continuous cheers. In the house I found my dear Lincoln, Charles and Thomas with the officers of the Troop stationed here and poor Mr Tomlinson, who had not deserted Clumber notwithstanding the situation of his wife – which devotion I shall not forget.

I could not believe that I was at Clumber, the whole was changed, every thing was removed that was valuable, such as pictures, ornaments, furniture, statues etc. and nothing but bare walls, and the house filled with men in all the rooms, with cannons, of which I have 10 [x] 3 pounders and 14 little ship guns and firearms, muskets and pistols and sabres planted in their proper positions and in all the windows. The scene was beyond description, the confusion and joy occasioned by my arrival might have formed several pages for the pen of an experienced novelist – before I went to bed,

I visited all the arrangements made in the different rooms. Lincoln, who had made them, shewed me and it [*pleased me?*] to observe the attention of the people to him and I learn that he is adored by all, that his ability to perform, his forethought, his kindness of manner and the pleasant way in which he has given his orders and run every thing has commanded universal admiration and has received the affectionate attachment of every mortal here – The preparations are indeed formidable –

1831

sufficient to repel 20,000 men – In the house there are 200 men, and out of it a great many more, including a Troop of Yeomanry of 70 men and horses. It was late before we retired, when I laid down I was not long before I fell into a sleep which was only broken at intervals, by thinking I heard something [*passing*?]

14 October I would not give any orders last night, not wishing without due deliberation to alter any thing that Lincoln had done – but this morning I determined to make a change in our mode of defence. I therefore settled that the Yeomanry should be dismissed, all but a Sgt. and 12 men, whom I kept until the next morning – I reduced the number of men to 20 picked men, who have been mainly old soldiers. I admit none of them into the house. I have made a barrack for them in the offices adjourning, where they sleep and mess, and I mount a chain of sentries in a ring round the house in the pleasure grounds. In this manner we shall command regularity and something like system and efficiency – I think that we shall not be surprised and shall be perfectly secure against all attack in this manner. Towards evening, I had made some progress in putting the house to rights, and making it more as usual, for I found it scarcely habitable, and my own room full of people with guns mounted and full of litter and dirt. I was obliged to take a small room for a bed room for the last night and this night – tomorrow I shall get into my own rooms and shall be able to send for my daughters who[*se*] rooms were occupied in the same manner. At night I went to see that all my arrangements were carried properly into execution, and found them well done – on my return home, from not knowing the countersign, I was taken prisoner by one of my own sentries – We shall soon be all together and comfortable again – I have heard of no fresh aggressions.

15 October My report of the morning was that two men had been taken last night, who pretended to be gentlemen and who said that it would be very disagreeable to be taken before me, who would know them – and offered 20 sovereigns to let them [*go*], they refused their money – but told them that as they saw that they were gentlemen that they liberated them. Nothing could be more unfortunate, there can be no question they were incendiaries and that they were the very people that we are looking for and who had been so frequently seen in various parts evidently bent upon mischief ... It is perfectly clear to me that the magistrates and authorities took no [*thoughtful*?] pains to prevent the infamous outrages at Colwick and Nottm Castle, for full 8 hours nothing whatever was done and the slackness in the performance of their duty on all occasions, especially regarding obnoxious persons has been signally remarkable, they shall hear more of this.

1831

16 October	[*A 'spy' is arrested at Clumber – much detail – sent to Worksop.*]
17 October	I went to Blyth today to confer with the General of the District, Sir H. Bouverie ... about the man taken last night. I have heard of nothing but tranquility today.
19 October	[*The Duke's Clumber tenantry express their loyalty and support to him. They also offer to volunteer for whatever defence duties he requires.*]

My dear Lincoln leaves for Oxford tomorrow ... he has in view ... trying for the highest honours [*degree*].

Dr Guisford, the new Dean of Christ Church, tells me that Charles and Thomas can be received [*there*] about 9 November.

21 October	... Lincoln writes from Nottingham that he has visited the Castle and found it in a woeful plight.
23 October	Intimation has been sent to me today that I should be upon my guard against assassination.
8 November	Charles and Thomas went to Oxford today, they will matriculate tomorrow and will remain for the remainder of the term. The loss of the company to me is great, they are charming youths, excellent and unexceptimable [*sic*] in every respect, I do not know of a fault that they have, nor do I know of a virtue that they have not. In writing thus I record the fact after reflection – they are like the rest of my worthily dear Children, remarkable examples of real worth, pure and unalloyed. They love what is right and follow it as a pleasure, vice and impropriety they shun and loath – and yet more cheerful, contented and sociable beings cannot be found. I am sure that my plan of sending the dear fellows to Oxford, not withstanding that they hold commissions in the army, will be highly beneficial to them. Wherever they may be placed they will hereafter feel themselves to be on a level with anyone. They are very good scholars and I have no doubt will very greatly improve at Oxford. – They started early this morning in a hack post chaise, it is the first time that they have had entirely to do for themselves. They will be as steady as two old men.
17 November	... the Lake was frozen over even up to the bridge yesterday and today a swan was frozen to the ice and was liberated with difficulty ... the thermometer was last night down to 21 degrees.
26 November	[*He mentions the* 'dastardly Newarkers'.]
8 December	My dear William returned home from Eton yesterday.
9 December	To my surprise ... my three dear Oxonians arrived home.
13 December	I have broached the scheme for ... a School of Medicine and Anatomy at Nottingham. [*This was eventually opened, on St James' Street, but closed again by 1836*]

1831

17 December   *[He mentions that his health is improving]* – after a new beverage which is very unpalatable to me but to which I think I shall be much indebted – brandy and water.

19 December   I have been blooded again with leeches *[near the base of his spine.]*

20 December   ... I have lately had correspondence with the Duke of Hamilton of a most agreeable and satisfactory nature on a subject of the highest and dearest interest to us. A short time perhaps may, as I hope, develop its results.

21 December   *[He notes that arson and poaching are prevalent.]*

22 December   *[He notes that his name has been omitted from the list of Commissioners appointed to investigate the October rioting in Nottingham. He is aggrieved, as he has never known a Lord Lieutenant to be excluded from such a Commission.]*

24 December   *[He records the gift of a painting from the Rev. Mr Newling – it is a portrait of the 1st Earl of Lincoln.]*

25 December   ... After Chapel we all attended the Sacrament ... afterwards we all *[including his Mother]* dined together – only our dear little noble Sailor ... was missing. My Mother is far from well.

27 December   Lincoln, Charles and Thomas are gone to shoot ... at Martin. Young Mr Canning is to join them there.

30 December   ... Leeches have again been put upon my back over the spine, rather below the shoulders.

Fig. 31 *Clumber House, circa 1835, drawn by Moses Webster.*

1832

1 January   [*In his usual retrospective on the past year he comments –*] ... it seems as if I had lost all my friends and I had everyone against me ... In this County I stand alone ... the mob is set against me. My tenantry is faithful and attached.

2 January   My admirable Lincoln left me this morning for Oxford ... he aims for a first class and I have little doubt that he will obtain it ... There is something about him that is of no ordinary character. –I am fully persuaded that he is destined for great things.

5 January   The clothing etc. was distributed to the poor today. I could not leave my room and be present at the distribution – they all seemed very happy and grateful and more cleanly and tidy within appearance than I have ever yet seen them.

6 January   I went down to the Drawing Room and had our evening's entertainment. [*He reports that they all missed Lincoln and Edward and that, in addition to himself, Charles was unwell.*] –This has been a very flat and certainly not a merry Christmas. The younger ones enjoyed the ceremony and the look of the plum cake and were delightfully happy.

8 January   [*Following a letter from himself to the King, on the subject of the Nottingham Commissioners –which he had sent via the Duke of Cumberland. The reply explained that he was excluded from the Commission in view of the offences, which included damage to his own property –Nottingham Castle.*] – They want to drive me from office – they expected I should resign on receiving such an insult.

14 January   [*He notes that the Nottingham defendants charged with damaging the Castle were* 'let off'. *Others were found guilty of attacks on different properties and were sentenced to death.*]

16 January   A delicious day with bright sun. I took a ride with [*Georgio – or possibly Georgiana?*] and on the airy part of the Forest.

19 January   My three dear boys left me today [*for Oxford*]. I came to Ranby and brought my remaining young ones with me.

1832

23 January Some relations of the condemned men at Nottingham came here today. [*They were seeking his assistance as Lord Lieutenant, in a petition to the King for clemency. He told them that he could not assist them but notes that it is the government ministers who were at fault and who ought to suffer punishment – not these poor devils.*]

30 January [*At Ranby*] – I have completed my 47th year ... In May Lincoln will come of age ... I have the satisfaction of thinking that he has fixed his choice for a partner on a person in every way calculated to make a happy and advantageous union.

13 February [*He postpones his trip to London*]
– My Valet has been taken very ill.

2 March I am busily occupied in beautifying and improving this delightful place. It is assuming a most interesting aspect on every side and in 20 years will eclipse almost every other place that can be named – That is – if it is allowed to remain in the possession of my family.

4 March I have been much shocked to see written in the Stone Temple across the water – and in an excellent hand – "The Kingdom of heaven Brethren is like unto a rump of Beef where you may cut and come again, therefore rejoice and be glad" – and again on Clumber Bridge "What think you of Christ reader and what does Christ think of you, he thinks that the Duke of Newcastle will go to Hell".

Fig. 32 *Clumber's 'Stone Temple across the water'*

5 March [*He mentions his*] – sense of duty and a wish to do good urges me to the very irksome ... tasks.

12 March Attended a meeting at Tuxford to establish a Dispensary there for the use of the poor – This has been a scheme of mine, and I never felt greater pleasure than in the accomplishment of establishing such an Institution. The meeting was very well attended and above £100 subscribed in the room. We shall have a donation fund of above £200 ...

13 March Came to Ranby for a night to see my mother ...

1832

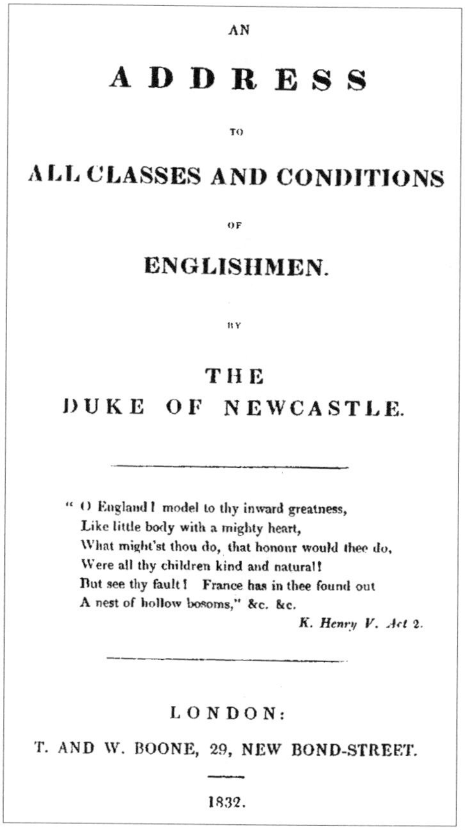

Fig. 33 [*There are several entries around this time which refer to his work in preparing to have his latest 'Pamphlet' published.*]

AN

ADDRESS

TO

ALL CLASSES AND CONDITIONS

OF

ENGLISHMEN.

BY

THE
DUKE OF NEWCASTLE.

―――――

" O England ! model to thy inward greatness,
Like little body with a mighty heart,
What might'st thou do, that honour would thee do,
Were all thy children kind and natural!
But see thy fault! France has in thee found out
A nest of hollow bosoms," &c. &c.
K. Henry V. Act 2.

―――――

LONDON:

T. AND W. BOONE, 29, NEW BOND-STREET.

――

1832.

30 March Left Clumber [*to go to London*] and reached Grantham where we slept. Georgiana and Charlotte are with me.

6 April My dear little children came from Clumber today.

14 April Georgiana and Charlotte and I dined today with the Duchess of Kent. The little Princess [*Victoria*] looked in excellent health, she is a charming and most likeable child – precisely what she should be.

1 May Made acquaintance with the Duchess of Hamilton and her daughter Lady Susan to whom Lincoln appears, and most justly as far as I can see, to be very partial. We drank tea at the Duke of Hamilton's this evening, only a family party and I and my daughters and Lincoln ... Lady Susan I like extremely, I think that she is the very thing for Lincoln and quite calculated to make a husband's happiness.

8 May I must here observe that I have been treated with utter indifference by all, those who were formerly my friends have kept away from me ... I have a stiff task before me ... I shall have to fight my battle single-handed.

12 May [*Sir R Peel refuses to join the Government*] – I honor him for it ...

19 May Dined at the Eton anniversary dinner, a small but very cordial meeting [*This is another occasion where he writes of his difficulty in making a speech.*]

22 May This is my admirable Lincoln's birth day. He this day attains his majority.

23 May ... Lincoln's birth day has been celebrated at Newark by the

1832

inhabitants and gentlemen of the neighbourhood, by those of Retford and neighbourhood, by my tenants who met at Tuxford and by my tenants at Boroughbridge and Aldborough. At Clumber I gave a dinner to all my servants, laborers etc. and here in London the same thing, the upper servants and friends yesterday, the under servants and friends today, they have been highly pleased and rejoiced.

25 May ... My heart aches, I am sick, disgusted and distrustful of all mankind, I see so much [?] and depravity, such a total want of principle and such horrible profligacy that I am ashamed of my species and bewildered amongst the maze of wickedness which on almost every succeeding day is opened to me.

Emblems of revolution are freely and publicly worn such as the coloured flowers, ribbons and [?].   All this must lead to something fatal most rapidly.

30 May [Mentions Lord Maitland, who was at Eton with him. He is touched that Maitland's father, Lord Lauderdale, has asked the Duke to carry his voting proxy. The Duke notes that Lord Maitland was known as 'Citizen Maitland' whilst at school, but his attitude to democracy has now altered.]

16 June ... The Cholera is approaching Clumber. There have been many deaths at Doncaster and Gainsborough.

23 June [He records that he is having difficulty with his plan to keep Charles and Thomas at Oxford. As army officers they are due to return to their regiments but the Duke wishes them to continue with their education and obtain degrees. A senior army officer tells him that it will not be possible for the twins to be away from the army for three years.]

27 June We dined with the Duke and Duchess of Hamilton. The young people became much better acquainted, we were quite en famille. Lincoln is much attached to Lady Susan and she is evidently partial to him. She is a charming person and when they know their own minds fully, I have no doubt that the determination will be such as we Parents anxiously desire.

30 June We went to see the Surrey Zoological Gardens which are just established, they are very pretty and will in a short time be a very beautiful establishment.

3 July ... A case of cholera occurred at Normanton Inn near Clumber – a man died there on Saturday night.

5 July Charles and Thomas came home from Oxford today – they are very well.

10 July A Ball at the Duchess of Hamilton's – it was the first that Charles and Thomas have been at, they danced a little but made

so much confusion that they gave up. Poor Lincoln is going tomorrow and only staid for this Ball – Lady Susan Hamilton seems to be as partial to him as he is to her and as soon as Lincoln has taken his degree I hope that they will be united.

11 July   Lincoln returned to Oxford today. That is, he went to Cuddesden about 7 miles from Oxford where he is going to be in the house of a Mr [*Saunders*?] with whom he is going to study for his degree, it will be hard and dull work but I am sure that it will be advantageous to him and that he will hereafter always have to congratulate himself upon having done it. I fear that he will find it dreadfully irksome at first after the succession of gaiety which he has had in London.

Fig. 34 *'Lincoln' (by George Richmond)*   Fig. 35 *Lady Susan (attributed to Sir Francis Grant)*

13 July   Having received a letter from Lincoln which, in addition to what he had told me before he went away, still further authorised and commissioned me to settle matters for him – I [*have*] seen the Duchess and Lady Susan Hamilton and found the latter fully prepared to give her consent and whole heart to my dear and admirable Lincoln – and thus that point is settled, and when Lincoln has taken his degree, they will be united – Lady Susan has shewn herself in a still more amiable and valuable light since I mentioned the matter, and I should do her the greatest injustice if I did not own that her behaviour has been as perfect a thing as I can imagine, from a warm hearted, open, generous, amiable and most engaging girl. She is not less good than beautiful, and I hope that by God's blessing my deserving and admirable Son has the fairest prospect of being as happy in the wedded state as any one ever was.

1832

14 July   ... I find that Lady Susan has considerable expectations and that she will have money of her own, independent of what he [*her father, the Duke of Hamilton*] will also give her. But this I never knew till now – I am truly rejoiced at the event – it is most desirable in every point of view.

19 July   The more I see of Lady Susan Hamilton the more I like and admire. She is not a common person, and possesses a mind in devotion of many things – full of talent, spirit and energy, but not yet tempered by the most [?] permissive graces. Beauty in face and figure, without affectation, the picture of good humour and happiness.

Her mother, the Duchess of Hamilton, is a most extraordinary woman. She is the handsomest, and the most perfect woman in appearance that I ever saw, with a dignity and pervading grace and elegance which must be seen to be understood. Her talent is of the very highest order, with a soul and elevation of mind that excites reflection in the beholder or rather hearer, a devoted mother, she would do any thing for her children and this devotion they repay be unbounded affection – it is an edifying sight to see her and her daughter together, the maternal instinct of the one and the watchful attention of the other, waiting as it were upon every turn of her Mother's countenance. The Duchess's singing is superior to that of any professional person that I ever heard – her science and execution in music is the same. Her conversation is what one would expect from such a person and all that she does, says or thinks is marked by superiority – I think my invaluable Lincoln has an abundant source of happiness in store for him and that God may bless them both with his choicest blessings, making them shining ornaments to benefit by their example and their virtues.

28 July   [*Saturday*] – Arrived back at Clumber.

29 July   In looking around today I have been much pleased ... the Terrace is beautiful.

31 July   This place is in real beauty, I never saw it so much so – the Terrace is now a most enjoyable lounge and the Pleasure Ground [*shady?*] and various now that it is quite interesting to us all.

3 August Attended a meeting of the Tuxford Dispensary. There has been a great deal of squabbling and so there was today. [*He indicates that he brought the meeting to order and was praised for his efforts. He was told he had* 'saved the Institution from being destroyed'.]

4 August [*He writes that Lord Manvers, on behalf of several gentlemen, has called at Clumber to suggest that Lord Lincoln should stand*

as candidate for the Northern Division of the County – this despite the differences they had with the Duke over his political opinions.]

5 August The people about here are in terrible alarm about the cholera – it has been very bad at Retford amongst the lowest and worthless class, and several in the neighbouring villages have taken it home from thence –a woman at Walesby died in this way a few days since and her children took the disease – one is dead ...

At Newark and Nottingham there have been few cases recently.

6 August Mr Gladstone who is to come in on my interest at Newark has just published his address – He is a friend of Lincoln's and a very talented and highly principled young man, as he tells me, for I do not know him.

7 August ... I rode over to Ranby today. My Mother ... looks thin and not very well.

8 August Sir R. Bromley came here today to ask me if I would let Lincoln stand for the Southern Division of the County ...

10 August [*He writes of the jury decision to allow him £21,000 compensation for the damage to Nottingham Castle. Notes that he expected between £25,000 and £30,000 but that he is glad the business is over.*]

13 August [*He reluctantly accepts that he has lost the battle with the Army to allow his twin sons, Charles and Thomas, to continue Oxford studies and also retain their commissions. They have been ordered to return to their regiments by the end of the month. He therefore advises them to resign their commissions.*]

18 August The Duke of Hamilton arrived here today. He is so kind and cordial that it is a pleasure and true satisfaction to have him with us.

20 August Riding about a great deal to show the county to the Duke of Hamilton we went to Welbeck – I never saw it look more wretchedly in every particular.

23 August The Duchess of Hamilton and Lady Susan [*have*] arrived.

24 August Lady Susan seems greatly pleased with every thing here and admires her future abode excessively.

25 August [*He has been upset by an argument over Lady Susan's wish to see Lincoln at Clumber. Her mother is also in favour of this but Newcastle is appalled and sees it as quite improper. However, he has given way, as he knows that Lincoln is also in agreement with Susan on the matter.*] – I deeply lament ... it will have a very bad influence.

29 August On our return from seeing Worksop Manor, we found to our surprise Lincoln, who had arrived only 10 mins. before us.

1832

31 August *[Following a long talk with Lincoln over the question of accepting a parliamentary candidature for the South Nottinghamshire Division]* ... he thinks it will neither be wise nor fair towards his intended Wife that he should be severed from her so early, nor be kept so long in London ... I am quite of the opinion, and always was so, that a newly married couple at first starting cannot live too quietly and domestically, their habits become firmed and settled and they rarely go on amiss afterwards, if such a mode of life is relied upon as being the most agreeable.

1 September The Duke of Hamilton left us this night ... the marriage is to take place in the end of November.

2 September *[The decision having been made that Lincoln will accept the call to stand for the election in South Nottinghamshire]* ... I cannot say that I am pleased with the idea, but I believe that we have done politically well by aiding the well disposed.

4 September ... we rowed on the water and took the Duchess of Hamilton to see the leopard at Hardwick ... In the evening we had music.

11 September Today Lincoln returned to Cullesden to resume his studies – but all hope of his gaining honors is at an end ... The Duchess of Hamilton and Lady Susan also went today.

14 September On riding thro' Worksop today I perceived that those whom I saw and met behaved towards me very differently from *[how]* they have of late years. All seemed curious and pleased to see me, and everywhere were pulling off their hats and trying to catch my attention – What has effected the great change I know not, but that it is not so only here but elsewhere is too evident not to be remarked *[Could it be that the populace were looking for an invitation to the wedding festivities?]*

18 September *[He has agreed with Hamilton that he, Newcastle, will give a £3,000 per annum allowance for Lincoln – Hamilton will add £1,500. Out of this Newcastle suggests that £500 be 'pin money' for Lady Susan.]* – I know this is not enough but I can do no more and I shall be put to my wits end to do so much.

22 September I have been during the greater part of the day at Markham Church and Parsonage ... ready for consecration in the ensuing Spring. I have looked at the old church with Dawkins, the Vicar, and we agree that it will be best to pull down great parts of the Old Church, reduce it in size and rebuild the bad parts, making it fit for the performance of funerals and even for service if necessary.

25 September The heat has been very great today, it was 72 in my bedroom with the window open and the sun excluded.

26 September Came to Ranby for a few days.

1832

27 September	[*The King has indicated that he does not wish the twins, Charles and Thomas, to resign their army commissions.*] I prefer the arrangement and shall adhere to it.
29 September	Returned from Ranby.
6 October	Lincoln returned tonight. [*From Oxford.*]
15 October	All my 4 girls are ill with exceedingly bad colds.
16 October	My dear Lincoln left ... for Oxford.
17 October	Robert is placed in the Upper School ... a remarkably intelligent and clever little fellow.
19 October	[*Regarding the Hafod Estate, he notes that the asking price is about £100,000 for the House, library, statues, pictures, furniture, china and wines. He believes it may sell at £65,000.*] I shall offer £50,000 ... if one could discover a rich mine there I should then be completely set up in the world – for at present my means are very inadequate to my wants.
22 October	[*Having dismissed his previous solicitor for being 'high and mighty'*] The new solicitor, Mr Henderson, arrived this afternoon.
29 October	Saw two swallows today, the weather is extraordinarily mild ...
2 November	Went to Combermere Abbey [*via Mansfield, Alfreton, Ashbourne, Cheadle, Newcastle and Woore*] ... the road was beautiful ... the entrance to Cromford is the most striking thing I ever saw ... there is a passage of a road thro' rocks on the right which beats anything of the kind.
3 November	It is many years since I was here ...
5 November	Lincoln is to be married on the 26th.
6 November	I have agreed to give Lady Susan £1,000 a year should she be a widow without children during my life time.
7 November	[*Travels to Devil's Bridge and notes that the distance is 94 miles.*]
8 November	[*To Hafod*] ... beautiful ... enchanting and surprising ... the House is bad and falling into decay very fast ... the water from the lead mines kills all the fish ... there is no wood and very little game or grouse ... no village near at hand ... no market town near ... no doctor nearer than Aberystwyth. I have made up my mind to give £40,000 and no more ...
9 November	[*Back to Combermere Abbey – via Newtown*] ... Flannel manufacturing has increased the population from 700 in 1801 to 7000 in 1832...
10 November	[*Regarding the forthcoming wedding*] – All is now settled to the entire satisfaction of the Hamilton family and I think that this Union will prove to be what I fully expect an honor and happiness to both families.]

1832

14 November [*Back to Clumber via Newcastle, Leek, Buxton, Bakewell and Ashford.*] Arriving at my own door, I found that only my two youngest girls were at Clumber – at this time Lincoln's carriage was seen by the company coming over the bridge – he shortly arrived and I had the happiness of seeing him and my little dears perfectly well.

15 November Lincoln started canvassing ... at E[*p*]perstone ... I drove over to Ranby [*found his mother unwell*] ... brought back Georgiana and Charlotte to Clumber.

16 November [*In Nottingham*] – The fog was so thick that I could not see the Castle. I felt heart sick at being in the neighbourhood of the scene of so much villainy, spoilation and malicious mischief. [*He then moved on to Leicester*]

17 November [*To his Portman Square house in London.*]

20 November [*Back to Clumber.*]

21 November My mother I find is sick and does not go to Scotland.

22 November We left Clumber not before 2 today, we called at Ranby in our way ... We arrived at Wetherby at 9 o'clock ...

23 November Came to Carlisle tonight.

24 November We breakfasted at Gretna Green which is kept by a man who was once my Valet, he tells me that since the death of the blacksmith he himself marries the people who come there – he showed me the form, the register and it is a most infamous business and ought to be stopt (*sic*) by law.

25 November [*At Hamilton Palace*] ... This is a noble house ... I never saw so good, grand and faultless a house. It is truly palatial.

26 November Lincoln's marriage has been postponed until tomorrow ... after their marriage they go to Lord Belhaven's place near here – which will not be agreeable or convenient.

27 November This day my very dear and admirable Son was married to Lady Susan Hamilton ... [*Dinners were provided for the Tenantry in the Stables and Outhouses.*] The Gentlemen and superior tenants and vassals had dinner in the town –in all above 3000 were dined.

7 December The Duke of Hamilton and I rode over ... to see the newly married couple – Lady Lincoln looked thin and not well.

8 December ... called on Sir Wm. Maxwell who served with and knew my father in America.

10 December [*Lady Lincoln has been taken ill with faintings.*]

11 December [*Heard from Mr Tallent, his agent in Newark, that Mr Norton had given up the electoral contest and that Lord Lincoln had no competition.*]

1832

15 December   [*Arrived back at Clumber – via* 'Rusby ford, Newcastle, Durham, Darlington, Catterick Bridge and Boro'bridge'.]

At Worksop, whilst we were changing horses, a crowd collected and soon a band of music appeared. On leaving the Inn we were saluted with cheers from the bystanders, and to our surprise found ourselves moving on at a foot's pace preceded by a band of music and a large crowd which attended us to the end of the Town, where they halted and gave us hearty cheers – this is something quite new to me. We found all the inmates of Clumber well ... Lincoln arrived from Scotland half an hour after us.

17 December   Lincoln has been elected today ... I wished much to have heard him speak. I thought of disguising myself so as to hear him amongst the crowd – it took a long while to make this disguise, procure the wig and the consequence was that on arriving at Newark, I was too late. [*Later in the day, Lincoln told him that he would have recognised him even with the disguise!*]

18 December   Lincoln returned to Hamilton Palace today.

25 December   We have passed a very happy Christmas Day ...

28 December   [*Lincoln writes that Lady Lincoln has*] become very weak and has been obliged to keep to her room ...

31 December   ... I close this eventful year! It had been a year of sorrow, sadness and disaster to Britain ...

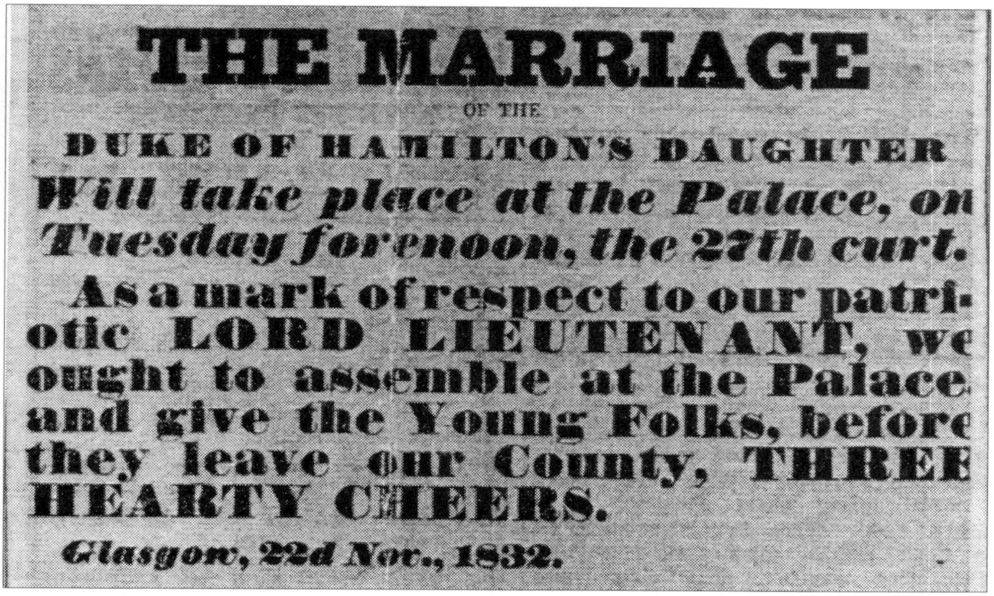

THE MARRIAGE
OF THE
DUKE OF HAMILTON'S DAUGHTER
Will take place at the Palace, on Tuesday forenoon, the 27th curt.
As a mark of respect to our patriotic LORD LIEUTENANT, we ought to assemble at the Palace and give the Young Folks, before they leave our County, THREE HEARTY CHEERS.
Glasgow, 22d Nov., 1832.

Fig. 36 *A handbill, in circulation for the celebrations at Hamilton Palace.*
[*This copy taken from 'The Hamilton Advertiser' 12 July, 1941*]

NUPTIAL FESTIVITIES AT CLUMBER.—The preparations which have for some time past been going forward on a splendid scale at the seat of the Duke of Newcastle, for celebrating the recent nuptials of Lord Lincoln, the eldest son of his grace, with the daughter of the Duke of Hamilton, were completed a few days ago; and on Friday week the illustrious couple were expected at Clumber. The noble bride and bridegroom were to be met at Worksop by a numerous escort of the duke's tenants, tradesmen, and other persons of the neighbourhood, wearing white wedding favours; the cortege would then proceed to Clumber, where accommodation had been made for the substantial entertainment of several hundreds of individuals, by throwing an awning over the court-yard, so as to form a dining-room. The specially-invited guests were to be entertained in the grand banqueting-hall, when the duke's massy service of gold plate would grace the table. To afford to the poor of the neighbourhood an opportunity of seeing the arrangements, and partaking of the good cheer so liberally provided, the court-yard tables were to be opened on Saturday to all comers; and these were expected to be pretty numerous. This is the first time Clumber has been the scene of such festive doings since the death of the late Duchess of Newcastle, some years since.—*Sheffield Mercury.* 1833

The band continued playing and the cannons firing till the hour of dinner, when as many as could be conveniently accommodated were regaled in the true spirit of baronial hospitality. Some idea of the immense provision may be formed when we state that it included 9 oxen, 600 head of game, a cart-load of hams, 25 sheep, 50 stone of bacon, a similar supply of veal, 500 loaves of bread, 200 plum-puddings, a suitable quantity of pies, tarts, &c., 167 gallons of punch, and 13 hogsheads of strong ale. A flourish of trumpets obtained silence, and grace being said by the Rev. John Mason, of Tuxford, the Duke's Chaplain, upwards of 1,500 persons immediately commenced operations upon the abundant store set before them.

Fig. 37/38 *Two newspaper cuttings relating to the festivities – See Diary 11th and 16th January 1833*

1833

1 January   I have lived to see my admirable Son united to a young and beautiful female who unites virtues, mind and heart, with exterior graces and accomplishments and in every way fitted for his wife – I have only to wish most sincerely that my two eldest daughters were also married to men equally worthy of and suited to them – but alas, where are they to be found? I have never yet seen the young man that I should really like for them.

I have been robbed of my boroughs, abused, ill treated, and pillaged. [*Here he notes a public softening towards himself.*]

2 January   Went to Martin this afternoon. [*During the night, four poachers were captured by his men in Piper's Wood.*]

4 January   [*Returned to Clumber.*]

6 January   [*The Duke sent out a general invitation to his tenantry to meet Lady Susan at Clumber on the 11ᵗʰ January.*]

7 January   [*It was decided to build a* 'temporary place to hold 500 persons at dinner'. *This appears to have been formed by erecting a canopy over the inner courtyard to the east of the house.*] ... It started today ... it will be a beautiful building.

8 January   The country ... is wild with speculation and delight. I wish I may be able to satisfy them ...

9 January   The building is nearly roofed in today ... dining 800 persons. I have invited all my neighbours to dine with me on the 11ᵗʰ and I shall forget all differences and ill treatment. The only exclusion is Lord Surrey. [*Heir to the Duke of Norfolk and living at Worksop Manor.*]

11 January   The day is over and well concluded. We met Lincoln and his dear lady ... at about 3 miles on the other side of Worksop on the Chesterfield road, nothing could be more agreeable or handsome than their reception in Worksop and the procession thro' the whole line was beautiful. The Worksopians escorted them to my gate, whence they were received by my tenants, who formed a line and proceeded by the former headed by flags and music

When they were set at the door, my guns fired a full salute. The dinner was a fine sight – I should think that at least 1200 dined here. – In the evening we had fire works ... I had a large party in the great dining room.

12 January This day all the villages and poorer people had their feast ... the people were assembled here about 1/2 past 12 – and began dinner at 1 – above 1000 people marched together from Worksop and made a beautiful appearance – the scene was delightfully gay. We let them in at the gate of the Court until the new building was filled which held about 600, then when they had done were sent away entirely off the premises and [an]other 600 took their place – In this manner we must have fed at least 3000, and we could have done more if our provisions had not failed, but there literally was not a scrape of bread, beer or [broken?] victuals left, and some people with tickets were obliged to go away empty – The consumption must have been enormous – When dinner was all over we had the fire works ... [then] dancing to the Band ... at length they got together into a regular Ball – They all went away about 7 in a very orderly manner evidently highly gratified with their entertainment.

16 January This evening the Servants had their Ball – I must say I never saw a prettier or a better arranged thing – The music was in the centre and the dancing was in the length from N. to S. as described below. The other divisions were for the Supper and the [clothed?] lines then the curtain placed to sheet out the supper, which was drawn up when the Supper was ready. Two stoves were placed in the dancing rooms and the

Fig. 39

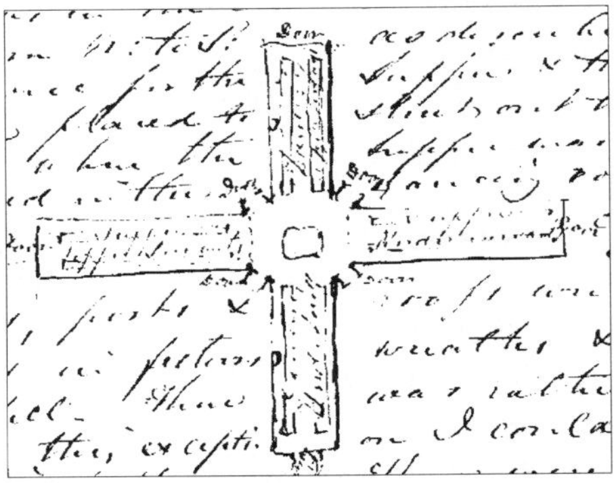

upper servants in the both cases kept separate from the under servants – The sides, posts and rooms were ornamented with evergreens in festoons, wreaths etc. and had an extraordinarily pretty effect. There was rather a deficiency of light but with this exception I could not have wished for anything better. There were two transparencies in the [?] of the roofs to the Supper rooms immediately above the curtains. The whole seemed to give great satisfaction and I never saw people more really pleased – Some of us (that is all my children) danced with them which delighted them exceedingly – At the last before the supper I stood up in a reel and they were all exceedingly pleased with it – in short they were truly gratified and we not less so to see them so. There were above 400 present.

This ends our festivities and nothing could have gone off better than they all have done. This last I think the best of all.

18 January Lincoln and Lady Susan went yesterday to Stoke [*Hall*] from thence to attend a ball at Newark, which was particularly well attended and they were received in a very flattering manner, the more so as I had complained of the backwardness of the Newarkers towards myself on former occasions – for which reason I objected to go amongst them, having a remembrance of the outrageous indignity shown to me there on several occasions and never resented or [*repaired*?] by the town of Newark.

21 January My dearest boys left me this morning. Charles and Thomas for Oxford, Robert for Eton. Lord Douglas [*brother of Lady Susan*] also went this morning, so that such a blank in our party is most sensibly felt by us. Lord Douglas is a charming young man and liked by us and by all. He is very good looking, amiable, modest and [?] and cannot fail to interest those who know him.

30 January This is my birthday ... 48 is a pretty good age. A few years and 60 will stare one in the face, if I should reach it.

9 February ... Poor Mundy has had another paralytic attack, I fear it will take him off.

14 February ... The Duke of Hamilton planted a cedar tree here today near the London approach road. Caroline and Henrietta [*did*] the same.

21 February The dear Lincoln's left us today. He is gone to attend parliament, as he thought that he could be absent no longer he was uneasy about it, but there seemed to me little call for his attendance just now, for what can any one do now who thinks rightly, he is perfectly impotent, he can only express this by his voice and his [*vote*?] but who cares for either now? ... We missed them [*the Lincoln's*] from the moment they left us, both are most delightful companions, she has become quite one of us and is every thing that I can desire for my beloved Son.

23 February I am now at last [*closing*?] with the purchase of Hafod, but I shall not get it at such a bargain as I expected. I am obliged to offer £56,000 for it as another person has offered £55,000 – it will be dear – but I think I can make it answer.

25 February In order to make the Hafod purchase I must sell somewhere and I have made up my mind to part with the Yorkshire property [*Aldborough and Boroughbridge*]. I shall be truly sorry to part with it, but I must make some sacrifice for general advantage. It is now that I feel how I have been robbed by the reformers, for if the Boroughs had been still existing. I might have obtained at

1833

least £200,000 for the 4 seats independently of the landed property. I could have sold the whole for a certainty, for £350,000 – probably a great deal more.

26 February I hear from my Lawyer tonight that I am all but the purchaser of Hafod at 55,000 Guineas or £57,750 – infinitely more certainly than I intended to give, but still, the more I think of it, a good purchase - ...

27 February ... I am completing the new approach road from London by Tuxford and Haughton Park. I have taken pains with the whole and I think that the line of trees and plantations such as to produce a beautiful and varied effect. I never did anything in this way more to my satisfaction. The passage through the last wood I have studied very much ...

28 February ... I am about to add a Gold medal to the Eton Scholarship. This medal is to be given to the 2nd best.

5 March Wrote to Edward ...

9 March I am sadly hampered and perplexed about the Hafod purchase ... Edward Pryce Owen is bidding against me in Chancery and writes the most insolent letters in order to deter me from being a competitor. He threatens to lay all the proceedings before the public "to show a Tory leader in his true colors" as he says ...

11 March The spring is very backward ... The [*muscaris*?] are only now in flower, the snow drops going off, crocuses in full blow.

18 March [*Left Clumber for London, staying overnight at Grantham*]

19 March [*Arrived in London*] We came at an excellent pace

.... By letter I learn that I am the purchaser of Hafod for £62,000 an enormous sum and more by 12,000£ than it is worth at present whatever may be made to it by laying out money there. I have been much played upon by the parties concerned in the Sale and driven up to this [*price?*]

20 March ... My lawyer was with me ... I cannot place much confidence in him or his tribe.

22 March I am at last really the purchaser of Hafod – I have sent a person this evening to Hafod to look after every thing and and see that all is properly dealt with, to examine the inventories and finally to seal up every thing.

25 March [*The Duke presented* 'some petitions' *in the House of Lords.*]

5 April This is Good Friday. We all as usual went to Church and all who were old enough staid [*for*] the Sacrament. ... Lincoln and his admirable wife attended with us and made me feel proud and thankful ... There were with me my two eldest daughters, Lincoln and his wife, and my 3 sons Charles, Thomas and William ...

1833

May God preserve and guide them in all goodness ... to the benefit of mankind.

19 April   I have been ill with the influenza ... Many deaths, among them Lord Foley quite suddenly.

22 April   Caroline broke out with measles.

24 April   Went to the Levee and presented Lincoln. I also presented some addresses for the better regulation of the labour of children in Factories.

5 May   ... Lord Combermere told me today that on his estates in the West Indies he has 500 slaves, valued at 80,000£. At £7 a head he would receive no more than about £3,500 – What a gross injustice and shameful interference with property Mr Stanley's proposal will be.

7 May   Came to Hartford Bridge with William who is going to a private Tutor (Mr Thompson) at Westgreen House ...

9 May   Went to the Drawing Room today with my two daughters, meaning to be [in] the party when Lady Susan was presented – but we never saw anything of her or Lincoln, which was a great disappointment to us.

31 May   Attended a Pitt Club dinner ... After dinner, my health was given which I scarcely expected, however I endeavoured to address the meeting as usefully as my want of practice and extreme disinclination enabled me – It seems that I was successful, for all that I said met with marked attention and very great applause, indeed I hardly knew myself, unused as I am to anything in the shape of a kind or friendly greeting; this is the first public applause that I ever received ...

2 June   The 'Belvidere' is coming home from the Mediterranean ... we shall see dearest Edward for a few days.

4 June   Mr Gladstone made an excellent maiden speech last night ...

5 June   Lincoln told me yesterday that his dear wife is in a family way ... [confinement due in January] ... I greatly rejoice at this event ...

10 June   ... in the afternoon we came to Hartford Bridge where we found Lincoln and Susan, William and Robert.

20 June   Charles and Thomas arrived this evening from Oxford ... They are two fine fellows and do themselves and me the greatest credit – their conduct is admirable.

21 June   This morning, at ½ past 6 my dear Edward arrived, he was soon by my bed as I desired that he should come the moment that he arrived ... I put on part of my clothes and went with him immediately to see his brothers and sisters as I wished to have the pleasure of witnessing their first meeting – it was a real treat to see their natural affection and joy at meeting. We have had

1833

a long and most delightful day. I sent directly to William and he arrived this night by the coach. Robert came in the morning from Eton – so that we are all, thank God, united again ... [*there follows much praise of Edward's qualities and his high standing with his naval captain.*]

24 June My Mother came to London today to see Edward ... She is remarkably well – dined with us and did not seem at all fatigued by the journey.

3 July Georgiana, Charlotte and Edward are sitting for their pictures.

6 July My dear Edward left us this morning ... for Portsmouth ... May God bless him and protect him and preserve in him that purity of mind which is now so admirable.

7 July [*Notes that he has consulted Sir Robert Peel on* 'the best course' *for Lincoln's parliamentary contribution. Comments that he is glad that* 'the first year has passed without Lincoln taking part in debates' – *indicates a concern about the distractions in Lincoln's life.*]

12 July The Duchess of Hamilton, who is at Leamington, is very unwell, she has been attacked by spasms and being already in a weak state of health, I fear that the consequences may be serious.

I sat for the last time to Mr Wyon for the completion of a profile which is to be used for the medal to be given to the second Eton scholar – it is very well executed.

7 August ... I have paid away nearly £30,000 of money and must have done much good to my unfortunate tradesmen and others who were greatly in want of their money ... I shall leave in whole perhaps nearly £8,000 owing ...

8 August [*Left London for Clumber – slept at Stevenage*] – my two eldest girls and four boys are with me. We go in two carriages – two others will follow tomorrow with Miss Spencer and her young two, and the rest of the servants.

9 August ... a very pleasant journey ... we arrived here, at Clumber, at 9 o'clock.

10 August In looking about today I found everything in a very satisfactory state – All my outdoors operations have succeeded perfectly and all the garden departments in the highest order and condition.

12 August My Mother came here today. She tells me that the Princess Augusta tells her that she is charged by the King to send me a message respecting the lace of the Notts' Militia which he wishes to be changed from gold to silver! What a vast scope of mind a man must have to think of lace when revolution is placing the throne as well as every institution in the most slippery and precarious situation! How happy the country which in times of such difficulties and dangers possesses a King with such an elevated and extensive mind!!

1833

15 August [*Mentions having made peace with the doctors of the Medical School of Nottingham following a disagreement with them.*]

16 August ... My barley and oats are all in today and harvested without the least injury from the weather – The wheat begins tomorrow, it is the finest crop I ever saw here.

20 August My vases are arrived from near Bath where they were made.

We commenced putting them upon the Terrace two days ago. They are not so fine as I could have wished them to be, but still they are very handsome ornaments and I am very glad at last to have them to adorn my Terrace.

23 August The smallpox is very bad about here – numbers have died who have neither been vaccinated or inoculated. Several of these [*who*] have been inoculated have taken the disease but it has died away and not proved fatal.

1 September We have had tremendous winds with rain, which have done much mischief in some places. All my harvest is in.

2 September Went out shooting with my three sons. Yesterday being Sunday we could not of course go out. Our sport was not very good, the scent was particularly bad and the birds tho' [*small?*], wild. We killed between us 25½ brace, 9 hares, 1 [?].

4 September ... Here I am very busy with my house, preparing to do up the Great Drawing room and to finish the Library – My house is like a workshop. But whilst I am about all this, I cannot but reflect that in a few years my property may be wrested from me and all that I am doing here, either be destroyed, or be for the benefit of some fierce Republican, or low but rapacious scoundrel of a Revolution[*ary?*]

12 September ... My Drawing room is now ready to receive the plasterers – the windows are out down to the ground, the new frames put in, the whole room cleared and nothing but the bare walls left. The Library looks really superb, where I have fitted up a small side complete, to see how things fit and how I like it.

20 September [*Left Clumber for Hafod – although with detours, it was 27th when he arrived.*]

30 September [*Says he intends to promote the building of a harbour in the Hafod area.*]

1 October Charlotte's 21 birthday.

[*Notes that the house at Hafod has been unoccupied for 17 or 18 years.*]

4 October [*He mentions his mouth disorder having been treated by the use of leeches, applied by Mr Williams of Aberystwyth.*]

1833

15 October   [*He writes in praise of the 'Welch' – especially of the women*] – for figure and manners [*they*] would not disgrace but adorn a Court.

17 October   Steam carriages are now running on the common roads about London at the rate of 11 miles an hour ... wonders will yet be worked by this means.

24 October   [*At Aberystwyth*] – Some black game, 11 in number arrived today from Arran, in the care of a man kindly sent by the Duke of Hamilton. I soon dispatched them to Hafod where I hope they may succeed.

11 November [*Starts the journey home to Clumber*] ... At Newtown I bought flannel, to encourage the manufacturers ... I bought enough to clothe a small town – I must dress every body in flannel this winter.

13 November [*Having slept at Derby*] ... Arrived back at Clumber ... I looked into the marble works and was surprised to see there the finest model of a greyhound as large as life that I ever saw – it was perfect ... Found everything well here and in beautiful order – Sent to Lincoln who is at Ranby and will be here tomorrow.

Fig. 40

Greyhound figure on South Gate pillar, Clumber

14 November Lincoln and his dear Lady came here this morning. I have been very busy making their new apartments ready ...

15 November By a letter from Edward, I learn that his ship is ordered home ...

19 November [*Receives word that his action, in arranging for a doctor from Aberystwyth to tend the* 'Welch poor near Hafod', *has been met by* 'deep and unbounded' *gratitude for his* 'act of mercy'.]

27 November This is the anniversary of my dear Lincoln's marriage, we have observed it here with rejoicings ... I do not suppose that such another as Lady Lincoln could be found, certainly not one containing so many and rare qualifications.

2 December   We performed a curious operation today by reinstating a Cedar Tree which had been half blown down by the late hurricane. The tree is a very large one, of 70 years growth – we applied the crab which is used by the masons for raising stone ... I had no idea before of the force of this machine.

3 December   Today my dear Twins are 20 years old. [*Still at Oxford.*]

9 December   This has been a grievous and afflicting day to me. I will not state wherefore but it strikes at the roots of my happiness [*Possibly a disagreement with his son, Lincoln.*]

1833

11 December ... Charles, Thomas, William and Edward are home ...

12 December ... All is arranged for the consecration of my New Church at Markham Clinton which will take place on the 27th.

14 December My private grief embitters my days – and it is the more poignant as it could not be looked for. May God in his goodness effect an alteration.

20 December My preparations for the sale of Aldbro' and Borobridge are now complete. They are valued at 146,000 ... I think that it to be very well sold at 170,000.

23 December ... Edward went this morning to Portsmouth ... Charles accompanied him. It is a great pity that he is obliged to leave us at Christmas time.

25 December We have passed a very merry Christmas Day, the young ones dined with us for the first time at a later hour of 5 o'clock – highly delighted of course.

27 December This day the New Church at Markham Clinton was consecrated by the Archbishop of York. Nothing could be more successful than all the arrangements. The ceremony is very impressive and imposing, the prayers and additional services very beautiful and in every way worthy of the admirable Church of England. I greatly rejoice that this work is finished, it has been a long while in hand but for want of a parsonage house I could not complete it much sooner with any satisfaction to myself. The Church must have cost me above £10,000 and the Parsonage and grounds full and above £3,000 – more.

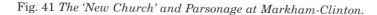

Fig. 41 *The 'New Church' and Parsonage at Markham-Clinton.*

1833

28 December   I have prepared Edward today for receiving the Sacrament tomorrow. I have always done this to all of them and it is delightful to see the genuine piety and good feeling which these dear children exhibit upon such occasions.

29 December   We took the Sacrament today ... I had the happiness and blessing of being accompanied at the altar by 7 of my children.

30 December   Lincoln and his dear Wife left us this morning for London ... the more one knows Susan the more one must love and esteem her.

31 December   [*Following damage caused by more high winds, which affected:*] ... a large and magnificent Cedar of Lebanon, in the pleasure ground close to the house, which was quite necessary for hiding the Offices. I shall try to reinstate it with the crab ...

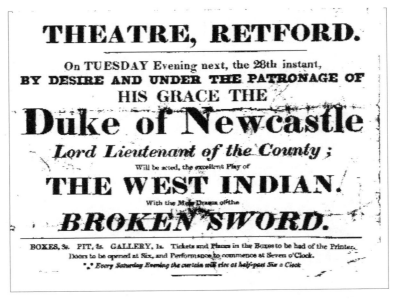

Fig. 42 [*28 January 1834 entry refers*]

1834

3 January	[*Unsuccessful attempts to raise the Cedar – see 31 December 1833.*]
6/7 January	[*Success in raising the Cedar but doubts that it will survive as the main roots had been damaged.*]
10 January	Edward is very unwell ...
12 January	Edward is much better ...
15 January	I have at last had the good fortune to find a Tutor that I approve of. Mr Dalton came here today to see and settle with me ... my dear little boy [*Robert*] will no longer suffer from neglect ...
22 January	... Robert's new Tutor arrived yesterday.
26 January	This night's post has brought me a letter from Lincoln, announcing that Lady Susan was safely delivered of a very fine boy at 1/2 past 10 yesterday morning ... [*He notes that it was a difficult birth.*] Charles is gazetted as Cornet in the 1st Life Guards ...
28 January	We went to a Retford play which I ordered – [*See Figure 42*]. It was a dreadful night that the people will the more appreciate the compliment paid to them. I understand that it has given them great satisfaction. We filled two landaus. The house was full and the audience very hearty.
29 January	Excellent accounts of Susan and Lincoln's little baby. Lincoln sent me a lock of his hair which I shall keep as a treasure.
31 January	My dear little Robert went to Eton today with his new tutor, Mr Dalton. I miss him much and my family is now reduced to 5 and dear Edward just on the point of leaving me for his ship.
1 February	Everybody has left us today. The Duke of Hamilton started for London ... The day after tomorrow I shall go to London to be present at the King's speech and to watch the Debate and proceedings of Ministers. I shall only stay for a few days and then return here. I consider [*it*] to be a duty to be personally present in such awful times.

1834

3 February ... left Clumber and reached Eaton late at night. Edward is with us.

4 February Arrived in London ... I have seen my little Grand child – he is a very fine one and quite healthy and perfect which is a great blessing.

10 February Went with Edward today to Salthill, where the 3 dear fellows from Oxford and Robert met us, we dined there and after taking an affectionate farewell of one another, we returned to London and arrived in time for dear Edward to start by the Mail for Portsmouth ... it will be long before we see him again, he goes first to Jamaica [on the 'Blonde'] and then round Cape Horn to the western coast of America, where his Captain will be stationed as Commodore.

14 February ... I left London ... arrived at Biggleswade ... where I slept.

15 February ... arrived at Clumber ... having dined at Wansford.

27 February The weather has been continuously mild during the whole of the winter and the spring is now extraordinarily forward. Most of the shrubs and many of the trees will be in leaf in a fortnight. The blackthorn is in full blossom, so are the apricot and peach trees in my garden.

28 February My dear little Robert is far from well at Eton ... something caused him much pain with nausea. I shall be very anxious about him, knowing how much he suffers from such attacks and now poor fellow he has only strangers about him.

2 March The thermometer was never lower last night than 47 – an extraordinary heat for this time of the year. Several rose trees are out in full leaf, the birds are making their nests and singing and the trees bearing more the appearance of the end of April ... The season tho' beautiful is however unhealthy, people especially children are dying in numbers at East Markham. 14 were buried in one fortnight and 9 died last week in the village of Egmanton.

3 March Came to Ranby to stay for a few days with my Mother.

8 March ... Mr Parkinson told me today that some quick [hawthorn] which was planted in the last autumn has already grown five inches – an event quite unexampled I should think. The lilacs are showing flower and some of my rose trees in as full leaf as they ever will be.

9 March I wrote to the Duke of Cumberland ... about a title for my little grandson who has none and therefore cannot bear none and must be plain Mr Clinton which does not seem to be what it should be. [The King had already refused such a request] I was called Lord Clinton during my grandfather's lifetime.

1834

12 March	[*His 'Yorkshire Estate' – Aldborough and Boroughbridge –was offered for sale today but only reached £50,000 and was withdrawn*]
16 March	William came home today from Oxford. Charles and Thomas remain there during the vacation to read for their degree. This is their own doing and very praiseworthy of them ...
18 March	A self-taught artist of Nottingham [*Mr Janus*] is now taking my portrait ...
20 March	[*Mentions that there have been frosts during the past week*] – My gardener tells me that he thinks the wall fruit is all killed.
21 March	My dear Robert came home today from Eton – he is looking very well ... his illness has kept him back, but still he has made much progress.
23 March	I have been invited to allow myself to be put in nomination for President of the Royal Society of Literature. I have declined it on the grounds of unfitness as well as from literary disqualification as from want of leisure.
24 March	Tomorrow or the next day I expect Lincoln and his new family. The dear little baby will for the first time breathe the air of Clumber. May he live to adorn it and be a blessing to his family and to his country.
25 March	To my surprise Lincoln arrived at past 11 o'clock tonight.
26 March	The dear arrivals are very well today. The baby I find extremely improved. He is a beautiful child and a really fine little fellow – May God bless him.
2 April	Farmers are getting worse every day, even my tenants are complaining and I shall have to lower my rents if the present wretched times continue – it is vastly perplexing.
9 April	Whilst out rabbit shooting today, Lincoln flushed a woodcock, he went to the place from which it rose and then found its nest, which had 4 eggs in it but they were broken and the young birds already hatched! ... Mansell knows of another nest ... with 4 eggs in it ... of late years so many woodcocks have remained and bred here that we may well suppose that they are becoming natives of our bounty.
15 April	Lincoln left us this morning [*His departure had been delayed due to Susan's illness.*]
16 April	Left Clumber and slept at Mansfield.
17 April	Arrived in London ...

1834

18 April   William left me today for Oxford.

[*The Duke spoke in the Lords today, against a proposal that a Musical Festival be held in Westminster Abbey – he noted that he will have* 'stirred up a hornets nest' *but wrote that he had* 'discharged my conscience'.]

24 April   [*Received news that Thomas had failed his degree – he rushed to Oxford to console him – and noted that Thomas intends to* 'try again'.]

25 April   [*Still at Oxford, he noted that Thomas was to study at home and retake his degree in October.*]

2 May   [*The Duke's back trouble returned, following horse-riding on the previous day. However, he went ahead with his speech in the House of Lords, opposing the Westminster Abbey plans for a Musical Festival – but, noting that there was no support for his opposition, he decided not to put a formal motion on the matter.*]

3 May   ... Charles joined his Regiment on the 1ˢᵗ – he went to a field day today. I dined at a public day at Lambeth Palace ...

10 May   [*Thomas is recommended for a vacancy in the 1ˢᵗ Life Guards.*] – He will not abandon trying for his degree in October next.

15 May   My two daughters and I went to the Drawing room today ... I never saw so few people that I knew, and every body who can muster a dress coat and a plume of feathers goes to a Drawing room.

17 May   Thomas was gazetted yesterday as Cornet in the 1st Life Guards.

22 May   Lincoln's dear little boy was christened today by Dr. Hodgson, Dean of Carlisle – we assembled a little after 6 o'clock ... the Duchess of Hamilton being the God mother, the Duke and I the God fathers. The dear little fellow was called Henry Pelham Alexander – he looked beautifully [*sic*], indeed I never saw a nicer and handsomer child – May God bless him and make him all that he should be.

After dinner we had a party – and this finished a very pleasant evening. I should observe that this took place at the Duke of Hamilton's, where Lincoln and Susan are now living.

24 May   Dined at the Eton dinner today. Lincoln was in the chair ...

29 May   Dined at the Pitt dinner today. [*Reports that he had been told that he was regarded as their defender in* 'this hour of peril'.]

8 June   We heard from Edward from Jamaica two days ago [*letter dated 9ᵗʰ April*] he was ... remarkably healthy.

Tomorrow, I set out for Oxford to attend the Commemoration ... [*The Duke of Wellington's installation as Chancellor.*]

1834

10 June   *[The Duke reports that he was amongst those who today received honorary degrees. Says that each recipient was met by undergraduate responses, signifying approval or disapproval – and that he was received by a 'kind and favorable' response.]*

13 June   ... I shall never forget the days that I have passed here ...

14 June   *[On leaving Oxford]* – William returned with me. We stopt at Eton and saw Robert ... he looked superior to all the boys ... in coming out of school.

19 June   The King and Queen went to the Opera tonight. We were there ... no enthusiasm or loyalty – it is all gone.

20 June   Went to a Ball at the Palace.

21 June   A grand dinner at the Mansion House.

22 June   The eldest Mundy, Edward, an excellent man, died about a week ago.

5 July   *[The Duke, with three of his sons and two daughters, were invited to join the party on board the Lord Mayor's steamer, which escorted the Royal Yacht down the Thames. Queen Adelaide was on board the Royal Yacht – the Duke had (a few days earlier) indicated his disgust that the Queen should be leaving England at this time.]*

15 July   Henrietta is declared to have the scarlet fever – it is a great annoyance just as I am about to leave London.

16 July   Henrietta has the complaint mildly, but it is thought advisable that we should all leave the house – it is a very great inconvenience and an annoyance.

17 July   Thomas went by the coach ... to Cheltenham ... on to Barmouth in Wales ... to read for his Degree. My three daughters and William went this evening for Clumber.

18 July   My dear little Henrietta is going on as favorably as possible.

23 July   Working all day – fagged to death and can scarcely move – I shall rejoice to lie down at night.

25 July   ... I have bought a house for Lincoln which I have given to him. The house is next to the Duke of Somerset's at the top of Park Lane and is the most complete, convenient and prettiest house in London. I buy it new, fitted up and furnished within two months ... for £13,000. The furniture etc.etc. is very handsome and the whole thing most to be coveted.

27 July   *[Back at Clumber]* Left London yesterday at 6 o'clock, travelled all night and arrived here at 10 to breakfast ...

29 July   Robert arrived today from Eton ...

31 July   Lincoln arrived this afternoon ...

6 August   Henrietta arrived today. She looks very well ...

1834

8 August   [*Boro'bridge sale continues.*]

We had a game of cricket today. Lincoln, William and Mr Dalton [*Robert's tutor*] against Mr Dawkins [*the new Vicar of Markham Clinton*], me and Robert – we were shamefully beaten but it gave us plenty of exercise, considering that some of us had not played for years, we did pretty well ...

9 August   [*Boro'bridge sales are estimated to be in the region of £28,000*]

12 August   A letter from Edward dated Rio [*de*] Janerio June 12 ...

14 August   [*Writes that he will pay for Hafod with his 'new mortgages' of £62,000 – Also that he had raised the monies for Lincoln's new house.*]

15 August   Lady Lincoln has been very unwell for some time. [*He gives his opinion that this is due to her having sat on damp grass.*]

16 August   [*Having noted some days earlier that there was a vacancy for a new appointment as Knight of the Garter and expressing his personal hope that it be given to the Duke of Hamilton*] – ... That miserable rat-like looking Duke (yclept) of Norfolk has been made a K.G. – he deserves it as little as any man in the Kingdom ...

17 August   The weather is more enjoyable than it has been for years – we are almost always out of the house setting in the colonnade or elsewhere, without any other covering than that worn in the house. My terrace is every thing now, and is unceasingly beautiful and agreeable – It is the delight and admiration of all who see it.

22/23 August   [*He mentions Susan's illness and says that* 'she is for a time unconscious'.]

26 August   [*Boro'bridge sale* 'is going on promisingly'.]

1 September   Went out shooting – we slept at Mr Dawkins parsonage at Markham Clinton on the preceding night, and we were out early and late, but I never remember on the first day of the shooting to have had such bad sport and to have killed so little.

4 September   [*Lincoln and his family had gone to Ashton, Lancashire. This was to a 'neglected' house owned by the Hamiltons.*]

9 September   Left Clumber [*for Hafod via Shrewsbury.*]

15 September   ... 8 South Down lambs arrived from Clumber ... to improve the breed.

1834

17 September   I had the 'Thetis' ... [*made ready to be sent*] by my wagon tomorrow to Clumber.

Fig. 43 *"Thetis dipping the Infant Achilles in the River Styx" – by Thomas Banks R.A.*

29 September   [*He reports that he had been made very welcome at Aberystwyth.*]

8 October   [*Back to Clumber.*]

9 October   The Drawing room ceiling is completed within two days work and the walls are fit for the last coat of plaster so I shall have the convenience of the room in the winter.

10 October   Thomas arrived this evening.

11 October   [*Travelled with Georgiana and Charlotte to join Lincoln at Ashton.*] ... left at 10 o'clock – arrived about ½ past 2. Lincoln had sat up till 2 for us – and was in bed, but soon got up to welcome us to his abode.

12 October   Very tired and up late ...

16 October   ... a letter arrived announcing that my Mother had taken very ill with inflamation on the chest ... I shall leave this place for Ranby early tomorrow. My dear Mother has no one with her and must be in a most forlorn situation, on a sick bed with no one whom she loves near to her.

17 October   After a rough journey in an open carriage, with high wind and rain, I arrived here at about 1 – I did not drive up to the door for fear of disturbing my Mother, and I sent to speak to the servant – his answer was "The Duchess is just alive and that's all" This was sad and dreadful news ... [*she had*] not spoken since 2 o'clock and was quite insensible. As soon as I had recovered and collected myself a little, I went in to see my dear Mother, but how altered! Death was upon her – I took her hand, it was cold and nearly [*inanimate?*], I spoke, but she could not hear the voice which a short time before would have gladdened her. I looked, but her eyes could not meet mine, they were closed and sightless! ... I would have given the world to have had even a sign or acknowledgement from her, but the person was gone, nature was spent and death near at hand.

1834

I had no resource but to take the chilly hand of my dying parent, to press it to my lips and to offer up a fervent prayer of forgiveness of all errors of misconduct, if I had committed them, to hope that I had her last blessing and to beseech God Almighty to receive her precious Soul into his everlasting habitation of bliss.

Sick at heart and worn down, I retired and with my clothes on laid down on my bed, having settled with Mr Russell [*the doctor*] that if any change should take place that I should be summoned instantly – at about 1/2 past 7, he came to say that the scene was drawing to a close, but that my dear Mother was still utterly unconscious and that he did not see the least likelihood of any [*sign?*] of returning animation even for a moment. He was right – at 1/2 past 8 on the 18th in the morning my dear and excellent Mother expired without a sigh, a groan or a struggle!!!

What a contrast to her life, which has been one continued scene of trouble, agitation, trial and disquietude. It has often been my astonishment, how my dear Mother could support herself through what I have seen her undergo – her mind must have been of the highest order to have enabled her even by the strong aid of Religion to support herself through a long life of trial with such fortitude and heroism.

When every thing was prepared, some more entered the room where the remains of my dear Mother were laid. I wished to take a last farewell of those remains which had long been known to my sight and which had contained a Soul that loved me and all her children beyond herself. All was peace, silence and solemnity – Every thing which decency and love and affection required had been done. I was satisfied and retired ...

19 October   The pain and anguish which I first felt surrounds at every step. I am obliged to look at the letters, at the papers and to search into every thing. From having been so much absent since the Spring I have most unfortunately been very little with and alone with my dear Mother, so that her wishes of late have not been so much known to me. I would give anything now to have known them, that I might punctually execute them.

21 October   To my surprise Lincoln was announced this morning after breakfast. I had requested him not to come knowing how much he would be wanted at home and how inconvenient it would be to come here – but with his usual diligent kindness and amiable attention and right sense of duty he determined to come and I am glad that he has done so – besides which it enables us to come to several conclusions which without him I could not. His conduct and that of the others is beautiful and honorable to human nature ...

1834

22 October [*Talked with Lincoln about his Mother's affairs and his own –* ' in case of anything happening to me ...']

Both of the Houses of Parliament have been set on fire and totally destroyed ... about a week ago.

23 October [*Returned to Clumber*] – it seems like a dream. What has one short week produced?

24 October [*His Mother's funeral at Markham Clinton*] ... ... The severed Parent who I have this day left in the grave was born on the 5th day of April 1760. She was tall in person, rather thin than otherwise. Her manners and appearance announced that without a doubt that she could be nothing else but noble. She was possessed of elevated and very strong mind and very considerable abilities. Her disposition to do good was unbounded and ever uppermost in her mind, this was as regarded herself and the rest of the world, but to her family and children her affection and devotedness knew no bounds, there was no sacrifice let it be what it would, that she did not make or would not have made for them – Her charity, kindness and active benevolence was universal, her piety that of the Truest Christian and every thing she did had a deference to it – but it was not lip-service and hypocrisy, it was genuine, sincere and unaffected. Her trials through life had been very great so much so that I have frequently wondered how she had endured them with her sensibility, and yet have retained such cheerfulness, serenity and high spirits. Her mind was always at work, and this was her only weak place, it sometimes disturbed her and others too much, but it arose from a keen anxiety to benefit all she loved and valued ...

25 October ... My dear Mother has most unfortunately left everything in trust and I can proceed no farther independent of the Trustees ...

26 October Mr Mason [*Vicar of Tuxford and Chaplain at Clumber*] with his usual good sense gave us a very feeling and appropriate sermon.

27/28 October Lincoln, Caroline and Henrietta and I left Clumber in the afternoon and slept at Ferrybridge and arrived at Ashton after a very pleasant journey at 8 o'clock.

30/31 October Nothing to record than the enjoyment of a peaceful and happily accorded domestic circle. Susan is quite one of us and is thoroughly amalgamated as a child of our house.

4 November ... Thomas went up for his Degree yesterday ...

7 November My dear Thomas is at last successful, he obtained his degree on the 5th and in a manner entirely creditable to him.

8 November A letter from dear Edward dated Falkland Islands in July ...

1834

14 November	Susan (Lady Lincoln) has been very unwell and confined to her room – Her health is by no means satisfactory to me ... she is not what she ought to be.
16 November	... dear Lady Lincoln is better.
17 November	... dear Susan ... is very far from well.
18 November	Left Ashton ... arrived at Skipton ... Susan was better this morning.
19 November	...we went a new road by Keighley, Bradford and Wakefield to Doncaster, it is an excellent road, no hills and good horses ... arrived at Clumber at 1/2 past 6.
22 November	Our party in Retford and Bassetlaw seem bent on having one of my sons [*Thomas*] ... I have told them that we do not deserve the honor and that it will be declined.
1 December	Wrote to Edward – also to Charles and Thomas.
3 December	[*He mentions that the twins, Charles and Thomas, are 21 today.*]
9 December	... The dear Lincolns and their little boy came this evening – she is much better but very thin.
21 December	[*New government formed, under Sir Robert Peel – the Duke notes his own great disappointment at not being asked to be a Minister.*]
22 December	[*At Ranby, he has two visitors in connection with the purchase of the estate at Cwmelan – he agrees to buy it for £23,200 – says it is upwards of 40,000 acres and a very good buy.*]
24 December	The Duchess of Hamilton arrived yesterday.
25 December	[*He notes that they all attended chapel and received the Sacrament.*]
29 December	We all went to attend a Newark Dispensary Ball, of which Lincoln was Steward ... [*£107 raised*] – I have now made peace with the Town – I had resolved never to go there again.
30 December	Having left the Duchess of Hamilton here and Susan who was not well enough to go, we returned home today. I stopped for some time at Newark to see Mr Gladstone ... I have put him right in many particulars.
31 December	... As a politician I am shunned and discouraged, as an individual ... no one seems to care about me ... feeling myself valueless, but I must bear it, I cannot cure it. I cannot change my nature and I do not desire to lose my conscience ... End of the Year 1834.

1 January ... I seek to be useful but my efforts are abortive ... heartbreaking, humiliating and painful ... Had I not a proud spirit, had I not a view beyond worldly reward, I should sink in despair ... so blessed in my family ... I have laboured hard to increase my pecuniary condition.

[*He notes that he has allowed Charles to stand for election in Bassetlaw.*]

2 January Charles, accompanied by Lincoln, commenced his canvass this morning at Worksop.

3 January [*Charles had problems making speeches at the farmer's rooms in Retford*] – due to his diffidence and want of confidence in himself – I have cheered him up ...

5 January Mr Gladstone ... was elected today for Newark.

12 January ... Lincoln was elected this morning without any trouble ... my dear Charles is beaten ... beaten, but we have humbled our enemies ...

22 January An artist ... Parke ... is modelling my bust for the Duke of Hamilton, who means to have it (and one of Lincoln) executed in marble ...

23 January A great break up of our family. My dear Robert returns to Eton ... Charles and William, one to join his Regiment at Brighton, the other to Oxford ... we miss them most excessively.

25 January This is little Henry's birthday – today he is one year old, a grand event in his little life.

27 January Susan, poor dear Soul, is suffering again dreadfully ...

[*He again refers back to the time she sat at Sion, with her* 'feet in wet grass'.]

28 January [*The Duke and Duchess of Hamilton depart for London, to prepare for their sick daughter's arrival there*] ... better not done, fretting and worrying their dear child by over kindness and anxiety ... it plagues poor Lincoln to death ... it will poison their happiness ... set a stricter guard [*on*] parental meddling and fidgeting interference.

147

1835

31 January   [*He records that he strongly disapproves of the new Prime Minister, Sir Robert Peel. Sir Robert had indicated that he is to be a Reformer on a grand scale.*

Reports that Mr (Rev) Dawkins had an accident whilst they were out shooting today. Although thrown to the floor when his gun went off accidentally, he was not badly hurt.]

1 February   My House Steward, and the artist Parke, very gallantly took two poachers this morning who had been shooting close to the house about 1/2 past 6 this morning. The men were taken with each their guns [*sic*] and 3 hen pheasants.

2 February   Rode over to Ranby with Lincoln – [*Lincoln took several 'fixtures' from there to move them to his London home.*]

3 February   Lincoln went to London today ... I have done all in my power to prevent this absence – but in vain – his itch for politics and to commence business in office overpowers every other feeling ... I could not have done such a thing – home is the first care, when all is right there, then other matters may receive due attention – She poor thing [*Susan*] is far from well ... nothing in my opinion is more objectionable than the separation of young married people, they ought not to think that they can do without one another – if they do, they must be indifferent to one another and various unpleasant consequences may be likely to ensue.

4 February   Susan was very unwell in the night Lincoln's self-gratification has, I fear, caused this. [*They had had to send for the doctor.*]

8 February   Violent thunder and lightning this evening ... large triangular hail fell ... Susan is not so well this evening. Lincoln must return.

10 February Susan is much better and was up today ... I saw her, and to my surprise found that she would on no account have Lincoln here – she said that his return would 'fidget her death' ... This is a Hamilton fashion not a Clinton fashion – it is what, unfortunately she has been accustomed to see in her parents and most unwisely wishes to adopt in her case – I now find that I have been doing poor dear Lincoln much more injustice than he deserves.

11 February Lincoln arrived this afternoon from London. He has brought a bed carriage with him and means to convey Susan to London as quickly as possible.

13 February Lincoln, Susan and little Henry went away this morning ... Susan looked very ill.

17 February Good news from London – Susan arrived without fatigue or inconvenience.

18 February This is my dear Edward's birthday.

1835

24 February   Left Clumber at ¹/₄ before 9 – arrived in London ¹/₂ past 1 – I dined on the road at Wansford.

27 February   Lincoln is unwell ... Susan is worse than she was in the country.

28 February   Lincoln is better today.

2 March   [*The Duke took his seat in the new, temporary, House of Lords. He did not approve of the arrangement*] – given us a little hole that will not hold more than 250 people.

3 March   I have been busily employed today – amongst other things I have had an audience with the King and asked Him to grant me other letters so that I might have one to give to my little grandson. His Majesty was very kind, consented to my request and begged me to put the matter into the hands of someone at the Herald's College which I shall do tomorrow.

4 March   Wrote to Edward.

5 March   ... went to the Herald's College today about the new titles. I put a good many on the list and must needs reduce them for they tell me that they would cost several thousand pounds for the patents.

Bought a good many Statues and busts at Rope's Sale – a beautiful Statue of Mercury and of the Poet Thompson [*does he mean James Thomson?*] by Rope. A magnificent Statue of Bonapart made for his sister – with many busts, some antique and some modern – one of Eve I think the finest thing I ever saw.

9 March   Called on Sir Robert Peel by appointment ... a long conversation about the additional titles – he placed the matter before me in a new light, especially that of detraction from the ancient by inferior modern titles – I think he has [*dissuaded?*] me from desiring to obtain what can be no honor and may be thought to bend the other way.

11 March   [*Returned to Clumber – stopped at Eaton on the way.*]

15 March   During my absence, Lord Manvers has thought fit to mark out a road up the centre of the Clumber Park Lane, which he has with great industry formed and shaped and has cleared away every thing which obstructed the line in its course.

He has stubbed up trees, cut down others and lopped and initiated others so as to disfigure and injure not only the scenery, but actually the property where this has been done. All this has been done without giving me the slightest notice of it, and he has entered upon my property and injured it and has turned away the road and directed it with a new course, all without my consent and knowledge and entirely of his own free will – It is shameful to see the mutilation and havoc which has been made. I have written him a very strong letter and have not spared my remarks upon his outrageous and most unneighbourly conduct.

1835

16 March Lord Manvers has sent an answer to my letter, but refuses to give any explanation of his conduct, as he says that the tone and temper in which I have written precludes his doing so and he expects that I shall prosecute him for the outrage – I shall do no such thing – but I shall take other steps, both to stop his proceedings and to make him know that he shall not do such things with impunity.

20 March I thought it proper to send Lord Manvers a notice of trespass, to secure myself against any farther aggression. The notice extends to all my estates – so that in hunting he will be a good deal puzzled to know what to do. It will serve him right, if it gives him much annoyance – he has behaved most outrageously and unwarrantedly and deserves all that I can do against him.

23 March ... Clumber Park Lane, which gives me a good deal of trouble. Lord Manvers is acting very slyly and cunningly, evidently under legal advice, and means to bring the matter that he has himself created before the Magistrates in petty sessions. This indecent act is entirely his own doing – The Duke of Portland has written to me today, to compromise the dispute as he calls it and to refer it to arbitration – I replied that I wanted no arbitration, that my case was clear, I had not offended, I was the sufferer – the whole aggression belonged to Lord Manvers who from his likeness to the animal both in appearance and habits – I call Porkus. Whether he will be able to sustain his aggression I know not – in no case shall I submit to any decision against me, because I am convinced that none can be made with justice. I am told that Lord Manvers is alarmed at what he has done, and wishes to back out if he can – My discharge is a great annoyance to him, it cuts up his darling hunting and is a capital lash him.

25 March Robert has been very unwell but is now better.

26 March The Duke of Portland called on me today, as mediator and pacificator from Lord Manvers. He brought me a message from Lord Manvers, acknowledging that he had been quite in the wrong thoughout the affair, that he could not justify his acts and that the manner of effecting them was reprehensible, that he was very sorry for what he had done and that he hoped that I would forget and forgive – Of course after such an ample avowal and apology I could not not [sic] but assent to the proposals of peace. I requested the Duke of Portland to inform Lord Manvers that I must require Lord Manvers to restore everything in the Lane to its former state, as much as possible – and this the Duke of Portland assures me will be done – Thus ends the offensive bully of my marine neighbour, who fancies himself always on ship board and in true Captain Jackson fashion orders – "make it so".

1835

30 March	I came here (Ranby) last night ... brought Georgiana and Charlotte to assist me – we have been hard at work all day.
31 March	[*Back to Clumber.*]
6 April	... I left Clumber this afternoon [*for London*] and went as far Grantham where I slept.
7 April	Arrived in London between 8 and 9.
8 April	[*Saw his solicitor about the sale of Aldborough.*]
	[*Heard that Sir Robert Peel's government had resigned.*]
10 April	... 3 Peers have been made. We shall have all the Jew Brokers, Bankers and Tradesmen in the House of Lords at last.
	[*More paper work completed on the sale of Aldborough*] – I have yet about £30,000 worth to sell.
14 April	[*A letter arrived from the King noting that, after all, the Duke would not be pressing for* 'inferior titles'.]
15/16 April	[*Return to Clumber – slept at Stevenage*] – a bad accident detained us a long while – a gig ran against one of our horses and drove the shaft into its mast – Found all well on our arrival which is always a great blessing.
20 April	I sent a draft for £23,200 to settle for the Cwmelan purchase ... today ... I never yet had to do with any one who has throughout conducted the business in a manner so perfectly honorable and gentlemanlike as Mr Peel – I could almost say that he has proved an exception to a rule.
25 April	In writing to me, the Duke of Cumberland invites me to write another pamphlet ... I may spare myself that trouble ... no one seems to attach any value to my opinion ... my motives have been mistaken and I pass for a violent and extravagant man, merely because I am firm to what I believe to be right ... For this I have been shunned and avoided as a dangerous character to associate with ...
27 April	Nothing new today – Snow today and snow yesterday.
30 April	... soaking rain today ... I have lost a great many sheep.
1 May	... I have settled to remit 10 per cent to my Tenants at the coming rent day, it is in fact at the rate of 20 per cent on the years rental, and this I fear will in reality be but a poor relief to many of them.
2 May	William arrived safely in London and would arrive at Oxford last night – He is going to try in earnest for a 1st Class.
8 May	My new cascade which has been at a stand still since last autumn is now actively finishing up under Mr Grey's direction, I think that he will make a very successful operation of it – The effect will be bold and good as it now appears and the

1835

> construction is ingenious and well managed. I am also settling everything about my library so that it may now be finished out of hand.

10 May More rubbish Peers are made ... This is all most shameful and hurts me exceedingly.

15 May Letters from my dear Edward dated Valparaiso Feb 2.

16 May [*Mentions that the judges have awarded Rufford to Lord Saville – in a dispute between Lord Scarbrough and Frederick Lumley.*] – I am glad of it ...

19 May Left Clumber very late in the evening and reached Grantham.

20 May Arrived in London about 12 at night.

22 May This is my dear Lincoln's birthday, he and Susan and several of our relations dined here [*Portman Square*] to celebrate the day. Lincoln is very unwell.

23 May I learnt this morning that Lincoln's illness proved to be the measles, which he has very fully and is very much disturbed by the complaint and has a great deal of fever – I found him very uncomfortable and his wife does not seem to understand or to turn her mind much to nursing – I shall therefore take the affair upon myself until he is well – There are many comforts of a sick room which I have supplied for him, I being but too well acquainted with the matter ...

Robert went to Eton this afternoon.

25 May Lincoln is wonderfully better today ... The small pox is raging in an extraordinary manner everywhere – Georgiana and Charlotte were revaccinated this morning ... the effect wears out in 7 to 10 years. The others have been done two years ago.

28 May This is kept as the King's birthday. We went to the Drawing room which was prodigiously crowded – Both the King and Queen and others were kind to us – They made enquiry after Lincoln.

3 June Presented several addresses at the Leveé today, which the King received very graciously and complacently ...

5 June Robert has taken the measles.

7 June Lincoln has given the measles to another person. The Duke of Hamilton's niece Miss Orde has taken the complaint.

8 June We all dined with Lincoln today, to celebrate Susan's birthday, her real birthday is tomorrow ... she is 21 ...

11 June Charlotte has the measles after all.

13 June [*Robert arrived in London from Eton*] Charlotte is better and going on most favorably.

1835

15 June   Henrietta is rather unwell today.

18 June   [*Waterloo Day*] We had a very good meeting at the Carlton Club.

21 June   Sunday – Went to Church – walked afterwards as is my custom with my children, and passed the rest of the day with them – a practice which I cherish and anxiously wish that I could hope to see perpetuated by Lincoln – His wife is giddy and he suffers himself to look complacently upon a vital evil – She is seeking happiness elsewhere than at home in the domestic circle. It is a vicious poison which affects and influences every relation of life. The prospect of what I see resulting from it and what will assuredly follow grieves me to the Soul and [*strongly?*] embitters my thoughts.

13 July   Lincoln's conduct is most distressing to me – it breaks my heart and destroys my peace of mind by day and by night.

15 July   [*At the Duke of Wellington's house, along with some 60 others, to discuss the forthcoming Municipal Corporation Act – as usual, Newcastle spoke his mind – he was against the measure.*]

25 July   [*Another private meeting – he found no support for his opposition to the Bill.*] – the tide was the other way.

26 July   [*Spent much time preparing to speak on the Bill in the House of Lords*] ... flurry in general disturbs my reason and destroys what powers I may possess.

28 July   [*Spoke in the Lords on the Bill. He said that, as the Bill was to go to Committee, he would not oppose the 2ⁿᵈ reading but registered his opposition to the principle of the Bill.*]

[*On the 31 July 1835, the Duke signed a codicil to his will. This effectively cancelled the previously intended bequests to his son and heir, Lord Lincoln. The Park Lane house, which he had purchased for Lincoln, was to be left to 'my youngest children'. The Hafod estate bequest was transferred to son Charles and the Yorkshire properties to his daughters. None of these actions are referred to in his diary.*]

11 August   [*Gave notice that he had decided to vote against the Bill going into Committee. Says that he was 'tricked the other night' into being refused leave to speak until after 2 a.m.*]

12 August   [*He again spoke in the House of Lords*] – ... harassed by ... my lamented and unfortunate situation as to Lincoln ... [*I am*] ... worn down and weary and really unwell ... I lost the thread of my argument ... I floundered about and hearing people laughing, I naturally thought that they were aroused at my [?] efforts and I thought of a speedy retreat. I wound up abruptly and as well as I was able ... I detest speaking and therefore, of course, perform my task with evident dislike and distaste – duty alone would induce me to ever open my mouth.

1835

13 August   [*Reports that he has paid for the Hafod estate without the aid of a loan.*] – Tomorrow my family leave me for Clumber. I hope to follow in a few days.

14 August   All my dear children left me today for Clumber ... Tomorrow I have to go to Windsor to a grand Garter affair ... in the new Hall – It comes very inconveniently.

15 August   [*Writing of the Garter Knight's meeting in St. George's Hall, Windsor*] – the effect ... was truly superb and magnificent ... reached London about 3 o'clock. I have seldom been more completely done up.

16 August   Today I am quite unwell.

17 August   I was very unwell in the night ... extraordinarily faint. I was able however to attend the House in the evening ... The Duke of Cleveland made a very unwarrantable and uncalled for attack upon me for former occurrences which I repelled and told him ... I did not owe my dukedom to my borough. The House cheered for a long time – I find now that I have really been of some use – I have by zeal and perseverance raised an approach to a [*popular*?] feeling ...

18 August   My children have arrived safely at Clumber – I am better today but I am not well yet.

20 August   [*In the House of Lords*] – said a few words expressing my reservation of the Bill.

25 August   ... I left my Codicil at Coutts today [*see 31 July 1835 above*]

27/28 August   On the road ... I dined wretchedly at Hatfield ... had some tea at Wansford and laid down on a bed with my boots off for an hour ... arrived here (Clumber) at 1/2 past 7 in the morning of this day – breakfasted at 1/2 past 8 with all my dearest children ... at night enjoyed the fresh country air and a good bed.

29 August   This place is looking beautifully.

1 September   ... joined my 2 Sons who were out shooting ... a great quantity of game.

2 September   [*The Duke went to Sheffield, some twenty-five miles west of Clumber.*] ... never having been there altho' so near ... I bought what I wanted in plated goods and cutlery for Hafod where I debar the entrance of silver, as plated things are quite as useful and will not attract thieves – I mean no reflexion on the Welch – Rodgers is the best Cutler in Sheffield and Stuart and Co. the best grate manufacturers. I saw beautiful castings which will suit me perfectly for fitting up the Library and Drawing rooms here – We returned at night.

5 September   [*He had received news that he had* 'received leave for a loan from the Government to Aberystwyth harbour'.]

8 September   [*Left Clumber, with Georgiana and Charlotte, to travel to Hafod.*] – stopped at Lichfield – the house full of race people.

9 September   [*Travelled on from Lichfield*] – to New Town – where we slept and fared very well.

10 September   [*Travelled on to Hafod in heavy rains and high winds*] ... Charles and Thomas were on the box and had a miserable journey ... We left Caroline and Henrietta with Miss Spencer at Clumber to follow on in 2 days.

12 September   [*Heard from Clumber that both Caroline and Henrietta had measles.*]

14 September   The Hogarth ... being perfectly obscured ... Mr Bate, by his cleaning it has exposed to view and a splendid picture it is ... worth £1,500 to £2,000 – also a Salvator Rosa ... a Hogarth sketch, which was pasted to strengthen the back of an unworthy picture, of course I shall rescue the sketch ... We also found a very spirited sketch by Vandyke.

15 September   ... Mansell [*his Clumber gamekeeper*] has been here – the effect of a good Keeper is evident ...

17 September   [*Received good news from Clumber about his daughters' recovery from measles. Miss Spencer is full of praise for the way the girls behaved.*]

19 September   ... Some servants arrived here this evening from Clumber which they left 3 days ago.

20 September   Mansell and his wife, at my suggestion have come from Clumber to see their nephew who is Keeper here. [*Mrs Mansell was gravely ill.*]

21 September   Poor Mansell's wife died this morning ... There is not a soul who does not seem to be moved and affected by it ... The long journey in dreadful weather in an open carriage probably gave her cold, deranged her system, and disordered the brain in some way ... Poor Mansell is in a deplorable state – Tomorrow I will endeavour to comfort him.

22 September   I went to see poor Mansell today – poor honest fellow, he is dreadfully afflicted.

23 September   ... Poor Mansell went away this morning ...

24/26 September Went to Aberystwyth ... saw the harbour, went to a Play where the inhabitants and neighbouring gentry received [*us?*] very kindly.

28 September   My very dear and delightful little boy Robert returned to Eton today.

1 October   This is my dear Charlotte's birth day. We have all heartily congratulated her on the event ...

1835

3 October	My dear children Caroline and Henrietta arrived this afternoon from Clumber.
10 October	Caroline and Henrietta went with Miss Spencer to Aberystwyth today ... The Duchess of Kent and the little Princess [*Victoria*] are touring about every where ... they are now at Ramsgate.
13 October	My pictures here are nearly restored ... The Assumption of the Virgin ... highest class. A Descent from the Cross by Vandyke is a noble and splendid performance ... The Southwark Fair by Hogarth needs no comment ... The pictures in the Drawing room here would be worth at a sale not less than £6,000.
18 October	We received letters from dear Edward today ...
23 October	Went to Rhayader, accompanied by Charles and Thomas in order to see and look over Cwmelan ...
28 Oct – 2 Nov	[To Aberystwyth] The works at the harbour have done infinite good ... This has been mainly effected by my coming into the country. Mr Parkinson arrived here yesterday from Notts' ... for the purchase of land at Cromwell ...
3 November	We, that [*is*] Charles, Thomas and I arrived here [*at Dolclythis?*] this evening having left all my dear daughters at Aberystwyth for sea bathing which 3 out of the 4 require. [*As part of their recovery programme.*]
7 November	[*Back at Aberystwyth*] – found all my dear Daughters quite well and much improved by sea air and bathing.
8 November	... examined the Castle [*Aberystwyth*] ... I should like to buy it [*off?*] the Crown and preserve this old and interesting memorial of former times.
9 November	Returned to Hafod ...
12 November	Left Hafod and arrived and slept at Newport.
13 November	Arrived at Combermere ...
15 November	[*He mentions having been to Church in the morning but having refused an invitation to attend another Church in the evening. His reasons were that it would have been* 'for parade – it is not a matter to make so light of'.]
17 November	Left Combermere ... and after a most tedious and disagreeable day's journey arrived at Clumber ... we seemed to be stopped by a thousand delays and were finally obliged to go round by Derby to Alfreton from Ashbourne.

1835

18 November	Went out shooting for a few hours with my 2 dear Sons [*the twins, Charles and Thomas.*] ...

This evening the Aurora Borealis [*Northern Lights*] was most beautiful and curious..I never saw it before wear the same appearance. The night was quite light between 9 and 10 o'clock and the lights kept flashing in rays from all quarters and seemed to concentrate in point just over the Terrace where there was a beautiful and most singular play of lights – Such appearances are magnificently grand. |
19 November	My very dear and excellent Sons left me today to join their Regiment – if they were not so steady and well principled as they are I should dread their residence in London. Their absence will be a serious loss to me.
23 November	Nothing new that I know of.
25 November	I called in Dr. Williams to see my Housekeeper/Kerrod, who is dangerously ill.
27 November	I have purchased Mr Pocklington's property at Cromwell for £6,600 – I have done this to possess the whole of the Lordship ...
28 November	[*He heard from the Duke of Hamilton that Hamilton had been offered* 'the Garter'.]
30 November	I am most actively engaged in finishing every thing up here and hope to get into my Library and Drawing room. This will be a great comfort, and Clumber will then be itself again.
2 December	Our excellent and valued Kerrod is sinking fast and she cannot live many hours – I saw her today and could not but admire the [*sublimity?*] of the sight ... the death bed of a dying Christian with a mind at ease from a clear conscience and a heart dedicated to God and her duty, she calmly meets her death ... A more excellent attached and faithful creature never existed – Her ability is equal to her virtue. She has been in my family, first in the nursery, for about 25 years – Her loss is truly irreparable ...
3 December	This is the birth day of my dear Twin Sons – May God bless and protect them ... [*he had heard that they were both unwell – also that son Robert was doing well in his studies at Eton.*]

We lost our excellent Kerrod this morning, she expired at 5 o'clock ... |
8 December	The remains of poor Kerrod were buried today at Markham Clinton – I had them laid there, being well assured that she would have wished to be laid nearest to the spot where those will rest who she most loved and venerated.
10 December	My dear son Robert arrived this morning.
18 December	William arrived from Oxford today.
23 December	The winter has set in with unusual severity.

1835

25 December   Our Christmas party has never been so small – besides my Daughters only William and Robert are here – It is a lamentable falling off from that full and happy reunion which used to mark our Christmas parties heretofore.

30 December   ... Will not Sir Robert Peel now see his errors in consenting in any way to remodelling the Corporations?

31 December   This is the last day of an eventful and most disastrous year ...

I have been greatly afflicted ... I fear that I have continued grief in store for me – I am wounded to the heart ... on public grounds I have had to suffer ... materially affected my health ... I have laboured ... but have effected little in public or private matters.

THE DUKE'S SPEAKING DIFFICULTIES:

Throughout these Extracts, a recurring concern of the Duke's is his reluctance to speak in public. In attempting to understand his problems in this regard, it is interesting to read the following piece. The date of the item is believed to be 1836.

"When he used to address a speech to the House of Lords, he spoke in a loud, husky, screeching tone of voice, and accompanied his extravagant expressions with a more extravagant gesticulation. In the delivery of a speech, he neither regarded grammar nor heeded logic ... As to argument, there was no attempt at it; the style was clumsy – the diction inaccurate. His speeches were, every one of them, only a tissue of the most violent diatribes against the liberals. In denouncing them, his Grace resorted to so much bodily violence, that it was almost ridiculous to watch him, except that it was somewhat fearful to witness his anger ...

The Duke of Newcastle, as a speaker, is all energy and animation, and nothing but energy and animation. To describe his manner is impossible; and perhaps it may be imagined best by simply stating that, in his more violent moods ... one cannot look at him and listen to him without involuntarily giving vent to the exclamation – "What a passion he is in!"

1 January   ... It is only lately that I have made the discovery, but I can now plainly perceive that my countrymen do me justice and I enjoy their good opinion – At last it seems, justice is done to me, and I am no longer considered to be the wretch which heretofore I have been reproached to be and scarcely worthy of human notice on Christian consideration ... I have solemnly devote[d] my self to the sacred service of God and my country ... I am but too sensible that I am unsupported and almost lonely ...

Our family party is the smallest that we have ever had and is sadly diminished. All however have been very merry and happy and peaceful and altogether we have passed a most amiable day, inter changing our presents and in the cheerful pleasures of society.

2 January   I have today received a letter from Edward who gives a good account of himself [*from Callao, dated September 15th*] – [*Also letters from Charles and Thomas*] – stating that they are heartily sick of London and pining for the country.

3 January   The cold yesterday and the day before was intense ... the rain froze instantly – a vast deal of illness in the country and many deaths ...

4 January   I have written to the Town Clerk[s] of Newark and Retford, intimating to them that I resign the corporate offices which I hold of Custos Rotulorum in one and High Steward in the other – My offices die with the Corporations but I take the opportunity of the short temporary continuance [*in offering*] the Chief Magistrate of the Towns to restore into their hands what they had conferred upon me.

5 January   The Conservative Newspapers are urging the Conservatives to make a general effect at the opening of Parliament, to overthrow the vile and despicable administration by which we are cursed and disgraced ... nothing will do, short of the expulsion of the Papists from the House of Commons.

1836

6 January [*A deputation of the Clergy of the Deanery of Retford called at Clumber. They requested that he convene a meeting on the subject of raising monies for the* 'very meritorious Irish clergy'. *After much thought he agreed to do so, although he thought it wrong that the clergy should have to rely on charitable gifts.*]

9 January [*He notes a newspaper report that*] – a Cabbage cures and even prevents intoxication.

11 January Came to Sir R. Bromley's [*Stoke Hall*] to attend a Newark ball tomorrow – my two daughters and William are with me.

12 January As usual when we go to Stoke or the Newark Ball we have snow – it came down the night before last ... We went to the Ball tonight which was tolerably well attended – we were very well received – The room was dreadfully cold and we were most happy to leave it on our return home. We have a large party here.

13 January Returned home today – it is my dear William's birth day – he is now 21 – and a noble and most delightful young man ... I have had his fortune made out and I find that he will have about £725 a year, not a bad provision for a younger son. The servants are all now drinking his health and a fine row they are making. I am afraid some of them will be a little the worse for it, but I like on these occasions to excite and busy out their hearty good feelings.

15 January The meeting at Retford today went off very well. I was in the chair ... The subscription in the room amounted to £391.

17 January William has been by no means well lately, ... and causes me some uneasiness ... he has a pain from the shoulder to his chest which stops his breathing freely and looks unwell besides.

18 January Very busy all day with my work people, except when interrupted by visitors. I am doing my utmost to get into the Drawing room in the course of the week. My Library, now nearly approaches completion also.

20 January I rejoice to see William more himself again today.

22 January ... Lord Winchilsea and his son and daughter are here, ... but I cannot get him out shooting.   My dear boy Robert left us today for Eton.

28 January The Drawing room is finished in its temporary state and the furniture put in today – we inhabited it in the evening and found it to be a most pleasant and agreeable room; tho' spacious yet perfectly warm – and it was really quite a pleasure to be able to move about without tumbling over furniture or people's legs.

1 February We took our leave of shooting today – We were 4 guns at Bevercotes but where we formerly saw 100's, we now only saw 10's – This I attribute to the alteration of the gun law, the sale of game and the advantage and inducements given to the poacher.

1836

2 February   A very busy day of preparation for my journey to London tomorrow. The Duke of Hamilton has kept me up in anxious conversation until nearly 1 o'clock when he started (it is snowing hard) for London, where he is going to be made a K.G. ...

3 February   Set out from Clumber at about 7 o'clock this evening, reached Grantham at 1/2 past 12 where we had tea and laid down on a bed for an hour when we proceeded on our journey and arrived in London at 5 o'clock. The snow is deep at Clumber and as far as Wandsford, it disappeared gradually until we lost it near London.

4 February   [*Went to the House of Lords*] ... I observed that the Duke of Wellington and friends were very shy of me I know not why, but I shall heed it not. I depend neither upon their smiles nor their frowns.

5 February   [*Attended a Chapter of the Garter, following which, the Duke of Hamilton was elected as a Knight of that Order.*]

7 February   [*He mentions an interview with* 'one who I have always most tenderly and affectionately loved' *– probably his son and heir, Lord Lincoln.*]

9 February   Left London at 1/2 past 2 this morning and arrived at Clumber at 1/4 past 10 ... I breakfasted at Alconbury Hill.

12 February   [*The Committee of the Central Agricultural Society requested that he should become their President*] – this needs a good deal of reflection.

13 February   Received today a small packet of corn sent to me by dear Edward from S. America. He says that it has 7 heads.

   The Assistant Poor Law Commissioners [*waited?*] upon me today ... They seem disposed to act most properly and I shall give them all the assistance in my power.

15 February   A railroad is projected from London to York by Lincoln which will pass through Walkingham, my consent to which was asked for today ... Such a railroad would be of immense importance to Lincs. – it is difficult to perceive of what other particular benefit it can be, or how it will be supported.

17 February   I have Hopper, Architect, here consulting him about every thing projected to be done here and at Hafod.

18 February   This is my dear Edward's birth day – He is now in his 21 year ... the dear creatures begin to show me up for an elderly gentleman

19 February   [*Went over to Ranby to search for correspondence between the Duke of Wellington and General Robert Craufurd. The General had died at Almeira, and his papers were believed to have been entrusted to the custody of the Duke's step-father, Sir Charles Craufurd. No such papers were discovered.*]

1836

20 February [*Back at Clumber – he interviewed* 'Mr Kerr, a medical gentleman' *for a position at Hafod*] – I afterwards came on to Kirklington ...

21 February Went to Church with Adml. Sotheron and family ...

22 February Attended the meeting of the Thurgaton Incorporated Workhouse which was very fully attended and every appearance of an intention to oppose the proceedings of the Poor Law Commissioners. The attempt was made by Mr John Beecher's friends and others connected with Southwell and the poor house. I would not take the Chair and maintained a neutral position until I had heard all the statements on both sides. I then thought it required of me to give an opinion and to express my sentiments and I was fortunate in giving satisfaction to those present. I was assured that I had settled the point for the Commissioners by declaring in their favour and with the more effect from the peculiar line which it took, thus giving encouragement to the Commissioners and securing the good will and confidence of those who I wished to persuade and influence ...

After the meeting I stopped for a short time at Kirklington, took leave of my good friends and rode home ...

23 February [*He makes critical comments about Lord William Bentinck's failure to attend an election meeting at which Lord William was a candidate.*]

27 February [*Left Clumber for London*] – reached Grantham for the night.

28 February This being Sunday went to Church at Grantham ... slept at Biggleswade.

29 February [*Arrived in London*] – Thomas has been unwell ... Robert is also ill at Eton ... [*mentions his own lumbago.*]

1 March ... The Dinner of the Festival of the Welch Charity held at the Freemason's [*Tavern?*] went off very well. The collection made was £1040.

7 March [*Records that he is afflicted by a problem* 'in my loins' – *he also mentions a parliamentary debate where views were expressed about* 'setting aside the young Princess Victoria' – *he opposed the idea.*]

8 March [*Attended the House of Lords, still in their makeshift accommodation*] – whilst there I saw the new plan for the House of Lords designed by Charles Barry, which certainly is a beautiful and appropriate design and which he himself told me would not cost above half a million – £500,000.

12 March [*Mentions a mutiny of British troops in India – he blames Lord William Bentinck.*]

1836

19 March ... A very large party at the Duchess of Kent's for her nephew who is to be the King Consort of Portugal – we were there.

21 March A Ball at the Duchess of Kent's at Kensington. The Princess Victoria danced all the dances but waltzes, and danced very prettily and like a lady – her manners and behaviour are very agreeable and in all respects what they should be. The Princes of Saxe Coburg and their father were there, the eldest son ... is betrothed to the Queen of Portugal, I do not envy ... him poor fellow – if he does not please, he will be poisoned - We did not reach home until between 4 and 5.

22 March ... Robert came home from Eton this morning.

23 March Went to the King's levee today [*He reports that he presented a petition on Church matters. Notes, with disgust, that another petition was presented by a Mr Gully – an ex-prize fighter, now an M.P.!*]

27 March By a letter from E. Dawkins [*Vicar at Markham Clinton*] I learn that he has executed my commission, and the loved and honored remains of my dearest wife and 4 children and my dear sister Charlotte have been moved from Bothamsall and have been deposited in the vault of Markham Clinton Church –

It is an ease to my mind to think that this, the last act of honor to their memories and beloved remains, has been properly executed.

28 March [*In the House of Lords he gave notice of a question regarding*] – the number of Roman Catholics now and in 1799.

30 March [*In the House of Lords he raised the question, but was told that the information was not available – he notes that he received no support.*]

31 March ... This being Good Friday, took the Sacrament as usual and with as many of the family as were able to attend with me – snowing heavily ... fear for our flocks [*especially in Wales*].

2 April ... Susan is again pregnant, her confinement may be expected in August. She is still out of health ... spasms ... convulsions.

9 April I have just heard of the death of poor Henry Mundy, after long and great suffering ...

12 April [*Attended a meeting at the home of the Duke of Wellington.*]

13 April Dined at an immense dinner of the City Conservative Association in Covent Garden Theatre, there were about 1100 persons present ...

15 April Went this evening to the great musical festival at Exeter Hall [*proceeds for the Charing Cross Hospital*] – when we arrived there, instead of going to our places, we found an order from the Duchess of Kent inviting us to her box – We did not desire the

1836

change but obeyed and remained there the whole evening. The Duchess and Princess Victoria and a large party were in the box, H.R.H. as usual was most kind to us.

16 April   [*Attended another meeting at the home of the Duke of Wellington*] – I qualified [*my opinions*] not an iota ... My remarks made no visable impression – The House of Lords is lost.

19 April   Went to see Burke's statue of Sadler, which is just cast in plaster. I suggested some alterations which I think will improve it if they succeed, I really think that it will be as good a work as any one would produce. In the evening went with Robert, Lincoln, Charles and Thomas to Astley's [*circus*] and were much amused.

20 April   [*Attended a Ball given by the Goldsmiths' Company.*]

21 April   My dear Robert returned to Eton today – He is a delightful and admirably disposed boy and his noble and beautiful countenance is but an idea of his mind.

23 April   Came to attend a dinner at Windsor Castle given by the King to the Knights of the Garter being St. George's day. The King seemed very well, the Queen not so, she is a mere skeleton and I was told had been spitting blood ... she is much beloved ... Lady [*Delisle?*] one of the King's natural daughters, told me that the King was dying to get rid of his present ministers ... I told her that ... it should not be done by halves ... This she will mention to the King and I hope that it may do good.

24 April   I slept at Eton last night and this morning went to Chapel for the first time since I left the school [*thirty-four years ago*] ...

Fig. 44 *School Yard, Eton, by Percival Skelton (1852).*

much painful reflection. I have today been settling every thing relating to the scholarship, so that now the deed of settlement may be made out which will fix the foundation as long as this College exists. [*He requested that the boys should be allowed* 'a full day's holiday without exercise' – *this was agreed.*]

– I have been very happy to give pleasure to these boys.

27 April Dined today at the Duchess of Kent's – I sat by the young Princess [*Victoria*] and had a great deal of conversation with her. I like her extremely – Whilst she is lively, she is amiable and good, her manner is very pleasant and all her ideas correct and well regulated – she is clever, well informed, expresses herself remarkably, is without any affectation and is [*very?*] agreeable – She promises well for the future – this is saying a good deal for a girl of a little more than 16 ...

28 April A Ball at the Mansion House ...

30 April Dined at the Royal Academy today ...

 1 May ... it is as cold as Christmas ...

 5 May ... yellow green fog.

11 May Attended a meeting of the Protestant Association ... Lord Winchilsea in the chair ... I was called upon to move a resolution I was tongue tied, and floundered about ... made me appear, what I truly was, an [*egregious?*] fool ...

15 May This night I parted from my dear children that I leave behind, as I and Charles and Thomas go to Clumber tomorrow for a week.

16 May Arrived Clumber at 1/2 past 11 – breakfast at Stevenage, dinner at Grantham.

17 May This place is looking beautifully ... the beeches are in full leaf here, so are the thorns and larches ... but the lilacs and oaks are rather behind those in or near London.

20 May It is almost a phenomenon to see the fruit trees now in full blossom, and all the forest trees disclosing nearly their full leaves. The Cedars will be in bloom about tomorrow or the next day – a few rhododendrons are opening their flowers, in general most flowers are backwards.

22 May This is my dear Lincoln's birth day – we celebrated it here by drinking his health – not a very splendid, but not the less affectionate celebration.

23 May It has been so cold today that we are all quite perished – winter has come again and the vegetation is suffering from the severity of the weather – rain is much wanted, there is scarcely food for the stock.

1836

25 May	[*Set off for London* 'with regret' – *slept at Grantham*.]
26 May	[*Arrived in London*] found my 4 dear Girls quite well.
27 May	... we attended a concert at the palace.
28 May	[*The King's official birthday*] – we went to the Drawing Room ... 3000 persons had been counted.
	Today I have a large family dinner to keep Lincoln's birth day.
31 May	Went to see Giraffes, which have arrived at the Zoological Gardens.
	[*Comprehensive description of the* 'Nubian men' *who accompanied the animals.*]
6 June	Came to Salt Hill to see Robert ... my 4 daughters are come with me.
8 June	There are 92 coaches of all description which pass by Salt Hill in the 24 hours, an almost incredible number. We returned to London this evening.
17 June	In the chair, as President, at the general meeting of the Central Agricultural Society ... it was a troublesome one – so bad that I threatened to leave the Chair.
19 June	Caroline is indisposed in the same way as last year.
21 June	My two youngest Daughters were this morning [*perfectly?*] confirmed at Lambeth by the Archbishop of Canterbury. Robert was confirmed at Eton during the last week and now all my children have been confirmed ...
28 June	My dear William arrived yesterday from Oxford for a few days.
29 June	I have more or less doubted the justness of phrenological deductions – today I called upon [*Deville?*] and asked him for a description of my qualities – he felt my head and wrote it down for me, and in the course of a very long conversation with him, and most especially by his reasoning and demonstrations from various casts in [*his*] possession, I am convinced that when cultivated as a science it must furnish facts which are indispensable for a knowledge of character and faculties.
5 July	Caroline and Henrietta, with Miss Spencer, went to Clumber this morning.
6 July	... I have made arrangements for paying all my London bills. I am proud and much pleased with my performance.
8 July	[*Left London for Clumber*] – Slept at Stevenage, dined at Wandsford.
9 July	Arrived at Clumber at 4 o'clock.
10 July	The country air is most enjoyable and [*renovating?*]
13 July	... I had expected the Duchess of Kent was coming north this

1836

year and I was about to prepare for Her reception here. I learn however ... that such is not to be the case ... This is a good hearing for me and will ease me of a good deal of inconvenience – Altho' I should have received our future Queen with the highest gratification.

15 July   ... A letter from Charles at sea in the Downs states that he and Thomas were very sea sick indeed ...

17 July   Thomas writes from Cowes where he and Charles now are ... May all good attend them. Excellent and exemplary young men as they are ...

21 July   Attended the Assizes at Nottingham and returned here at night.

24 July   My terrace here is now in high beauty – I have by some late purchases added what was wanted in ornaments, and I must acknowledge that it is ultimately almost all that I could wish it to be.

26 July   My dear Robert arrived today from Eton ... He drove thro' Oxford and found William well, hard at his books.

I began my corn harvest today ... my hay is all in.

27 July   Robert is as happy as the day is long – I played at cricket with him this evening.

2 August   Charles and Thomas arrived this morning from London.

9/11 August   [*Left Clumber – slept at Derby – on through Newtown to Hafod*] – William arrived from Oxford – Miss Spencer and my two youngest daughters arrived.

Fig. 45 *During his stay, William painted this unique depiction of the Hafod mansion.*

1836

13 August	A letter from Lincoln, announcing that Susan was brought to bed and had presented him with another boy.
16 August	My harvest at Clumber is all in. [*Finished in 15 days.*]
23 August	... My dear and noble Caroline's birthday.
29 August	This is my dear Henrietta's birthday, she is this day a charming girl of 17. I do not know of a fault that she has except being short.
30 August	My works here [*Hafod*] are advanced a little ... the repairs and redoing of the house are completing, the rain and weather is at last kept out.
31 August	William tried to leave us this morning for Oxford but failed in finding room on the Mail.
1 September	My dear William has gone at last ... I shall now be extremely anxious for his success at Oxford.
2 September	[*He notes that the Queen Regent of Spain's general has been murdered*] – Papists are barbarous and bloody – Protestantism is the Christian religion.
4 September	A letter from Edward dated Callao April 19.
8 September	[*He mentions*: 'My mines at Cwmelan']
15 September	Went to see the Cwmystwyth mine works ... I left a present for the men which pleased them excessively ...

Fig. 46 *Old mine-workings at Cwmystwyth* [*September 2000*]

16 September	My dear son Robert left us for Eton [to]day. He went by the Mail, the first time that he has travelled in a public conveyance. [*On 18 September, the Duke notes that his Valet, [Henry?] Vachel, accompanied Robert to Cheltenham.*]
27 September	[*Mentions a Mr Haslam*] – 'an ex-surveyor who has long been

1836

employed by the Ordnance' ... when all the right people are in place ... I may then be enabled to finish as it ought to be, my house at Clumber, as well as at this place.

30 September ... I hear from Notts that the turnips, [that] were very fine when I left it, are now destroyed by lice and flies and grubs, there is no grass, hay is selling at £9 a ton, if bad weather comes there will be a great malady among the cattle – our prospects are now bad.

3 October ... arranged the purchase of as much of the Crown property at Newark as I can compass – it is very unpleasant to see a property go away which, tho' only leased, has for nearly a century been considered as secure as a family property.

7 October My tenants here have paid their rents well. I wonder how they can pay at all, miserable as they appear ...

8 October Caroline and Henrietta went with Miss Spencer to Aberystwyth.

11 October Today the sale of the Crown Estate of Newark – of which my ancestors and I have solely been the Lessees – is to be sold.

14 October [*He heard that he had been able to buy* 'nearly all the lots' *at the Newark sale –* 'almost £13,000 worth'.]

Robert has hurt his knee and leg very much, by falling thro' a trap door in a shop in Eton.

21 October [*He reports having spent* 'about £67,000' *on the Newark sales.*]

23 October I have learnt today, with deep regret, that William, by the advice of his Tutors has abandoned the idea of going up for honors.

29 October [*Mentions his new Steward, Haslam.*]

7 November My dear family from Aberystwyth joined me today. The weather is very severe, and a fire side with one's family around it is a cheery and a happy event.

8 November Very busy about every thing – more of my English colony is arrived and I am beginning to change the face of things very visably.

12 November Hard at work to settle every thing – with so much and so many points to attend it is no sinecure.

13 November A wretched day, pouring with rain, and we could not go to church – I read prayers to my family at home.

14 November Charles and Thomas left me this morning to join their regiment.

16 November If my servants had had every thing ready, I should have been off [*in time?*] this morning, as it was I left Hafod at a little after 9 and arrived at Shrewsbury at 1/2 past 8.

17 November I have been detained for a long time this morning, in consequence of my carts, which were on the road to Clumber, being stopped at a turnpike gate 3 miles out of Shrewsbury –

1836

The gatekeeper required a penalty because my name, as he said, was not properly put upon my carts – I resisted the payment and he stopped them for above 3 hours – I tried every device in my power to get the carts through the gate, but without force, which I did not like to use, it was impossible, the men were saucy and inexorable and locked the gates not only against me but others as he knew that if he opened the gates that I was determined to push through –

– after squabbling for a long time, I could not be detained any longer, and not choosing to pay the penalty, I left one of my horses and have endeavoured so to arrange matters that the man shall gain nothing by it – he is a known [extortioner?] and I have done this for the public good and to bring a supposed construction of the law to issue – The point is this – The Act requires that the Christian and surnames shall be painted on the carts – this in the case of a titled person is as superfluous as it is ridiculous and I will not do it. If I put my Christian and surname only, I shall not be known, and am quite determined not to put both – and I shall try the point – I have ordered an action to be brought against the man – and I think he will have no cause for congratulating himself upon his ingenuity or [extortion?]. The public will be rejoiced, for he has been the nuisance of the neighbourhood for a long time ... reached Clumber at 1/2 past 11.

18 November   This morning my dear sons William and Edward arrived by the Mail – Edward is but little altered – [Caroline and Henrietta are due tomorrow.]

19 November   Lincoln and his wife and family arrived today – I made my acquaintance with my new Grandson [Edward] who is a very nice child – I imagined I was happy in having so many of my family around me, but in the evening the post brought me astounding news, nothing less than that Charles had declared himself to a Miss [Madge] Orde, niece of the Duchess of Hamilton – a miserable poor creature with nothing whatever to recommend her. I cannot conceive how she could make an impression on my man – I would not have him link himself to such a person on any account – the idea and the event makes me wretched – mine is a life of disaster and this is a cruel one – I have most decidedly refused my consent.

22 November   Charles' affair never quits my mind. [Records that he suspects the Duchess of Hamilton has 'promoted this grievous and truly lamentable affair'.]

27 November   The Exchange at Nottingham has been burned by accident ...

3 December   This is my dear Sons (Charles and Thomas) birth day.

1836

7 December	Robert arrived this morning ...
9 December	[*Records that he has dismissed Mr Dalton, Robert's tutor*] — as he was not properly calculated to educate him. He is a disagreeable ill mannered man, and does not possess the art of teaching ...
24 December	Yesterday it began to snow, today it has snowed heavily also and there is nearly 2 feet depth of snow on the ground ... The trees are weighed down with the load upon them.
25 December	With the exception of Charles and Thomas, who cannot leave their regiments, we have passed our Christmas very happily together. We all took the Sacrament as usual and passed the whole day in the house, as the snow is so excessively deep on the ground and it has continued to snow during the whole day ... I dread the mischief to the poor and to the cattle and stock of all kinds.
26 December	We are almost snowed up here — the mails are stopped ...
27 December	We are shut out from communication from London ... The North mail went thro' Worksop at ¹/₂ past 6 this morning but we have heard that it was quite stopped before it reached Ollerton ... [*Snow*] 10 or 12 feet deep in many places.
28 December	Today, at about 3 o'clock, we received the post that should have come by yesterday's mail — These letters came by horse from Retford, the Ollerton road not being open yet ...
31 December	Here finishes the year 1836 ... I have endeavoured to stand rooted to the center, where Truth abides ...

Fig. 47 *A wintry scene at Clumber Bridge.*

1 January ... I do not look forward to tranquillity, there is too much mischief afloat, to permit of a calm ...

2 January The severity of the weather is beginning to be much felt by the animals, the hares and rabbits are becoming very thin and weak, the birds also are dying – The sheep are fed entirely upon dry food, my farmer gives them a great deal of chopped straw, as hay is very scarce.

6 January ... The weather began to soften yesterday evening ... the birds and beasts will now find a little food ...

10 January Went to Newark accompanied by my Daughters and Lincoln to attend a Ball there – it was ill attended due to the state of the weather.

11 January After looking about at various parts of my property here, we returned to Clumber – Susan was not well enough to go to Newark.

14 January [*Adml. Mundy is* 'to be advanced from a mere Companion to Knight Commander of the Bath ... Sir George Mundy']

16 January Robert's new tutor, Mr Penrose, came today – he is a modest unassuming young man with good abilities and I think will make a good tutor for Robert. Poor dear little fellow ...

17 January Lincoln, William, Edward and Mrs Thompson went from here today, to attend a dinner at Newark, which is given by the constituency of the Southern Division of this county to Lincoln.

19 January Lincoln came home this evening – I understand that he acquitted himself extremely well ...

20 January My Nottm paper arrived this evening. I have read Lincoln's speech and think that it does him credit ... He is rather fond of detail ... he will cure this as his ideas and views enlarge.

21 January ... We enjoyed an excellent days shooting, we were five guns and killed [89?] pheasants besides a due proportion of hares and rabbits.

1837

23 January   What is called influenza is prevailing to a serious state at this time. We have it in this house, many of the servants ... Georgiana and two daughters and now Susan have been severely attacked.

26 January   My dear Robert left me this morning for Eton ... Susan is very unwell ... nor do I see any immediate prospect of her cure.

29 January   Susan is no better and is very weak. Lincoln is anxious to worship his juggernaut, the House of Commons ... There is again very deep snow ...

30 January   Susan remains in the same state ...

31 January   A heavy and most grievous affliction has fallen upon us, I forbear mentioning what it is, any further than that it concerns me as a parent in a manner least expected of anything that could happen to me. [*This was the delicate matter of an intimate relationship between Susan and her brother-in-law, William.*]

3 February   The Duchess of Hamilton arrived today ... weak state ... hearing of her Daughter's state she determined to leave London ... it is miraculous what a woman may and will do if she pleases – the devotion of women is one of the most remarkable traits of their beautiful character.

6 February   William went this morning with Mr Thompson. The Duke of Hamilton arrived about 5 in the afternoon.

11 February   The Duchess of Hamilton returned to London today – she is gone to prepare for a journey to Paris ...

13 February   Lincoln set out for London at a little after 6 this morning. Susan left about 1/2 past 10 ... The Duke of Hamilton ... travels in her carriage.

17 February   Lincoln writes that Susan arrived in London in 3 days from here ... Lincoln is in great misery. I feel for his trying situation.

18 February   This is my dear Edward's birthday. He this day completes his 21st year.

20 February   I went today to call on Lord Scarbrough at Rufford. He is making thorough alterations and repairs there, and not before they are wanted, for every piece of wood appears to be as rotten as tinder ... like touchwood ...

1837

Lord Scarbrough shewed me about the lower part of the house which I had never before seen – this is the curious and ancient part – here is the crypt and the groined gothic arches and columns ... the whole general building is still extant in good preservation, and Lord Scarbrough means to clean all the patchings and interferences away, so as to shew the whole in its pure and original state – it was built in King Stephen's time – I was not before aware that a building of such antiquity and curiosity existed so near to me.

Fig. 48

Crypt at Rufford Abbey.

27 February   Lincoln is unwell, perhaps with influenza – Susan is something better.

10 March   My little book is out at last ... it is now before the public.

11 March   Went to Nottingham to attend the Assizes ... There was a large attendance of County gentlemen, we dined with the Judges – Edward went with me.

12 March   [*The Duchess of Hamilton and Susan left London for Paris yesterday.*] – Winter has returned again.

16 March   Robert arrived this evening.

20 March   I have the pleasure of hearing that my book is much approved of ...

24 March   ... The thermometer last night was at 19 and the lake quite frozen over from the cascade to the lake head ... This being Good Friday we all took the Sacrament, Caroline was a communicant for the first time –

27 March   Snow again today ... the ewes and lambs will suffer dreadfully and there is nothing for animals to eat.

1837

29 March	Lincoln has arrived at Paris. Susan has been attacked by spasms so severe as to affect the brain.
2 April	Mrs Fitzherbert [*the Roman Catholic wife of George IV*] ... is dead ... [*at the*] great age of 93.
6 April	Winter weather still continues ... the lake frozen over at 9 o'clock this morning ... greatly injuring the vegetation – grass there is none and turnips have all been finished for some time ... Such extraordinary weather is probably as heretofore by Haley's Comet.
20 April	Mr Haslam [*Estate Agent*] kept me for some time again today ...
24 April	[*He mentions the* 'insensitivity' *of the Duchess of Kent. Says that it will cause a rift between the King and Princess Victoria.*]
27 April	Very late this afternoon I was able to uproot myself from Clumber – we reached Grantham.
28 April	Arrived in London ... Lincoln is arrived from Paris.
15 May	... Went to East Sheen with Edward.
16 May	Went to the Exhibition today – the first in the new Gallery ...
17 May	... I was at the levee today – and presented some Addresses. The King was ill and feeble and was seated – Lincoln and Charles went with me.
18 May	... Went to the Drawing room today, where I presented Caroline. [*Princess Augusta presided, as the Queen was ill. Georgiana and Charlotte accompanied their sister.*]
24 May	[*Princess Victoria is 18 today*] ... a Ball at St. James' ... which we all attended ... Princess Augusta again officiated ... the Duchess of Kent and the Princess [*Victoria*] were also there ... as usual we went up to the Royal party on the first occasion – but to the surprise of us all, the Princess would not notice any of us – what this may mean I know not – This however is certain that it exhibits exceedingly bad manners, and to say the least of it is blameably [*sic*] rude and impolite.
1 June	... A Ball for the distressed Spital Fields weavers – the Opera House was fitted up for the occasion ... above 2000 present.
16 June	This evening Lincoln has set out on a foreign expedition – I never feel without anxiety when any one about whom I am anxiously interested goes abroad – from knowing foreigners well, I have a great [?] of their deadly contact and contamination – I wish too to see natives love and delight in their own countries ... which should be the first and dearest and truest objects of their love and affection.

1837

17 June   ... The Duke of Norfolk is about to sell Worksop Manor, he has never offered any part of the estate to me – The Duke of Portland has treated for it but the associations were broken off on a difference of £70,000 as I am told ... [*Newcastle had met Lord Aberavon at dinner today and Aberavon indicated that he might buy it himself.*]

20 June   The King died about 2 o'clock this morning. At 11 o'clock a Privy Council was held at Kensington ... The little Queen took the oaths ... She spoke ... with extraordinary distinctness and in a tone of voice so sweet and agreeable that every one was particularly charmed by it. She went thro' the business with a calmness and dignity that surprised every one and when the Councillors kissed her hand she received all most favorably without making the slightest distinction.

23 June   [*Commenting on the young Queen's good qualities, he wrote*: '... we may have to thank Providence for bestowing upon us so rich a blessing.']

24 June   Came to Salt Hill for a day or two to see Robert ...

25 June   Went to Church at Farnham ... Saw the Birmingham and London rail road which is forming close to this place. We observed a shameful proceeding upon it, namely that the laborers were working on a Sunday as on a week day and this is the first time that I have ever seen such a thing in England and I must confess that it shocked and hurt me to see such a rare sight.

26 June   ... went down to Eton to see the boys at cricket ... shewed my daughters all about the college.

27 June   Went down to Eton today ... settled about the deed of endowment for the Scholarship. [*He then returned to London.*]

28 June   Appearances are not favorable or auspicious of the wise policy of the new reign – All the appointments which have been made are from the reformers and the Queen sees none but those of that class ...

[*He notes that Sir J. Conway has been removed from his command of the Army and replaced by Lord William Bentinck*] – a dismal change.

29 June   We are going on very ill ... I am in great alarm.

30 June   Parliament will be dissolved between the 15th and 21. As Lincoln's interests have been represented to be affected by his absence when others are canvassing – His Brothers, Charles and Thomas have in the kindest, and most disinterested manner undertaken to go into Notts. by the Mail tonight – [*Charles went to Nottingham; Thomas to Newark.*]

1837

4 July   There is talk of many new Peers ... Mr Denison, now M.P. for Notts' S. Division is to be one of them – his father is in business and was a bagman and used to carry samples about the country, which Old Mr Sutton of Kelham has since told me of. His Brother was made a Bishop about a month ago and if this man is made a Lord, this family may indeed wonder, as others will, at its strange elevation.

7 July   Charles and Thomas returned from Notts today and in the afternoon left for Windsor, where they have to attend the King's funeral tomorrow.

8 July   Today all the shops are shut and nothing is stirring but people going to Windsor. [*He does not comment on his reasons for not attending the funeral.*]

9 July   [*Mentions that Sir William Clinton was one of the Canopy bearers at the King's funeral.*]

13 July   This morning Charles, Thomas and William took their leave of me, to go by steam packet to Antwerp – this is their first absence from their native country – I shall feel very lost without them ... Lincoln ... remains in Paris ... has sent for his children – I have however stopt their going until he has well considered this point which he has decided upon very precipitately and immaturely –

14 July   Attended a Chapter of the Garter today ... kissed Her Majesty's hand.

15 July   I have been right glad to learn ... that Mr Denison resigns the contest and consequently that Lincoln [*will*] not be involved in a contest.

17 July   ... Lincoln has determined upon having his children over to Paris – I deeply lament this – I know very well how it will all end – it will end miserably ... but my poor son is blind – and in nothing more than his distrust of me and indisposition to adopt any opinion of mine as fit for him – it is equally ungrateful and unwise and will too assuredly carry a sting with it which will punish –

19 July   Lincoln's children left London for Boulogne. I went to the Queen's first levée today ... between 13 and 1400 persons present ... After the levée there was a Privy Council at which, with others, I was sworn in as Ld. Lt. [*Lord Lieutenant*]. [*The Queen*] shewed by her manner that she entertained no bad feeling towards me – on the contrary, she accompanied her courtesies with a most obliging smiling manner ... she performed her part admirably ... precisely as I would wish to see my own daughters ...

20 July   My dear Edward left me today for the Mediterranean. I took him down to the steam packet, 'Don Juan', lying below the London Docks.

1837

21 July   ... Mr Tallents [*his Newark Agent*] and I arranged Lincoln's address to his constituents ...

25 July   ... Lincoln arrived from Paris this evening, he is remarkably well and left Susan certainly better, tho' in a miserable state.

26 July   Lincoln left London for Notts about 12 today ...

29 July   Bassetlaw election is over ...

31 July   Caroline and Henrietta went to Clumber this morning with Miss Spencer, we shall follow tomorrow. Robert came home from Eton today.

1 August   Still here ...

2 August   ... my 2 eldest Daughters and Robert and I sat out from Portman Square and reached Biggleswade ...

3 August   ... we arrived at Clumber [*via Newark.*]

4 August   [*He heard today that Mr Knight had been successful in the Bassetlaw election, and that Foljambe (of Osberton) was third.*] Rode over to Welbeck but did not find the Duke of Portland.

Thus we have all 4 conservative members for Nott's county.

5 August   Today I have examined my ship 'Lincoln', which has been taken out of the water and was intended for thorough repair and considerable alteration. I found her so entirely decayed by dry rot, which with every plank we removed appeared to be rising up the hull, so that in all probability hardly a piece of wood was free from taint, that I [*at*] last determined to condemn her and, I think, I shall build another in her place, of my own timber. It is scarcely five years ago that she underwent a thorough repair and was then found to be very rotten, but now she is too far gone to make even any repair [*achievable?*]

6 August   Lincoln left me this evening for London, from whence he will immediately proceed to Paris, to join Susan and his children.

11 August   My Daughters gave us a little fête today at their garden – first a breakfast and at night what they called a Chinese fête, with lanterns and other illuminations, a collation, fireworks etc. etc. – all very prettily and very nicely done.

14 August   My harvest began on the 7th ...

15/16 August   [*Spent with Mr Tallents on business matters.*] – and then occupied the rest of the day with Mr Nesfield and others.

17 August   [*With Mr Brickley, about Nottingham business matters.*] – he is negotiating with the Midland railway company for such land as they require from me in the King's Meadows ... he had asked £320 an acre. [*Expects to settle at £300.*]

Lincoln writes that ... Susan looking rather better ...

18 August   Edward has written from Malaya.

1837

20 August   [*Notes that a party is to be held in the Nottingham Castle yard on the 29*th*.*]

22 August   ... left Clumber ... reached Cheadle late at night.

23 August   We left Cheadle – [*Arrived at Combermere Abbey too late to attend the wedding of Miss Cotton to Lord Hillsborough.*]

28 August   [*Moved on to Powis Castle and found Robert there with Lord Clive.*]

30 August   [*On to Hafod*]– found Caroline and Henrietta quite well.

8 September   I have today purchased Pugh's desirable property at [*Pontrhydygroes?*] for £3,000, which will pay about 3½ per cent ...

11 September   ... Lincoln has gone to Lausanne with Susan and their boys – The Duchess of Hamilton accompanies them. Charles and Thomas and William were at Venice when I last heard from them and Edward was at Gibraltar just about to take his passage to Malta.

20 September   [*Mentions Fredr. Mundy* 'the third of the brothers', *being ill.*]

21 September   ... Combermere and Son and Lord and Lady Hillsborough arrived today.

24 September   This is the only Sunday out of the last 3 that we have been able to go to Church.

25 September   As Worksop Manor estates are again on sale, I wrote to Lord Surrey requesting the refusal of it. His reply is obliging and I think I have secured the refusal or at all events of as much as it would be desirable for me to purchase.

27 September   Drove Robert in my pony phaeton to the [*Pentre Brunant?*] Arms to meet the Mail ... Robert is gone to Eton ...

28 September   [*Busy on Aberystwyth Harbour matters.*] – I have no money to lend but I promised to try if I could procure it and have written by this post to Messrs Coutts to ask them to lend £3000 at 5 per cent, with security of a mortgage on the harbour dues now amounting to £600 per [*annum?*], with a debt of £800 for money borrowed in addition to the £3,000 now required.

29 September   A letter from Charles in Vienna.

30 September   [*The Duke is warned that the Aberystwyth Trustees are* 'in high glee', *because they believe that they have* 'found a hole in my pocket'.] ... I will make them ashamed of themselves.

2 October   [*He notes that some titled* 'born gentlemen' *are reduced to living off wages received by working as coachmen.*] – This truly is the depth of degeneracy!!!

1837

6 October   [*Records that he has been inspecting his stock of animals.*]

Two years ago ... consisted of ... Scotland black face and Cheviot sheep – and Highland and Ayrshire Cattle – these last are good of themselves and want little improvements, the Cheviots are thrivers and the wool excellent, but they are not good in shape. I have brought a beautiful Leicester ram from Clumber, to cross with them and I expect some fine and beautiful sheep from this cross. I shall try the same ram with some mountain native sheep. The black faced Scots are beautiful and magnificent animals to look at but their fleeces are bad and wool coarse. I mean to try a South Down ram to the black faced ewes, which will [*improve?*] the wool materially and will probably produce an admirable animal in all respects. – If I succeed I shall try to establish the black faced breed on the hills and the other Cheviots on the lower and enclosed grounds.

7 October   A letter from William today announces his and his dear Brothers arrival in England.

9 October   My 3 Sons are arrived this evening, all well.

11 October   [*Writes that the young Queen is* 'in the hands of vile Ministers and her Mother' ...]. A letter from Lincoln today from Lausanne ...

12 October   A letter from Edward from Malta dated Sept 19th. [*On board the 'Sapphire', as mate.*]

13 October   [*Mentions the poor agricultural prices in Wales.*]

17 October   Went to Aberystwyth today to see the harbour to be prepared for the Harbour meeting tomorrow ...

18 October   Attended the meeting – a trap was evidently laid for me but I did not fall into it ... gave them my mind very fully ... condemned their underhand and paltry attempts to upset me in public estimation.

19 October   ... I returned to Hafod ...

21 October   Today I planned a very extensive improvement here – creating a village and a Church and enclosing a large tract of ground ... I propose to enclose from the new farm to the hills surrounding Pwllpeiran bog and flats.

27 October   [*Mentions the potential for the mining of copper and lead on his land.*]

29 October   [*Bemoans the sale of the Royal Stud at Hampton Court.*] ... Foreigners buy the best of our mares and horses and take them out of the country.

30 October   Charles and Thomas left us this morning early for London ...

2 November   My [*drainers?*] from Notts' are arrived ...

1837

3 November	[*Went to Devils' Bridge to arrange* 'for the new buildings and alteration of the Inn ... I like my new tenants the Norrison's very much ...']
5 November	The Curate Mr Jones read the prayer for the King's deliverance from the Powder Plot and gave a very good sermon on the subject.
6 November	A very disturbing letter from my dear Lincoln, the villainous Doctors who he employed at Paris [*to attend Lady Lincoln*] ... have demanded £18,000 for their attendance ... after the lapse of only one day, [*they*] actually arrested him and carried him before a [*judge?*] ... what trouble and disaster have been brought upon him and us by his unfortunate connection with the Hamilton family.
7 November	[*Mentions that, with new purchases, his Hafod estate will comprise* '50 to 60,000 acres'.]
8 November	[*Left Hafod – slept at Hereford.*]
9 November	After having breakfasted, we went on to Stoke Edith ... we have passed the remainder of the day very pleasantly under the hospitable attentions of [*Mr?*] and Lady Emily Foley and a very agreeable party in the house. The house is a very ugly house by Indigo Jones, the grounds are very extensive and the woods fine ...the trees [?] are like everything else, growing freely in a most fruitful soil – we saw the mode of making cider, and some beautiful Herefordshire cattle, bulls and cows, also some excellent South Down sheep.
10 November	[*Travelled on to Lichfield*] – ... we passed by Eastnor Castle – a modern castle by Smirke and in my opinion a very poor performance – the building is as uninteresting as the situation in which it is placed ... it could not have been safe, as it is commanded by ground within bow shot of the castle ...
11 November	We inspected the Cathedral at Lichfield – built by Roger de Clinton. At Derby we stopped to see the china works ... I had not seen it for about 30 years. Arrived at Clumber at 1/2 past 8 found our dear Henrietta and all well.
13 November	I received today a very kind letter from the King of Hanover ... [*previously the Duke of Cumberland.*]
15 November	A letter from Lincoln ... the affair with the Doctors remains as it was ... I much fear that it may cause much trouble and embarrassment.
17 November	Left Clumber [*for London*] this morning, called at Thoresby on my way and found them at home ... [*slept at Eaton.*]
18 November	... drove straight to the H. of Lords ... took the oaths and my seat. Dined at the Duke of Wellington's ...

1837

25 November   I gave notice last night for the presentation of a Petition for the exclusion of Roman Catholics from seats in Parliament ... [*He was persuaded to postpone this. – Commenting on the Ministers he wrote* 'they are a tricky, pettifoggery wretched crew'.]

28 November   I presented the Protestant petition this evening ...

1 December   ... drove to Coutts, with whom I had much need of conferring relative to the purchase of Worksop manor, should I be able to trial for it ... The sum will probably be not less than £350,000 ... left the Strand a little after 12 and arrived at Wandsford where I sleep at 1/2 past 9 – very glad to get in.

2 December   Arrived at Clumber at about 4 and found all my dear family here quite well – dear creatures I am well pleased to be with them again.

3 December   This is Charles and Thomas birthday ... They are admirable young men, an honor to my family and a real source of comfort to me under all circumstances and on every occasion.

5 December   ... wretched weather, gloomy dank and foggy – chillingly cold.

6 December   My dear Robert arrived this morning from Eton ... excellent health.

7 December   ... The particulars and price of Worksop Manor has been handed to me – the price set upon the whole is £420,000 – a price so preposterous that no one can go near it – it would not pay 2 per cent – probably not more than 1 per cent.

10 December   Lincoln and his family arrived [*in England*?] on the 8th. Susan, he writes, is the better for the journey.

16 December   Charles arrived today to our universal joy.

22 December   My new chimneypiece for the Drawing room is at last arrived and we have been busily at work today fixing it.

Fig 49 This chimneypiece, in white marble, was purchased by the Duke at the Fonthill Sales. In the early 1900's it was located in the Yellow Drawing Room at Clumber. This room was on the (relatively unchanged) eastern side of Clumber House and may be the one referred to at this point in the diaries.

1837

24 December Mr Tallents, my Agent at Newark and become my confidential man of business, died on the 22nd. In him I have lost a real and valuable friend as well as a man ... whose judgement and ability I could completely rely and whose zeal and integrity were unwearily exercised for my advantage – He is in every sense a most irreparable loss to me.

25 December We all took the Sacrament today. [*Except for Robert, who was not yet confirmed.*]

30 December This morning my dear Charles left us for Windsor ...

31 December ... Thus finishes the year 1837 ... [*He then entered around 250 words regarding the wretched state of the nation.*]

Fig. 50 *Worksop Manor – showing the North front, following the partial rebuilding in the 1760's.*

1 January · ... In reviewing the past year, I find that I have been less publicly active than usual ... I am willing to stir when I can hope to do good ...

In my family some matters have grieved me to the soul. My dear son Lincoln has been subjected to severe trials ... Thomas arrived today from Windsor ... He is not very well. Clumber, I trust, will set him up ... He had 3 radical companions in the Mail – [*Thomas Slingsby*?] Duncombe one, a Mr Griffin and another Mr G. has been very active in Canada by his own account ...

3 January · Went to Belvoir Castle on a visit for a few days.

Thomas accompanied me ... This is the first time I have attended one of these great annual meetings, altho' I have been frequently invited. We were 35 or 36 at dinner. Dukes of Wellington and Sutherland, Marquis of Salisbury [*and Exeter*?] with their Ladies – Lord and Lady Wilton, Aberdeen, Forrester with a vast many more.

4 January · [*Birthday of the Duke of Wellington*] – this is a great gala – many went out shooting etc. I preferred looking all about the house and place ...

After dinner I had to give the Duke's health.

5 January · This day is a hunting day ... Belvoir hounds met at Croxton Park ... I turned my horse to see the house which Mr Gregory is now building at Harlaxton ...

Left Belvoir Castle this morning and returned to Clumber, where I found Mr Thompson had arrived yesterday, he brings me news from Lincoln who he has seen at Leamington that Susan is somewhat better ... Sir Wm. Clinton arrived after us today.

10 January · A great deal of snow has fallen for several successive days.

11 January · I have completed the filling of my new ice house today, it holds 326 loads.

1838

22 January	My dear Robert left me today on his return to Eton.
26 January	An interesting letter from Edward dated Smyrna 15th Dec.

22 January   My dear Robert left me today on his return to Eton.

26 January   An interesting letter from Edward dated Smyrna 15th Dec.

27 January   Major General Sir R. Jackson, who commands this district, being here, I have communicated to him fully what I have learned by letter, and what all my opinions relative to secret combinations amongst the manufacturing workmen ...

29 January   My dear Thomas left me for Windsor today.

30 January   I have today completed my 53rd year.

3 February   ... We returned home from Thoresby.

8 February   A break in the weather ... The frost has lasted almost uninterruptedly for 5 weeks.

9 February   Pursuant to agreement, the Duke of Portland came here today, to discuss certain points relative to the purchase of Worksop Manor Estate. He came with the full intention and expectation of outwitting and out manoeuvring me, or, in his view, of jockeying and taking me in. Before he left my house, I think he was fully sensible of his mistake and found that he had over shotten his mark. He wished to come over me by his superior wealth and greater skills in such conductings. I wish to have all the portion of land between the road from Ollerton and Worksop, turning to [the] right on Sparken Hill following that road to Worksop town. Then up to the canal as far as the Duke of Norfolk's property goes, on the Clumber side after the canal, up to the Osberton estate and by that boundary to Clumber Park side. The Duke, in compact with Mr Foljambe [of Osberton], does not choose that I should obtain this portion and uses every means known to the lowest unfairness to make me put up with less – a very small portion within the old road – This I cannot consent to ... he bullied, tricked, shuffled and prevaricated – he tried the same acts today, in a manner the most degrading to himself, but without avail, I made my stand and met him upon his own ground, he feels that he is defeated and has begun to cry for quarter – He agrees to try if Mr Foljambe can be prevailed upon to acceed to my pretensions. He moreover requested that I shd. today fix a price which I could give for the whole estate if I would not consent to his proposed [partition?] – as I did not agree to it, I declared to him that I was ready to name a sum, and asked him if he on his part was prepared to name one (for it was agreed that whoever named the highest sum was after that to have the privilege of treating for the estate unmolested by the other party) – Here he [receded] again and declared that he should not be ready to do this for at least 3 weeks to come. I then [?] upon his shuffling conduct, which was not pleasing to him, and putting his tail between his legs, he left me with the

1838

understanding that Mr Foljambe was to be applied to ascertain if he would give way, and if not then we are in three weeks time to state on paper the sums which each of us will give and the highest sum named is to terminate the completion of the lowest bidden. I never was more disgusted with the conduct of anyone, [*than*] with that of my knavish neighbour this day –

14 February ... Lord Manvers came to consult upon and talk over with some unpleasant private business – upon which I rendered him all the assistance in my power. [*He gives no hint of the subject under discussion.*]

16 February A great deal of wild swans have been upon the rivers and the lake here this winter – they are white and a good deal resemble the tame swans – there is also a vast variety of wild fowl brought to these rivers by the extreme severity of the winter.

I started out on an avenue today to run from Apley Head to Carburton – if it grows well it will hereafter be a beautiful feature of the Park.

19 February I have resolved to try to buy the whole of the Worksop Manor property – I find it impossible to [*reach terms?*] with the Duke of Portland who tires me out and disgusts me with his barefaced jesuitical deceit and eternal and tortuous trickery.

21 February The negotiation with the Duke of Portland and Mr Foljambe is at an end ... I have written today to offer £320,000 for the Worksop estate ...

22 February William went duck shooting by himself and [?] 10 couples of ducks, 1 teal, 1 snipe and 1 hare. Surprising sport for this time of the year.

I believe that I am making good progress with the purchase of the Worksop Estate. I probably may get it for £380,000.

25 February Our eyes are at last treated with a view of verdure.

26 February Our verdant prospects have been very transitory ...

Mr Mously to whom I have confided the purchase of the Worksop property called here today and he tells me that he is confident of buying the Estate for me – certainly he thinks for 380 ... [*perhaps £350,000*] ... I shall have made a famous purchase.

3 March Today I am thrown into a peck of trouble. 4 or 5 material things are gone wrongly at once, and serve to distress and perplex me.

5 March Having had occasion to remonstrate with and censure my Stewards in Wales and here, both have resigned, so that, in vulgar language, I am likely to have a pretty kettle of fish ...

6 March ... my people have begun ploughing today but the ground is in such a state that it is halfway up the horses' knees.

1838

8 March ... I am near terminating my negotiation for the purchase of Worksop Manor ... [*I have*] offered £340,000 for the whole ...

10 March Marked out a line of a new approach road from Carburton Lodge to this house which I think will come into the principal road near the Bridge and will be rather a striking feature about the place ...

12 March Saw Mr Wilmot [*Agent at Worksop Manor*] today about exchanges with Lord Scarbrough.

15 March ... I shall be detained here until the conclusion of the Worksop purchase, should it be concluded – this event is delayed by the Duke of Norfolk's illness ... [*indicates that he has now offered £350,000*] ... and if that is not satisfactory, then shall the estate and woods ... be valued and if the valuation should prove to exceed that sum I am to pay all the excess up to £370,000 ...

16 March ... The Duke of Norfolk's solicitor ... [*suggested that the sale can be concluded at £375,000*] this narrows the business ... [*he increased his offer to £365,000*] ... It is not known that I am treating for the purchase beyond £320,000 which I bid in my own name – It will, I presume, make infinite surprise [*when*] the real purchaser is declared.

18 March This is my dear Georgiana's birthday which we have all celebrated with the sincerity which our love for one of the most amiable and excellent of beings has necessarily inspired. She planted a Deodora Cedar of Lebanon on the pleasure grounds lawn.

Went to look at my new avenue and found it planted as far as from the foot of Apley Head to the turn of the road.

Fig. 51 Lime Tree Avenue, still a beautiful feature of Clumber Park.

1838

22 March   I rejoice to be able to record that I am at last successful and have begun the purchase of all the Worksop Manor properties at as I think a very fair price – namely £370,000 – this is a great and most desirable event for my family and the [*possession?*] of Clumber.

25 March   I have been informed today that the Duke of Portland has got wind (too late) of the purchase of the Worksop Manor Estates and I suppose has expressed his vexation and disappointment. He has but himself to thank for it, as he drove me to do as I have done.

28 March   Lincoln writes [*from Leamington*] that Susan has been taken suddenly and alarmingly ill with inflammation in the bowels ...

30 March   ... My purchases of Worksop manor is now secured as I learn by this post from Mr Mousley – but the vendors are not very well pleased to learn that I am the purchaser – What however [*will*] the Duke of Portland make if it?

31 March   Lincoln writes that Susan is better and considered out of danger ...

2 April   I have today completed the marking out of both sides of the new approach road from the gates near Clumber bridge to Carburton bridge ... it now only requires that the road shall be formed and stoned. The avenue from Apley head is planted as far as the end of Hardwick Wood – the new bit of road to the back from the front of the house is made and sundry plantings completed ...

3 April   [*Records that £20,000 deposit is due today on his recent purchases and that Mr Mousley is acting on his behalf in London.*]

4 April   The Duke of Norfolk, Ld Surrey and Ld [*Fitzwilliam?*] signed the contract yesterday so that now there is no question of my being the purchaser of Worksop Manor. I have always feared some trick for they are not well pleased that I am the purchaser and the Duke of Portland it may well be understood is mortally disappointed and I never was certain of what he might be able to effect – The point is irrevocably settled.

My dear Robert came home from Eton today ... He is an excellent boy.

7 April   Mr Mousley came here today to confer and settle all things relative to the Worksop purchase. Poor Fredric Mundy also came on his way to [*London?*] ...

8 April   Rode to Worksop Manor to shew the house and such part of the estate as lies on the way to Mr Mousley, who was surprised and pleased beyond measure with both. The house is a most noble and admirable structure and kept in excellent order. The offices are excellent and commodious and dry – They are strongly arched under the whole of the principal mansion.

189

1838

13 April   This being Good Friday we have all taken the Sacrament ... The coronation is fixed for the 26th June ... on a very economical scale.

14 April   ... This day put my Sigismunda picture by Correggio or [?] into the hands of the cleaner (Mr Corbett) and stood by whilst he removed the old varnish with his fingers. I had the satisfaction of seeing it turn out bright and pure.

16 April   I learned today that it is Ld Surrey who has promoted and carried the sale of Worksop Manor – the Duke of Norfolk is greatly against it and has done his utmost to prevent it. We were all there today – my daughters saw the house for the first time, that is within the house – the more I see of the place the more I am delighted with the purchase and the less I cease to wonder that I ever could be and actually am the purchaser of such a magnificent accession to the already magnificent Clumber.

18 April   William left us for London today.

19 April   Wrote a long letter to Sir R. Peel ...

20 April   I have had a day of a thousand incessant worries until I am quite tired out. Several things might be noted but I have not the energy to write them.

23 April   I was told today that a timber merchant at Worksop intimately acquainted with the Manor Woods had said that the timber upon the estate was worth at least [£200,000?] – I also heard from some authority that the Duke of Portland was astonished when he heard that I had bought the estates – and when it was confirmed to him he exclaimed – well, now the Duke has me –

24 April   Yesterday and today I have been most fully occupied with the business of my new purchase – Yesterday land and wood valuers etc. with whom every necessary arrangement was made and today with Mr Mousley.

27 April   Very busy with various improvements out of doors ...

30 April   ... the Coronation ... is postponed ...

2 May   William returned from London this morning ... [I am] wearied to death with my preparations for going – having a bad cold upon me ...

3 May   [Left Clumber at 10pm – slept at Newark.]

4 May   [Arrived in London.] ... found Lincoln here, stayed up talking till 4 o'clock ...

8 May   ... settled to sell my properties in the Town of Nottingham, immediately, we expect it to fetch above £60,000 and it does not give me now above £1,100 a year – as most of the land is unoccupied and intended for building purposes.

1838

10 May	Attended the Queen's Ball this night – This is the first that has been given at Buckingham Palace ... The Queen danced the whole night and did the honors most gracefully and agreeably.
11 May	Charles and Thomas who came up for the Ball returned to Windsor.
12 May	Dined at Lambeth Palace.
18 May	Susan, Lincoln and their children went thro' London today on their way to Kew where they have taken a house.
22 May	This is my dear Lincoln's birthday – he dined at [his] home to our regret, but we drank his health and many happy returns.
25 May	... William arrived today.
26 May	Called at Kew today. Lincoln has a very bad cold ... I am very much alarmed for the inmates of this very small and ill-situated house.
30 May	My Daughters have never seen a horse race, I took them to Epsom ...
4/6 June	[Spent at Eton and Windsor, then returned to London.]
8 June	I have received information that yesterday I became the purchaser of the Crown Manor of Newark ... I have thus obtained, in spite of enemies, all that I formerly possessed at Newark ... the whole is now my own property ...
	The Manor £3,900, the Castle Wharf 2030 and Old Toll House 180 ... My purchases of Crown property at Newark have amounted to above £71,000 –
	and altogether in Notts within the last 2 years to not less than £450,000 – little short of half a million of money – which is pretty well for one who has no capital at command.
9 June	Thomas came from Slough to London yesterday by the rail road in 35 minutes – from its being entirely new it was jerking and uneasy.
13 June	Dined today where the Duke of Wellington was ... [Comments on Wellington's failing health.]
16 June	[Dined at Sir Robert Peel's.]
18 June	... The Queen has a Ball tonight ... I and my daughters will not go – and I shall state why. [He comments that it is an inappropriate day – Waterloo Day – and also that the invitations had been distributed over several days but his had only arrived today.]
20 June	Went to the levee to present William – when I brought him up the Queen said "what another of your sons", as though there was no end to them. Tomorrow Henrietta will be presented, then all my daughters will be out and Robert will be the only one not in the world.

1838

21 June My sale at Nottm has turned out most unfortunately ... not £4,000 has been sold and about £10,000 expected by private contract ...

22 June Henrietta was presented yesterday by the Duchess of Hamilton ... I was deprived of seeing her ...

25 June ... We were at a Ball at Ld Fitzwilliam's tonight ...

27 June Nothing but Coronation thought of – it worries me to death. I shall be heartily glad when it is all over.

28 June This is the Coronation day of the Queen.

29 June Went to see the fair at Hyde Park today.

2 June A Ball at the Queen's ...

3 July Heard from Edward today from Malta ...

5 July ... a ball at the Duchess of Gloucester's given to the Queen.

9 July A fine parade of the troops in Hyde Park.

10 July ... afternoon party ... then to the House of Lords.

11 July A fine fête at Syon House given by the Duke and Duchess of Northumberland ... dinner, fireworks and dancing ...

13 July A Ball at the Duke of Cambridge's at which the Queen was present. She danced, as usual, all night.

19 July Called upon Ld. Scarbrough to try to induce him to exchange Morton for Wellow and some other estate, perhaps Maplebeck – if this can be effected Clumber will indeed be complete – Ld. Scarbrough is very civil and neighbourly and well disposed to do what is accommodating and agreeable – He does not object to the exchange but wishes for time for consideration.

20 July Poor Lincoln disclosed to me the melancholy state of his distress. Lady Susan has been greatly in the wrong and to such a degree that Lincoln feared a separation must take place. I urged patience and forbearance and wishing to see if something cannot be done to effect an accommodation. It grieves me to the soul to see his happiness thus disturbed and possibly destroyed, we must try all before abandoning hope.

21 July I have had a painful task today upon the grievous subject of yesterday. It is a heartrending business and I fear that a happy result is hopeless, but so far as the present is concerned. I trust that I have been enabled to ward off any present and immediate act ... it afflicts me to the soul to see the miserable position of my dear and suffering Son – God's ways are inscrutable ...

22 July Rode over to Kew to see and dine with Lincoln in his solitude and wretchedness ... Susan remains much the same ... Her mind is under a wrong influence ...

1838

23 July   Went to the H. of Lords for the last time today, not meaning to go there again whilst I remain in London if I can help it.

24 July   [*Writes that he had been awake all night and that he had written to Susan and Lincoln.*]

25 July   ... I have seen Lincoln today ... Susan is better ... no spasms.

26 July   [*attended*] the Queen's Ball tonight. It was thinly attended ... Charles is lame on the heel and could not go. The Queen danced with Thomas ...

28 July   Just returned from Kew where we have been to dine with and take leave of them. Susan is greatly better ... May God ... make them good, exemplary and prosperous ...

2 August   Left London 1/4 before 8 and reached Grantham a little after 9 ...

3 August   [*Left Grantham*] – breakfasted at Newark where I had business ... particularly the Castle Wharf ... I shall try to do something with it which shall make it productive but detract from the Old Castle as little as possible.

4 August   [*At Clumber*] – Charles and Thomas arrived today.

7 August   A letter arrived from my dear Edward dated Portsmouth ...

8 August   ... I have seldom much enjoyment of the country as my time is much taken up ...

9 August   Perpetual rain ... unfavorable to the harvest ...

           [*Wheat selling at £4.4.0 a quarter.*]

10 August ... My Steward (*Parkinson*) is about to leave me ... I believe I have made a good choice in appointing Mr Edward Wilmot ... £800 a year ...

11 August Lincoln with his family went in a steamer ... to Antwerp.

           Mr Mousley and Mr Hassell came early this morning [*regarding land valuations at Worksop*] – afterwards we rode over the farms on this side as far as Sloswicks a ride of 14 or 15 miles.

13 August Rode with my family to see Elkesley parsonage which Mr Thompson is about to alter and make a fit residence for a clergyman – it might be and will be a beautiful thing in good hands.

14 August Commenced my harvest today – the crops are excellent and the corn in a very good state for cutting ...

15 August Lincoln and Susan have arrived safely at Antwerp ...

16 August Left Clumber early this morning [*for Hafod*]. Stopt at Derby ... reached Birmingham rather late in the evening.

17 August ... left Kidderminster, where we found a wretched accommodation and only three rooms and 5 beds amongst us –

1838

18 August   ... [*Edward caught up with them whilst they were out walking*] – ... [*he*] ran on and flew into our arms – it was a delightful meeting and most singular in the Welsh mountains.

22 August   The rain so perpetual, the weather so cold, the Sun so rarely seen ... The poor people cannot get their turf and will not be able to lay in any fuel for the winter and even now have not where-withal to bake their bread –

25 August   [*He bemoans*] ... the palpable inefficiency of my Steward, Mr Haslam, who I believe has done his best, but is not a man of business or skilled in estate affairs.

27 August   The people of this country have become actively unpleasant to me ... worry, thwart and perplex me ...

30 August   [*Describes a land ownership dispute with a neighbour, Lord Lisburne*] – determined to keep my temper ...

3 September   Went today to Rhayader with my 5 sons to shoot grouse in the neighbourhood ...

4 September   Out again ... I and William to Cwmelan [*where they killed 10 1/2 brace*] – and the others went fishing and killed 85 salmon and trouts.

9 September   ... Here ... my people have gone to sleep ... it is no easy task to drive things on in this country ...

11 September   My harvest at Clumber is all in and very well gotten – it must be the most valuable stack yard corn and hay that ... I have ever had.

12 September   Wrote to Susan today ... at Frankfurt when I last heard ...

    [*Heard from Mr Curtis, a magistrate residing at Sutton-in-Ashfield, that 350 people had enrolled in the*] – 'National Association for political purposes' – training diligently by night ... some muskets and arms have arrived from Birmingham.

    [*He intends to advise Mr Curtis*] – watch the traitors vigilantly but secretly.

16 September   [*Notes that the sale of his remaining Yorkshire property had gone well – £20,000 worth already sold, another £5,000 to come from private contracts*] – thus ends the once famed possession of Aldborough and Borobridge which used to send 4 members to parliament.

18 September   Mr Haslam [*Steward*] is going to leave me and his successor Mr Kendall came today ...

19 September   ... The Birmingham rail road opened the day before yesterday ... 112 miles from London which can be travelled in 3 hours – The trains will travel night and day upon this road. [*First class single fare £1.12.6d.*]

1838

21 September	My dear Robert left me this morning for Eton.
25 September	Riding about the different farms with my new Steward.
28 September	I have had a most unpleasant day today ... [*No detail given.*]
3 October	[*Looked at possible 'mining grounds' – notes that the mine at Cwmystwyth makes about £13,000 a year.*]
4 October	A letter from Lincoln from Munich ... all well.
6 October	Came to Aberystwyth for a day or two ... The breakwater has advanced considerably ... In the town they have established gas lighting and a supply of water and sewage only is now wanted to make the town complete ... improvements originated by me, when first I came here 5 years ago, I wrote a paper which was published recommending all these improvements ... all but one of them has been accomplished ... population about 6,000 ...
7 October	We all went to Church ...
8 October	... returned to Hafod.
9 October	Mr Walker of Chester called to confer on mining matters ... his Mr Taylor will arrange to survey the ground ... Mr Walker tells me that mines are not worth more than 4 years purchase.
13 October	... Snow ... bitterly cold.
14 October	... a hurricane with a deluge of rain ...
	- The announced marriage of the Queen with a son of the Duke of Saxe Weimar ...
18 October	... I left Hafod at 4 o'clock in my little open carriage, Caroline with me in the carriage and 2 of my sons on the box – it was a dreadful day pouring torrents of rain, with a strong driving wind blowing a hurricane ... arrived at Newtown ... we had no Servant with us ... [*slept*] ... on to Welch pool we found the others.
19 October	We finally arrived at Lichfield [*after dining at Shrewsbury*] ...
20 October	[*Left Lichfield, breakfasted at Derby ... on to Clumber*] – we found Miss Spencer who was perfectly overjoyed to see us again – This place is in the highest order, and has improved beyond description, even in the short time since we left it – the growth of the trees is something miraculous ..
21 October	Sunday – nothing new today – looking about the place.
22 October	... Shot upon my new Manor of Worksop for the first time – plenty of game.
27 October	... The donkies 2 male and a female which Edward procured for me at Malta have at last arrived in London ...
30 October	... I am expecting Sir Robert Peel in a few days, I mean to collect the gentry and yeomen as numerously as time will permit – it will do most good to unite our desultory allies, at this critical moment.

1838

1 November   Sir R. Peel came today, tomorrow I shall have from 40 to 50 persons to dinner and I trust that it will do good and give satisfaction.

2 November   My feast went off admirably. [*Mentions the Dining Room – used for many years as a lumber room for the library and other furniture*] – became a splendid banqueting room and entirely on this occasion eclipsed all its former beauty and magnificence – ... 40 to 50 persons, 40 were placed at one table by leaving out the sideboard, and those who could not sit at the first table had a table to themselves in the end corner of the room – Such a reunion of people has not occurred before in Notts in any one house.

I had but two refusals, one from Mr Ramsden, the other from Welbeck – As it was to meet Sir Robert Peel, to promote good will and cement our union – I invited [*our*] principal yeoman, or gentleman farmers, who do not ordinarily come to our houses and they were perfectly delighted at the attention. 14 of the party were ladies, [*including Lady Sh....... ?*] every one seemed to be pleased and in the best humour and I never before saw any meeting which gave such entire satisfaction. In the morning we went out shooting. Sir R.P. is an excellent shot, the weather unfortunately not favorable – so that we were driven home an hour and a half before dinner time. I therefore appraised Sir R. of my intention to propose his health at the dinner – when the time arrived, I gave the Queen and Constitution and Church and State as the first toast ... My guests and the ladies were delighted to have the opportunity of hearing a speech from Sir Robert – In all this I flatter myself that I have hit off exactly what is right ...

3 November   Out pheasant hunting today we killed 86 – beside other game ...

4 November   We went to Worksop Manor and I shewed Sir R.P. the house and the extent of the estate, he advises me to pull the house down, and I think that I shall eventually follow his advice – especially as the furniture has been removed from out of the house ...

5 November   The donkies which Edward bought for me at Malta at last arrived, the poor animals are in a deplorable plight, wounded and bruised all over, their bodies mere skeletons. The mare is 15 hands high and a surprising creature and very gentle – the two stallions are not so large, but very fine animals and very savage and untamed – Edward paid 50 [*Guineas*] for the mare.

1838

12 November   I launched my new ship today – She looks very well upon the water and does credit to the builder. The two men who have been principally engaged in building her are father and son of the name of Spencer – and singularly enough, the father of the elder Spencer (with him) built the old Lincoln in 1814 or 15 – the former employed by a builder of the name of Ratsey, the other now built by one of the name of White – both of the Isle of Wight.

Fig. 52

13 November   ... my Sons Charles and Thomas left me today to join their regiments in London.

16 November   I have had the best rent collection that I have yet known and my new Steward (Wilmot) has collected a larger sum by nearly double that has heretofore been paid to my account by any former Steward – this is a great satisfaction to me – it gives me confidence in my new administration.

17 November   I am quite incapacitated by a sort of attack of cold, toothache and swelling of the face and gums – I suffer very much.

19 November   [*Still unwell*] – ... I can hardly open my mouth.

28 November   I have discontinued my journal until this day from the state into which I was thrown by the inflammatory attack ... I now feel remarkably well in health, but reduced in bodily strength.

30 November   ... I went downstairs this afternoon for the first time.

3 December   I have today for the first time been made acquainted with an idea of some objection to the Worksop Manor title. I think nothing of it and believe it to be some juggle of the lawyers – however, it [*obliques?*] and constrains my operations – I cannot proceed with my sales to Messrs Foljambe and Machin or with the sale of timber which is a most material loss.

I went out today for the first time nearly approximating to 3 weeks.

4 December   A letter from Lincoln from Rome ... Susan is pregnant and would probably be confined about the end of March.

1838

5 December	[*Mentions that Robert had now finished his time at Eton but not yet arrived home.*]
6 December	[*Notes that he has been involved in an accident*] – a table fell upon my great toe and has crushed and injured it ...
10 December	I am quite laid up with the state of my foot, I must lose the nail.
13 December	I find that the man who I left at Hafod as Steward ... is most unworthy ... I shall instantly discharge and supersede him.
	The vast estate of Rossington, belonging to the Corporation of Doncaster was sold today by auction. [*It adjoined the northern boundary of the Duke's 1,500 acre estate at Martin – his bid of £90,000 for Rossington was unsuccessful.*]
14 December	An incendary fire took place on the premises of a tenant farmer [*Low?*] at Maplebeck ...
17 December	My toe is very bad today –
20 December	... I can only get about upon crutches.
21 December	Went today in the carriage to see Shire oaks and the intervening part of the Worksop Manor Estate – I was delighted with all I saw – The Estate possesses every advantage is in very good condition and is admirably allotted –
	For the 254 acres which Mr Machin wishes to have near his own house and property I have asked £28,000 and after seeing it I am confident that it is worth more –
	Of Mr Foljambe for the 300 acres adjoining Osberton Estate I have asked £45,000 and these sums they must pay or they will not have the estates.
23 December	My toenail came off today and now I hope that I may begin to mend.
24 December	.. This is Christmas Eve!!! With what wonderful rapidity this last year has escaped! ...
25 December	This morning as usual after the usual greetings, we went to Chapel and all received the Sacrament ...
	I have been greatly disturbed to learn by today's post, that dear and excellent Old Rowlands has suddenly failed and is sinking fast – I shall never see him again, from my earliest youth I have ever known him the faithful and affectionate and devoted friend of our family – His place cannot be supplied, the void will be great and painful.
27 December	Dear, good and excellent old Rowlands is gone! He expired on the night of Christmas day – His nephew [*Peter?*] Webster tells me that on the day preceding his death he prayed for me heartily for me and all my family! I do indeed lament that I may never again see his long known countenance and that the last of

1838

the old connection is now swept away. Rowlands was of a good Welch family of Pwllheli in Caernarvonshire. His brother was valet to my grandfather and is painted in the shooting picture. Griffiths ['old Rowlands'] just deceased was Butler and so continued to my grandfather's death – he had formerly been with my uncle Lord John at Oxford. In his exterior he had all the manner and appearance of a high gentleman of the old school – he was full of life and spirits – remarkably temperate and moderate in all things and I believe as good a man as could be found – his zeal, affection, devotion and attachment were unbounded – he would have gone to the world's end for me – his intelligence, activity, energy and integrity were remarkable and gained him the respect and confidence of all ranks – He was as faithfull in his duty to God as in his discharge of those that were due to me – He was a beau ideal of what a servant could and should be – His age about 88 and retaining his faculties to the last.

31 December ... I have arrived at the end of my book, oddly enough [*meaning that he had also reached the last page in this particular volume*], and of the year 1838 ... My health ... has been unusually good until latterly ... Politically I have been a cipher, and so I intend to remain unless I am called upon for exertion which is not likely ...

End of 1838

Fig. 53 *"I suppose that it must be the largest basin out of a single block in the world".*
[Fig. 52 – See Diary entry – 25 January 1839]

1 January ... Time passes quickly on and I begin to find that my years yet to come, in the common course of events, may not occupy many more books ...

By God's blessing I will be a firm upholder of his worship and of that Christianity which, as I think, is most pure in the Protestant faith held by the Church of England. There is an awful struggle before us, Popery is making every effort against us and more successful than could have been supposed in these times – the contest will be fierce, but the issue is not doubtful. Popery will eventually fall and at no distant day ... the contest will be one for life or death ...

2 January Attended a meeting at Worksop for the purpose of considering whether we should not displace the schoolmaster, who has proved himself very unfit for the situation – We did replace him. The Duke of Portland, G[*ally*?] Knight and other subscribers were there.

3 January [*He received information that* 'the people are arming'.]

6 January [*He was told that* 'the country is to be divided into 49 divisions by the party now hatching mischief ... ']

7 January A most curious storm of wind arose in the night ... it has done very great damage ... the [*lead*?] has been blown up on the roof of this house and trees immeasurable have been ['rooted' *or* 'rocked'?] up and broken ...

9 January Came to Stoke [*Hall*], Sir R. Bromley's, with my 4 daughters and Edward, to attend a ball at Newark tomorrow.

10 January The ground, as usual when we attend a Newark ball, covered with snow ... Henrietta is unwell with one of her bad sick headaches and is not able to leave the room and go to the ball. – The ball was very well attended ... William was one of the Stewards officiating most assiduously ... The Newarkers seemed much pleased with our presence and were more civil and attentive than on many former occasion.

1839

11 January	We did not return home here [*Stoke*] until ½ past 4 this morning ... Henrietta is quite recovered. We have a spring day today and the snow quite disappeared ... [*He notes reports of storm damage around the country*] ... at Hafod the house and wood have sustained much damage.
12 January	Returned to Clumber this afternoon ... last night there was a dance at Stoke which lasted till between 2 and 3 o'clock. Stopped at Newark on my way, did business with Tallents and went to see the building of the new warehouse, near the bridge on the Castle Wharf.
14 January	Arrived at Drayton Manor. [*To see Sir Robert Peel.*]
17 January	Out shooting today ... my host's [*political*] sentiments, as far as I have heard them, coincide with mine – I think he will do well for the future.
19 January	... returned by way of Nottingham but reached it too late to see any thing, to the great disappointment of my daughters, who never before passed through it ... [*reached*] Clumber ... 9 o'clock.
20 January	I find that in the late tempest we lost about 1500 trees – above 1200 in Clumber and above 200 in Apley Head.
23 January	As I was out shooting today at the Decoy, I had the misfortune to sprain or rather to dislocate my ankle which, however, fortunately came into its place again – The pain and swelling has been very great and I am again unable to get about.
24 January	... I attended a meeting at Newark ... all the Clergy of the County and many of the gentlemen ... [*regarding extending education on the principles of the Established Church.*]
25 January	... My large marble basin for the fountain arrived today – the waggon which brought it was drawn to the terrace and now remains there with the package upon it. I shall erect a stage like a ship's way and slide it from the waggon down the reservoir, keeping a sufficiently high elevation. I am quite pleased to have it here at last – it must be three years since I expected to receive it, but there has been so much difficulty attending the finding of so large a block without a flaw, and then in making and transporting it, that I began to think I never should obtain it – I suppose that it must be the largest basin out of a single block in the world.
30 January	This being my birth day, Combermere, with the kindest intentions and in the kindest manner proposed my health after dinner at a very large party now in the house. Of course, I was obliged to reply which is never a pleasant task ...
31 January	The Duchess of Sutherland is dead ...

1839

1 February   A singular invention and discovery has been made, by which the objects in a camera obscura are fixed upon a material, so as to form a permanent representation of the scene reflected ... The discovery was promulgated in France by M. Daguerre, which induced Mr Talbot immediately to announce and exhibit similar specimens of his preparation – and [it] appears that he made the discovery several years ago and was just about to make it known to the scientific world – it is singular that such an extraordinary discovery should be declared simultaneously.

2 February   The last of my guests left me today and we have a clear house.

4 February   [Started out for London] – my leg is better and my cold also ... slept at Wandsford.

5 February   ... breakfast at Eaton ... London 1/4 past 6 ...

7 February   I have today learned with extreme concern the death of Admiral Sotheron ... quite unexpected – he had been ill for some time ... He had long been my esteemed and most attached friend. I knew him first when he succeeded to the Kirklington Estate on the death of Mrs Whetham, nearly 30 years ago ...

9 February   Left London for Worthing accompanied by Charles and Robert ... I am come to place Robert with a Tutor.

10 February   Went to call upon Mr [?] at Tanning to make his acquaintance.

11 February   ... Left Worthing for London – [bad road conditions] – we were 7 horses on the road.

15 February   [Left London with Charles and Thomas] – slept at Stevenage ... [mentions 'people calling themselves Chartists'].

16 February   Arrived at Clumber at 10 o'clock found all well.

17 February   Ground covered with snow ... I am laid up with a fresh complaint, a dysenteric disorder of the bowels.

18 February   Better today ...

19 February   A letter from Lincoln of the 11th from Genoa. Susan not very well.

20 February   The Duke of Portland and Ld Manvers called here today by appointment – They wished to confer with me upon the state of the country and to consult what would be the best to be done to provide for the security of this county. The arming of the people seems to have created great alarm especially about Mansfield. The Duke of Portland proposed to endeavour to establish an armed association of defence to which proposal I assented [altho'] I think it is scarcely required here ...

24 February   I was out on horseback today and about my work again and putting things in train, which for a long time I have been unable to look after.

1839

25 February	[*A police officer called to tell the Duke that* 'an Inspector, sergeant and 30 men' *had arrived for duty at Mansfield and awaited his orders.*] ...

I determined to go and see the Duke of Portland and told the Inspector and his Sergt. to follow me there. I found the Duke of Portland ... he feigned entire surprise at first ... I then saw into the whole business ... and I was confident that my hypocritical friend was at the bottom of the whole proceeding. The men had been sent out at his request and to satisfy his alarmed cravings. His Grace is dreadfully alarmed for his Mansfield property ... the expense of these men will be enormous, not less than £12 a day, and I am confident that the county neither will or ought to sanction it. His Grace has also artfully contrived a general meeting of Magistrates, to consider the state of the county ... This is all very right to a certain extent ... [*but*] I am the [*Lord Lieutenant*] of the County and he might be frank with me.

26 February ... [*Went to Mansfield Woodhouse to call on Col. Neal, Senior Magistrate at Mansfield.*]

3 March A letter from Lincoln dated Paris 28 Feb. – all well ...

4 March Attended a General meeting of Magistrates at Southwell ... went off very well upon the whole ... and will be beneficial.

6 March ... deep snow ...

7 March Lincoln and his family are arrived in London.

The Duke of Portland called upon me again today ... I certainly shall not be a dupe to his sly and subtle manoeuvres.

11 March The Duke of Portland is acting very unpleasantly towards me.

I have felt it incumbent upon me to remind him that he is not the only wise man in existence.

14 March I have at last concluded the purchase of the furniture etc. at Worksop Manor. I am to pay £3,600 for every thing remaining. I shall sell the greater part of it and I fear that I may then find that I have given too much ...

In another letter from Ld. J. Russell, he informs me that ... I cannot arm and train the special constables ...

16 March Attended the Assize at Nottingham – I took the opportunity of meeting and speaking with the gentlemen of the Co., relative to the state of the county. In the grand jury room I read a long paper which I wrote this morning ... I afterwards dined with the Judges ... and afterwards retired to the Inn, where I had a good deal to do which kept me till between 11 and 12. At Mansfield the people were up and about at that late hour, they assembled near my carriage and ['*growled*' *or* '*grumbled*'?] when I drove off. I reached Clumber a little after 2 o'clock.

1839

18 March   I met the Duke of Portland today ...

19 March   ... Went to Worksop Manor yesterday and today to settle various things in and out of the house – not a very easy task.

22 March   Just returned from Nottingham where I saw the General of the Brigade, Major Sir C. O'Donnell, and some of the Magistrates... I have ordered the Yeomanry to be held in readiness ... [*There was concern over a public meeting to be held on the 25th.*]

25 March   Robert arrived today ...

27 March   ... I rode to Mansfield ...

28 March   ... I am informed ... that Oastler eulogised me to a Nottm mob and was cheered – wonders will never cease!

29 March   We all took the sacrament after service today.

1 April   Timber sells freely at present ... I could sell any quantity of larch that I could cut down – without doing injury to the woods. I cannot cut down above 60,000 feet of larch which I am selling for the rail road, at 1s 8d a foot, taking the trees as they are cut down – in oak it is the same. Ship builders from Hull have applied anxiously for such timber as I can let them have, one man said he should be happy if I could let him have £30,000 of timber – oak sells from 2s 6d to 3s 6d a foot.

2 April   ... One of my works is nearly completed. The avenue from Apley Head is finished nearly up to the West fields and in a few days it will be completed to Carburton bridge.

4 April   Mail coaches are being discontinued everywhere and by railway substituted for them ... I shall be surprised if the regularity of the post be not seriously affected.

6 April   ... we miss dear Robert who returned to Tanning yesterday ... He is a charming youth and every body likes him.

8 April   Susan was brought to bed yesterday ... morning of a girl – their first ... a fat, strong, large baby but not so pretty as the boys were – Susan had a very good time and was well.

12 April   A letter yesterday from Mr Keary my new Steward in Wales ...

13 April   ... My new Steward, Mr Wilmot, laid before me the result of his and Mr Hassell's consideration of the best arrangement and allotment of the Norfolk [*Worksop*] property, and it is arranged that nearly 400 acres shall be allotted to accommodation land and quarters, to be let at from 3 to 4£ per acre. The people will gladly take the land at this price and thank me for it.

15 April   This spring is more backward than the last – hitherto we have had perpetual E. and N.E. rain cutting and drying – Yesterday and today the wind is come round to the westward – the larches are beginning to flower, and the shrubs are beginning to

1839

look a little green-ish, but there is no grass and vegetation makes scarcely any progress. There are more turnips remaining this year than ever I knew – many whole fields are yet untouched.

16 April   [*He bemoans the* 'infamous set' *that* 'surrounds the Court'.] –

For myself, neither I nor my family will go near the Court whilst the miscreants who infect it remain there.

18 April   ... went in the afternoon to Worksop Manor to meet the auctioneer (*Payne*) and select such things as I wish to retain at the Sale.

23 April   [*Started for London – slept at Grantham.*]

24 April   Arrived in London at 9 this evening – Found Charles here ... Lincoln came later.

30 April   This evening I received a letter from Ld John Russell informing me that the Queen had no further occasion for my services as Ld. Lieut. and Cust. Rotuloram of Notts. – This has arisen from an altercation with the Ld Chancellor, who wished to put men into the Commission not recommended by me and to whom I objected – he however at last put them in, upon which, I wrote to him in a manner not very courteous and for this I have been dismissed from the Lieutenancy – it is true [*that?*] 3 days ago the Chancellor wrote a few lines to me sending me a copy of my letter from Clumber, presuming it was written in haste and enquiring if I wished to withdraw it – to which I replied that if he would withdraw his appointments I would withdraw my letter – upon this followed my dismissal.

1 May   Called upon the Duke of Wellington ... [*he*] advised me to be quiet and told me that I was in the wrong. Afterwards I went to Sir R. Peel ...[*he*] advised me to write a letter ... [*I*] told him ... it would not do to have any appearance of begging to be restored – In the evening called on Ld. [*Lyndhurst?*] he was of the same opinion with the others, that I was in the wrong – I afterwards went to Ld Mansfield and he put the business on the right footing – he recommended the high ground – short apology, [*remonstrance and allude?*] to past services – On going home and late at night I went to work and wrote my letter, which tomorrow morning I shall send for his inspection.

2 May   Ld Mansfield approves of my letter ... Lincoln afterwards came in and I shewed it to him – we cut a good deal of my letter, condensed it and put it in good shape. Afterwards I had a long interview with the Duke of Wellington ... after [*going*] to see others I went home, made a few alterations in my letter, copied it off – Rode along to the Home Office and left my letter for Sir J. Russell.

1839

3 May   The public press has taken up my dismissal warmly – The kindness of friends is overpowering, many have shown a warm [*action?*] on what concerns me-

[*Receives a reply from Lord John Russell, Home Secretary – no reversing of the dismissal was offered.*] ... here the matter is ended ... It now appears that Ld. Scarborough is to be my successor.

4 May   ... the Queen is despised and disliked ...

6 May   ... the Queen was groaned at and insulted when she passed thro' the Square today on horseback.

8 May   ... Out at 1/4 past 9, I was at the rail road station and about 20 minutes before 10, I started [*on?*] the train of the Birmingham railway – This is the first time that I ever was on a rail road. I went in my own carriage – and alone – and I must say I did not at first altogether relish the experience – The novelty, the noise, the speed, the irresistible force, all impart an impression of astonishment ... In less than 41/2 hours we arrived without the slightest incident at Rugby, 82 miles where I left the railroad and posted to Nottingham where I arrived at 7.

9 May   ... rode to the reviewing ground on Bulwell Common at 12 o'clock ... In the evening I dined with the Col. Moore and the officers – could not leave the table till past 12 o'clock - after sitting at the Inn drinking tea, I left Nottingham for Newark, where I did not arrive before 3 and went immediately to bed.

10 May   William, who is Captain of one of the Troops of the Sherwood Rangers came into my room at 8 o'clock, before I was up, and gave me an account of all going on here ... The Regiment assembled in a large field at Holme, belonging to my tenant Wells ... Dined with the officers, as yesterday, and had to make a speech ..

11 May   This morning the Sherwood Rangers marched to Mansfield – poor fellows ... The post arrived and brought intelligence that Sir R. Peel, who had been charged by the Queen to form a Ministry, after having completed his arrangements had been obliged to resign, as the Queen refuses to part with her Court ladies ... Sir R. has been caught in his enemies trap ... He should have known better than to insist upon a point which was sure to meet with resistance on the part of our obstinate, spoiled and inexperienced young Queen. Arrived at Clumber in a sorry mood – which is not and will not be relieved by society – for I have no one with me and am in perfect solitude.

13 May   ... Went over to Ranby and brought from there the tithe deeds for Lincoln's use, who means to raise a mortgage upon the Estate.

1839

14 May   The Duke of Portland called this morning, he is anxious about raising armed associations and wishes to form one at Worksop. – I then drove over to Mansfield to learn how things were proceeding there ... Winter has returned, again it has snowed most of the day. Mr Mousley came this evening on business.

18 May   After riding over to Worksop Manor to see how all the arrangements for the Sale had been made – I met my carriage on Norton common and went to Mansfield.

22 May   [*To Nottingham, via Mansfield.*]

23 May   [*From Nottingham to Rugby – via Loughborough and Leicester – he caught the train from Rugby at 2.30 pm and arrived in London* 'at 7 o'clock without any accident ...']

24 May   I found a very unpleasant account here, respecting the state of my affairs – Mousley's letters are full of complaints and he appears as if he wished to get rid of a business which he can hardly manage from its magnitude. He tells me that unless I can instantly find 50 or 60,000£, to complete my purchase, that the Duke of Norfolk will cancel the agreement and that I shall lose my deposit and the estate – he represents all the difficulties but offers no remedy or expedient to dissipate them. Went to Coutts to ask them to advance the money, they demurred and referred me to their Solicitors who gave me no encouragement – I am at my wit's end now to obtain the money to complete the purchase and am and have been prodigiously perplexed and harassed, to devise means and to prepare to meet so immense a payment. I have been consulting and contriving and tomorrow I shall see Mousley who is unwell.

25 May   A long conference with Mousley – at last he has made a proposal which I think must be successful. The trustees are to be requested to give up the first claim on Nottingham and take a second on Worksop etc. I am to offer Nottingham, with Cwmelan, Dolyclettwr and Park Lane House, as security for £55,000, and I write to Coutts to propose a conference on the 27th.

27 May   Called on the D. of Norfolk and proposed to him to grant me an extension of the period for completing the purchase – he was very civil and said that tho' inconvenient he would consult his legal advisers and hoped that there was no doubt as to his being able to accede to my request – I then rode to Coutts where I found Mousley. and after explanation and debate Mr Marjoribanks and Coulthurst, said they hoped that they may be able to accommodate me – I am to obtain the rentals from Wales by the 29th or 30th and then a decision is to be made.

1839

28 May   ... [*The Welsh rentals had arrived.*] ... the valuation of the Nottm.
Property ... amount to an enormous sum, somewhere about
£180,000, I think, for 91 acres in the Park and between 80 and
90 in the Meadows – present rent about £600 ... In the evening
a letter from Mousley ... he had at last settled with the Bankers
and I am to have £55,000 on the security named above ... I trust
that I may now reckon upon some remission of my anxiety ... I
am, besides this, distracted by numerous other calls upon me
which I cannot answer and must from necessity postpone.

5 June   Went to the levée today – Being stripped of my Lieut. uniform
and having only the black full dress which I wore at the king's
funeral, I put it on thinking it must be appropriate for the
occasion, and I have reason to think that the reflection which it
conveyed was neither lost upon Her Majesty or the company
present.

I observed that I was an object of remark to every one who
knows me by sight.

6 June   In the evening to a party at the Duchess of Gloucester's. The
Queen etc. were there. As there was dancing, the Queen of
course figured away in every dance – She was very glum,
ungracious and unamiable and must have given more offence
than pleasure ...

10 June   Attended at the H. of Lords, to settle about a Nottm. enclosure
bill relating to the open lands near to the Park – I wish to insert
a clause to enable me to make a tunnell [*sic*] for communication.
This the parties were unwilling to grant.

11 June   [*Went to Coutt's bank, where it was agreed that the Settlement
date for the purchase of Worksop Manor etc. would be the 12ᵗʰ –
the monies to be advanced by Coutts would be on a joint bond
with the Duke and Lord Lincoln.*]

12 June   ... [*Dealt with business*] – about the enclosure of the land
between the Ropewalk and the Derby road ... I afterwards
proceeded with Lincoln to Mousley's chamber in Stone buildings
... we went to Coutt's ... signed various deeds ... their loan which
will now be £67,000 ... [*we then*] met all the Duke of Norfolk's
people ... I am now in possession, the title made over to me – I
have paid the whole purchase money amounting to £370,000 –
with interest added – My family was great and possessed much
consideration before – but this places it upon a pinnacle –

The conclusion makes me very happy and the possession is truly
honorable to me and mine – and when I consider that I have
obtained it fairly and justly and by the sweat of my brow I feel
consciously satisfied with the result.

1839

18 June   We were yesterday invited to a Ball at the Palace but we have been so [*slighted*?] and disrespectfully treated (besides the state of the Court) that I would not go – and thus mark my sense of the treatment.

24 June   An offer has been made to me to purchase the stone from the Steetley quarry for building the Houses of Parliament on terms of permitting the Govt. to work the quarry themselves, exclusively, and to pay me a Royalty of 3 halfpence a cubic foot.

26 June   Dined at Ld. Mansfield's ...

27 June   ... been for some time with business concerning Lincoln which harrasses him and me very severely.

29 June   My dear Lincoln's business is settled more prosperously than I had hoped for ...

4 July   We met this morning at the Duke of Wellington's ... on my return from dinner I found that William had arrived.

8 July   Confined to the house with a very bad cold.

11 July   This morning Lincoln came over before I went out ... [*the Duke expresses his happiness at this meeting. He then went to the House of Lords, on to Buckingham Palace and back to the Lords in the evening.*]

13 July   Went to the tilting ground ... ludicrous exhibition ...

16 July   ... I am wretchedly straightened as to money and shall not have enough left to pay my travelling expenses.

17 July   In the evening went to Astley's with many of my family ...

20 July   Attended a large meeting at the Duke of Wellington's today, the theme was the Irish Corporation ...

25 July   I went down to the H. of Lords ... [*He intended to raise the question of the appointment of Nottinghamshire Magistrates – over which he had been dismissed as Lord Lieutenant. However, he was warned that should he do so, then the correspondence between himself and the Lord Chancellor would be made public.*]

28 July   I have suffered very greatly all night and day, with a violent tooth ache on one side and a very painful gathering on the other – yesterday an offending tooth was extracted which caused this malady ...

29 July   Went to my Dentist and had the other tooth extracted to my very great comfort ...

30 July   Passed a wretched night.

31 July   ... I have now great difficulty in opening my mouth and masticating my food. [*He had again called on the dentist and had yet another tooth extracted – very painfully and having pressed the dentist, at length, as to the necessity.*]

1839

1 August   ... I feel much worse ...

3 August   I remain in the same state ...

8 August   Sir B. Brodie opened the tumor ...

11 August   Better today ...

12 August   [*He set out to take the train to Derby but was obliged to go to Birmingham.*] – Here I had the delights of a good night ...

13 August   [*Travelled by rail from Birmingham to Derby*] – reached in safety ... ready for a good breakfast ... went on [*via Mansfield*] to Clumber.

14 August   Saw the Duke of Portland this morning. [*Regarding 'Chartist' outbreaks.*]

15 August   [*Unwell again.*]

22 August   ... I am now in better health.

23 August   Left Clumber this morning ... reached Shrewsbury ...

My dear Caroline attains her 21 today – May God bless her and grant her long and good life.

24 August   ... [*They arrived at Hafod*] – we have been welcomed to Wales by the usual torrents of rain.

25 August   [*Sunday*] ... not gone to Church and have read prayers at home.

26 August   I have been looking about near home with Mr Keary at the works which have been going on and I have the satisfaction to find that whatever he has done, he has done well ... He appears to be respected by all here ...

Craigie [*an estate cottage*] has been enlarged and done up and is remarkably pretty – the roads are in good order, other houses putting in order and, as far as our present limited means go, all has been done ... that could be done.

27/29 August   [*Rain.*]

30 August   ... I was very ill yesterday with damp cold rheumatism and tooth ache. I am much better today.

1 September   Another wet day – we could not go to Church. I read prayers at home.

3 September   Went this afternoon to Aberystwyth to be ready to attend a Play which I bespeak tomorrow at the theatre.

4 September   The people here are much pleased to see us. I visited the new pier this morning ... about 200 yards are now built ... the Harbour is improved beyond expectations ... [*He then reports, with much detail, the manner in which the crowd greeted him on his way to the theatre.*] ... I proceeded ... in procession and there had a frequent repetition of their kind feeling. I should be very insensible if I were not, as I am, much gratified by their kind and grateful feelings of expression towards me.

1839

5 September	... I first came here 6 years ago. The change [*in the town's improvement*] is entirely attributable to me – Harbour, gas lights – water works – sewers, cleansing water closets etc.
6 September	Torrents of rain ...
7 September	Very high tide ... I am bathing here in the warm bath – and have received benefit from it as well as from the air.
11 September	[*Still at Aberystwyth – having treatment for throat trouble.*]
12 September	... rain every day ...
16 September	Went to a play ...
17 September	I have been tormented by tooth ache ... Dr. Williams administered creosote and the effects have been so magical and effectual as to remove all my aches and ailment ...
18 September	... Before leaving Aberystwyth, I determined to give my two dear Sons a view of North Wales ... [*went to*] Tan y brolch where we slept
19 September	... breakfasted at Beddgelert – 'The Goat' is a very nice Inn and remarkably clean and comfortable – we went to fish – only caught 4 trout ...
20 September	Returned to Aberystwyth ... travelled in a light carriage and often with 4 horses.
21 September	[*Returned to Hafod via Devil's Bridge.*] – to see the improvements which I have been making at the Inn ... may be when finished ... one of the best Inns to be found any where ...

Fig. 54
The 'Hafod Arms Hotel'

23 September	[*Went grouse shooting.*]

1839

27 September   ... the rain continues ...

1 October   This being a fine day we determined to go over to Rhayader to shoot on the moors. We had been told that the grouse were very plentiful but the word of a Welshman is very like that of a Gascon, not to be believed and so we found it ... We slept at the Red Lion, as usual, a horrid place, stinking and dirty and ill regulated.

2 October   A very rainy day ...

3 October   [*Back to Hafod.*]

5 October   The deed which I executed a few days ago and forwarded to the Rev. Hides, Vicar of Greasley, giving the site of Chapel and Churchyard at Brinsley to the Church for ever, arrived just in time and the Chapel and ground was consecrated by the Bishop of Lincoln on the 1st of this month.

6 October   [*Went to a church service in Hafod, where he was astonished at the Minister's behaviour*] – singing ... and accompanying himself upon an accordion – it was a painful and very unbecoming exhibition and what I presume could only be met with in a Welsh Church.

7 October   [*Pheasant shooting.*]

8 October   [*To Aberystwyth*] – ... I and William went to accompany Robert who goes by the mail tomorrow on his return to his tutor at Tanning.

9 October   At 8 this morning, my dear Robert left us ... so agreeable, cheerful, droll, amiable and good humoured ... We returned to Hafod this afternoon.

11 October   [*Mentions his lack of success in making his mining interests pay.*]

12 October   This was a rainy morning, and my companion William and I opened some of the boxes containing the books and arranged them in view – we found them in a bad state with damp and the worm had begun upon several of them. I mean to select the best and all the [?] for Clumber.

14 October   Robert is arrived safely in London.

15 October   It is said that Parliament is to be assembled in November to deliberate upon the Queen's marriage to one of the Coburgs – This family is so distasteful to the Country, and however good the youth may be, the match will not go down and will cause much opposition and general discontent and dissatisfaction.

17 October   We are still engaged in unpacking the books here, out of the cases in which they have been laid whilst the house has been repairing and altering. Amongst them are many magnificent and rare books ... there are some valuable treasures among the books – the library, I am confident, is worth at least £20,000 ...

213

19 October	[*With Mr Butler, on mining matters.*]
20 October	[*With Mr Whitling regarding* 'building matters here'.]
21 October	[*Mentions the report of a rich copper vein on his estate.*]
24 October	... This is Norrison's housewarming at the Devil's bridge – he expects a large company.

[*The Duke carried on with the sorting and selecting of books at Hafod.*]

29 October	Snow today and very cold ...
30 October	This afternoon I completed the purchase of L.Pugh's property – a very great acquisition to Hafod ... I paid down today £3,100 – ten per cent money and I expect that it will easily produce [?] £120 a year. Mr Pugh is a singularly sly, slippery, knavish man ...
4 November	[*A new school was opened at Hafod – the Duke providing a dinner of roast beef and plum pudding for the 47 children who were present today.*]

The sight of meat and plumb pudding was probably new to almost everyone present. A knife and fork were equally strangers to their hands ... I was really astonished to see the capacity of one little boy ... I then said a word to them, by way of encouragement and admonition – to this, poor things, they were very attentive. I then made them all go out at the door one by one and as they passed I made them a present of a shilling each. There are about 50 just now in the school, boys and girls ... The children took away with them each a large portion of the remains of the plumb pudding.

5 November	We have overhauled nearly all the books here ... the MSS are splendid and unique.
6 November	... Found the keys of the remaining bookcases and cupboards and discovered some grand books ... one ... a gigantic and splendid M.S. I should say priceless ... The Library is a prize and will ... make the Library at Clumber one of the best in the Kingdom.
12 November	[*Rode around the estate farms with the Agent, Mr Keary.*]
16 November	... our book work was completed today, it has taken 3 of us hard and close fagging for 6 weeks – 23 cases of books are packed for Clumber
19 November	[*Set off for Clumber, travelling through the night. The journey took 14 hours from Hafod to Shrewsbury.*] We arrived at Lichfield then to Sir R. Peel's home at Drayton Manor. [*Sir Robert was away seeing the Queen but arrived home on the 21st. They spoke of the Queen's forthcoming marriage. The poor health of the Duke of Wellington was also noted.*]
23 November	Immediately after breakfast, William and I left Drayton Manor for Tamworth ... it is a rail road station ... arrived at Nottm. at 10 minutes past 2 ... arrived here at Clumber at 7 – found all my dear children ready to receive me and quite well – they had just sat down to dinner of which we readily partook ...

1839

24/25 November [*Newark electoral matters discussed.*]

26 November   Lincoln came over here [*from Ranby*] on the 24th and in a manner worthy of him, which I shall never forget, tended his hand to one who is deeply penitent and by which means, the ground is laid for future union and good understanding. It has given an ineffable relief to my mind – tho' my heart still bleeds for the inward sufferings which I observe.

I rode over to Ranby today – Susan is by no means well ... she is with child again ... the dear little children are charming and in the highest health.

27 November   The building commissioners are at Worksop, also the builders [*Messrs. Grissell and Peto*] – they are examining the Steetley quarry, but it is decided that the stone from there is only to be used in the inside of the building, the exterior is to be either of Anston or Mansfield stone. The terms which I have offered are £130 rent, if they get more than 1/2 an acre to [*pay?*] for it – a lease for 7 years.

28 November   ... Lincoln was over here again today, his repetition of kindness and the visible progress which has been made in his feelings, gave the greatest comfort and consolation to the object of it ...

30 November   My dear William left me today for London from whence he will proceed to France by Dover and Calais. He will then proceed to Tours ... He has for so long been my amiable and constant companion that I must miss him excessively.

2/3 December   [*Political discord noted at Newark – the Duke refuses to allow Lincoln to canvass there, fearing* 'nomination' *accusations.*]

4 December   Lincoln and all his family came her today. The Duchess of Hamilton accompanied them. It is a great joy to have them again under my roof and to watch the characters of the children – They are charming children and I trust will one [*day?*] become an honor to their family and the Country.

5 December   Went today with Sir Richd. Westmacott to Markham Clinton, to decide upon the proper site for the monument to my dear and lamented wife. I think I helped him out of a difficulty and eventually placed the work in the situation most favorable to it.

9 December   ... Sir R. Westmacott left me today. The monument to the memory of my dear Wife is partly fixed in Markham Clinton Church.

10 December   [*Set off for Mansfield, in poor weather, the horses having problems due to the slippery conditions. He writes that he had to walk part of the way and that the journey took nearly two hours.*]

Then on to Nottm. and caught the train [*1.30pm*] for London [*arrived at 10pm*].

1839

12 December	William took Robert to matriculate – they returned from there this evening and Robert is entered upon the University [*Oxford*].
17 December	[*Has heard that Edward has received a letter 'of the most disagreeable description' from the Admiralty.*] – ... these gentlemen will be thrown upon their backs if they do any thing unjustly by my Son, nothing shall save them from my unrelently [*sic*] determination to obtain punishment and vindication by some means or other.
19 December	... William goes by tomorrow's packet to Havre ... it will do him good upon the whole ...
20 December	My dear William went away from here this morning ...
24 December	Left London this morning by the 9 o'clock train and arrived at Clumber at [?] in the afternoon.
25 December	Again I have been permitted by God's goodness to pass another Christmas day with my dear family ...
28 December	I had a long conference today with the Duke of Portland and Lord Manvers on the subject of the representation of this County ...
29 December	[*Rode over to Welbeck ... the Duke of Portland indicated that none of his sons* 'would like to represent the County'.]
30 December	Attended the Quarter Session at Nottingham today – [*where he spoke against the formation of a new County police force.*]
31 December	... Here ends a very eventful year – chequered with good and evil ... I am most uncomfortably impoverished, I have no money and am dreadfully harassed for payment which I have no means of effecting. In another year I may expect to be more at my ease but not at present. I am most inconveniently straightened in my circumstances.

1840

2 January — We have a large party in the house and I have the satisfaction to observe that they are all pleased and happy. Charles and Thomas joined us yesterday. William and Robert are the only absentees. The poor Duchess of Hamilton is exceedingly unwell ...

3 January — Many of us rode today to see the quarries at Steetley and the boring for coal ...

6 January — Attended the Quarter Sessions at Retford. I am now endeavouring to acquire what I ought to have known long since, namely an insight into the conduct of public business in the Country, particularly that part relating to the duty of a Justice of the Peace. I wish to make myself a better country gentleman altho' it may be late. Hitherto my early entry into high situations has been a hinderance to my acquirement of those things which if I had not been so placed I should have been more familiar with.

9 January — A few days ago the Duke of Portland gave me notice that an immediate outbreak of the Chartists was expected ... however nothing occurred ... the stopping of the Mails will be the signal.

10 January — Went to Newark to attend a ball there ...

11 January — ... returned to Clumber.

13 January — ... Col. Rolleston obligingly asked us to Watnall, where we came this afternoon.

15 January — Left the Ball room at Nottingham at ½ past 4 – My two Daughters returned to Watnall, I went with Lincoln to the Inn where after dressing for travelling, packing up etc.etc. we laid down for a short time on sofas and chairs, all the beds having been engaged ... [*They caught the 10.30 am train and arrived in Portman Square, London at 9pm*] – had some tea and something to eat and immediately went down to the Duke of Wellington's. [*They had been due to dine there but arrived too late.*]

16 January — The Queen went down in person to open the Parliament ...

1840

20 January   Lincoln and I were down at the Station at 6 o'clock, but the train was just starting and tho' we ran to catch it we were too late. My carriage and servants were on the train and started without us – we were able to wait for the [*8.45am?*] train and caught up my carriage, which was waiting for me at Rugby. At Nottingham I received a letter from Lord Manvers, which he wrote by permission of the D. of Portland ... signifying that ... he thought the aristocracy ought not to endeavour to force a second member down the throat of their opponents ...

I came here [*Clumber*], where I have the pleasure of finding all well.

21 January   Wrote to Ld. Manvers giving my opinion ... I would have no compunction at forcing anything down the throats of my opponents.

[*Mr Tallents, Agent at Newark writes to report that* 'every palpable iniquity, bribery and trick' *is giving concern to their cause.*]

22 January   ... I went over to Welbeck ... found Ld. Manvers with the D. of Portland – he is an awkward man to deal with, wants humouring and tickling a little and you may overcome most of his scruples and crochets.

24 January   [*Reports the loss of the election at Newark, by 9 votes*] – by the most scandalous practices – money, kidnapping, suborning intimidation by brute force ... it is a great blow to us.

27 January   Lincoln went to London today ... The Duchess of Hamilton also left us today, we all regret her [*absence?*] extremely, as well one may, superior as she is to almost every living woman ...

28 January   Robert is arrived at Oxford ...

31 January   ... Charles and Thomas were obliged to go this morning ...

4 February   Attended a meeting of general Sessions at Southwell this morning [*on the subject of a new County police force.*] ... I remained silent.

6 February   [*Mentions* 'the horrid system and doctrines of Socialism' *and the* 'blasphemy and immorality' *of it's exponents.*]

8 February   Prince Albert is arrived [*In England*] ...

10 February   This day our Queen Victoria is united with Prince Albert of Saxe Coburg – We all drank their health ...

12 February   ... Went to Haughton School today and met the Trustees there. Found the School in a wretched state – the boys miserably taught and ill disciplined. The House and premises more like a large pig sty than anything else and dreadfully dilapidated. We did what we could to incite the schoolmaster to exertion, but I fear that it is in vain – the defects are habitual and long continued and not capable of correction – a new man and a new system are I am persuaded the only remedy - I gave order for putting everything in complete repair.

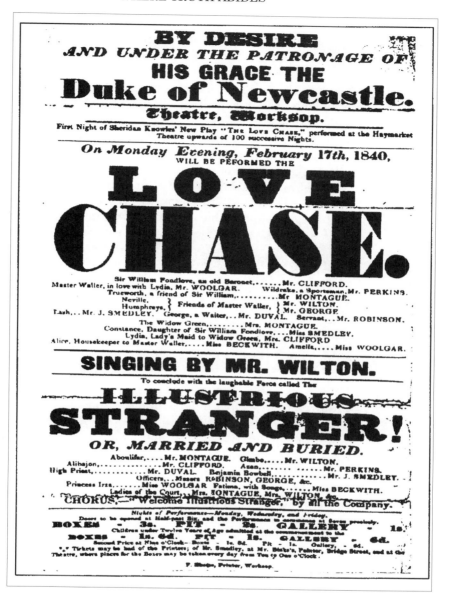

Fig. 55

18 February I bespoke a Play at Worksop last night and I thought it might produce a good effect if I opened the house in honor of the Queen's marriage.

I was not mistaken – the measure has given the greatest satisfaction ... I never before was in the Theatre, which for scenery and decorations on the stage was particularly well conducted. The company too was unusually good for a country theatre.

[*The Theatre was probably in Castle Street, Worksop.*]

1840

19 February   ... The same old stale routine seems to be going on at the Palace. The same familiar dinners and the same riff raff invited to them – A poor look out !!!

20 February   [*Records the death of Lord Mansfield*] – I myself have indeed too great cause to lament him as a friend ... – Lincoln arrived from London today.

21 February   In the course of my ride seeing them at work at the Roman Catholic Chapel at Worksop – I went in and was much pleased with the decoration of the interior. The whole is remarkably well designed and executed. – The altar is beautiful and for its size striking – The Priest, Mr Jones, was there and invited me to see his house adjoining which I did and was much pleased with the

whole arrangement – Mr Jones is very unlike a popish priest and like other people – He is a quiet, well disposed and agreeable man and never offends in his vocation, mixing with others without introducing his opinions.

Fig. 56

24 February... I have been busily employed as usually at this time of the year, in thinning out, opening, lopping and here and there planting.

25 February   Went to survey the practicability of draining the lands at Gamston, without disturbing the mills which I have considered as the offending cause of the wet [*On return to Clumber, he learnt that a serious accident had occurred whilst Charles, Lincoln and Edward had been shooting. Edward had shot estate tenant Robert Candlin* 'all over the head and face'] – Candlin was taken home to Hardwick and doctors instantly produced, one being at Clumber – Poor Edward is disturbed beyond measure and attends the man with the most feeling assiduity. The man is blind at present ...

28 February   [*Notes that a letter of his to the editor of an Irish newspaper, the 'Statesman', has been printed in that paper.*]

Candlin is in some respects a good deal better ... Poor Edward is unremitting in his attention upon him.

The boring for coal at Shireoaks has proceeded to 65 yds 56 of which thro' sheer stone. The stratum in which they now are is supposed to be immediately upon the coal measure –

1 March   My poor cousin Lincoln Stanhope has died suddenly, he was 4 or 5 years older than me but we were boys at school together ...

1840

3 March   My little letter to an Editor [*see 28 February above*] ... has created a great sensation – I wish I could speak [*meaning that he would like to have expressed himself to his fellow peers in the House of Lords*] ... alas I have neither head nor tongue for speaking.

4 March   Took a long ride with Wilmot over the distant part of the Worksop property.

5 March   Again with Wilmot looking over the woods, drainage etc.

6 March   ... rode with Wilmot over the forest farms, marked out the fences, discussed the arrangements upon the spot – in the evening we went to the Theatre at Worksop, it being the Manager's benefit – we were much amused by the company in an excellent Farce, 'Love will find out the way', very droll and entertaining – the parts were excellently well sustained.

9 March   Looking over parts of the estate with Wilmot – went to see the farm in Haughton Park which Mansell is to have. So long as I have been accustomed to Mansell as my Keeper, I can hardly imagine him as one of my principal tenants.

He is an admirable Keeper and a superior man, and I have no doubt from what I heard him say today that he will be as good a farmer as he has been a gamekeeper.

The farm being vacant and he, feeling that he is getting rather old for his business, wishes to retire and enjoy his otium cum dignitate in the cultivation of a farm, close to his old haunts – Bred up on the soil and devotedly attached to my family, tho' I part with him as my Keeper with regret, yet I favor his wish with real pleasure.

10 March   In the course of my ride, looked at the former Priest's house and Chapel in Worksop Manor Park – it is now mine, as the other Chapel and house are completed – the Priest, Mr Jones mentioned that his priest predecessor was buried in the garden of the old house – his name was Physic –[*this should probably have been 'Fishwick'*], Jones says that he was a great scamp, that he buried him as deeply in the ground as he could, 6 or 7 feet from the surface, and threw in quick lime over him to destroy his remains – a curious confession!!! But he added probably the future inhabitant of the house may not like to have Physic so near to him, and if this should be so and that it is desired, I will gain the right and remove his bones. This anecdote is so characteristic that I am tempted to insert it here.

11 March   Wrote to William today ... [*in Bordeaux.*]

One of the Maltese jack asses brought by Edward from Malta died today. I still have another Jack, and a Jenny which is in foal.

12 March   [*Records that Edward has been appointed as mate on the 'Cambridge'*] – we shall feel his loss exceedingly ...

1840

14 March   War is declared with China. Our dear Edward went this morning – May God bless him wherever he goes.

16 March   ... wished to see Payne the auctioneer about the sale of Worksop Manor house and he promised to come tomorrow ... I have seen Woodhouse about the coal boring today – he is quite confident as to the results – he anticipates a fine coal mine and a sale of at least [*100,000 tons*?] in a year – which will amount to about £30,000 – and the royalty to about £2,500 or £3,000.

Lincoln arrived this evening from London he is thin and not looking well –

Edward was to go his ship today.

17 March   Went to Worksop Manor house to meet Mr Payne, the auctioneer – we looked over the whole of the house critically – whilst my determination is to sell the house, we could not but regret deeply the necessity for destroying such a noble pile, so grand and beautiful in architecture and so truly admirable as a specimen of durable and consumate art in building – I venture to state that there is nothing exceeding it in this or any other country. Notices are to be instantly given and circulated and the sale taken place in June – Our enquiry was how the house could be pulled down, it is so circumscribed that it has the strength of [*rock*?].

18 March   This is my dear Georgiana's birthday – we have all heartily congratulated her upon the event, with the warmest wishes for her future welfare and happiness.

Messrs Grissell and Peto have written to say that it is at last determined to use the Steetley stone for all the inside work and interior [*works*?] of the Houses of Parliament and asking to work the quarries for that purpose at a royalty of 3 halfpence per foot – which is but a poor price.

19 March   Georgiana and Charlotte continue so unwell with cold or influenza that I am not able to go to London today ...

20 March   My dear Daughters are better today.

[*He records that he has 'positively declined the honor' of chairing a meeting on 'the case of the Irish Corporations'.*]

23 March   Lincoln and his family went this morning to Ranby.

24 March   The ground covered with snow and snow storms throughout the day... This evening after dinner, a member of the Dublin Corporation [*Rev. Gregg*] arrived from London ...

25 March   ...we left Clumber this afternoon and went to Nottingham where we slept.

29 March   We heard yesterday from Edward who was taken very unwell with what they termed muscular rheumatism at the back of the neck ... ... broke out in blisters ...

1840

30 March	Heard from William from Bordeaux ... He is going on to Rome and Naples.
1 April	We had a little amusement this morning becoming the day ... [*unfortunately, no other detail given.*]
3 April	Charles and Thomas have been to Sheerness on a visit to Edward.
5 April	The Queen believes herself to be pregnant ... rather soon to suspect such an event ... she is a strange self willed, unreasonable little personage. We went to the Levee today ... I made my bow and passed on, making my bow also to Prince Albert who stood [*at*] Her left hand. He is a well looking young man, good countenance, with dark hair and complexion. Hitherto all agree in speaking well of him.
7 April	[*He called at the Admiralty to urge that Edward's promotion be implemented.*]
9 April	I have been trying with much anxiety to find someone who will lend me a sum of money ... that is to the end of the year when I shall receive payment for timber etc. but at present my immense purchases have so impoverished me that I have not been able to pay my bills for the three years past and my creditors are [*pushing*?] and impatient ... at present and for some time I have suffered greatly from distress and humiliation.
10 April	... Lincoln went to Ranby this morning. Robert came home from Oxford this evening.
14 April	... I presented some petitions in the House of Lords.
17 April	[*Good Friday*]... the service was very long ... we did not get out of morning service until 3 o'clock.
18 April	[*Edward arrived – on leave for 10 days.*]
20 April	Left London at 1 p.m. by rail road and arrived at Nottm. at 1/2 past 9, being delayed at Derby etc. by the holiday people who were very numerous – Robert is my companion - I come all this way to attend the meeting tomorrow on the Rural police business.
21 April	[*Left Nottingham for Southwell ... arrived late and found the 'Rural Police' meeting had started*] I objected to the whole proceedings ... I deeply lament the decision of the meeting – it will assuredly lead to [*nuisances*?] and deplorable evils. Arrived at Clumber ... I have done my duty ...
23 April	Today is my sale of timber – I expect a good one. I learn this night that most of the timber (standing) sold remarkably well, oak 3s 6d and 4s a foot and beech grown in Clumber (felled) [*14s*?] a foot – When all is sold up it will produce from 8 to 9000£.

1840

24 April   I left it [*Clumber*] on the sweetest morning I ever beheld ...

          [*Caught the train at Nottingham and arrived in London at* 'Euston Square Station'] ... less than 12 hours from Clumber.

27 April   Went to see the progress made in building the Houses of Parliament ... If I were a builder or Clerk of Works I should be ashamed of such work – and I shall think it my duty to report my opinion to the architect Mr Barry.

28 April   Went with many of my family to see the Polytechnic Exhibition ...

29 April   Effected a loan ...

30 April   I am very sick at heart ... nothing goes well with me. I am very unhappy – nor can I ease my mind by unburdening it to any one.

1 May   Robert returns to Oxford this evening.

          [*The Duke attended a dinner at Goldsmiths' Hall*] – The Goldsmiths are an agreeable, intelligent and worthy body of men and it is a pleasure to go among them.

2 May   [*Attended a meeting at the Duke of Wellington's*] – Dined afterwards at the Royal Academy ...

4 May   [*Spoke in the House of Lords, on the Irish Corporation Bill.*]

9 May   Dined at Lambeth Palace today – Lincoln accompanied me.

12 May   There was a ball yesterday at the Palace but neither my daughters nor I were invited. Charles and Thomas were invited and went there.

13 May   [*Reports that beneficial changes at Court were due to the influence of Prince Albert.*]

16 May   [*Attended a morning concert at the Academy. He observed* ' the manners and deportment' *of Prince Albert – and he was favourably impressed.*]

22 May   This is my dear Lincoln's birthday, to celebrate which we had a family dinner.

23 May   [*Attended the Eton dinner with Lincoln.*]

25 May   The Queen's birthday is celebrated on this day went to the Drawing room with two of my Daughters. The Queen ... gives herself no trouble, speaks to no one, scarcely looks at people as they pass like flitting shadows.

26 May   My cold clings to me and keeps me unwell ...

29 May   ... there is a concert at the Palace tonight, but we of course were not invited – I am in fact better pleased to be away ...

30 May   [*Dealt with Hafod business.*]

31 May   Lady Lincoln seemed so unwell this evening that I thought it very likely that childbirth was commencing.

1840

2 June   I have seen Mr Woodhouse today who is conducting the boring for coal at Worksop. [*Notes that the boring has reached a depth of 130 yards.*]

4 June   [*He notes that the Queen had, for the first time, gone to Epson races.*]

6 June   [*Visited Thorpes, booksellers*] – I may purchase some MSS.

9 June   This is Susan's birthday. She, Lincoln and the Duchess of Hamilton were dining here ...

10 June   [*Reports that the Queen was shot at today.*]

11 June   We all went today to write our names down at the Palace ...

13 June   Webster, nephew to good old Rowlands, and who succeeded him in doing everything for me here [*as Butler*] ... was seized with a paralytic stroke ... two days ago.

14 June   Poor Webster died this morning ... he was a very valuable man to me.

18 June   We dined yesterday with Sir William Clinton.

22 June   Attended a Ball at the Palace ... [*The Queen*] – to me, she was kind and agreeable ... there is no opportunity for conversation.

23 June   Lady Lincoln ... delivered of a fine boy – is very well.

30 June   Not at all well – Making my preparations for leaving London – Charles and Thomas march to Windsor with their regiment early tomorrow morning.

1 July   ... I feel very unwell and country air is very necessary for me ...

2 July   ... Robert arrived today from Oxford – quite well and in improved looks and better [*stirred?*] mind ...

6 July   ... On my return home I found my dear Edward who had slipped up from Portsmouth for 2 days to see us before leaving England.

8 July   My dear Edward returned today for Portsmouth – it was a great delight to see him even for so short a time ...

9 July   Attended with 4 daughters and 4 sons at St George's Church this morning, to be present at the Marriage of Sir Wm. Clinton's 2nd Son, Col. Fredk. Clinton to Miss Mary Montague, 2nd daughter of Lord Montague. The alliance is an excellent one ...

11 July   [*Received a letter from William posted at Naples on 23 June.*]

13 July   ... I had Mr Robins with me today about the Sale of Worksop Manor house in one lot.

14 July   I was not ready for 2 o'clock, I therefore sent my daughters with the carriage by the 2 o'clock train to Birmingham ... [*whilst he finished his business matters*] ... went to take leave of Lady Lincoln, the children and the Duchess of Hamilton – took some coffee, and not long after, was seated with Robert opposite me in

1840

one of the carriages. We arrived in Birmingham at 1/4 past 2 – put up at the Royal Hotel ([*Dee's?*]). My daughters had arrived and were all asleep.

15 July ... Slept at Shrewsbury.

16 July ... Arrived at Hafod.

18 July The rain has continued unceasingly.

20 July Rain again – the poor people are in despair, they cannot get their turfs, nor is the prospect of harvest very cheering to them.

21 July ... If the bad weather should continue these poor people will be deplorably off – without fuel ... corn and potatoes.

24 July ... the same rain ... Nothing is so difficult as to get on and do any beneficial works in this country.

26 July [*Sunshine – but the hay*] – is mouldy and rotten.

27 July [*The hay*] – tumbled dried, dusted and turned about and collected into very large cocks.

28 July A letter from Edward ... William has arrived at Paris.

3 August Sir Richard Westmacott was extremely desirous that I should purchase his favourite and last work, the figure of Euphrosyne [*see 27 June 1827*] I have consented to do so, and it is mine for £500, it is a beautiful statue and equal to anything I know ...

4 August William is arrived in England ...

5 August ... We came over to Aberystwyth for a day – I drove over in the evening in the little pony phaeton ...

6 August Went to see the Pier ...

7 August [*Returned to Hafod.*]

13 August William is arrived at last ...

15 August [*Heard from Lady Susan that Lincoln was ill (bilious).*] – I think it proceeds from annoyance, acting upon a disordered system.

21 August [*Heard that Lincoln was still in bed but that the fever had abated.*]

28 August Went to Aberystwyth with my family to attend a concert ...

29 August [*Returned to Hafod, late at night and in dense fog. The Duke was driving and they had an accident near Devil's Bridge. The pony phaeton overturned and the Duke's left leg was hurt.*]

30 August [*Pain in his knee, also in his side and arms.*]

3 September Lincoln is arrived at Hamilton ... He had a very pleasant passage from Liverpool to Glasgow. Charles has been very unwell at Windsor ...

6 September ... the harvest is going on favourably enough here, which is a great point in such times as we live in.

1840

8 September	... I am much plagued and perplexed about my affairs ...
10 September	... my knee is much better ...
14 September	... I am about to repair and alter the Church here and to erect the monument to the Johnes family ... it will be one of the choicest buildings to be found anywhere ...
17 September	... I have a letter from Edward from Genoa dated 8th ...
1 October	This is my dear Charlotte's birthday ...
2 October	Charles and Thomas arrived this evening, we did not expect them ..
7 October	Worksop Manor House was put up for sale yesterday by Robins at his auction mart in one lot – it only reached 13,200 guineas and I had it bought in at [£30,000?]. At last they have cut the coal at Shireoaks – they have at present bored through 13 inches of coal but it is to be hoped that the bed is much thicker.
15 October	This is my dear Robert's birthday. Time has indeed quickly passed. He now enters his 21st year ... He returns to Oxford tomorrow morning ... Reading does not seem to suit and agree with him.
16 October	My dear Robert left us this morning by the Mail ... His absence always causes regret – He is a universal favourite.
18 October	I have been working hard all day, and now am writing at 4 tomorrow morning, in hopes of getting off in good time ...
19 October	... we arrived at Shrewsbury at little before [*midnight*].
20 October	Left Shrewsbury about 9 o'clock – dined at Lichfield and arrived at Clumber a little before 11. We were delayed nearly two hours between Alfreton and Mansfield, first by having to change a drunken post boy, after having come a mile from Mansfield – They are cutting into a hill and have left the road in a shameful state, there being no light to give warning, the post boy had gone too far on the upper road and a few yards further would have turned over the carriage. The carriage had to be put back and when this was accomplished it stuck fast in the clay – it was some time before we could procure ropes and assistance, as all the traces had been broken.
21 October	Lincoln and Susan were visiting Thoresby and called here on their way home to Ranby. [*He expresses the wish that all previous* 'difficult points ... may hitherto be right'.]
23 October	Went to Ranby to stay the night. My dear grandchildren are much grown and improved – They are fine and beautiful children.
24 October	Looked over all Lincoln's farming concerns here ... really excellent – returned to Clumber late to dinner.

1840

25 October   My poor clergyman [*John*] Mason is on his last legs ... I have
              known him from my boyhood. He is now perhaps my oldest
              living acquaintance.

28 October   Went to see the improvements at Rufford. Lord Scarbrough had
              just before arrived [*and*] came up to see us and invited us in to
              see the interior. All that has been done is in good character and
              [*closely?*] adhering to the period of its monastic celebrity – the
              hall is fine but gloom is the prevalent character and I should be
              very sorry to live in the house.

29 October   Attended an adjourned general meeting of the Magistrates
              today at Southwell [*Regarding the financing of the new Police
              force. The force of forty officers was reported as costing £2,200 in
              pay alone.*]

3 November   Attended a bazaar at Carlton [*Carlton-in-Lindrick, Worksop*],
              the proceeds to go to the building of a Church at Woodsetts – a
              bad wet foggy day but the attendance good not withstanding –
              This is the first of these affairs that I ever attended and I am
              not the more reconciled to seeing ladies transformed into
              shopkeepers. I am a matter of fact man and like to hear things
              called by their right names and see persons in their right
              places.

11 November   ... Attended in petty sessions a meeting at Worksop, and was
              glad to see the D. of Portland looking much more himself
              again.

13 November   [*After persistent and heavy rainfall*] – The disease amongst the
              cattle is a singular and great scourge – it affects all cloven
              footed animals in a similar manner. Horses also are
              dangerously affected, but not by the same disease.

17 November   A letter from Edward from off Beirout [*sic*] ... Henrietta had a
              letter from him off Alexandria.

19 November   Came to Ranby to stay two nights – All are well here except
              Susan ...

20 November   Walked about Lincoln's farms ...

21 November   [*Returned to Clumber*]

22 November   [*Remarks on* 'the Queen's accouchement'.]

              ... A proposal has been made to me to buy the House at Worksop
              Manor to rebuild precisely as it is, on the [*Norman?*] Castle
              estate on the Isle of Wight, the present notion is to give me
              £20,000 for it ...

24 November   ... My flocks and herds are unfortunately not free from the
              epidemic ...

1840

25 November	Attended the petty sessions at Worksop this morning, there was little to do. Major Walker brought his Policemen to be approved and sworn in, which was done. There is to be 1 Superintendent and 5 Constables for the Worksop district, which is very large. The more I see of this new system the more I dislike it.
28 November	We have a very severe frost just now – it set in 3 days ago and yesterday the lake was entirely frozen over from one end to the other – therm: down to 23.
30 November	The disease amongst the cattle is spreading thro' my herds and flock – it has not killed any but has made them wretched objects.
3 December	Charles and Thomas' birthday, which has been celebrated amongst ourselves – it is long since they have been with us on their natal day.
10 December	I sent poor Candlin, who Edward had the previous misfortune to shoot in the face, up to London to be attended by Alexander who is acknowledged to be the finest oculist ... the case is hopeless ... the optic nerves ... irretrievably injured ... This will be a sad blow for the poor fellow and is sensibly felt by all of us.
14 December	My two daughters are staying at Thoresby for a night ...
15 December	A letter from Edward today ... from Alexandria.
16 December	Mr Corbett has been here for some weeks cleaning the pictures ... All the pictures in the little drawing room and dining and some few others are finished – he is now doing them in the great drawing room and began the 'Finding of Cyrus' by Costigliona, it was in wretched condition, cruelly, covered with paint and dirt – from being barely visible he has brought out to being a brilliant picture and one of the finest I know – the Vandyke [its pair?] will come next and I have no doubt that it will undergo an equal change for the better.
17 December	Robert arrived this morning at 2 o'clock. He is looking very well.
18 December	[They went out shooting – it had been snowing.]
21 December	... The winter has set in early ... the frost does not leave the ground.
23 December	[He bemoans the news that Edward has again been overlooked for promotion] – This is too bad.
25/30 December	[Unusually, there are no diary entries relating to Christmas or family matters for this period.]

1840

31 December With this day we conclude the old year ... de mortuis nil nisi bonum ... for myself and what concerns my family, I have nothing to complain of and much, very much for which to be most thankful and humbly grateful. Prosperous I have not been, neither I or mine, but in that I may see the goodness of God, who will not permit the vanities of the world to dazzle and seduce by the bright illusion of success, or the giddy allurement of too much worldly enjoyment.

Fig. 57 *Worksop 'Abbey' and 'Ruins' – sketched by Emma Wilmot in 1846.*

I January	Again I am permitted by God's goodness to commence my Diary of another year ... with a full determination to do my best to deserve, as much as I am able, the blessings so graciously shewn to me.
3 January	Last night, or rather this morning there was a fearful storm of thunder and lightning ... more like masses of liquid fire ... hail came down instead of rain, and today it has snowed heavily ...
7 January	Came to Stoke [*Hall*] to attend the Newark Ball ... deep snow and intense cold ...
8 January	We did not appear very early this morning ...
9 January	Returned to Clumber – Charlotte and Caroline had accompanied me to Stoke – we found all others well on our return.
10 January	Much snow almost every day ... I saw people walking over the Trent, as we went from Stoke to Newark yesterday.
11 January	Attended the Sessions at Retford ... The roads in a wretched state ... I did not reach Clumber before ½ past 10. I had had nothing to eat since breakfast.
12 January	Attended a meeting at Worksop this morning for several purposes – to establish an Annuity Society from the surplus of the Savings Bank ...
	also to consider of the best means for repairing the Abbey gate house and the Ruin – The repairs of the Church and enlargement of the burial ground were also mentioned.
	I afterwards came in to Thoresby, where I now am, for a day or two.

1841

14 January ... returned home today.

15 January A letter from Edward of the 10th Dec ...

22 January My dear Robert left for Oxford this morning. William accompanied him to London ...

26 January Lincoln is now at Wilton ...

Wilton
February 1st 1841

My Dear Father,
... avert the evil which I dread ... I tremble to think of the sequestration of your house – prosecutions – foreclosings – and above all, the loss of position in society and the sacrifice of reputation which I know you value highly.

... make over the management of your affairs in trust to 2 or 3 friends of sound judgement and tried experience ...

I certainly should ... die with melancholy forebodings if I were compelled to leave my Children to the fate which so generally befalls a race of titled paupers.

I am ever
My Dear Father
Your most affectionate Son
Lincoln

[Letter from Lord Lincoln to the Duke – University of Nottingham Manuscripts and Special Collections Department – Reference No. C 12,853 / 1]

30 January ... I have today completed my 56th year ..

31 January Today cold and much snow.

4 February ... Some marble has been found in Scratta Wood, and a small specimen cut and polished – the colour is by no means bad and the quality very good – The bed found is only 6 ins. thick.

6 February ... Robert has had a bad accident in skating, he came into collision with another skater was thrown and pitched upon his head, which rendered him insensible – when taken home 10 leeches were applied to his head and he was very much better.

9 February ... Dear Robert is nearly well again.

10 February [*Notes that the Aberystwyth Harbour annual dues have been let for £1,021*] – in less than 5 years they will let for £2,000, and for this they have me to thank.

11 February A thaw at last ...

12 February A letter today from Edward announces that he is exchanged into the 'Princess Charlotte', but mentions nothing of promotion ...

15 February Thomas arrived today on leave from his regiment ...

23 February My large Vandyke of Rinaldo and Armida, is now finished and very perfectly restored ... tomorrow it will be varnished and the next day restored to its frame and its place.

1841

25 February   Lincoln and Susan have arrived in London from Wilton ...

Susan is pretty well again ... but like her mother ... it never can be calculated upon for 24 hours.

1 March   My grand avenue and road thro' the Park is now completely finished, it has been a heavy job but as I think very successful and a noble feature in the place.

2 March   I have made my arrangements for a new mode of selling the House at Worksop Manor – By this mode I expect to keep myself safe throughout and never to be at the mercy of [jobbing?].

7 March   Lincoln and Lady returned to Ranby yesterday ... She, poor thing, is very indifferent.

10 March   [Records that, once again, Edward has been passed over for promotion] – it is a grievous disappointment to me and will be heart breaking to him dear fellow.

12 March   I should have gone to Nottingham today with Lincoln to attend the Assizes, but I am not well ...

16 March   ... I am just now very busy in the grounds, altering, decorating and improving in time for producing an effect in the Summer ...

22 March   Mr Mousley came here today to settle all his affairs with me, we began at 1 and kept closely engaged in business until 8 ... dined and resumed our work about 11 and continued at it until the whole was finished on the 23rd at near 4 in the morning. I paid him his enormous bill of £5,200 and completely understood and satisfied myself as to every thing that had been transacted by him, how it now stood and how it bore upon the future ... I rejoice that I have finished it. I must fairly say for Mousley, that his work has been well done ... served me so well ... so much cleverness and ability. He may be a rogue and a sharp practitioner – but he possesses means of action which few have.

24 March   I have tried to sell my remaining houses at Boro'bridge but have not succeeded – I can buy, but I cannot sell ...

25 March   Came to Ranby to stay a day with Lincoln. Lady L. is unwell and in bed – She is seldom free from headache or spasms.

27 March   Returned from Ranby this afternoon. Susan was again in bed from bad headache.

28 March   I have presented Mr Younghusband to the living of Egmanton.

I hope that he may prove to be what is required in such a Parish, but in these days of strange and unsettled doctrine, there is no certainty of a man's worth and principles until he has been tried and evinced his worth by his deeds.

30 March   Came to Ranby with 4 daughters to stay a day or two. Susan is again confined to her room.

1841

31 March The wind has been very violent, in riding to Worksop to attend the Magistrates' meeting, I could scarcely keep upon my horse. Susan is better today and came down stairs.

1 April Returned to Clumber this afternoon – Poor Lady L. again in her bed – Her sufferings must be horrible.

3 April Attended a show of stallions for agricultural purposes – it was exhibited in a field called the Common at Retford. This being the first show, there were not many horses but the cart horses were very fine, two of the prizes were taken [by] two tenants of mine, Watson of Walkeringham for a very superior Cleveland horse and Booth of Markham Clinton for a cart horse.

5 April ... The weather continues wonderfully fine for the time of the year ... even the oaks ... buds very formed, others are out in leaf and in some places the black thorn is in full blow – there is also plenty of grass upon the lawns ...

6 April ... A ball of fire passed over the house this afternoon about 1/2 past 7, it came from West to the Eastward and broke over Hardwick Wood, where it dispersed and disappeared in sparks similar to the bursting of a sky rocket fire.

7 April A letter from Edward from Malta ... I am most anxious that he should be promoted.

9 April Good news by express from China ... The Island of Hong Kong is yielded to us – 6 millions of dollars to be paid us as an indemnity ...

This is Good Friday, and it was a gratifying and proud sight to see my 4 daughters and my only 2 sons here, attending at the altar with that reverence and devotion which mark a true, pure and Christian spirit.

12 April Engaged all day at the Retford Sessions. Not a very heavy day but some bad characters and aggravating circumstances, which made it proper to sentence two of the parties to 7 years transportation each. – A man of the name of Sleigh, a receiver of stolen goods and a great vagabond, pleaded his own cause and with great subtlety and ingenuity.

13 April Went today with Mr Thompson to Mansfield, to see a font which is being made out of stone, gotten from Mansfield Woodhouse quarry belonging to Lindley of Mansfield. The stone is certainly of a most beautiful colour and quality, but I doubt if it is better than that of Shireoaks ... I am to send a piece of the Shireoaks stone, which he will work upon and try it as a specimen.

17 April Rode over to Ranby with Robert, to see and take leave of the dear party there [*Lincoln was returning to London for the parliamentary session*] -

Lady L. is better and in better spirits but still very thin.

1841

21 April	The timber sale yesterday was very successful, that of this day is expected to be even more. The oaks are felled already in many places and I observe that they are obliged to put them standing up as the sap runs so freely.
23 April	... Robert left us this morning for Oxford [*During his stay at Clumber, the Duke had asked him what he intended to do when he left university*] – enquired whether he thought the Church would suit him. He without hesitation replied that he should like it ... We agreed that it should not be done lightly ...
26 April	William is gone to Nottingham early this morning ... He will be much instructed by witnessing the proceedings [*nominations for the election.*]
27 April	... William says that the villainy, venality and abomination of the worthy men of Nottingham is beyond all description – a good deal of tumult and fighting, 11 men sent to the hospital yesterday and 1 killed ...
28 April	... This is the first day of my sale at the Worksop Manor house – I am informed that it is gone off well ...
29 April	... My sale has gone off very well today, and the prices for which things have been sold is very good – but still the total amount is very small.
30 April	... This is the concluding day of my sale of the [*interior?*] of the Manor house – Few of the articles remain unsold and every thing sold this day even at a better price than on the former days. In a months time, I shall sell the remainder of the House, and there will be an end of one of the finest structures that was ever built.
1 May	Went for a day or two to pay Dawkins a visit at the parsonage at Markham Clinton – it is greatly improved, the trees have grown so much that they begin to make a feature in the place.
2 May	This being Sunday, attended service in the Church – I could not prevent my thoughts wandering to the once dear objects whose remains lay so near to me ...
4 May	William went to Newark today with his Troop of Yeomanry, to meet the rest of the regiment. Lincoln is already at Newark.
7 May	Lincoln went to London today ... Returns to Newark tomorrow. He expresses himself much pleased with his new avocation of soldiering .
10 May	Lincoln is returned to Newark ...

1841

Fig. 58 *Newark in the 1840's.*

11 May   Went this morning to Newark with my Daughters.

The Sherwood Rangers were reviewed in a field near Kelham bridge – we arrived on the ground as the regiment was trotting past – all went off very well ... they cheered Lincoln who was out with them for the first time ... they then cheered me, which was perfectly unexpected. I acknowledged the compliment as well as I could. I afterwards dined at the mess which was a long business – and did not get back to Clumber until after 2 this morning.

12 May   Lincoln is gone back to London.

13 May   William is gone to see the review and inspection of the Regiment today ...

15 May   Rode over to Elkesley, to see how the repairs to the church may be best effected – a very pretty church may be made by a little addition and the removal of several unseemly obstructions.

22 May   I was informed late yesterday of a meeting to take place at Retford today, to petition Parliament not to meddle or interfere with the Corn Laws, and was told that if I should go to the meeting it would be attended with very good effect and would give great satisfaction. I accordingly went there this morning, accompanied by William. Sir T. White was voted in the Chair – he is an excellent man ... I forebore saying any thing untill finally it was moved and carried that I should present the petition to the H. of Lords. I then thought that I ought to say something, more especially as I shall not be in London to present the petition – I rose and gave them a speech unburdening my mind and making remarks which appeared, and which I know, did give very great satisfaction ... The meeting went off well, without a dissenting voice, but people

were afraid of speaking out and were too much upon their good behaviour, I should have liked to have known more of the real mind of the meeting, by the description of their own thoughts and feelings.

23 May [*Heard that his speech had been* 'greatly approved of'.]

29 May The oaks are all out in full leaf but much eaten by insects and caterpillars ...

1 June My last sale of Worksop Manor House began today.

The items of this day's sale consisted of some remaining doors, windows, flooring and ceiling joists and sleepers etc. – they all sold well, but the amount is very small. I trust that the succeeding days will make more, or the sum total will be very low and disappoint me bitterly

Fig.59
*Worksop
Manor in the
early 1840s –
sketched by
Emma Wilmot*

2 June My sale today is a little more in amount and all the things are well sold, yesterday they were confined to the attics – today there were some attics but they descended to the ground floor – tomorrow the 2nd storey will be sold and then the roof will follow.

3 June ... Ld. John Manners offers himself to oppose Wilde at Newark. He will succeed without doubt – I am very anxious for a seat for William and I could seat him at Newark or Retford. My sale has got off well today but amounts to nothing.

4 June This day the sale is completed – everything is sold but the walls of the house and for them there was no bidders. The inside of the house, except the grand staircase which is not sold, but

1841

including the roof, doors, windows, floors, beams, joists etc. has only made £6000 – a mere trifle, and a sad disappointment to me.

The lead, of which there is much, has sold for a great price at 17, 18 and £19 a ton – the total amount will probably be between 5 and £6000 – this will only be ascertained when weighed.

12 June   Worksop Manor is rapidly clearing under the hands of the destroyers – in another week the floors, ceilings and most of the roof will be removed.

15 June   The weather being favorable, we went on a little expedition to visit Chatsworth – I have not been there for many years and was very desirous of seeing the extensive alterations which have been made there within those 20 years.

The extent and magnificence, and I must add taste of the alterations, greatly exceeds what I had any idea of. The new addition to the House is immense, the old house was so handsome and complete in itself, having four fronts, that it was no easy matter to add on anything that would not be ruinous in its effect. This however under the difficulties is well contrived, the fault is that the new building does not accord with the old and is tame and plain in its style (the plainest of Italian) – However it is a truly magnificent whole – I gave a preference to the library establishment and the dining room is very fine – the great use of marble pleased me. There are few pictures and [?] portraits – There is a statue gallery, but no antiques and in my opinion the modern marbles of very moderate merit – Altogether both inside and out I like the House, it is now made comfortable and is truly palatial also.

We then proceeded to the grounds, they are delightful, a good many people were seeing the place, it was a fine day and we were much struck with the gaiety of the whole place and scenery – The gardens, flowers, kitchen and terraces are seen to be good, as Paxton – the Duke of Devonshire's gardener – is a very clever man and one of the first rate gardeners – The great lion is the new Conservatory, which no doubt must be the largest and finest in the world – it is [?] 300 feet long and __ broad. I never saw any thing so well constructed, the construction in itself is a curiosity – It is 60 or 70 feet high – it is only just finished, the trees were only planted in the last autumn – The arboretum and walks in the wood which is taken in the pleasure grounds in a manner are most enjoyable, we lastly visited the terrace adjoining the house, all pleased beyond measure, and retired delighted with the view, to eat some dinner at an Inn newly erected in Edensor Village on the outside of the park – with good appetites, a capital dinner, and every thing the

1841

perfection of cleanliness and comfort, we enjoyed ourselves excessively and set out on our return home only a little before nine, in about 4 hours afterwards we found ourselves at Clumber.

17 June   William is gone to a dinner at Mansfield ...

18 June   I hear today that William acquitted himself excessively well yesterday ... My family is beginning to be known and esteemed and will soon be pre-eminently considered in the County and elsewhere ...

19 June   Lincoln has been in great tribulation about his children, who are all unwell, the infant dangerously with inflammation of the lungs and he expected to lose him – however he is now much better, and Henry too, who is confined to his bed with an attack nearly similar.

20 June   [Lincoln's letter reports that the children's health is better.]

23 June   [Heard that Lincoln is ill] – I wish that I had any influence to prevent and remedy all this, but alas, it is only by accident that I hear anything ...

the thunder and lightning have been formidable with a proportional quantity of rain ...

25 June   Lincoln arrived today ...

4 July   ... Lincoln is gone to Newark tonight, to be ready for his nomination tomorrow morning.

6 July   Lincoln's election went off admirably well ...

9 July   Lincoln left me this morning, on his return to London to join his family ...

10 July   Letters from Edward of the 19th Malta ...

18 July   [Heard of the death of Lord Feversham. Records that he was his kindest and warmest friend.]

19 July   [Left Clumber for Hafod, sleeping at Lichfield.]

20 July   We came on to Shrewsbury ...

21 July   Arrived at Hafod this evening – Rain as usual has been our companion on the journey.

25 July   Before I left Clumber, my bailiff had been to Mr Watts at Babraham near Cambridge to hire a South Down ram to use with my flock – He procured the best, but was to pay 150 gns for the hire of him for the season – I have not seen him but I am told that he is a singularly fine shearling – He was shown on the 23rd at the show of the Agricultural Society at Liverpool and won the first prize.

26 July   [Records the considerable alterations made at Hafod.]

1841

27 July ... William and Mr Thompson arrived ...

4 August ... I had a very awkward fall today. [*He had slipped whilst hurrying along the marble floored hall.*] I might have been killed ... I am truly thankful for my escape and preservation.

6 August Very late at night, my three dear sons arrived ...

23 August This is Caroline's birthday ... We are a strong family party, 4 sons and 4 daughters – Robert only is absent, Lincoln I hardly count as he scarcely ever is with us [*at best?*] a few days.

24/25 August We went to Rhayader to shoot grouse on the moors there ...

31 August ... Sir R.Peel has been sent for by the Queen ...

2 September [*He lists the new Ministers in Sir Robert Peel's government and then adds:*] – I confess that I shd have liked to have gone to Ireland, and I am convinced that I could do good things there, but I ask not, hint not, and no one (perhaps I am not fit) will drag me from obscurity.

18 September [*Very depressed, hints at continuing financial problems.*]

24 September Came to Aberystwyth this evening ...

28 September Wrote to Ld Aberdeen today to try if he will do any thing for William – Peel was testy and refused to consider himself at all for him – neither kindly nor altogether courteously – but such is the man – and one cannot make a blackymoor white.

29 September Went to call at Crosswood [*Lord Lisbourne's*] ...

Georgiana accompanied me in the little phaeton.

13 October Returned to Hafod from Aberystwyth.

14 October All my sons left me before quitting Aberystwyth.

15 October This is my dear Robert's birthday – He attains his majority today.

18 October I have a wretchedly bad cold and can think of and do nothing.

20 October ... The Johnes monument arrived today and is now lodged in the case in the Church ...

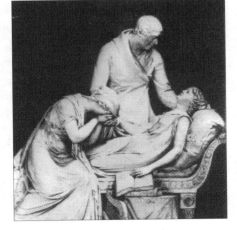

Fig. 60 *The (now badly damaged) Johnes monument.*

1841

Fig. 61 *Hafod Church in September 2000.*

25 October	... The Church is nearly finished, the monument in course of erection, the painted glass for the windows will be put up tomorrow.
24 October	Edward is at last promoted to his lieutenancy.
27 October	Edward has received his Commission and on applying for service has been appointed to the 'Harlequin' 16 gun sloop, Comm. Hastings – She is destined for China. I wish she were a larger vessel – E. seems to like his destiny.
31 October	[*Edward arrived, unexpectedly, on leave for a few days.*] ... Robert has passed his dreaded little go ...
1 November	We have passed the day in talking over all matters in any way relating to Edward's service and long absence from home – it is a long time to look forward and makes one melancholy to think that when we part tomorrow morning it may be never to meet again.

1841

3 November   The Johnes monument [*sculpted by Sir Francis Chantry*] is now in its place. Its erection was completed today.

4 November   William has been appointed as attache to the Embassy of Vienna ... I have a very bad opinion of it [*the diplomatic service*] and always dread its consequences upon individuals but there was nothing else for William to do, and he has rather a leaning to it.

7 November   My dear Charles is bent on not being idle. He seeks service ... [*Charles had applied for several appointments as A.D.C. to Army officers.*]

11 November   [*Left Hafod, travelled via Devil's Bridge to Welshpool.*]

12 November   [*On to Derby, dining at Lichfield.*]

13 November   Tried the railroad from Derby to Eckington – left at 9 and reached Chesterfield at 1/2 past 10 – where we learned that there were no horses at Eckington – we were therefore obliged to procure horses to take us from Chesterfield to Clumber, a tedious business and we only entered the house at 1 o'clock, truly pleased to find our journey at an end ... We found William here.

17 November   ... lake frozen over ... [*also snow*].

18 November   [*Reports on the relative merits of milk quality from his Shorthorn and Ayrshire cattle – the latter being found better in both quality and quantity.*]

22 November   This is my last day with my dear William. Tomorrow morning he leaves me for London, from whence he will go almost immediately to enter upon his new career and join Sir Robert Gordon at Vienna. Diplomacy is not a profession that I by any way admire – A foreign residence never improves an Englishman, foreign morality and habits are so unsuited and contrary to ours, that it is a fearful thing to launch a person into such a vortex of corruption – I have given him and fortified him by all necessary advice and I trust and believe that he will profit by it.

23 November   My dear William left us today ... to me it is a particular loss, as he has been my companion for so many years.

25 November   [*Mentions the* 'weak and silly' *of Oxford, in following Dr. Pusey's Tractarian teachings – and* 'calling themselves Anglicans'.]

10 December   It is rumoured that the young Prince is to be called Albert Edward – I hope not ... The name of Victoria has always been a drawback upon the Queen's popularity, and the same will attend that of Albert.

1841

12 December   Nottingham – Here I am on my way to London – I dined at Clumber and came on here in the evening – I shall go by the ¼ past 8 train tomorrow morning.

13 December   ... arrived in London at the Euston Square Station at ¼ past 3.

14 December   ... I have been made very miserable today by what I have learned of Ldy Lincoln's misconduct, I fully expected it, but never the less I was astonished as well as grieved when it was made known to me.

16 December   ... Lincoln's unhappy business has been one principal subject of occupation.

17 December   ... Lincoln ... has come to the resolution now of effecting an immediate separation with Ldy Lincoln. It is heart breaking ... he must trust in God for the issue.

19 December   ... Lincoln has been here this evening, I also saw the Duchess of Hamilton in the morning – I now thoroughly know the wretched subject which causes us so much inquietude ...

20 December   I have been up all night, Lincoln remained with me till late ...

[*The Duke and Robert then returned to Nottingham by train and on to Clumber.*]

21 December   [*Went to see Lady Lincoln at Ranby*] – She was up and in her bedroom and received me there ... I have seldom seen her looking better or more beautiful ... so fascinating, so intellectual ... [*yet making*] such confessions as she announced to me, besides how such a person, who is really a good and attentive mother, could almost unmoved contemplate an external separation from 4 of the most lovely and loveable children I ever beheld – or such a one who values first place should forego and sacrifice all the advantages which her present station gives her and sink into a degraded outcast of society ... merely to indulge in a sinful propensity.

24 December   [*Following Lincoln's request that Susan should be told* 'to leave his house for ever', *the Duke rode over to Ranby.*] – I have ... fulfilled my wretched task ...

25 December   My small family party (4 daughters and Robert) took the Sacrament ... we could not wish a happy Christmas knowing that that cannot be.

26 December   ... I rode over to Ranby ... expecting the removal of the children, should it be attempted ... [*mentions conversation with* 'Hill', *possibly butler or valet to Lord Lincoln.*] – Hill says Lady Lincoln takes scarcely any nourishment ... two large bottles that they supposed to be laudanum ... have been bought from the Chemist's – Their suspicions have been roused ... I am convinced that Ldy. L. subsists upon laudanum, [...?] and other stimulants and sedatives.

1841

27 December	Came on a visit for a day or two to Mr and Mrs G. Knight at Firbeck.
28 December	[*Henry Gally*] Knight is a very old friend and schoolfellow of mine ...
29 December	On my way home, I stopped at Worksop to attend the Justice meeting. We found a numerous bench and some very aggravated cases of assault.
31 December	... I have gone with two of my daughters to Thoresby for a night. I have come to the end of another year – I have done nothing, and it has done nothing for me ... but I doubt not that by God's aid, I shall overcome all difficulties and perhaps finally prosper.

1842

3 January   ... Charles arrived from London this evening ...

6 January   I have been to Ranby and had a long interview with my unfortunate daughter in law.

7 January   ... Robert left me this morning to return to Oxford ...

9 January   I have been to Ranby today ... [*Lady Lincoln*] is repentant, obedient ... her parents are her curse, if she can be kept clear of them she can do well ...

10 January   Lincoln arrived from London.

12 January   I went to Nottingham ... this morning to attend a meeting of visiting members of the Lunatic Asylum ...

13 January   Today I attended the adjourned Sessions at Southwell [*At the meeting, the Duke urged the abolition of the new Rural Police Force* – 'but it was negated by a small majority'.]

             ... wretched day [*snow and wind*] ... the inside of my carriage was nearly full of snow, as was the outside. In coming home, I was in frequent danger of being upset, and in Thoresby Park, my coachman lost the road and we had great difficulty in finding it.

15 January   I rode over to Ranby ...

17 January   ... Lincoln came this morning to shoot wild ducks with his brothers ...

20 January   Rode over to Ranby today – most dangerous riding ...

22 January   [*To London with Lincoln – they caught the train at Eckington.*]

25 January   [*To Windsor for the royal christening.*]

26 January   [*Returned from Windsor to London by rail.*]

27 January   ... By a loan from my 4 daughters and Robert, I have been enabled to pay off a considerable debt, with great advantage to myself and some advantage to them. I shall now (I trust) soon be clear of debt, and whenever I am so, I hope I shall not be tempted again to exceed my monies.

28 January   [*He travelled by train from London to Nottingham, then on by coach to Clumber.*]

1842

29 January	Went out shooting today – the snow still very deep, and hard walking.
30 January	... This is my birthday – it has pleased God to allow me to see my 57th year completed ...
1 February	Received a letter from Edward from Madeira dated 27 Dec ... The brig is notorious ... he calls her a diving bell ...
3 February	[*Records here the death of J. Rayner, who had been hunting in Clumber Park and was returning* 'to the kennels' *when his old pony bolted and the cart was overturned*] – between the Normanton Inn and the hill.
7 February	Thomas left me this morning for London.
15 February	Attended a meeting at Southwell, an adjourned Sessions for the purpose of electing a Chief Constable of Rural Police ... I afterwards went to Mansfield, where I joined my daughters who were waiting for me and we then came on here to Kirkby on a visit to Mr and Mrs Vernon.
16 February	We all went this morning to see Hardwick [*Hardwick Hall, Derbyshire*] – The roads to it are very bad – There is something very grand about the aspect of the house and surrounding Park – but the [*latter*] and the adjacent country are too bare of timber and plantation and the house itself is not so remarkable (for its good old style) as I had expected. Some of the [*pantheons?*] in stone carving are good but wanting in sufficient relief. The interior is, generally speaking, cheerless – the gallery is fine and a good model for such an apartment. I was rather disappointed in the general effect as well as in the style and detail of the building exteriorly and interiorly.
17 February	We returned to Clumber this afternoon.
19 February	In the course of my ride today over the further parts of Worksop and Shireoaks, I saw Steetley Chapel for the first time, it is well worth the attention of anyone who is fond of what is most choice in architecture – I was really surprised by the interior, I never remember to have seen any thing so elaborate and exquisitely worked as the mouldings and capitals – the proportion too of the arches is perfect and the effect quite striking. These remains are a perfect bijou.

Fig. 62
Steetley Chapel by Emma Wilmot

1842

7 March   Occupied the chief part of the day planning drainage near the house, to lay the pleasure ground more effectively dry than it is now, the same on the terrace and lawn – then at the Carburton fishpond, to arrange for its proper completion.

17 March   ... The D. of Norfolk is dead ...

21 March   ... Ldy Lincoln took a short walk upon the terrace today.

23 March   The weather is dreadfully cold ... I lost 10 [sheep] in one night.

24 March   ... I am engaged in making a new drainage in the pleasure ground and on the lawn ... at between 7 or 8 feet from the surface, we find a surprising quantity of water, which was out of and through a quick sand which flows with the water.

25 March   Ldy Lincoln was able to attend Chapel today ...

26 March   Went to inspect minutely the enclosure at Wellow and the allotment made to me, which is a very good and advantageous one ... it will be a very pretty little estate.

4 April   ... up to my eyes in papers ...

8 April   [On his way to London, he and his daughters visited Nottingham Castle and Park. He notes that this was his first sight of the Castle since the Reform Riots.]

14 April   I sat for my bust yesterday to Mr Behnes – it is for Eton College.

23 April   Went with my daughters to the water colour exhibition – a beautiful display ... Dined at Lambeth Palace – a public day.

25 April   ... attended a Ball at the Palace.

28 April   Attended the Queen's Drawing room today with two of my daughters. Her Majesty looked tired, serious and bored.

29 April   My new Clerk of Works went to Hafod this evening.

2/3 May   Nothing very worthy of note – balls and late hours are not very favorable to doing anything in the day – my journal falls a sacrifice too, to the unnerving business.

6 May   Heard from Edward from the Cape.

9 May   The Town is mad about the coming "fancy ball", as it is called, at the Court. We are not invited, and I am truly glad of it, for if I had been invited I shd not have gone ...

15 May   Wrote to William today ...

19 May   Today, I know not why, the Queen's birthday is kept, I dined at Sir R. Peel's ... afterwards went with my daughters to a humble squeeze at the Duke of Wellington's.

20 May   ... Tonight another ball, which finished me, I was quite done up – Besides this I have many heavy annoyances on my mind.

21 May   [More trouble with Lady Lincoln] – I fear that it is a hopeless case.

1842

22 May   This is dear Lincoln's birth day ... [*Susan has indicated that she cannot be reconciled with Lincoln*] ... poor dear Lincoln is to be pitied.

29 May   Had a long conference this morning with the Duke and Duchess of Hamilton ...

30 May   [*Heard that, once again, someone had fired at the Queen.*]

31 May   ... all the town has been enquiring at the Palace today.

1 June   A Levee today which was most numerously attended. I went and made my bow ... the Queen, poor thing, seemed to be oppressed and excessively fatigued.

3 June   Busy all day and night for it is now 4 o'clock preparing for going to Clumber tomorrow.

4 June   [*Caught the 11am train to Nottingham – arrived there at 5.30pm and at Clumber by 8.30pm*] – time enough to take a delicious walk in the sweet and cool air.

5 June   Everything is looking in the most flourishing state ... my grass is very short for want of water.

9 June   I have hardly had time to do all my matters at Clumber, but tho' rather incompletely done, I hurried away at 1/2 past 1 and reached the Station at Nottingham in good time to go by the 1/2 past 4 train. Having some time to spare, I looked about me in the neighbourhood of the Station and conversed with several people that I met – in particular with a man who told me that he was a stockinger out of work – that the greatest distress prevailed, that the people were starving, that the hosiers were still reducing their wages and that he did not know what would be the end of it.

He supposed that the object was to drive the people into a revolution, that both parties were alike and that between them the [*object ?*] was to crush the poor man – His last wage was 13s a week, out of this he had to pay 9d a week for frame rent, 2s 6d for house rent and 8¹/2 for needles leaving him the remainder to live upon – he said it was worse than nothing – I knew what he meant but I asked him why – He said because then he must go to the Bastile which would be something better tho' not much – He abhorred the Bastile – it is evident that there is a settled feeling amongst them that they will be driven in commotion – indeed, poor wretches, I know not what they are to do or what we can or are to do for them. I am so poor that I must reduce my labourers and that must lend to increase the general distress.

I arrived at my home [*Portman Square, London*] at 20 minutes past 11, and found all my Daughters well ... an hour afterwards, Robert arrived from Oxford.

1842

12 June   Lincoln came here to dinner today and brought his dear children with him. Ldy. L. still remains the same ...

13 June   I have seen the D. of Hamilton today.

14 June   I found Ldy. Lincoln in bed, where she has now been for some weeks ... a pitiable condition poor thing. Her sufferings must be excessive ... she was attended by spasms of faintings ... so that I could not enter upon serious conversation.

15 June   Called again today upon Ldy. Lincoln ... infinitely better ...

she wishes to go away somewhere and not again to return to and live with Lincoln untill she feels disposed to do so ... I say that is her fault not his ... I now give up the case, with deep sorrow that Lincoln should have ever had the misfortune to be united to such a woman.

20 June   ... made notes of a speech which I might make tomorrow, if I had more confidence in myself ...

21 June   [Decided against making a speech.]

24 June   [Prepared a long letter to Lincoln, regarding the matrimonial difficulties] – The worst of it is that the office and politics of the party so entirely engross his thoughts that he hardly allows himself to think upon any other subject.

[Travelled home to Clumber – firstly by scheduled train to Rugby, then by specially commissioned train to Nottingham.]

26 June   It has blown a hurricane ... It has broken many trees and made mincemeat of the leaves and flowers.

27 June   I have come here for the purpose of unsparing retrenchment ... I have already gone through three departments – Gardens, Game and Woods and grounds, and those which stand me in at least £5,000 a year, I have cut down to £1,000 ...

28 June   I have now investigated every item of expenditure ... I have limited the amount of each department – On the principal source of expenditure adding to the 3 named yesterday, that of building repairs etc. amounting to little less in the last year than £7,000 there will be a saving of nearly £5,000 – on the Stables, in the house, and in general management, I may fairly anticipate a reduction and saving amounting to full £2,000 more ... I may be enabled in a short time to get thro' my difficulties and feel myself at ease.

29 June   My dear Robert left me this morning ... to Oban in Argyllshire, going to read with a Tutor, to prepare himself for taking his degree ...

4 July   ... the Queen was again shot at yesterday ...

1842

5 July   [*Records that yesterday's gunman was*] a deformed creature, and a bad character ... a sound daily flogging for some weeks, would do him and others a great deal of good ... sending [*him*] afterwards to a penal Colony.

13 July   [*Records that Mr Gladstone's sister, Helen*] has become a convert to Popery ... It is very deplorable that such things should happen in England ...

19 July   [*Gives his thoughts on Peel's government –*] as dishonest and shabby as it was incapable.

26 July   I have come to the determination to let some of the more distant Manors ... they will lend to save expense upon them ...

1 August   [*Left for Hafod ...slept at Derby.*]

2 August   [*On via Uttoxeter, Stafford and then Newtown, where he slept.*]

I am very much indisposed ...

3 August   I felt really ill when I got up ... stopt for a short time at Devil's Bridge.

6 August   I am very much better today ... A letter from Edward by the overland mail – dated Singapore dated May 5 ... [*Edward had been ill.*]

8 August   That wonderful work, the Thames Tunnell, is at last finished and was opened a few days ago ...

21August   [*Records that Susan had left Lincoln and she had written to the Duke, giving the impression that she would return – the Duke did not believe her.*]

27 August   [*Travelled to London, via Ledbury and Cirencester.*]

1 September   Here I am at Clumber again ...

2 September   Lincoln came over from Ranby ...

4 September   ... Dear Lincoln came here this afternoon.

5 September   We went out shooting today ... we only killed 20 brace among 4 of us and 26 hares and a land rail [*corncrake?*] ...

7 September   Passed a great part of the day with dear Lincoln at Ranby ...

The conduct of the Hamiltons ... is odious, vile and abominable beyond description.

12 September   Lincoln came out to shoot today ...

13 September   I went to Ranby this afternoon ...

14 September ... I returned to Clumber this afternoon ...

19 September   ... I was out shooting at Worksop below Sparken Hill, when thunder came on and stop'd me. I was afraid of exposing myself to the wet, being already almost crippled by painful rheumatism between the shoulders, which quite affects my head also ...

Fig. 63 *A fine sketch of '<u>Sparkin</u> Hill', Worksop, by Emma Wilmot –circa 1843. Emma and Edward Wilmot (Agent to the Duke) lived at Sparken Farm, on the right, just around the next corner.*
This northerly view indicates a small area of the Duke's newly purchased Worksop Manor Estate.

20 September	Came to Langold for a day or two ...
22 September	Returned to Clumber this afternoon – on my way home went to inspect the sheep etc. for the sale tomorrow at Hardwick – they all looked well ... but I apprehend two enemies to a grand sale – the bad state of the times and the prospect of a bad day tomorrow ...
23 September	... soaking rain and stormy wind all day ... all the sheep were sold and 6 out of ten horses were sold, tho' at a very low price.
30 September	... Attended the Agricultural Show at Retford, it was holden in the Spa Meadow ... there were very few animals and none of a very superior kind ... [*He then went to dine at the Markham Clinton Parsonage with the Rev. Dawkins.*]
1 October	Robert has left Scotland on his return to Oxford ...
11 October	[*Travelled to London, by train from Nottingham.*]

1842

14 October   ... I fear that my dearest Son Edward has fallen a sacrifice to the climate ... The Hampshire Telegraph [*reports that*] Lord Edward Clinton has died of fever ... Charles and Thomas arrived this evening from Clumber – they say that their Sisters were fully persuaded of this result and that for two days they have been crying about it and thought of nothing else – Charlotte has dreamed about it and could not divert herself of the idea of its reality – God's will be done – it is a heavy blow.

16 October   I wrote today, to announce to my dear Daughters and to Robert what I had learned ... I shall be at Clumber on the day after tomorrow and on that account I wished to delay the sad intelligence as long as I could – Somebody had sent Robert the Hampshire Telegraph, which he immediately sent off by his [*servant?*] who returned shortly after with a letter from me detailing all I knew and exhorting him not to let the event have such an effect upon his mind and to prevent his taking his degree – This may be most difficult but I call upon him to rouse all his energy to effect it. It will of itself be a calamity if Robert shd again postpone taking his degree.

17 October   All hope is at an end – we have learnt today that Ld Morris of the 'Harlequin' has written to his brother, giving a full account of our dearly beloved Edward's death and many details which are intended for us. God Almighty has dealt most mercifully with us, in allowing this awful calamity to be broken to us so gradually, and above all by thus so soon dispelling that agony of suspense to which we thought we were doomed for the next three weeks – to the arrival of the mail ...

18 October   Left London by the 9 train and arrived here about 1/2 p. 6, found my dear daughters well, but of course it has been a mournful meeting for us all. Charles and Thomas came with me.

20 October   Lincoln came over here today from Ranby ...

22 October   Robert writes to me from Oxford in the most satisfactory manner, poor dear fellow, he has to suffer alone the grievous loss which has befallen him and to control himself and smother his feelings in order that he may not interrupt the train of his studies and lose his degree ... I shall rejoice when it is well over.

Saw several swallows today flying about the house – it seems to be passed (*sic*) their season to appear.

23 October   Mr Tomlinson of Elkesley did the service here today, he preached a most beautiful sermon ... I am very sure that there could not have been a dry eye in the Chapel ... Many a copious flow of tributary tears was shed to the memory of one so very very dear to us.

25 October   ... Saw several swallows yesterday.

1842

26 October [*Heavy snow was falling all day.*]

29 October [*Charles left for London today.*] I am now without any Son here.

3 November I have a male and female Maltese donkey here, for breeding the male had been turned into one of the paddocks and the female was in a stable and small paddock apart. The male contrived to open the gate and got at the female and he injured her in such a manner that she must die – he has bitten her in the most shocking manner all over, and in fact worried her – and he must in some manner have injured her back as she [*crumpled?*] up – I regret this the more at this time as my dear Edward had purchased them and sent them to me from Malta – The male is really ferocious.

4 November [*Robert wrote to say that he was ill with head pains and liver problems.*]

5 November The poor she ass ... is recovering by dint of extreme care.

My groom is extremely attentive and kind to the poor beast.

6 November I shall not be able to sell any wood this season [*meaning that the sale prices were so low*] ... the loss to my revenue will be ruinous – I reckon upon a regular annual income of about £5000 and this year I shall not make a shilling from them. Last year by great effort I barely raised £2000 from which expenses were to be deducted.

7 November My poor she ass is dead ...

[*Received another letter from Robert*] – he is very unwell and unfit for work ...

I cannot express how anxious I am about him and how grievously annoyed I shall be in addition to all other things, if he eventually fails and misses his degree.

8 November [*A letter arrived from William in Vienna.*]

10 November [*Robert's tutor has*] – recommended him to take his name off the degree list ... it troubles me beyond expression ... a great humiliation and a grievous disappointment and for my poor dear boy enough to break his heart ...

I immediately despatched a messenger with a letter to him, urging him to come here without delay that we may endeavour to cheer and restore him, for he is ill in health and wounded and afflicted in spirit.

12 November [*Received a letter from Captain Hastings, of the 'Harlequin'. Hastings confirmed that Edward had died on 12th May and that 'his remains had been committed to the sea'.*]

13 November My dear Robert arrived this morning ... he seems truly happy to be home again.

1842

21 November [*The Duke writes here about the appointment of Sir William Clinton as 'Lord Governor of Chelsea'. He expresses his disapproval of his kinsman having accepting such an 'inferior position' and accuses the Duke of Wellington of failing to acknowledge Sir William's true worth.*]

22 November [*Snow*]

24 November ... Attended an adjourned Sessions at Southwell – we had very hard work and much fighting about the Rural Police ...

25 November For some time, the engine which supplies this house with water has done so very irregularly and scantily, until at last it almost entirely stopped for a long while ... they looked up the culvert which admits the water from the lake, which was found to be entirely closed with the casts of trees. The culvert is a large brick culvert which will enable a man to pass up it, and one did so and cleared away all the roots which were merely fibrous like hair and so matted that the mass was at last impervious to water.

26 November The information was brought to me this morning, that as the foreman of the woods (J.Simpson) was going to his work he found a man dead in the plantation called the 5 thorns – The man proved to be Greaves of Retford fishmonger – He was found suspended to the back of his cart, his smock frock having caught upon some part of the back, the body was in an upright position but the head had fallen back – there is no apparent cause of death, except that it might have been caused by apoplexy, or in getting down he may [*have*] caught unexpectedly and may have broken his back ... he had been at this house ... then on to Carburton for rabbits and from thence to Day's house [*Budby Corner*] for more – and from thence he was going on to Hardwick.

30 November Lincoln came here yesterday ... it is such a comfort and pleasure to have him here ... Attended the Justices' meeting at Worksop today. The D. of Portland, 4 others and I made a full bench – I am in wretched spirits today – As I rode home, and afterwards, I felt as if my heart would burst – I really am most miserable – and hardly a day passes without some addition to my ills, annoyances and embarrassments – Where and how it will end I know not.

2 December [*Reports that Lord Combermere was at Clumber.*]

7 December ... My finances are in so bad a state that I must adopt some measure immediately for the liquidation of my debts and for regular payment in future ... purchasing when I was not even then in a flourishing condition first created difficulties for the payment of interest etc, the fixed payments now amounting to £31,000 a year – This I parried whilst I could sell the produce of

the estate well – but last year timber failed and what very little I sold was at not much above half the value of the previous year ... I am with a deficiency of at least £7000 ... to avoid worse, I have resolved to commit the management of my affairs to Trustees – My tradesmen's bill do not exceed £10,000 ... my bonds about £65,000 – The rest is in mortgages which may remain – but from £70 to 80,000 will be necessary to get me clear ...

12 December   [*Another check on his financial position proved even more depressing*] – Debts £15 to 16,000 ... Bonds £95,000 ... Lawyers bills from 4 to £5,000 – In all about £116,000.

14 December   [*Travelled to London by train from Nottingham.*]

19 December   Much concerned with accounts etc. and with lawyers I have [*now?*] every thing prepared but I have not yet decided upon a plan – what I am disposed to adopt, is to place the management of my affairs in the hands of a tried and experienced individual and let him prescribe what shall be done – A Mr Lindsay of Edinburgh has been particularly recommended to me – I have written to him today.

20 December   [*The diary entries for this date have been heavily deleted.*]

23 December   Left London this morning by the 9 train and arrived at Clumber at 7 – found them all well here – but there is something mysterious about them which I do not comprehend – it was so for some time before I went away, it is even more so now.

24 December   Mr Lindsay came here today from Edinburgh ... I have laid everything before him and he sustains no apprehension of being able to extricate me from my difficulties without resorting to a trust, but by assisting me to pursue the same course which would be followed by a trust if it existed – I myself am quite inclined to this opinion and hope to be able to adopt it.

25 December   This is Sunday as well as Christmas Day. We all received the Sacrament ...

26 December   Mr Lindsay left me today ... I think the plan eventually to be agreed will be to effect a temporary loan to pay off all the debt, bonds and simple contract – and in the meantime, to sell property in my own power and with the proceeds of sale to pay off the loan – the loan itself bearing an inferior interest to pay bonds etc., bearing interest at a rate of 5 per cent ...

30 December   ... Rode back with Lincoln to Ranby and saw his dear children.

31 December   Charles is very unwell today [*scarlet fever?*] ... his name appears in the Gazette as Captain in the Life Guards ...

We have arrived at the termination of one of the most eventful years in the history of this country and of the world ... what may the coming year be?

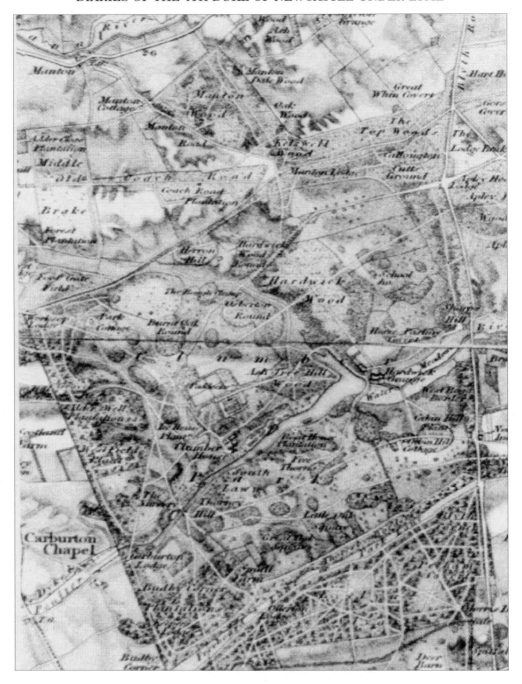

Fig. 64 *Map of Clumber Park – surveyed 1824 – revised circa 1840.*

1843

1 January   ... I never in my life was so extensively unhappy as at this time, and I have not been consoled by not one of my family greeting me on the event of the new year, and wishing me happiness, altho' it may not be very likely to befall me –

What causes all this, I know not, but it appears to be a systematic apathy and indifference for which I am totally at a loss to discover a cause.

2 January   Charles ... is better this evening ... sponged all over with vinegar and water, then put back to bed – he is more cheerful in himself ...

How it is, I know not, but on this day, I have had the happiness to observe a spontaneous and simultaneous change amongst my children, and what has evidently existed for a length of time, seems to have been suddenly broken through and dispelled – I can only suppose that "some enemy has done this and sown the tares among the wheat"

3 January   [*Charles is reported to have scarlet fever and small pox. It is decided to have Clumber House thoroughly ventilated.*]

... I am endeavouring to get the small house at the Manor ready for my Daughters and Robert to go to ...

Fig. 65
Manor Lodge, Worksop

5 January   ... My children went to Worksop Manor this evening.

1843

6 January	Charles passed a good night without opiate and thank God, is going on in the most favourable manner ... I rode over to see the new inmates of the little Manor House – they seemed very happy and amused by the novelty of their new abode ...
9 January	Charles ... had an excellent night ... two wings of partridge and a glass of Madeira for dinner ...
10 January	[*Went to London by rail – on the 12th he recorded that he had travelled through snow and high winds and had thought that the train would be blown over.*]
11 January	[*The Duke met Mr Lindsay, his financial adviser.*]
15 January	[*Wheat prices were very low – the Duke recorded that a quartern loaf was being sold for only 7d.*]
2 January	After church Thomas came and we walked together ...
23 January	[*Back at Clumber*] – I left London by the 1/4 past 9 train, and arrived here 20 m. to 7.
25 January	Went over to Worksop Manor to see my Daughters – dined and slept there ...
26 January	Went out shooting with Robert close by the Manor house, not a great deal of game ...
1 February	... Charles went out today for short time – after a confinement of above a month ...
2 February	Left poor Charles at Clumber with an amusing book or two ... came here to Worksop Manor ... for two nights.
5 February	Robert was very unwell ... I have remained at the Manor ... I went to church at Worksop with my Daughters, and afterwards visited poor old Jane Hutchinson with them, who is confined to her bed with a paralytic stroke – She has been the faithful and excellent dairy woman at the little farm for more than 30 years. Her attachment and interests is of the good old kind and it was quite affecting to observe her today – She was pleased beyond measure at our visit ...
7 February	.. deep snow and the lake frozen over ...
8 February	Rode over to Worksop Manor today ...
9 February	[*His daughters and Robert moved to Ranby today.*]
10 February	... Charles and I rode here (Worksop Manor), where we are now established for a few days, whilst they thoroughly clean and purify the house at Clumber.
11 February	... It has been a miserable day today snowing with a brisk wind all day ... I braved the weather and did work out of doors with some of my people here ..
14 February	Occupied here ... principally marking timber, so as to have the best trees and relieve them from neighbours, which are doing

1843

them great injury. The trees are of great magnitude here, and will make very considerable further improvement under judicious and careful treatment.

15 February   At last we are all united again. Thomas came from London last night ... his 4 sisters and Robert came to Worksop Manor to breakfast with us ... after luncheon, we all came to Clumber ... poor Charles was quite overcome with it.

16 February   ... one can hardly make oneself warm near the fire and at night it is bitterly perishing ... in my bed room, with a fire, it was 38.

17 February   [*He sent to London all his documents which related to the Hafod estate*] – with the deepest regret ... preparatory to the sale of all my Welsh property – a sum of £30,000 raised upon them to pay off all my outstanding simple contract debts.

18 February   [*Went rabbit shooting in the snow.*]

20 February   Robert returned to Oxford today ...

23 February   The frost and snow is quite gone – a charming day.

28 February   Thomas returned to London today. I this morning signed a mortgage deed to the Eagle Insurance Co. which lends me £30,000 and with this I shall pay all my debts – I engage to sell my Welsh Estates, with which I shall repay the money, and I hope discharge all my Bond debts – but times are desperately bad and a good sale may be impossible.

1 March   Came to London today ... Caroline accompanied me, as she will be glad to have something done to her teeth.

3 March   Having obtained my money, I have today been paying it away to many and have made many happy ... I find that my payments will exceed my means by upwards of £1,000.

9 March   [*Records that he was writing his diary at 2.30 a.m., after a day spent on matters related to the sale of his Welsh estates.*]

11 March   [*Returned to Clumber.*]

14 March   My dear Charles returned to London today ...

20 March   Out a great part of the day in the woods, inspecting and marking ... fine trees are coming forward in this park.

21 March   ... I have reduced my breeding flocks to 500 and something ewes, and yet I shall have more lambs than when I bred from 8 or 900.

24 March   ... my lambs this year are improved in shape and kind ...

25 March   [*Notes* 'with much pain' *that Lincoln had taken part in a Commons motion regarding bribery allegations at the Nottingham election.*] – I should oppose his endeavours ... I suspect that my dear Son has been imposed upon by Sir Robert and made a [test?] of for his crafty and [sapping?] purposes.

1843

28 March   My future Chaplain here, Mr Webster, came yesterday to look about him and make arrangements for his future residence ...

I have been in the woods marking trees with my woodsman, taking much pains with this department ... he has now adopted my views and has come well into my mode of managing trees and plantations, and I could now pretty confidently trust him in the woods ...

29 March   ... I met some farmers today returning from Worksop market, they gave a wretched account of the state of everything but barley ...

30 March   I have been vexed and annoyed by what Lincoln has done in the H. of Commons ... I deeply regret to appear at variance with one another – But in honor and duty to my country I cannot act otherwise.

31 March   I have now, within a very little, completed the payment of all my debts ...

I rejoice to observe that my dear Lincoln has had the good sense and good feeling to adopt the right course ... This is right and fair.

13 April   Saw 3 swallows the day before yesterday – the first I have seen this year ...

14 April   My Daughters and I, with the family, took the Sacrament today.

15 April   Lincoln rode over here today, he was looking pretty well and gave a good account of his children.

18 April   Lincoln and his four dear children came here this morning and staid untill the evening when they all returned to Ranby ... They are charming and most promising children.

23 April   Lincoln was called to London yesterday ... No man with a family should be in office especially when situated as poor Lincoln is – A man's family calls for and requires a man's almost undivided attention, to do his duty by them properly.

25 April   Mr Lindsay came today ...

10 May   We all went this morning to be present at the inspection of the Sherwood Rangers in Grove Park – it was really a pretty sight – the ground being handsome, the day fair and a large concourse of people – probably 2,000 ...

My dear Lincoln was far from well ...

I staid dinner at Retford and returned home by 1/4 past 12.

11 May   [*The Duke records that Robert has 'plucked' his degree*.]- it is a very galling disappointment and great vexation and adds immensely to the many mortifications and annoyances which crowd and fall upon me ...

1843

22 May   Robert arrived this afternoon.

29 May   [*Spent time with his Agent, Mr Wilmot.*]

13 June [*To London by train. His daughters and Robert travelled with him. William was already waiting for them in London.*]

16 June ... My rents are now all collected and Mr Wilmot reports most favorably of the result.

30 June [*Records that, unexpectedly, Lincoln had met Lady Lincoln at a royal wedding on the 28ᵗʰ.*]

4 July   [*Left London for Hafod – by train to Cirencester. Slept at Hereford.*]

5 July   [*Arrived at Hafod.*]

14 July [*Records that, in lieu of cash, his Welsh Agent has had to take tenants* 'cattle, sheep and wool and sell it for payment'.] – This must be ruinous to the tenants ... I wish I had sold this property ...

20 July We are all very busy here ... I very much wish that it should be bought for the Prince of Wales – it would be an excessively popular measure here in the Principality ...

21 July ... Lincoln writes that he has been to Bristol with the Pr. Albert to see the launch of the steam ship named Great Britain ...

13 August [*Records that Charles and Thomas have dined at Windsor with the Queen and that she had danced with Thomas. He also mentions that the Queen had been very pleasant.*]

20 August This is Sunday – we were all at Church today, with a numerous and most respectable and well behaved congregation, in a Church now rendered capable of inspiring veneration to Almighty God and decency of behaviour in this temple – I surveyed it with infinite satisfaction as I looked at it and participated in its service, in all probability for the very last time – For we go on Saturday next. I trust that the benefits which I may have been instrumental in effecting here may live after me, when I am gone and far away.

22 August ... Lincoln's 3 younger children have the [*whooping?*] cough ...

26 August Completed all my matters here, but not untill late in the evening, when I took my leave of this beautiful place for which I have done so much and which has been the source of much pleasure and very great interest to me ... my anxiety will be that I shall sell it to the best advantage ... tomorrow we set out on a tour of N.Wales to Liverpool.

27 August [*Visited Aberystwyth harbour and found that improvement work was at a standstill.*]

1843

28 Aug/2 Sept [*Diary entries for these dates record their tour of North Wales On arrival in Liverpool (having crossed the river by steam boat) they stayed at the Adelphi Hotel.*]

4 September [*They travelled by train to Crewe, then went on to Combermere Abbey.*]

7 September [*By train from Crewe to Birmingham, changed trains and then on to Derby and Chesterfield. They hired post horses and travelled home to Clumber.*]

9 September Went out shooting with William ... the heat great.

10 September ... To my great sorrow and mortification, I have heard of a clandestine marriage formed by my son Thomas ... by special licence at Christ Church, Marylebone, in July last, no one being present but the clergymen and clerk – the name of the woman is Brinton ... she is young, handsome and ladylike in appearance and manner ... it is thought that they have lived together before marriage ... Poor fellow, he has cut off his future prospects and inflicted a lamentable injury upon his family – I fully expected something of the sort from the manner in which they behave towards me, having no communication with me whatever, and concealing from me every thing of the slightest nature – I deserve very different things from my children to whom I have devoted myself from the moment of their birth – but so it is, and nothing produces an ameliorated change – it makes my life extremely miserable – as to my poor son – I shall not discard him, her I shall of course disown and never acknowledge.

13 September ... probably so fine a harvest has rarely been known.

16 September [*Charles arrived home.*]

19 September I am taking [*down*] the magnificent house at Worksop Manor and in order to do this in the shortest and best manner with least expense it was proposed to blow up one of the back walls. This day was fixed for the experiment – we accordingly went there this morning to witness this operation, many of our friends met us there and there were many people to see the sight. The weight of wall to be thrown over was computed at 400 ton weight, and the quantity of powder used was 42 lbs. All being ready the signal was given and 3 men lighted the trains which ignited the fuses – in about [1½ minutes] the first explosion took place, then others in succession which had an extremely fine effect and must have resembled the bombardment of a Town – the whole of the bottom of the wall was burst through and split to pieces but yet the wall stood. The experiment failed – it was really extraordinary how the superstructure of the wall could remain upright with scarcely

1843

any thing except a few loose stones to rest upon – we determined to try more explosions in the soundest parts – 7 push holes were drilled, charged etc. all but one were successfully exploded, but still the wall stood and we were obliged to give it up – it is evident either that the mining was not properly conducted, or the wall was so unusually strong, which it certainly is, that the ordinary modes will not effect its fall or destruction – I hope that our failure in this matter is not a harbinger of failure in the Auction room today. I do not anticipate a good result – such being a stranger to me.

20 September The auction is over – There was no bidding and the estates were brought in at my prices – I am told that the room was well filled, and many very wealthy men present, who came here interesting to be purchasers – but for some reason they did not bid a sixpence – it is expected that several parties will now negotiate privately – one Mr [Matherson?], by his lawyer, was to see Mr Henderson last night ... I am informed that the whole conduct of this sale gave the utmost satisfaction to all present – and has raised the character of the Auctioneer (*Smith?*) very highly in public estimation – I am rather sanguine in my expectation to obtain my own prices for the estates altogether, before many days have passed.

The attempt to explode the building at W.M. which failed yesterday, was this morning attended with complete success – it was blown up finely [*sic*], and all came down with a grand crash and without accident.

23 September ... For the last 6 weeks there has been little interruption in this beautiful weather, now [*and*] then a day's rain, but not above 3 or 4 of these during the period of 6 weeks.

28 September Went to Nottingham this morning to attend the Hospital Meeting. It was the worst I ever saw ... £117 was collected in the Church. There was a meeting afterwards in the Town Hall to elect a Physician to the Lunatic Asylum ... Dr. Williams was elected...

1 October ... nothing can be more prosperous than the whole state of nature hereabouts.

4 October ... My dear Robert has again been very unwell ... liver affected and rhuematism ... I shall be rejoiced if ever he gets over his degree – there seems to be a spell against it.

6 October Attended the Agricultural dinner at Retford, Lincoln was President and in the Chair ...

15 October Robert is better, but still far from well he has not yet been out ... I fear he will be unfit for taking his degree.

1843

17 October	When I got up this morning I was surprised by seeing the ground covered with snow ...
18 October	... Sharp frosts every night.
23 October	Quarter Sessions at Retford – which I attended ... Lincoln was called upon to take the Chair ... I was on horseback and did not get home till 9 o'clock to dinner.
26 October	Attended an adjourned Sessions at Southwell. The rural Police was the prominent point of discussion ... I gave notice of a motion ... for increasing the Salary of Gov. of the House of Correction, which is now only £260 a year ...
27 October	... The swallows left us here on the 22ⁿᵈ – but when shooting in a turnip field close to Worksop today, we saw [them?] flying about as in the summer.
3 November	Mr Lindsay came a few days ago ...
4 November	Took Mr Lindsay to Nottingham and met Mr Wilmot there – we examined and looked over every thing and every situation. [Mr Winter, his Clerk of Works, estimated that the Duke's Nottingham and Basford lands were valued at 'a little short of a million of money'.] ...
5 November	This being Sunday the particular [service?] for the day was read and Mr Webster gave us one of the cleverest short sermons on the occasion that I ever heard ...
8 November	To my infinite and inexpressible mortification Robert has again failed for his degree ...
11 November	Robert arrived here this evening from Oxford – Charles returned with him ... Robert is quite bald on the top of his head, his hair all came off during two days only ...
15 November	Came here, to Ossington, on a visit for a few days, I have not been for several years, and find the place quite altered ...
16 November	There was a meeting at Southwell today and Mr Denison took me there ... I made my motion [see 26 October above] and to my surprise not a single man in the room was found to second it – I was of course greatly disgusted, as either I must be totally deficient in sense of judgement or the gentlemen must be wholly disinclined to give me support – in either case, it will befit me to cease to take any part in public affairs. We elected Mr Roper to be Governor of the prison.
20 November	Engaged the greater part of the day endeavouring to work out a new system of pruning – by beginning at the top of the tree – I selected some of the worst cases of trees in the pleasure ground with trees of 60 or 70 years growth, and did not satisfy myself by the results as I have mutilated the trees without establishing a good leader as I could wish still, it will remain to be proved by

1843

the summer's growth whether or not the experiment be successful. In young trees the system is unquestionable, but in old trees at best problematical.

Fig. 66
Pleasure Grounds at Clumber.

23 November   The result of the receipts of my rent has not been nearly so good as I had been led to expect – even a ½ years rent has not been paid up by fully £1,500 – and the arrears now remaining amount to nearly £9,000 – I am sadly disappointed at this result and shall be greatly inconvenienced.

29 November   When in Worksop today attended the Justices' meeting.

Sir T. White received a letter intimating that the services of the Yeomanry, which he commands, would be accepted to attend the Queen when she arrives in Nottingham on Monday 4 December – they are all in commotion in consequence – it is a long way for them to go, and will I fear be found a great inconvenience both for time personal attention and expense ...

30 November   ... to Thoresby for a few days. Sir T. and Lady White and daughter were there. [*He records that the Yeomanry would only be lining the route for the Queen's visit to Nottingham – not acting as her escort. He wrote to Lincoln, to request him to make enquiries about the role of the Yeomanry.*]

1 December   [*Records that Lincoln had failed to obtain any change in the proposed arrangements.*]

2 December   Returned home this afternoon.

3 December   William went off this morning to meet his Troop, which is to assemble at Redhill.

4 December   Again a beautiful day. Charles and Robert went out to shoot wood pigeons and killed 13 – at this time of the year, a wood pigeon is as good a bird as can be eaten.

6 December   I have seen my Clerk of the Works from Nottingham today ...

7 December   Went to Southwell today to attend an adjourned Sessions. Remarkably small attendance of Magistrates – our business was soon over.

11 December   The last of the Windsors is dead. The Earldom of Plymouth is extinct.

1843

20 December   Larch is much wanted just now for some of the rail roads, it is also becoming very scarce – I have been requested to furnish 30,000 feet to a contractor who will give me 1s 6d a foot ...

23 December   Lincoln is at last returned from London, he rode over from Ranby today and is looking fully well – tho' getting too fat. Some of his children have colds, as every body has ...

25 December   As usual we took the Sacrament today - 4 Daughters and 3 Sons – and I trust that it may have been beneficial to us ... Happiness is no longer among us. No attempt is made to amuse or be agreeable to me – on the contrary, they all get together away from me, as if my presence were something noxious, it is a painful consideration, and destroys me. It is wretched, most grievously wretched for myself, but for them such impiety to their parent is a sin that must bring misery with it, and for them I grieve for their fatuity, with no other selfish feeling that than which a father who has lived for his children and loved them so well, must naturally feel – Vice is not the cause, they are virtuously minded and good but something possesses them which I cannot account for – The last Christmas I shall never forget, it was more like a thorough alienation than any thing else.

27 December   We had a large crop of cases at Worksop today occasioned principally by <u>Christmas festivities</u> – a saintly way of rejoicing among the many – some of the cases were striking, others curious.

                  The Duke of Portland mentioned that informations had been lodged against several offenders under the Act of Anne, for high betting - that his Son, Ld. George was to be charged for £160,000 – Ld. Eglington for £300,000 and many others for very large sums – If they should be convicted in the finality, the result will be serious indeed and most salutary – The Act imposes a penalty amounting to 5 times the amount, for every bet above £20.

30 December   My dear Charles left us this morning to rejoin his reg. at Windsor – He is to speak to Thomas about his deplorable marriage ... Lincoln returned to Ranby also this morning. His visits are very short and few – I scarcely see anything of him.

31 December   ... I have passed a wretched year, the most so of any in my memory – I do not know of one redressing circumstance to mitigate a series of untoward events, a succession of misfortunes, miseries, difficulties and disasters, which, but for God's gracious aid and protection human strength and mind could scarcely withstand ...

| 1 January | Thanks be to God. I again enter on a new year and, thanks again, this has been to me a happier day than the first of last year. My four daughters are with me and William and Robert ... |
| 3 January | ... Charles has been very ill since his return to Windsor ... |
| 8 January | My dear Sons Robert and William left me this morning. William stays a fortnight in London and then proceeds to Vienna ... I may never see him again ...

I came in the afternoon to Ranby to pass two nights here and see Lincoln and his children ... |
11 January	Returned to Clumber today. Lincoln goes to Newark to attend a Ball tonight.
16 January	Vegetation has for some weeks been in a very forward state – Many rose trees on the terrace have made shoots of several inches long, and the leaves are about to expand – several rose trees in the pleasure ground have never thrown off their leaves – On the terrace the marzerians [*daphne mezereum*?] are in full bloom – crocuses, snow drops etc. shewing – Such precocity has been rarely known, I should think.
17 January	... lake quite frozen over ...
21 January	An extraordinary sermon from my clergyman Mr Webster ... calling himself one of the high church ...
22 January	All my dear little grandchildren came here today, to pass it here and take leave of me, as they go to join Lincoln in London the day after tomorrow – It was delightful to see them so happy, so good and so agreeable. I saw them go with great regret.
26 January	I hear today ... that I have probably sold my Cwmelan property in Radnorshire ... for £25,000.

Ld. Combermere tells me that he has a pig now weighing alive 57 stones – an ox, I believe belonging to the D. of Devonshire, was lately shown ... which weighed a ton and 500 lbs ... |

1844

28 January   [*Heard that Arthur, his grandson* –] is alarmingly ill and his recovery very doubtful ... I much fear that we shall lose him, as he is a delicate child, tho' full of spirit and activity.

29 January   Little Arthur is out of danger ...[*!*]

30 January   This is my birthday, and all have been vying with each other to do all sorts of kind things by me – which has given me very great pleasure on every account – and it has seemed to please the givers, quite as much as the receiver.

31 January   ... We had the best days sport on the Manor hills which I have known this season ...

1 February   Before going out shooting today, one of my tenants Denman of Gamston Mill called here to speak to me. On the 24th he had written to me to inform me that on the previous day, on his return from Retford market, he found one of my sons (Robert) at my house – who said that he had run away from College – he asked to go to Retford and Denman took him there – but he did and wanted nothing there. D. brought him back with him – thought it best to acquaint me with the circumstances fully persuaded that it was Robert. I sent word to Denman that he had an impostor in his house and directed him to take the person before Mr Dawkins – From that time to this day I was surprised to hear nothing more about the affair, and I had learnt from Mr Dawkins that no one had been brought before him. Denman had called here yesterday but I was out all day shooting. This morning he proceeded to tell me that, on receiving my instructions, he went to the person and told him that he had appraised me of what had happened, and that I had desired him to take him (the impostor) before a Magistrate, Dawkins. The impostor was much agitated and exclaimed 'you have undone me!' – said he could not go before Mr Dawkins and exhorted Denman not to take him – he hesitated to do as I directed, but having two friends in the house – Baker of Gamston and [*Samping*?] of some place near Newark, he called them in and asked their advice and assistance. On seeing and hearing the person (the stranger) they said 'don't take him, let us speak to him in private – I think he has something to say, which he will not impart to you, but which he may tell to us' – accordingly they went with the stranger into a room, where they remained for above an hour. At last they came out and said 'Denman it is all right, there is no occasion for a Magistrate, the stranger is not a man, but a woman.' They soon after went away and Denman went to the stranger and mentioned what his friends had told him – he asked whether she really was a woman, to which she replied 'Yes' – Denman said 'you have taken me in so must not be deceived again, will you consent to

1844

see Mrs Denman that she may verify that you are a woman' – to which she assented – and he took the stranger upstairs to Mrs D., who was expecting every hour to be confined. On enquiry he learnt from his wife that the stranger was a woman, and a lady 'of the first quality'. The lady staid on and Denman did not know what to do with her, he wished her gone 'tho' she was very amiable', as his wife might suffer from having to attend to her when she should be preparing for her lying in. D. enquired what the lady meant to do, she said 'I shall go to York, where I can change my dress'. Since the discovery, the lady had been very much with Denman's wife and conversed with her very much and freely. The lady had said that from Gamston she would go to Worksop – on the 3rd or the 4th day after her arrival, I forget which – Denman went to her and said – 'my servant and gig are going to Worksop, if you have a mind he can take you there' – to which she assented and he took her to Worksop, from whence she was to go by coach to Eckington. Some little time after she was gone, Mrs D. told D. that the lady had confided many things to her, which she could not mention then and had not yet told him, as she was now in her bed and had even kept back her labor to be of use to the stranger. However, she told him that the last thing which the lady told her before she went was – 'I am the Countess of Lincoln, I assumed this disguise to see my children which Ld. L. debars me from' – and she showed her a letter which she had written with her name signed – she desired Mrs D. to divulge nothing untill she was clear away – thanked her, kissed her and departed. This is a marvellous story altogether and if not real, might be supposed to be incredible. What may be the reality, unfortunately cannot be immediately ascertained, and the misery is that these people will have been talking of it every where and spreading it all over the country – I desired Denman to keep silence and to enjoin his friends to do the same but I fear that it is too late.

The whole transaction has been sadly mismanaged by Denman, if he had obeyed my directions all uncertainty would have been avoided, and his duty was, clearly, to have informed [me] instantly when he made the discovery of sex, and not to have presumed to have taken the management of the whole affair into their own hands, where as he did not attempt to inform me of what had passed untill the 31st when I was out shooting, he coolly went away, and on the following day (1st Feb.) only, gave me information so serious to me and my family, as it involved the supposed conduct of two of the members of the latter.

5 February ... William arrived tonight about 8 o'clock from London ...

12 February Our dear William finally left us this morning ...

269

1844

22 February   ... Sir Loftus Otway has bought Cwmelan for £25,000 ... I gave £23,200 for it nearly 10 years ago ... may lead to the beneficial sale of Hafod ... I shall not accept less that £100,000 for it, besides the original purchase price for Dolyclettwr.

26 February   Trying weather for my lambs – this has been a very rough day, with wind and very heavy snowing all day.

29 February   Left Nottingham by the 1½ train, and arrived in Portman Square before 8 o'clock. Poor Charlotte with a sick headache, and I not a good deal better.

1 March   Charlotte has nearly lost her headache today – I dined with the Welsh men being St. David's day, at the Freemason's Tavern, Sir John Walsh in the Chair ... I had to speak ... the whole went off well and pleasantly.

2 March   [*Signed contracts for the sale of Cwmelan.*]

6 March   ... I have gone over the plans and estimates for my new buildings. They will consist of the Churches at Elkesley and Bothamsall – the latter to be entirely rebuilt – A Parsonage to be erected at Bothamsall, a farm house at Elkesley and another small one on the Clumber side of the Manton Farm.

8 March   Started by the ½ past 9 train and arrived at Clumber at ½ past 6 – the train has been made ¼ of an hour later and made a mail train and thus all the principal towns, Nottingham included, have a post from London twice a day ...

9 March   Very high winds today, some of the gusts were furious and have done a great deal of mischief. The flag pole here was blown

Fig. 67 *This picture by William Collins and dated 1822, pre-dates the terraces at Clumber Park. The flagpole is recorded here as having been erected in 1817. Having been destroyed in 1844, it does not appear to have been replaced until 1861.*

1844

down, but no wonder for it was perfectly rotten from top to bottom. It was put up in May 1817, the year in which we were all so nearly swept away in fevers – I remember watching the progress of its erection from my room, when my eyes even so weak that I could scarcely make out what was doing – The spar was of extraordinary length and straightness – I may not find it easy to procure another similar and equal to it.

10 March   ... A bull and 4 Ayrshire cows arrived yesterday from Scotland. The bull is a young one, but handsome and good in all his points – he is precisely what I want – 2 of the cows are beauties, the others good – I have now a large stock of Ayrshire cattle and shall have a fine breed.

13 March   Railroads are a rage this year and several are projected in this neighbourhood ... will bring the road much nearer to us ... from Sheffield to Worksop and Retford and thence to Lincoln, decidedly a straighter and better line ... I never expected that any line of rail road could be thought of so near to Clumber.

18 March   My lambing here is very nearly over ... from 560 to 570 ewes – about 32 are barren – about 25 have yet to lamb and there are 660 to 70 lambs – My flock is all Southdown – the ewes are in excellent condition and have plenty of milk – one was doing well by 3 at a birth, but a fox has taken one of them about 15 days old.

20 March   ... Great alarm is felt here at the strike of the Colliers in Staffordshire and some other places ... a universal strike and turn out is arranged for the 25th ... the consequences will be awfully serious ...

25 March   I wished to keep Thomas's marriage really secret, if possible – and had only told Charles of it – but somehow or other it has got wind and has been mentioned to Lincoln by a friend – he has spoken to Charles about it – who imparted to Thomas that the affair was known and he instantly decided to leave the regiment and resigned his commission without any previous communication to me ... his retirement would be his ruin ...

29 March   ... We are beginning to feel seriously the effect of the strike among the colliers – The stocks are very low and in a short time coals will be so scarce as to be hardly obtainable at any price – I have only 3 weeks consumption on hand and must husband my stock very rigidly ... The colliers have the public at their mercy ...

30 March   ... I went to inspect my improvements at Worksop Manor, they have made great progress and are assuming a settled form. The alterations are as much ornamental as useful, and have quite changed the place – they will after the first outlay be a source of

1844

emolument and the division and allotment into fields accommodate and give pleasure to very many townspeople – The destruction of the large house is going on fast, on the 1ˢᵗ April I commence taking down the Eastern Tower, and shall proceed downwards and shall clear away from thence to the opposite side until it is removed.

1 April   Plenty of fooling this morning – and a glorious day ...

5 April   This is Good Friday – we all took the Sacrament.

8 April   ... I opened tenders from various persons to build a farm house at Elkesley and alter and repair the Church there – at Bothamsall to pull down and rebuild the Church and build a Parsonage house – The lowest offer is £1,762, which with £1,000 added for materials, will make a total of £2,762 for these 4 articles, which seems to me to be remarkably reasonable – all is to be finished by the end of August.

9 April   ... The new brickyard at Bothamsall turns out a prize – it has been at work now about 10 days ... they will burn their first batch of 22,000 bricks on Monday of the next week ...

11 April   [*Went to Nottingham regarding the Park estate development.*]

12 April   [*Returned to Clumber.*]

13 April   Lincoln came here this afternoon ... on his way from Dublin ...

15 April   Found my people busily preparing for my different works.

18 April   They commenced the destruction of Bothamsall Church two days ago. It was my intention to have borne all the expense of rebuilding the Church, believing that the parish could not afford it, but I had reason to believe that it would be very agreeable to the parishioners to contribute towards it, I wrote a letter to the Churchwardens, making the enquiry and leaving it to them, if they desired it, to give in aid such contribution as might be agreeable to their feelings or suitable to their finances – They replied in a most pleasant manner and most cheerfully and gladly agreed to contribute £100 and all the [*carryings?*] for the Church and parsonage – and thanked me for affording them the opportunity of doing so.

19 April   I heard that on Sunday last, Bothamsall Church was [*fuller?*] than ever was known, and that this large congregation was voluntary to take leave of their old Church – This feeling is worthy of notice and does them infinite credit.

22 April   Went to Bothamsall to see how they are getting on – The scaffolding is now erecting to the Tower down – all the inside and roofs are removed – The bricks turn out admirably, but they are carelessly and ill made. I must change my maker, as justice is not done to as good materials as ever were used.

1844

Some ewe hogs, as they are called here – that is lambs of last year's, have been put upon the lawn which are really superior, and equal to any I ever saw – They do credit to those who have the care of them, and well repay the cost which I have bestowed upon them.

2 May The Duchess of Portland was found dead in her bed at Welbeck this morning – She was rather unwell with a cold or influenza, but not even attended by a medical man. This awful event is wholly unexpected.

My dear Robert has again failed his degree ... a result of such gross and flagrant injustice. It is really heart breaking, and I will [*not*] suffer it to rest here.

4 May On going to Bothamsall today I found the Church levelled to the ground. The Chancel only is left standing – The foundations of the Parsonage are commenced.

11 May ... I wrote a letter of appeal and complaint to the Vice Chancellor Oxford on poor Robert's shameful business.

20 May The Church at Bothamsall is now about a yard high from the ground level.

No rain, no pastures – stock starving, but corn looking well.

21 May Some welcome rain today.

22 May This is Lincoln's birthday – I have remembered and blest him, but I may look in vain for filial sympathy and affection – would that it were otherwise ... I dread retribution – sins of omission are frequently as bad as those of commission.

24 May Mr Lindsay came today ...

27 May Went through many matters relating to my affairs, and settled for an improved method of keeping the accounts, then went fully into Nottingham concerns – checked upon the plan of the new roads in the Park, and particularly as to the approach through the tunnel – and made arrangements for the sale of the Town property on the 19th of June – and of parts of Basford and the Park, as soon as proper preparations can be made.

29 May The Duke of Portland was taken very ill yesterday. I went to Welbeck to enquire - he is better today and had gone out in the carriage. I was informed that he was taken with a fainting fit ...

I was at Worksop to meet the magistrates but the court was adjourned as no Magistrates attended.

31 May The Duke of Portland is better – he called here today.

8 June A long day at Elkesley and Bothamsall with the architect [*Tremin?*] and the builders etc. – everything is finally settled, and the work may now proceed without any more alteration.

1844

There has been much to correct and arrange ... by good fortune, I yesterday discovered an excellent bed of stone at Bothamsall – with which the Churches must have been formerly built and with which they will now be rebuilt and repaired.

10 June   I forgot to mention that about the 25th of May, I saw a most extraordinary number of swifts flying about, and flying low which is also unusual, over the broad part of the lake – they were so numerous and active in their flight that it was impossible to count them, there probably were not less than 200 of them. Ordinarily we see a few say 6, flying about in different places and very high in the air – these birds were all together mixed with a few swallows and appeared to be intent in pursuit of their [*flock*?] – can it be the peculiarity of the season which has caused this increase of numbers and change of habit – skimming over the water? The weather being utterly without moisture and very cold may have caused this.

17 June   Went to visit my works today – they are making good progress, and I have now, I believe, put them into a good way. Whilst at Bothamsall all this afternoon a short shower of rain fell – and appearances promise more.

18 June   At last, thanks be to God, the rain is come in good earnest ...

22 June   Robert arrived this night from Oxford ...

24 June   I left Clumber at 5 o'clock this morning and arrived at the Nottingham station a few minutes after the 7 o'clock train had started. I went to the Inn, shaved and had some breakfast and left by the 8.20 am train, and arrived in Portman Square at 1/4 past 3 – wrote some letters, dressed, ate a mutton chop and went down to the H. of Lords ...

25 June   ... I sent to poor Thomas to come to me, that I may speak to him on his wretched business, but he is not come – Charles is here and a great comfort to me

26 June   ... arrived here, Clumber, a little before 8 – found all well.

1 July   Slept at Nottm. last night and was at the Station before 7, but as they were preparing to put my carriage on, I was informed that it could not go by that train, being a mail train. I consequently went by the 8¼ train and arrived in London at 3, had some dinner and went down to the House ...

[*The debate was on the diocesan matters relating to the 'Sees of St Asaph and Bangor'. The Duke records that he could not refrain from speaking on this matter and he sets out the main points of his intervention. The Hansard report for this day's debate does not include any mention of the Duke's speech.*] ... I have given myself much useless trouble ... I have not been

1844

successful in gaining converts ... I withdraw and shall not trouble them again untill I perceive a more favorable opportunity for taking a public post.

2 July [*Records that his friends, including Lords Kenyon and Powis, attempted to calm his distress over parliamentary matters.*]

4 July ... arrived at Clumber at 9 ... no good news about the sale of Hafod ...

6 July When in London, I saw poor Thomas on the 2nd and was grieved to the soul to see him as he was. He seems to have isolated himself from every body and every thing ... a state of ... inaction, which prostrates all exertions and makes him conclude that he will be happiest in doing nothing and being "left alone" – to exist and vegetate without being of any use to himself or any other human being ...

I greatly fear that I shall never induce him to leave this woman's side, to associate with fit society – or to employ himself and follow up his profession. The whole thing makes my heart ache and bleed.

14 July Nothing new. I have hurt my back by cutting wood too strenuously and cold and rheumatism has fallen into the weak place, which pains and inconveniences me very much.

15 July St. Swithin – and his usual concomitant rain, tho' not in very great abundance.

25 July ... I am just going to Nottm. to attend the Assizes ...

26 July I yesterday went over the Basford estate with the map and examined ... it in a very cursory manner but sufficient to convince me that it is a valuable estate – the crops are good and the estate is well managed and in good order – I shall expect to obtain not less than 150 per acre, minerals included, for my part of the estate and for some portions of it, some 50 acres, lying nearest to the race course and to the Mansfield road, I fully expect £400 an acre ... I should get about £150,000 for the whole.

Attended the Assizes today – and also passed a very considerable time in the Park – my tunnel is made – I went through it ... dined with the Judges, Ld.'s Denman and Coltman, and returned home, arrived here about 12 o'clock.

27 July [*Records that the sale of the Cwmelan estate was now closed. £25,000 was to be paid to Coutts bank 'of their mortgage of £158,000'.*] – I am getting on a little and in the course of two months hence, I shall probably have paid off £45,000 of debt.

29 July I had offered ... to Prince Albert that he should buy Hafod for the Prince of Wales ... but my offer has been civilly declined ...

30 July My harvest is begun with the oats ...

1844

2 August [*Mr and Mrs John Vernon came to stay at Clumber for two nights.*]

We went to look at the Bothamsall building ... I was greatly pleased with the look of the Church. The tower is nearly up and all will be [*ready*] for the roofing in a fortnight.

5 August Wrote to William yesterday ...

7 August The Queen was yesterday morning delivered of a Prince ... [*Alfred*]

8 August [*He records a tragedy at Nottingham, where a crowd, gathered to witness an execution at Malin Hill, had suffered several deaths and injuries in the crush which ensued.*]

10 August We rode this afternoon to see the Bothamsall works. The church is nearly rebuilt and makes a beautiful appearance – it is well built also. The Parsonage is also in a forward state and will be ready to roof in a fortnight. The roof is [*being put*] on the body of the church.

... Charles arrived from London.

15 August ... my corn is all cut and in sheaves ... The turnips never looked better.

17 August Rode to look at my works at Elkesley. The stone work for the church is in forwardness, and they will commence pulling down the aisle on Monday 19th ... The roof is being fitted to Weightman's farm house, which is a capital building. At Bothamsall the Tower is up all but the battlements and pinnacles, the rest of the church all done but for the finish. The Parsonage nearly fit to receive the roof – Bothamsall Church I consider to be a beautiful model.

23 August This is Caroline's birthday, and her Sisters proposed that we should give her a little fete – the day was fine and we were to dine on board the 'Lincoln'. The servants all had fruit and cake etc. in the pleasure ground opposite and some wine to warm their stomachs – they walked about there and rowed about in the boats and amused themselves and seemed very happy. It happened to be the last day of harvest for the women and they came dressed out in their best and appeared on the opposite side. We sent them some provision and they were much pleased. All went off well, no accident, all pleased, and no people could conduct themselves more admirably. Our own immediate party were all delighted and happy. At times I could not prevent the intrusion of many sad thoughts and deep, very deep, regrets.

26 August The Bishop of Lincoln began his confirmation in this county today. He commenced at Tuxford – I have asked him to abide here during his stay in the neighbourhood ...

1844

27 August   My harvest was finished yesterday ... Mr Thompson told me that a field of spring wheat of his at Elkesley will produce him 6 gns an acre.

Elkesley Church is taken down – that is the entire aisle. When the aisle is rebuilt then the other alterations will be made. Bothamsall Church is ready to roof in – it is really beautiful. The pinnacles only are defective and must be altered.

28 August   The Bishop of Lincoln came here today, after his confirmation at Worksop. He leaves me tomorrow morning and goes to Ollerton and stops at Mr Cobham's at Edwinstowe.

2 September   [*Monday – out shooting – killed 21 brace – a very hot day.*]

4 September   Charles was called to London this morning, to attend a review with his Regiment tomorrow morning.

In the afternoon we went to Markham Clinton, where we stay the night on a visit to Dawkins.

5 September   Looking about my farms and other things in the neighbourhood of Markham Clinton returned to Clumber in the afternoon.

11 September   ... I am busily preparing for my departure. I shall go to Hafod the day after tomorrow, my family in the course of a week will go to Bridlington for sea bathing. I shall not stay more than a week at Hafod and then shall join them at Bridlington.

12 September   ... Charles returned from London today.

14 September   ... I had a very unsuccessful journey by railroad, I did not get into Liverpool untill 1/2 past 10 at night ... The country however thro' which I went was beautiful and interesting in the extreme – United with beauty and cultivation of the land, the [*swarm?*] of towns, villages, villas, manufacturing, steam engines, chimneys, factories, storehouses – roads, canals, railroads, and masses of human beings, is truly astonishing. When I passed Whitwell, I found the corn still green and standing ...

15 September   [*Left the Adelphi Hotel at Liverpool – took the steam boat to Birkenhead – missed the Chester train and 'posted' there instead – slept at Llangollen.*]

[*Notes that at Trevillan, between Wrexham and Chester, there was*] – a very singular modern church, a sort of hybrid of Grecian, Gothic and English ... which might be a good model for changing the style of Markham Clinton Church.

17 September   [*Arrived at Hafod.*]

18 September   ... engaged in packing up the spoils of this place –

two renowned chimney pieces and various beautiful ornaments. The chimney piece which I remove from the Drawing room I replace with one from Worksop Manor – also very fine and costly.

1844

19 September ... I have been astonished by the receipt of letters. One from Lady Lincoln announces that she is with Lincoln at Ryde, thoroughly reinstated as his wife – wonders will never cease! – this is the greatest of them all. I have not received a line from Lincoln for above 2 months, nor have I heard a syllable about him – she says that he is ill and that she has gone to nurse him – a pretty nurse truly, after all that she has done, and intoxicated with laudanum. I am lost in wonder and conjecture I know not what to think or to conclude – I only know that it must be a long while before she enters my house – she must prove herself to be worth something before I can blow hot or cold upon a matter of such grave importance.

20 September [*Two letters arrived from Lord Lincoln*] – He states that this change of sentiment probably arose from the good advice of Lord Douglas [*Susan's brother*], "but more particularly from the fact that the Duke and Duchess of Hamilton for their own convenience have become very anxious to get rid of her" – I dare say they do, and so would any one else who knows and feels what she is – and so Lincoln who has branded her with infamy to all his relations, friends and even acquaintances, banished her from his house and forbidden all communication whatever with his children – allows this woman to come back to him when it suits her mood or convenience, knowing that she hates him and does not disguise it, and that his temper and hers can never agree for a week – What will people think – assuredly, if she is fit to be received by him and whitewashed of all her sins – his preceding conduct to her must have been nothing less than atrocious – I believe Lady Lincoln to be vicious, deceitful, heartless and good for nothing and Lincoln's misery will be worse than ever. ...

The other letter from Lincoln is one in answer to mine written about a month ago and does him no honor as a Son or a man [*no detail given*] ... I pray that [*his actions*] may be errors of judgement and not of design.

22 September Nothing new – this is Sunday – I am not very well and have not been out much today.

25 September Left Hafod ... arrived in Lichfield ...

26 September [*Lichfield to Tamworth – train to York – on to Bridlington.*]

27 September ... I took a warm bath this afternoon and was much the better for it.

2 October ... The Queen in her steamer passed this place today at 12 o'clock, on her return from Scotland – she was accompanied by 4 other steamers – there were many ships in this bay at the time, and the scene was remarkable for animation and interest.

1844

3 October   ... excruciating rheumatism or something like it which is now subsiding but has left my left arm with a weakness ...

22 October   [*Reports that he has continued to suffer from rheumatic pain.*]

31 October   Poor Mr Mason who so long did the duty at Clumber [*as Chaplain*] is just dead ... I have known him from my boyish days ...

8 November   Received a few lines from William yesterday ...

11 November   [*Started for home, via Beverley, slept at the Victoria Hotel, Hull.*]

13 November   [*By train to Eckington, then on to Clumber.*]

15 November   Saw a swallow skimming about today as in summer ... not able to do much today, far from well.

19 November   Mr Lindsay came today – my affairs are improved ...

20 November   ... I am now working my way through the debts which beset me and if I could part with Hafod, I should be positioned in a flourishing condition.

21 November   Went to visit and inspect my works at Elkesley and Bothamsall. Weightman's farm house is nearly finished – it is a capital house – Too good indeed for a farmer –

The Church is not finished yet – more must be done to it, but the architect has committed faults – and has not contrived well. The vestry is half up – the pewing in a forward state. The Church at Bothamsall is as nearly perfect as can be – The pinnacles are not good and the end (east) window of the Chancel should be lengthened, when this is done the interior as well as the exterior will [*be*] quite a model for a parish Church – it is really beautiful. The parsonage house also, pleases me very much. The elevation, with the exception of the great chimney flue on the outside, which I never like, is faultless and extremely pretty, I think, and the interior is convenient, well arranged and good. I corrected a few faults but they are trifles – Bothamsall is truly well adorned by these buildings.

22 November   My rents were concluded yesterday. The receipts do not amount to the full 1/2 years rental ... [*arrears standing at between £8,000 and £9,000.*]

23 November   Mr Lindsay left me this morning ... an excellent man ...

I have been invited to Windsor Castle to attend the Chapter of the Garter on the 12th of next month – but I shall excuse myself.

24 November   I have sold the railroad shares which I held ... the price given for 100 shares was 105 1/2.

1844

25 November	Rode to look at my works at Bothamsall. The alterations which I proposed the other day have been executed and look remarkably well – by lowering the east window, I have given an importance to it and a proportion which will have a striking effect on entering, especially if I fill it with painted glass. I never saw a Church of its size that pleases me better – I think it now perfect.
27 November	We were agreeably surprised to see the Duke of Portland come into the Magistrate's room today at Worksop ... in the face he looked pulled and pale – I fear that he will not last long.
28 November	I went out shooting today ...
29 November	Charles left us this morning his leave being expired ... it is melancholy to reflect how broken up my once happy and affectionate family now is.
5 December	If the accounts of the papers are to be believed a general strike of the Colliers is recommencing ...
6 December	A sharp frost set in yesterday. The lake was frozen over this morning with thick ice ...
9 December	The full rigor of winter prevails – everything is bound up and dead ... There are many people out of employment – this severe weather will be dreadful to them ...
11 December	Wrote to William today ...
12 December	[*Records that there had been many accidents on the roads and railways in recent days*] – accidents appear to be like misfortune and like them seldom come alone.
14 December	... This morning at breakfast at Firbeck, where we have been staying for a few days, on Mrs [*Henrietta*] Gally Knight asking for some water, she was informed that there was none, as the well had become completely dry ... We returned to Clumber today.
25 December	... Our party is very small for this once happy anniversary and affectionate reunion of all my family – Some most loved, are not [*here*] – some far away – others not able to come and some not willing to come. I have heard that Lincoln, Lady Lincoln and his children are at Ranby – I have heard nothing of him for months – We all communicated, that is my 4 daughters, Robert and I and there was the largest attendance I ever knew in this Chapel, which was a very great satisfaction – there were in all 40 communicants.

1844

26 December   I forgot to mention that on the 21st a large deputation from the Newark and Sheffield by Mansfield railway came here, to persuade me to approve of the measure, but I would not give them an affirmative answer – as I wish for the Nottingham and Lincoln communication by Newark – and for the Sheffield and Lincolnshire by Worksop on the other side ...

29 December   ... I have now sold all my house property in Nottingham.

The contract for the last house in Pelham St. was signed yesterday, and deposit paid ... I have still a few lots of building land in old Thurland paddock or rather where the Hall stood, unsold – they go off heavily.

31 December   ... A letter from William ... ill for 3 weeks ...

Clumber and Worksop Estates

Expenditure for the year July 1844 to June 1845

	£	s	d
Land tax	973.	8.	1
Tithes	1,360.	11.	5
Estate Repairs	940.	4.	10
Sundries	3 780.	5.	5
Clumber House	1,948.	11.	1
Park and repairs	2,318.	12.	5
Gardens	690.	9.	2
Timber	1,005.	9.	6
Taxes and parochial rates	731.	9.	2
Insurance	197.	5.	0
Coals	386.	3.	0
Gamekeeper account	1,297.	14.	0
Gratuities	449.	0.	0
Expenses of the Office	202.	2.	4
Brickyards	1,191.	19.	11
Small Farm	40.	17.	0
Haughton and Hardwick Farms	783.	11.	4
Miscellaneous Disbursements	247.	15.	11
Agent's Salary	800.	0.	0

Note – The auditor's report accompanying these figures is critical of the Agent's book-keeping. He comments that they are 'greatly deficient in real check', and that they do not compare well with the 'precise uniformity' of the previous Agent's work.

[Source - Manuscripts and Special Collections Dept. – Ref. NeA451]

1 January [*As in previous years, the Duke entered his thoughts on the year ahead, including:*] – hope for health, prosperity and happiness ... that my dear children ... be all that they should be ... [*that*] I may be contented and resigned.

Attended the Justice meeting at Worksop + 4 Magistrates besides myself. The Duke of Portland, by letter, intimated that from age and infirmity he must henceforth discontinue his attendance on the Bench. [*They all signed a letter of regrets and good wishes to Portland.*]

A wretched, cold, foggy and chilling day. We have passed a very pleasant evening in our small party – my daughters all contributed some very good, pretty and well executed music.

3 January The Church at Bothamsall is at last covered in and the whole work drawing towards completion – I have not seen it for a fortnight or more, and am more than ever pleased with it, the carvers are now finishing the heads, figures and bosses which add greatly to the finish and general appearance – all the upper rooms of the parsonage are finished plastered and painted.

6 January [*Here, he records what he calls* 'two natural history stories'. *The first relates to the singing of a bullfinch, as heard by two of his daughters and Robert. The bullfinch was said to imitate many other birds, including blackbird, thrush and nightingale. The Duke suggests that the bird was tame and had escaped from its cage. The second* 'story' *is of a dog, which lived at the* 'Little Farm' *and was renowned for imitating the crowing of a cockerel.*]

9 January [*Sir Robert Peel replied to a letter from the Duke, regarding the purchase of Crown lands – e.g. portions of the Hafod estate. No details are given as to the content of Peel's reply – see 8th March below regarding the parliamentary events that followed this entry.*]

22 January ... I had an excellent sale of timber yesterday – prices having risen greatly, and many strangers attended which caused an

1845

extraordinary competition – several lots were unsold but ... I gained an excess of above £500 ... shall try another sale.

27 January   [*Snow – the first of this winter.*]

30 January   This being my birthday – my dear children have endeavoured in the kindest and most amiable manner to mark their attentions and to make up, as far as they can, for the deficiencies which they as much as I deeply lament – my four daughters and Robert are the whole amount of my family here – Charles tried to come but could not get leave. They made some very nice presents of their own manufacture in the morning, and in the evening set up a little novelty in their own rooms – and gave me some very pretty and well selected music and many other little agreeable and well contrived circumstance – I have been much delighted with them and their deeds.

31 January   ... To my surprise I received a letter from Mr Gladstone announcing to me that he had removed office altogether and had resigned – giving as his reason that what Sir Robert Peel was going to do regarding public education was so contrary to his known opinions ... that he could no longer remain in the same Cabinet ...

... Lincoln ... is to have a seat in the Cabinet!!! – Retaining his present office [*First Commissioner of Woods and Forests*] – against which if youth and inexperience were not a decided objection – there are many others that make such appointments objectionable ...

The Cabinet will now be composed of submissives and time serving boys, pupils and parasites of the wily and suspect – Peel – for such he is – he gets the unwary into his net and then blasts them for ever ... this he will not do with Lincoln ... I have often counselled him (Lincoln) upon this point but now he has deserted me and my counsels also altogether and follows his own heart's lusts, and poor fellow, he must take the consequences ...

1 February   ... as regards Lincoln ... it would really be too shocking for him, as my Son who have ever supported the Protestant Established Church of this country, to set cuckoolike in Mr Gladstone's seat ... Lincoln's career of undutifulness and office worship, endeavouring to gain as much as he can of the world, at the risk of losing his soul, is a wretched contemplation – He was once every thing that I could wish, my hope and my pride – His marriage with that vile woman his wife has been his ruin and disregarding all my counsels and throwing himself into unworthy hands has lost him – He is now a bad Son, and exposes himself to all the ruin ... God grant him a speedy view of his previous error, and endue him with humble mindedness and contrition.

1845

4 February   ... I am still in hopes that Lincoln has not taken a seat in the Cabinet – it would be ruinous to him – I wish from my soul that he had more independent and a higher mind – but he is too much like an office clerk, and has all the pedantry of a mere official drudge – He sees nothing beyond office and gaining a majority, never mind how – in the H.of Comms. – I wish he could and would take a high line I should be proud of him – As he is he annoyes me beyond measure – to see him the tool of such fellows as he [*assortes?*] with, vexes me to the soul.

I see that the E[*arl*] and C[*ounte*]ss of Lincoln are gone on a visit to Windsor ... what an indelicacy of mind this marks in poor Lincoln – how can he suffer such a woman to appear before the Queen under a mask, knowing as he does what she is ...

5 February   ... I observe ... that Lincoln is really put into the Cabinet – no experience, and has done nothing to distinguish himself above others, and can be little beneficial in council, such an elevation is as useless as it is uncalled for – this I must in candour state.

7 February   ... all I undertake fails and that I am doomed to disappointment, whilst others succeed without any difficulty ... very afflicting and very trying ... hereafter I may hear the blessed words – 'Well done thou tolerably good but faithful servant, enter thou into the Joys of the Lord'.

11 February   Some madman or wantonly mischievous fellow has destroyed the celebrated Portland vase in the British Museum, he was seen to smash it to pieces with one of the sculptured stones which was near ...

15 February   Charles is come from London this evening on leave for a few weeks ...

21 February   ... Sir R.Peel is transcendent – He rules the roost most supremely and carries all before him – He makes black white, turns every thing inside out, wills and it is done ... there is something beyond human ken in all this ... it makes one shut one's eyes and shudder as if on the brink of a precipice.

25 February   ... the thaw seems to be complete – unluckily, I am just now engaged in clearing the mud out of the lake under the terrace and before the ferry and the carts are in full work carrying it away through the pleasure ground – if the ground is very soft I shall have to stop this tomorrow ...

26 February   Attended the Justice's meeting at Worksop ... the market was stated to be flat.

28 February   Extremely cold today – it is very favourable to my mud clearing ...

1845

1 March	A maiden old lady, a Miss Vessey of Gateford near Worksop – died yesterday at a very old age – being 95 ... her property goes to Mr Machin.
2 March	[*He mentions* 'the ministerial bottle holders and parasites'.]
4 March	My wood sale today has not been prosperous ... the lots sold fetched £728. I realised about £60 more than my valuation – I shall try the sale again in 3 weeks time ...
5 March	[*Heavy snow. He records that no sowing, planting or digging was possible.*]
8 March	[*The matter of the sale of Crown lands, mentioned in his diary entry above – see 9ᵗʰ January – had been raised in Parliament. Lincoln had spoken on the subject but, in his father's opinion, had not sufficiently defended him from accusations of wrongdoing.*]
14 March	... My dear Charles left us for London this morning ... it is impossible not to lament his absence.
15 March	A great deal of snow ... my lambs are now dying and ewes also ...
16 March	... from 20 to 30 lambs have died in the last two nights.
	All my town property at Nottingham which was sold has been settled for – I have paid off £7,000 of [*Mr Horvard's?*] mortgage and £11,000 and upwards of [*Messrs Smiths?*] Bond and within the last year have now reduced my debt and the interest upon it by something more than £3,000 a year – £8,000 would pay every farthing that I owe including lawyers bills and purchases – if I can get my means paid up, which I am struggling for, I shall be clear of all debt.
17 March	... I am writing this at ½ 8 a.m. ... the Sun is this instant trying to peep out ...
18 March	... This is Georgiana's birthday [*her 35th*] – I called upon Robert to propose her health after dinner which he did with a good deal of humour and amused us all ... Georgiana would not be outdone, and to our surprise rose with great steadiness and composure and addressed us in a very neat and remarkably well expressed speech, which pleased us as much as it surprised us – it really was extremely well done – and she showed what she could do, if she chose to take advantage of an opportunity.
20 March	Quite the dead of winter ...
21 March	Good Friday – We all took the Sacrament ... I think there were no fewer than 38 besides the Clergyman.
22 March	The snow is nearly all gone ... – William writes from Vienna ...

1845

24 March Finishing all my tree planting today and tomorrow – The lake is still without its water, the river only being confined to a memory in its natural channel – the mudding, as much as I shall do this year, will be finished in 5 days and then I shall let the water in again ...

Fig. 68 *The River Poulter, seen here in 1988, when the Clumber Lake was affected by subsidence. The river flows west to east (right to left on this photograph). The derelict hull of the boat, 'The Lincoln', is visible in the distance. Beyond lies the estate village of Hardwick.*

26 March [*A letter of the Duke's, relating to his purchases at Hafod and written to the Editor of the 'Standard' newspaper, had appeared in that publication.*]

27 March The appearance of my letter has caused many well wishers to write to me ...

28 March [*Many more letters had been received*] I shall keep these documents amongst my most precious archives – I would not change my situation for any other in the Kingdom.

30 March I continue to receive letters ...

2 April Resumed our rides. Rode with my daughters and Mr Dawkins to see how things went on at Bothamsall. Dawkins had not seen the Church or parsonage since they were finished – he was pleased with them but discovered some errors and deficiencies.

8 April Rode over today to settle the allotment of the pews by the wish of the parishioners. The Church will be reopened on Sunday week (20th) for public worship.

1845

An attempt to fire the extensive plots of heath on Worksop Common was made on Sunday last but was discovered before much mischief was done – Kilton Wood was on fire during the past week said to be by accident. The heath was wilful mischief.

9 April   We have altered the days of holding the fairs at Worksop and they have been very bad of late years. To give it a good start and a spirit – I sent a good many things, beasts and sheep – as an experiment and for the first time some horses – Of these latter I sent six, two of high price – I sold two of the six, the first I believe that were offered for sale at a Worksop fair – In the next year no doubt there will be several horses – Of the beasts and sheep – the whole lot was sold and very highly approved – my Down wethers were admired by all.

13 April   My Bailiff, Kirkwood, came early this morning to tell me that a wholesale robbery had been committed and that 25 sheep had been stolen and taken away – There seems to have been much neglect and mismanagement from not counting the flock – on this account no one can say when these sheep were taken – but it is thought that they were taken on Thursday night – this being Sunday, and only now mentioned, I have set on foot enquiry in every direction ...

... [I have] a good deal to settle with Mr Thompson about Elkesley parish affairs ...

... I did not open my post bag untill very late – it's contents were such as to rouse and invite me to immediate action, and I wrote a hurried and possibly not sufficiently considered address to 'My Countrymen' on the present state of affairs especially as regards the encouragement of Popery [the Maynooth College Bill] ...

[the address is] to be carried in all the newspapers ... and generally circulated throughout the Kingdom – I wish it may produce the effect which is intended.

14 April   I find that there is much reason to apprehend that my own Shepherd has been concerned in the stealing of my sheep. He has been frequently seen late at night in Retford, and has been often drunk, and his conduct upon enquiry has been very questionable, and when he has been out he has been in very low places –

He lives at Hardwick, and has a wife and a large family and has an excellent place.

15 April   [Records that his people at Hardwick waited all day for the Police Inspector to interview them regarding the missing sheep. The officer failed to arrive.]

1845

17 April To my shame and unspeakable regret Lincoln has made a speech upon the Maynooth measure ... identifying himself with all its evil ... this follows from being connected with bad men and deserting the councils and his allegiance to his parent and best friend. I am grievously hurt at this ...

18 April I received many letters respecting my address ... as Lord Manvers says in his quaint way – 'The firm of Bobby Peel and Co. which is fast breaking up, will stop payment and be completely resolved' – ... Then will come the immense solution – Parliament will be dissolved ... This is almost an Utopian idea, but if we are fit for it, by God's help, it may be accomplished ... I cannot conceal from myself that if any one can be instrumental in accomplishing this end, I am probably the only man in the country in a position to bring it about – I write this in the privacy of my Chamber and before the God who, for his wise purposes, may be conducting such a frail and inefficient mortal as I know myself to be, to perform deeds far beyond my presumed and estimated strength ... Oh, that I had my Son with me and not against me in the fulfilment of all that may be good, great, glorious, generous, elevated and Christianlike !!

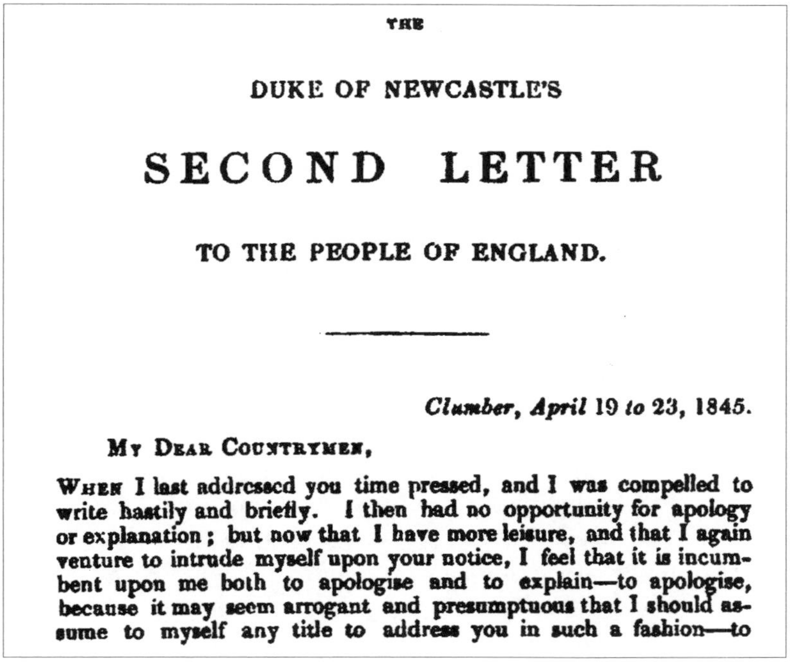

THE

DUKE OF NEWCASTLE'S

SECOND LETTER

TO THE PEOPLE OF ENGLAND.

Clumber, April 19 *to* 23, 1845.

MY DEAR COUNTRYMEN,

WHEN I last addressed you time pressed, and I was compelled to write hastily and briefly. I then had no opportunity for apology or explanation ; but now that I have more leisure, and that I again venture to intrude myself upon your notice, I feel that it is incumbent upon me both to apologise and to explain—to apologise, because it may seem arrogant and presumptuous that I should assume to myself any title to address you in such a fashion—to

Fig. 69

21 April ... I have received several letters from the country, all hearty, approving and ready to lend every aid in their power – one begs to be allowed to print and publish my letter for general circulation ...

1845

25 April   I sat up nearly all night, that is to 6 this morning to finish my [*second*] address ...

30 April   My people are busy in the woods, felling and barking the oaks and chestnuts – The oaks, as last year, are fully as forward as other trees ... the lilacs are only now opening into leaf, not as yet shewing any symptoms of flower ...

5 May   Nothing new today – I have again no renewed prospect of selling Hafod.

6 May   [*Mentions that his Clumber sheep were being sold at 6d a pound.*]

15 May   [*Sent his 2nd Address – see 25 April above – to London today.*]

19 May   [*Records that his Address was published in the newspapers today. It's publication coincided with the 3rd Reading of the Maynooth Bill in the Commons.*]

25 May   ... as might be expected, my last letter is being attacked in the newspapers ...

26 May   [*Outlined here his plan to attend the House of Lords on the 2ⁿᵈ June, when he intended to interrupt the Minister's statement on the Maynooth Bill*] –

... I shall impart my scheme to nobody, as surprise will be every thing ... I fear that I shall make but a lame figure in the business ... I am sanguine enough to think that it may be successful.

29 May   ... my shearing is nearly over ...

31 May   Left Clumber about ½ past 1 and arrived in London at ½ past 10 ...

2/4 June   [*Records that the Maynooth debate took place but makes no reference to a personal contribution.*]

4 June   ... I believe that I have at last found a purchaser for my Welsh properties, Hafod and everything, for £106,000 ...

6 June   [*Returned to Clumber.*]

13 June   Went to see how my works were going on at Bothamsall – building wall to parsonage garden – remaking end window to chancel to receive painted glass, and other things – found the builders' work at the Church miserably ill done, so rough and ill laid as to be most unsightly if examined into.

15 June   [*Left Clumber, to travel to London. Stopped overnight at Nottingham*]

16 June   ... nearly 4 o'clock before I arrived in Portman Sq., very tired, very hot, with a bad head and quite put out, I had to dress, shave, dine and collect and read my papers before going to the House of Lords ... I of course made a very bad speech but still got out a great deal of what I wished to say ...

1845

17 June ... my Daughters and Robert arrived about 1/4 before 8 and found me asleep upon my bed ... we soon forgot all our cares in dining and retiring early to bed.

18 June Waterloo day – the Iron Duke had his usual dinner. I almost think it will be his last – As a soldier he has done a good service, as a politician irreparable injury ...

22 June We were all at the Opera last night ...

23/24 June [*Sat on a 'railway committee' in the Lords.*]

27 June At a musical party at Mr R. Cavendish's ...

2 July Went with my Daughters and 2 Sons, to see the Plate Glass Works at Blackwall ...

5 July Went to see the bookbinding establishment of Messrs Westley and Clarke in Friar's Lane near St. Paul's ...

8 July Accompanied my Daughters to a very pleasant party at Sion ...

16 July [*Reports that Draft contracts had been completed for the sale of Hafod. Also mentions that, since 1833, he had spent some £58,000 on that estate.*]

[*He enters here an incident which had occurred whilst he was walking in a London Park. He came upon two men, said to be father and son. The older man, aged 85, had fallen down and was foaming at the mouth. The Duke offered assistance and went to call a hansom cab to send the man home. Eventually, the man revived and the Duke gave him a sovereign and also paid the cab fare. The men told him that they did not wish to give their exact address and merely said that they wished to go to 'a place at the foot of Highgate'.*]

17 July We went to the Opera this night ...

18 July A letter from William in Munich – He has been borrowed from Vienna ...

21 July [*He attended the House of Lords, where the Irish University Bill was being debated. He spoke in opposition to it.*]

23 July [*Charles returned to his regiment, although unwell.*]

25 July I just finished every thing in time to refresh myself by cold washing, shaving and dressing myself then breakfast and then off to the embarkation place. [*They then sailed to Ramsgate on the steamer 'Little Western'.*]

5 August Charles arrived this afternoon ...

11 August At last my sale of Hafod is accomplished ... deposit of £10,000 ... remaining 95,000 he will pay on the 31st Jan 1846 ... altogether I have made a very good bargain ... I shall be a gainer of £6,000 a year by the transaction – and of £1,000 a year by the former sale of Cwmelan ... I thank God for His goodness to me ...

1845

14 August	... my two sons left me this morning ... some sort of amputation [*division?*] seems to prevail among my children – they shew me because I am their best friend and wish them well. I am too sore and hurt to trust my pen.
23 August	... it is Caroline's birthday [*her 27th*] – we availed ourselves of it and made a trip to Margate – dined there and looked about us ...
29 August	Henrietta's birthday [*her 26th*]– at the solicitation of my quartet we made an excursion, going to Minster, Richboro' Castle and Sandwich ...
13 September	Made a tour of the Isle of Thanet and to Reculver ... to shew the whole at a view to my Daughters ...
19 September	[*They took the 'Ramsgate Packet' steamer to Calais. His daughters were seasick.*] I had almost forgotten this Town and situation ...
27 September	[*Back to London, via Dover.*]
1 October	[*Home to Clumber.*] This is my dear Charlotte's birthday [*her 33rd*] ... she has a bad cold, and is not able to enjoy any thing.
4 October	... to Bothamsall to view the state of the Church and parsonage.

No work could be worse executed than it is – the shameful scamping of the work now begins to show itself but too evidently, and in another season it will be infinitely worse – The parsonage as a living house is wretched from the miserable manner in which everything has been done. All the carpenter's work is dropping to pieces – and much of the stone work nearly as bad – it is papered now ... for Mr MacGregor to reside in it – but it will have to undergo a complete repair in the Spring when all the cracks, settlements and bad fittings have done there worst ... it will cost one many hundreds of pounds to put all the deficiencies into a habitable state.

Fig. 70 Bothamsall Church, 155 years later.

1845

5 October   Mr Thompson did duty here today, as Mr MacGregor is gone <u>to be married</u> ...

My harvest is of the wheat and remainder of the barley ...

6 October   ... in the afternoon went to look at all my horses in and out of the Stable – my young things have grown and improved greatly this summer – It is admitted that I have some of the best young horses in the County – I send to shew some tomorrow at the Retford show ...

8 October   Yesterday was the Retford agricultural meeting ... I was not able to go ... A two years old filly of mine took the first prize.

Today was the Worksop fair ...

15 October   Mr Lindsay arrived today ...

17 October   Today we went thro' all our business of detail and all the prospective arrangements for the next year with Mr Wilmot ...

21 October   Went in the morning to see the ploughing match, and afterwards dined with the members of the Laborer's friends Society – I as President was in the Chair ...

24 October   Attended an adjourned Sessions at Southwell ... a committee of 3 Magistrates [*was*] chosen to investigate serious charges against Mr Roper, for misconduct in his office of Keeper of the House of Correction at Southwell. These meetings always sicken and worry me – I see so little good and so much folly and inanity ...

25 October   [*Left Clumber to travel to Combermere Abbey.*]

31 October   [*Rode to see Sir J. Hanmer's estate in Flintshire.*]

3 November   [*Visited Trentham.*]

5 November   [*Back home to Clumber, via Normanton and Mosborough.*]

10 November   Planning a change of walks in the pleasure ground ...

13 November   Lord and Lady Combermere came here yesterday ...

14 November   ... the whole public mind is engaged with potatoes and railways.

19 November   [*Lord and Lady Combermere left Clumber.*]

20 November   Some railway surveyors made their appearance in the Park Lane and on the Bothamsall side – they were instantly discharged – this day they came into the Park, but could do nothing as we sent them off and I pulled their flags up etc. – and finally the head of the survey told me that I should [*ruin?*] it. The railway nuisance is absolutely intolerable.

21 November   Called upon Mr Foljambe today to consult with him how we can best oppose ourselves to the pestilent railway projects, which are about to destroy our properties in all directions – and for no definite purpose. I saw his new wife, Lady Milton [*Selina*, daughter of the Earl of Liverpool] and like her very much.

1845

24 November	Parts of the new farm house, which I last year erected at Elkesley are giving way already, a chimney is one foot out of the perpendicular – it is very mortifying and expensive – all Mr Tremin's works are equally disgracefully erected.
25 November	I have planned several alterations, which to me have long been eye sores – but I have not had the energy or courage to rectify them – Two things I am wishing to accomplish, both involving enlargement and breadth – clearing away obstructing trees and forming openings and groups, and admitting as much distance as this place is capable of – widening the water in several places and improving the outlines at various points which [?] are neither natural or handsome. What I propose is a correction of what I did many years ago, when I was a tyro in the business – I yesterday began to remove the points of land before the boat house, which will add greatly to the apparent breadth of the water and will greatly improve the scenery. I shall then commence operations opposite to the house, and deal very unsparingly with the opposite banks, which I think will be the most striking improvements I shall have made here – The Lincoln terrace in the pleasure ground I have almost completed.
27 November	Poor Thomas tells me that he has suffered greatly in his railway speculations ... the madness of speculators must be suicidal ...
29 November	... a great many women and ladies are turning Papists ...
1 December	We have devised a very good way of promoting the comfort of the poor, by establishing coal clubs in my villages. – The widows and [impoverished?] have a ton of coal given to them – and the others will by subscribing be able to purchase coals at a moderate price.
3 December	The first snow today ...
20 December	... Lincoln I now find to my sorrow and deep displeasure, is with Peel in all his vortex of abominations.
23 December	... It is stated that Lincoln is moved to the Board of Control, of which he knows as much as of the mountains of the moon, – but he must be rewarded for his faithful service to his wretched Judas – The idea of all this, and that Lincoln of whom I once thought so highly and so proudly, should be steeped in all the wickedness and unworthiness of passing events under Peel, shoots into my heart, grieves and wounds me beyond all power of description.
24 December	Today I have a letter from Mr Gladstone, who tells me that he has accepted the office of Secretary of State for the Colonies and War – he enquires whether I will again bring him in for Newark – I have replied – certainly not.

1845

If Charles will consent to stand and will engage to cooperate with me, and not with Peel – I shall put him in Gladstone's vacancy ...

25 December   Christmas Day, we had an early service – and the largest number of communicants I ever remember here, that is among my household and servants. Our own party as small as last year – and no family friends in addition ...

[*He wrote that he had a postal delivery today.*]

26 December   Charles does not relish standing for Newark ...

The Duke of Portland called here this afternoon and we talked over our elections and politics ...

29 December   ... I have been very busy for some time with my Lincoln terrace walk which I have now completed and which has been a very difficult and delicate job to manage so that it shall look well – and natural – one end has had to be raised, the other lowered 3 feet so as to make it level to receive the vases – to do effect this properly required a great deal of contrivance – I consider it to be a most successful work, and a great ornament to the place.

Fig. 71 *The 'Lincoln Terrace' in Clumber's Pleasure Grounds – circa 1910.*

1845

30 December   I have had a long conference with the D. of Portland today ...

31 December   [*The Duke attended the Justices' Meeting at Worksop. On returning to Clumber, he found Mr Tallents, his Newark Agent, had arrived to discuss the election.*] ...

I have here arrived at the end of another year ... I am only more and more wretched in that particular – Lincoln is utterly strange to me, I have had no communication with him for a year and a half – and he is, I fear, very bitter ... Charles thinks it better to lean to Lincoln than to me and is polite but no more – Robert has deserted me without a pang, and gone over to the same quarter – William is away, poor Thomas I believe is the best affected to me.

1846

1 January ... deserted by my children ... Lincoln is setting the wicked example – May God forgive him and them ... In financial matters, by assiduous attention and great self denial, I am at last beginning to behold and feel an extrication from my difficulties ...

5 January Went this day with my Daughters on a visit to Ossington ...

7 January [*Returned to Clumber.*]

10 January Poor Frederick Mundy is dead ...

13 January ... This is William's birth day – singularly enough I received a letter from him this morning ... we drank his health in affectionate remembrance.

15 January ... In forming the ground behind the nearest Seat on the Lincoln terrace, one of the workmen found a silver coin about two feet below the surface and precisely in the centre of the back of the Seat, in the slop [*sic*] of the bank – it is a shilling of Philip and Mary 1554 – I have the coin.

Fig. 72

21 January [*To Nottingham, to sleep there and be ready for an early train to London.*]

22 January [*Following a difficult journey to London, he reached Portman Square at 5.20pm. Later, he went to the House of Lords.*]

27 January After going to Coutts and several other places, I left London by the 12 train and reached here at Clumber at 1/4 past 9 ...

Charles accompanied me here and remains on leave for a few weeks.

28 January Looking about at the extensive works ... wonderful day ... the birds singing beautifully as in spring.

1846

30 January	Two of my daughters and I returned from Thoresby this morning where we have been on a visit for a night ... [then] went out shooting with Charles.
	This is my birth day and they have all kindly made all the fun in their power to amuse me upon the occasion ...
5 February	Attended a Vestry meeting today at Worksop where they would have me in the Chair ... This noble Church will now be restored to its pristine beauty.
9 February	... To my infinite surprise, I have learnt this day that Lincoln has accepted the appointment of Secretary to Ireland, vacates his seat and will be at Newark this evening – there never was any thing so ill advised, and as I am driven to do so – I shall oppose him ... Mr Hildyard comes forward to oppose him.
10 February	My old and excellent friend Mr [Henry] Gally Knight is dead ...
14 February	Charles returned to London today ...
17 February	My friend Gally Knight was buried this morning at Firbeck in the Church there. He has left Firbeck and some other estates to his widow, for her life ... has left to Sir Thomas White, who was a relative, the Langold estate, a beautiful estate, which is contiguous to his own place ...
18 February	[He heard that his cousin, Sir William Clinton, had died.]
19 February	I have sent a short address to be published about Lincoln's election and I hope it may do good, opposing free trade and other bad practices, lamenting Lincoln's espousal of them, desiring him thoroughly beaten, and suggesting to him to resign. This will be a service to him and the county.
	[At this time, Lincoln had compounded all previous difficulties with his father, by declaring that he was not averse to 'a connection between the Roman Catholic Church and the State'.]
22 February	[Notes that his letter had been published and 'The Times' had sided with him and condemned Lord Lincoln.] – I have had great pleasure in acting cordially with the D. of Portland and Lord Manvers ...
25 February	Went to Worksop to attend the Justices' meeting ...
7 March	The D. of Portland called and remained sometime to discuss election and other matters ... he is nearly 78 years old.
9 March	[To London by train from Nottingham. He then went on by hackney cab to a meeting at the Duke of Richmond's house.]
12 March	A densely thick fog, which lasted the greater part of the day – I could not see to write without a candle ...
13 March	My letter appeared in the Morning Post this morning ...
	[Left London and returned to Clumber.]

1846

14 March   Looking about at my works, many things have been done in my absence and I am delighted with the effect especially of the new walk, which opens very beautifully upon various scenes – Spring has made most rapid advances – Every thing is aforward here, I could almost think forwarder than near London.

17 March   The same beautiful weather continues and all idea of famine or deficiency has entirely vanished – The price of potatoes is even lower than last year, notwithstanding all the outcry upon the subject.

18 March   ... Much snow this afternoon ... wind very cold.

19 March   Much more snow in the night, and lying thickly upon the ground and trees ...

25 March   ... Corn was selling today at Worksop from 58 to 62.

1 April   This is the commencement of our first Petty Sessions at Worksop – but only 3 Magistrates including myself attended ...

2 April   Rode to Welbeck, to bear a message to the D. of P. from the Magistrates assembled yesterday, on a subject which the Duke referred to them and also to confer with him on several other points – found him remarkably well and long may he remain so.

3 April   Owing to Lincoln's neglect in not signing and immediately returning some deed ... we are placed in a very awkward position with the purchaser of Hafod and many other parties ...

5 April   ... Mr Henderson arrived ... having brought with him the deed signed by Lincoln ... Altho' my heart is in Hafod and Wales, which have so much interested and delighted me, yet in a pecuniary and advantageous [way], the Sale was absolutely necessary and will relieve my mind of so much anxiety, that I must on the other hand rejoice at its completion ...

6 April   Rain without ceasing since yesterday morning, the people could not work on digging the lake and moving the soil.

7 April   All is done, Mr Henderson informs me – and now I am no longer a Welshman ... I must say that they owe me a deep debt of gratitude ...

By this measure I realise £5,000 a year in saving of interest alone, for I pay off all my bond debts bearing 5 per cent and £2,000 a year spent upon the place by absorption of the income. I may consider myself a gainer of £6,000 a year at least ... and may now find my income superior to my expenditure ...

11 April   ... The farmers, it seems, are so favorable to me, that they have sent me a message requesting that I will take the Chair at the Retford agricultural meeting in October ... I particularly dislike being Chairman any where – but I must consent to give them satisfaction – They well merit it.

1846

14 April   Saw 2 or 3 swallows today.

15 April   ... Attended the Petty Sessions at Worksop – the tedious process of swearing in Constables was the principal business.

19 April   I went today to see my estate at Walkeringham – it was so wet however and so drowned with rain and flood that I could not get about much – it is a fine estate and greatly surpasses my notion of its value and condition. I went to see the two draining engines ... 40 horse power each and lift or rather propel 100 tons in a minute.

24 April   I am still busily proceeding with my ground works they turn out beautifully and every thing that I anticipated, but they have exceeded the estimates of time and cost by the double.

25 April   Rode to Bothamsall with my Daughters and settled what should be done to repair effectually my new Church, and put it and the Churchyard into complete order.

29 April   ... Lincoln is canvassing the Falkirk burghs ... A more offensive reception of a candidate never was given to anyone ... he thinks nothing but place and power and cares not what he does or what he loses provided that he may obtain and maintain that paramount object.

30 April   ... Lady Lincoln has been obliged to go to Brighton for the benefit of her health ... How little could I have guessed even that Lincoln could ever be brought to act thus!

1 May   A charming Spring day and mild ... The lilacs barely shew color and it would be difficult to glean a sufficiency to make a garland or deck a May pole.

4 May   Went to see the Cattle and sheep which are to be sold at Hardwick tomorrow by auction – they are very good.

5 May   [*Noted that Lincoln had been elected at Falkirk.*]

6 May   My works digging and widening the lake opposite to the house, are now drawing to a close as they ought to have done a month ago. I must have a good deal unfinished for the autumn – such as the deepening the new cuts nearly 2 feet and sloping the banks – I now shall only have about 6 inches of water merely to make appearance for the Summer.

7 May   Mr Tallents came here today, by appointment, to give account of his Stewardship ... [*the Duke entered here very critical comment on Mr Tallents (his Newark Agent) having* 'turned from the setting to the rising Sun'.] I thought it prudent to pardon him and continue him in my service – His youth and a regard for his late father induced me to act thus.

1846

11 May   I have had the pleasure of paying all my remaining country bills – and now I rejoice to know that I am out of debt here, and in a few weeks I shall pay my London bills, and then I shall be clear and my mind at ease.

12 May   *[Recorded that he was clearing his business matters, in order to leave for London.]*

13 May   *[Occupied on business matters with his Worksop Agent, Mr Wilmot.]*

            ... ordered all bills in the office up to Christmas 1845 to be paid and cleared off – so that after this not a sixpence will be owing to any one in the country ... by degrees I shall hope to extinguish ... my mortgage debts.

15 May   I learn today from Charles, that Lincoln has the gout in his feet and heart (as I read his writing) ...

16 May   ... The cutting of my lake was finished yesterday, the water is let in and the work looks extremely well.

17 May   At work again all day altho' Sunday ...

19 May   I have again been obliged to cry "wolf" – Altho' up at 5½ in the morning – I found it utterly impossible to complete in time.

20 May   At last ... we all left Clumber for Nottingham ... *[arrived at]* Euston station at 10½.

21 May   ... Dined this evening at Lord Combermere's ...

22 May   I was grieved to learn today that Ld. Manvers has been operated on for the stone ...

            Went for a short time to the H. of Lords this evening.

27 May   Holiday today for our comfort. Derby day ...

31 May   Much disturbed today with the affection of the bowels ...

2 June   ... William has been appointed first attaché at Constantinople, I can hardly believe it, I have heard nothing of it.

3 June   ... William gets £300 a year by this appointment.

17 June   ... dined at Combermere's – a large political party.

18 June   ... Waterloo day ... went to a ball with my daughters ...

7 July   In the H. of L. tonight – on Ld. Vyvian moving the 3rd reading of the Sheffield and Lincolnshire *[railways]* bill, I told the house that I greatly objected to the bill and moved that the debate upon it be adjourned to Thursday week ... Brougham stood my friend and supporter, two of the *[ministers?]* also backed me and I finally carried my point – I believe for the first time in my life.

8 July   *[With other Peers, he went by steamer, to dine at Greenwich.]*

10 July   *[Returned to Clumber.]*

11 July   Rode over to Osberton to see Foljambe about the railways ...

1846

12 July   Altho' Sunday yet in the afternoon, I took a very long walk over the farmed grounds – Wheat, oats and barley are looking well, but the turnips have suffered a great deal ...

13 July   Done a great deal today and finished with a long ride to Bothamsall, Elkesley etc. looking at the buildings that are doing in these places – Satisfactory.

14 July   ... The D. of Portland called here and with Wilmot had a long talk ...

15 July   [*Travelled to London by train.*]

17 July   [*Spoke in the House of Lords debate.*] – I made the best fight I could ... but as I perceived that it was evidently useless to divide, I withdrew my motion.

18 July   Dined at the D. of Richmond's ...

19 July   [*Recorded a joke that he had heard regarding Sir Robert Peel. Peel had cut his foot on a broken washing bowl and it was said of him that* "he had cut another of his Supporters".]

23 July   [*Recorded that of his two bank accounts with Coutts, he had £60 to £70 in one and about £200 in the other.*]

24 July   Teeth matters of my Daughters keep me in London ...

25 July   [*He sensed that a plot was being hatched to make way for Gladstone to stand again at Newark.*]

27 July   Left London this morning by Dover railway, from the station at London bridge at $11^1/_2$ and arrived at Ramsgate ...

30 July   I have just made a very desirable purchase of Mr Norton, of the Brewhouse Yard and gardens [*Nottingham*] ... I have given £3,500 for it ... it will yield about 4 per cent ...

3 August   [*Recorded that the new owner of the Hafod estate is planning to pull down the 'Moorish Palace' and rebuild it as an 'Italian Villa'. Also noted that Salvin was to be the architect and Nesfield the landscape gardener.*]

6 August   The little dwarf that they call Gen. Tom Thumb is exhibiting here – we went to see him today ... (14 years old and 25 inches high) ... he shook hands with me ...

11 August   I hear that Robert is gone to Scotland ... during the time I was in London he always contrived to keep out of my way ... I learn to my grief that he is doing no good.

31 August   [*Preparing for a Channel crossing to France.*] – My Coachmaker has sent me such an inconvenient carriage with such very small boxes ...

1846

We are to start at 7 in the 'Princess Alice' ... and make the passage in two hours.

AT THIS POINT, THE DIARY ENTRY READS:
"FOR THE HIATUS – SEE MY FOREIGN JOURNAL".

[This 'Journal' does not appear to have survived.]

26 October   *[At Clumber]* - I yesterday closed the journal of our foreign tour, merely expressing very briefly my thoughts which yesterday brought to my mind ... *[He also noted that he had visited a government minister and reported his opinions on what he had seen and heard in France. He did not enter here any detail on those opinions.]*

30 October   ... I went out for a few hours shooting.

2 November   ... Charles arrived this evening from London, to our great joy and satisfaction ...

3 November   A rainy morning but when it cleared a little, I rode over to Retford, to attend a meeting for the propagation of the Gospel in foreign parts, but found myself late ... returned without entering the meeting ...

4 November   Attended the Justices' meeting at Worksop.

6 November   Lord Manvers has been very unwell – went over to see him ...

29 November   I began yesterday to cut down the large lime trees and others which obstructed the Lincoln terrace.

Fig. 73 *This portion of a sketch, drawn by Emma Wilmot (c1846), indicates the density of tree growth in the Pleasure Grounds – many having been planted in the 1760-1780 period.*

303

1846

30 November	The cold is very severe. The lake quite frozen over.
1 December	Charles left us yesterday – he is the only one now who visits us ...
7 December	... the ice breaking up – I have been enable to fill all my ice houses, with ice from two to three inches thick – the large house was filled 3 days ago.
14 December	The frost is now intense ... out door work must soon be at a standstill ... many are now out of work.
19 December	... I came to London today and brought Caroline with me, who has something to have done with her teeth ...
23 December	[Returned to Clumber.]
25 December	... Took the Sacrament with my dear Daughters ...
26 December	... An Egg, perfectly formed, was taken from the inside of a partridge which was prepared for dinner – Such a production must be a very great curiosity at this time of the year. I have preserved the egg with a ticket attached to it.
29 December	... I and two of my Daughters went to Thoresby to stay there on a visit for two nights.
31 December	... Returned home this afternoon.

1 January   I here again begin a new year ...My four dear Daughters, who have been all amiableness to me, are the only members of my family who are with me on this day of former family greeting, affection and festivity. Alas! These times are gone by, and I fear, never can return.

4 January   Charles arrived this evening – to our great pleasure – he comes to assist me in doing the honours to a very large party assembling this week –

Lord Stanley and a great many others.

5 January   ... I am now fitting up my library – I have had the things here for some years – but left them in their boxes, untill more prosperous times might enable me to open the doors of my house – it and the other arrangements in the house will be finished tomorrow and on the 7th it will be opened for the first time in honor of a company which I trust may never disgrace it ...

6 January   ... My library is to be opened in it's best garb ... it certainly looks very beautiful and very magnificent.

7 January   ... some of my guests are come today.

8 January   ... We sat down 28 altogether.

9 January   Today we went out shooting on the Manor hills – we were 10 guns ... we killed 118 pheasants, hare and rabbits, no woodcocks ...

10 January   Sunday – My pews had hardly ever been so full ... afterward walked about to see the place.

11 January   Lord and Lady Stanley and many others left us this morning ...

14 January   The last remnant of our party ... left us this morning, and we went to Newark in the evening to attend the Ball ...

15 January   Returned home today not well and very much starved with the cold – What must the poor people feel with deficient clothing and empty stomachs? –

We are to increase wages to [*13 shillings and 6 pence*] a week.

1847

18 January	Came to London this afternoon ...
23 January	... dined at the Carlton Club ... [*In the absence of Lord Stanley, Newcastle was prevailed upon to take the Chair at a 'large meeting of Protectionists' – some 60 to 70 were present. Lord George Bentinck (rival to Lord Stanley as leader of the group) proposed Newcastle's health.*]
24 January	[*The Duke met Lord George Bentinck again. Mr Disraeli was present at this meeting.*] ...
25 January	[*Returned to Clumber.*]
8 February	Snow today ...
12 February	... I received news today of the death of the D. of Northumber-land ... He was a very old friend and schoolfellow of mine, we were in the same form at Eton ...
21 February	A letter from William ...
26 February	I am informed that Robert is gone to Ireland ...
8 March	I have now nearly completed all the cutting, deepening, widening and clearing the lake, and in a few days I shall be able to let the water in again ...
	The sloping down to the banks will now be passed to a conclusion, and by the end of the month I should hope to [*have*] most of the turf laid on, and the work all but completed.
9 March	... A plant, a fir tree, of very extraordinary growth has been shown to me, now growing in a young plantation joined in on one of the oak squares, between it and Thoresby border. – It is the greatest curiosity I ever saw – it is of no species that I have ever met with – in leaf and growth it is most like the araucaria but not so [*spearious?*] as it is – it is now about 9 or 10 years old – about the 2nd or 3rd year it pushed out lateral branches – as described in the drawing and the following [*year*] some other, but very short – the lower branches are very crooked and irregular – from the short upper tier of branches – the yearly growth for 6 or 7 years of between 2 and 3 feet unusually is regularly marked – but no lateral branches whatever – its growth is great and lusty, it is particularly healthy and most singular in appearance.
10 March	On rising this morning, found the ground and trees covered with snow ...

Fig. 74

1847

13 March Went to the Assizes at Nottingham ... I had a walk in the Park and made a survey of what had been doing, and found many things done of which I had no knowledge. My Steward Wilmot has been playing many very awkward tricks and I fear that he is little better than a rascal. [*Returned to Clumber very late at night.*]

15 March My lambing is going on well ... there are many doubles ...

24 March Today the Fast was observed here with great reverence and a general participation. I never saw so full a congregation in my Chapel – there must have been 100 people present.

27 March My digging and cleaning in the lake require another day to finish – tomorrow is Sunday – but on Monday I shall ... fill the lake and right glad I am that the tedious and tiresome work is completed, from the bridge to the Temple.

28 March [*He noted that 722 lambs had been born and also that 30 ewes were still to lamb.*]

29 March The Duke of Portland is very ill ...

2 April Good Friday – We all received the Sacrament ...

3 April A letter from William at Constantinople, he intimates to me his intention of marrying if I approve of his choice, and has treated the whole matter in a manner most becoming to himself and extremely agreeable to me ...

4 April My new clergyman for Bothamsall and the Chapel here, did service for the first time today – his name is Chapman ...

5 April [*Mentions that the temporary building, used for the proceedings of the House of Lords since the fire, was being 'broken up'.*]

13 April A fine day but cold – Saw a swallow.

14 April Worksop fair – went over to see the stock shown for prizes ...

21 April ... I may consider that I have finished my long and heavy works at the lake and adjourning ground, and we all agree that the whole has an admirable appearance and is most successful and enjoyable to survey.

22 April [*Slept at Nottingham.*]

23 April Left Nottm. this morning by 10½ train, arrived safely in London ¼ past 4, and found myself again with my Daughters in Portman square.

[*Dressed, dined and went to the House of Lords.*]

29 April J.Sutton of Kelham called here today and announced to me that he intended to stand for Newark ... he called himself a conservative ... [*The Duke declined Sutton's request for support.*]

1847

2 May   Sunday, but much of it dedicated to my vile railway business ... my daughters and I managed to make a good walk – tho' sometimes driven to take shelter.

4 May   Went to the Academy exhibition ... In the evening we went to the Opera to witness the first appearance of Jenny Lind ... makes one wish that she were one's partner for life ...

[The Queen and Prince Albert were also present at this performance of Meyerbeer's 'Robert le Diable'.]

Fig. 75 *Johanna Maria (Jenny) Lind – the 'Swedish Nightingale' by Eduard Magnus (1846)*

9 May   ... I believe that there is scarcely a doubt that many of the servile adherents to Peel, Lincoln I fear among the number, will ... join the Reformers ... I write this with shame and grief ...

14 May   On this evening we went to a Ball at [*the*] Palace – On going up to the Queen, to my surprise I found H.M. quite gracious in appearance ... For some years Her Majesty has been pleased to be absolutely rude and uncivil to me and my Daughters – an excellent assembly and very pleasant ...

22 May   [*The Duke sponsored a 'Collecting Dinner' for some 30 members of the Lords and the Commons.*] – All went off very well ...

24 May   [*He noted that the Duke of Buckingham was having financial troubles and that Stowe was to be sold.*]

6 June   ... Lincoln brought in a motion about colonisation for Ireland a few days ago ... poor Lincoln is weak and vain ...

7 June   I have for some time been looking out for a seat for Charles – it has been at last decided that he should go to Sandwich ... [*mentions that Charles was* 'laying close siege to a lady who he hopes to marry'] ... I shall have to pay a large sum of money for him, which tho' very poor I do not in the least grudge ...

1847

9 June   ... paid every thing of bills up to Xmas last both in town and country and all taxes and every other payment up to this time ... In the evening dined at Combermere's – a large political and pleasant party.

10 June   ... I was called before a Commons Committee today to give evidence respecting the Great Northern deviation by Tuxford – the Co. is endeavouring to give me the slip, but I was strong among the parties in the Committee room and I think that they will now see the propriety and necessity of adhering to their engagement.

11 June   [Heard that the Tuxford railway deviation would be approved] – this will be an advantage to the town and neighbourhood of Tuxford I believe and am assured.

A grand Court Ball this night – the Queen as before, kind in her manner to us ...

12 June   ... Charles arrived from Sandwich ...

13 June   ... Charles went to Windsor ...

16 June   ... went to the Duchess of Sutherland's Ball to the Queen at Stafford House ... home between 3 and 4 o'clock.

17 June   Charles went yesterday morning to Sandwich ...

We all went tonight to the Opera to hear Jenny Lind once more ... I cannot disguise from myself the sentiment of deep interest which I entertain towards her ...

18 June   Went today to the British Museum ...

19 June   ... dined at Lord Eglinton's ...

21 June   ... Thomas dined here ...

23 June   [Returned to Clumber – left his daughters in London – he slept at Nottingham.]

24 June   ... I am nearly prepared to begin some expensive works, in order to bring the upper part of the [Nottingham] Park into play for the erection of houses ...

I dined at Nottingham and came on to Clumber this evening.

25 June   ... I have had a long and tiresome day with Mr Heming who is to be Mr Wilmot's successor as my Steward – He is one of the hardest and closest bargainers I ever met with – money seems to be his great object – but I must hope that he will take as good care of my money as of his own. He is to have a salary of £800 to cover every thing – to take and engage in no other business besides mine – to live in Wilmot's house [Sparken, Worksop] and to take his farm but at a reduced rent of £160 instead of £200, and to give a bond of security of £12,000 ...

1847

26 June ... I went to Welbeck but could not meet the Duke of Portland. I went on to Worksop ...

27 June Sunday – Mr Chapman did the duty here very well ... [*he indicates that he had previously been very upset by something Chapman had done.*] ... I rode over to Welbeck and saw the Duke of Portland ...

29 June Charles informs me that he has proposed to Miss Grant and that she has accepted him ... he thought that she had a large fortune of £5,000 a year but he now learns that this is not so – but about £2,000 now and 1,000 more when her mother dies ... I anxiously hope that I may find her what I wish her to be, and a suitable person for him and not a burden on our family, as Lady Lincoln is ...

30 June Went to Worksop today, not to do justice but to see the Magistrates ...

1 July ... I have had incessant work all day indoors and out – every day I have been so thoroughly tired, that it is a joy to get into bed, but it is not quite so easy to leave it in the morning.

2 July [*Busy with paper work, especially with a claim for tithes* 'which is claimed out of Haughton by the vicar of Walesby and which if proved by him would take from me perhaps above £400 a year.' *The Duke thought that he had found the evidence to deny the Vicar's claim.*] – Went to Nottingham to sleep ...

3 July [*Travelled to London*] – walked in Kensington Gardens – Charles is here and tells me that Mrs Grant withholds her consent, unless I will agree to make a settlement upon Charles, as she wishes her Daughter to marry someone who has more money – a very silly and unreasonable request as I think ...

4 July [*The Duke met Mrs Grant and told her that he could not make the required settlement on Charles.*]

9 July ... Mrs Grant ... withdrew her daughter ... the intended marriage at an end . [*He makes it clear that, in any case, he did not approve of Miss Grant*] – The thing is too revolting and disgusting.

10 July ... Had another photographic portrait taken of me one having been taken yesterday, neither of them please, tho' excellent impressions.

[*He had also called on Lord and Lady Kenwall, regarding William's stated plan to marry their daughter*] – To my infinite surprise and annoyance I found that they had thrown poor William over ... my family seems to be peculiarly unfortunate.

11 July [*Returned to Clumber*] ... we are now settled here and quiet for a time will not be disagreeable.

1847

13 July   ... took my daughters to see the effect of all my works ... They were surprised and delighted at them – in the evening I rowed them on the water, and we were all equally pleased with the improvements in it.

14 July   A charming day for quiet enjoyment but vastly hot, too hot to move – we dined under an open tent on the lawn in the pleasure ground – most agreeable.

15 July   Another overpoweringly hot day ... St. Swithin does not weep today.

17 July   ... fine crops of wheat ... here usually they are very moderate.

          [*On this day he indicated that he was again very depressed by personal matters.*]

19 July   [*Had a 'conference' with Rev Pocklington, Vicar of Walesby, regarding the Vicar's claim to the Haughton Tithes.*]

20 July   [*Heard, to his surprise, that Thomas had gone to stand in the election at Canterbury.*]

22 July   [*Learnt that Charles was in 'bad spirits' at Sandwich.*]

25 July   [*Records that he has raised money for Charles' election expenses.*]

31 July   Poor Thomas has lost his election for Canterbury, I am truly sorry for him ...

3 August ... Charles has been defeated at Sandwich. This event was wholly unexpected ...

4 August Mr Lindsay left me this morning ... Lord Henry Bentinck called here this afternoon ...

5 August Gladstone is returned for Oxford – I grieve at it most sincerely, no return has given me more pain ... Although I consider the man himself to be of no weight and not likely to be an authority in any thing, yet he is a man of indefatigable application ... altho' pretty nearly unintelligible, so involved and mystified is the style of his speaking and writing.

11 August Prize fighting – principally on Lindrick Common, has increased so very much of late years, and has become so notorious and such a scandal to the neighbourhood, that a meeting was holden this day at Worksop to consider [*action?*] to put down the nuisance – and it was wished that I should take the Chair – it was found to be a difficult thing to devise means to meet all the points of difficulty – as the meeting place is on the borders of three counties – It was finally resolved that we should form ourselves into an Association to indict, and to appoint a Committee to watch the movements of the Fancy, and a professional man to conduct the proceedings – Mr Appleton [*Vicar of Worksop*] to be the Chairman of the Committee and Mr [*John*] Whall – the Attorney.

1847

12 August	[*Reports that his potatoes, wheat and barley crops are looking to be of poor quality.*]
16 August	Much rain today ... my white turnips are going off very much from grub.
18 August	The Postmistress of Worksop informs us that it had been telegraphed to Chesterfield that Louis Phillippe had been shot ...
19 August	The report of yesterday circulated by telegraph, proved to be a hoax ... – I asked the price of some small 2 years old Highlanders today and the man told me about £5 to £5.10 ... My corn harvest ... is most abundant and excellent in quality.
23 August	Today my harvest was finished ... a more abundant harvest or one in better condition was never gathered in at Clumber.
24 August	My lawyer came this morning ...
25 August	Left Clumber ... Sheffield for Manchester by the 12.15 train ... no other train to Crewe until past 5 ... They were obliging enough to give me a special train, which cost £10, and I arrived here at Combermere Abbey in good time for dinner.
26 August	[*Recorded that today's 'Standard' newspaper carried an item about his correspondence with the Editor of the Times. He claimed that the Editor had been 'decrying the nobility'.*]
30 August	[*Returned to Clumber.*]
31 August	... I have settled to open the shooting campaign tomorrow morning – I wish I were not alone.
2 September	I was so excessively tired yesterday that my only resource was to take a basin of soup – change my clothes and throw myself on my bed, where I slept – untill my daughters came up to bed – I then pulled off my clothes and went to bed – but was not recovered when I arose in the morning, being stiff all over as well as tired.
4 September	... I walked for 4 hours and am not tired – I shot ill and only killed 12½ brace ... I killed 4 hares and a rabbit besides.
	[*The Duke then drew a line across the page of his Diary, making the following entry.*]
5 September	Very remarkable – about ¼ before 5 o'clock this afternoon,
	I happened to look out of my room towards the East and two remarkable straight lines in the form of an inverted v – thus ^, white; and most distinctly visible – it was cloudy and stormy wind from N.W. by N., almost instantly the clouds cleared away and shewed a cross in the sky of large dimensions – it may have lasted for a minute or two and passed into and away with the passing clouds – How could these straight lines have been formed and what can it mean?

1847

7 September   [Out shooting with Mr Vernon.]

8 September   Justicing at Worksop. Afterwards went to inspect the Church –
they are going on very well – and, under Mr [Rev James]
Appleton's supervision, I trust that all will be made secure, as
well as rendered beautiful to the eye – It is fortunate that Mr
[Rev Thomas] Stacye died [in his ninetieth year], and that Mr
Appleton succeeded him in the nick of time, for without him I
am persuaded that the Architect would have thrown the Church
down.

10 September   ... Wrote to William today.

14 September   Most unpleasant reports reached me today about Lincoln's
family – there are various reports in circulation, one that Lady
Lincoln has run away and nobody knows where she is gone,
another that Lincoln had received an anonymous letter and that
he had turned Lady L. out of the house – and several other
versions – what seems to be certain is that something has
happened, and that Lady L. is no longer living in Lincoln's house
... I am not at all surprised at whatever may have happened – I
felt certain that Lady L. was incapable of doing her duty, as a
wife or a mother ... [I] warned Lincoln ... that he had forfeited all
right to divorce an infamous woman ... Lincoln has now no real
friend, his judgement of late is quite perverted ... He most
undutifully broke with me on account of this woman, and has
ever since done every thing to vex and annoy me, to indulge his
now wayward and bad temper – he is totally altered from what
he was before marrying this bad woman of bad blood.

16 September   ... Charles tells me that Lincoln went to Arran on the 13th.

Lady Lincoln has been staying at the Duke of Hamilton's in
Portman Square ...

their children are at Brighton with the Governess!!! ... what can
induce him to trust his children, in such a place to the care of a
governess – when it is his duty to have them under his own eye
and ear.

17 September   [Noted that the Dukes of Beaufort and Buckingham were
financially ruined and that their houses and other assets were
being sold.]

19 September   Charles arrived yesterday ...

20/21 September [Out shooting.]

28 September   [Travelled to Filey, for a 'seaside holiday'. Went by train from
Eckington – dined at York.]

30 September   Rode over to Scarborough ... the railway is destroying it, and
brings in such an influx of low strangers that good families are
leaving the place.

1847

3 October   Went to Church here – If I were to build a Church, I should like to take this for a model ...

I heard yesterday from Worksop that the walls of the noble Church there had been safely set upon their legs again ... these walls are now upright which have been for many years a foot and [a] half out of the perpendicular ... excellent foundations have been given – it has been a very clever business and should be recorded.

Fig. 76 *Worksop Priory, in the mid-19th century, drawn by James Baldock*

6 October   ... The delightful and most interesting Jenny Lind left England yesterday for Hamburgh ...

9 October   [*Records news from his Hardwick farmer, Kirkwood, regarding the good quality of the crop of potatoes.*]

15 October   Charles arrived today ...

21 October   ... Lord [*Balcunes?*] is one of my mortgagees, and not a pleasant one. The railway by Worksop takes some of the land in his mortgage, I thought I might take possession of the money paid for it but Lord B. objected and has plagued me much about it ...

27 October   ... Wrote to William today ...

28 October   Left Filey today and came to Scarborough. [*Reed's Hotel?*]

31 October   Sunday ... Charles left us for London.

1 November   [*Left Scarborough for York*] – we commenced 'lionising' without delay ...

2 November   ... we arrived here at Clumber at 4 o'clock.

4 November   I have received notice today that after Christmas the interests on my mortgages will be increased to 5 per cent, a circumstance which will be ruinous to me, as it may make a difference to me of between 3 and 4,000 a year [*he also expected an increase of $2^{1}/_{2}$ and 3 per cent in Income Tax*] ... I shall be obliged to discharge all extra laborers and servants and live in the humblest way, so as to live within my means and keep clear of debt.

1847

6 November	A letter from William ... Charles arrived this evening ...
13 November	Lord H. Bentinck who came here this evening tells me that his brother Lord George had just arrived at Welbeck ...
16 November	Lord George Bentinck was here today ...
19 November	... Our party here has broken up today, the Combermeres go early tomorrow morning.
20 November	Closely engaged most of the day with Mr Heming my new Steward and successor to Mr Wilmot ... Executed many deeds for and on account of the Nottingham and Lincoln railway which affects my property at Newark – and also two building leases at Nottingham.
22 November	[*Travelled to London*] ... in time for Lord Stanley's dinner ...
23 November	I took the oaths and my seat today ...
27 November	... I went to the Dentist by 9 am and started by the 10$^{1/2}$ train ... I went to Newark and took post horses from thence ... but they were all very slow ...
28 November	Sunday – nothing new – and unceasing rain.
29 November	... very great deal of wet, but not too much for this part of the country ... the springs are very low and no water in many of the wells – such as at Bothamsall ...
30 November	Charles left us this morning ... I had a letter this morning from William, dated Constantinople Nov. 13th ... [*he was*] very ill with fever ...
6 December	[*Records that the Haughton Tithes question has been decided in his favour. Complains that the law was unfair, as it allows a clergyman to make a claim and forces the rightful owner to pay for his own defence.*]
7 December	[*Another letter from William.*]
13 December	I have at last succeeded in reducing the arrears on the Clumber collection [*rents*] which used to be 8 or 9,000 to less than 2,000£ which is the case now ...
22 December	Went to a musical evening this evening at Worksop, where they formed themselves into a Society to play together and cultivate music scientifically – The Society is just formed and calls itself "the Philharmonic Society" – a violin player by the name of Radcliffe is at the head of it, who is a good musician and a very respectable man. I never heard him before this evening, and was agreeably surprised by his playing ... The orchestra consisted of about twelve – 3 violins, 2 violin cellos, and different wind instruments ... I shall do what I can to encourage it and advance it to maturity ...

1847

25 December	Our Christmas party has been very small – only my 4 daughters – but we have been very comfortable and happy together.
29 December	[*Noted the death of Frederick Mundy – 3rd son of General Mundy.*]
31 December	Snow again this morning. ... The prospect all around is most gloomy ...

Fig. 77 *A splendid drawing at Clumber (c1846), by Emma Wilmot, wife of the Duke's Agent.*

1 January   ... I am alone here with my dear Daughters, but all goes on most pleasingly, and we have been very happy congratulating, giving and receiving gifts.

3 January   ... We resumed our evening concerts again today – my 4 daughters and I. Harp, piano forte, treble and bass concertinas, and violin – after [*reading*?] it terminates the evening most agreeably.

7 January   ... I had all the Worksop musical performers here to play in the form of a concert, and I admitted all the servants and all the people in the Park who were able and liked to come, and some others to witness the performance and they all appeared to be much amused and highly gratified – they were all arranged on seats on one side of the fireplace, we on the other, the musicians in the angle between the end window and the third window – I engaged our friends to dine early and we entered the great dining room at seven o'clock – it made a charming music room – and the performers acquitted themselves to the surprise of every body – they are in truth very much improved since I first heard them – the whole went off exceedingly well and gave great satisfaction.

8 January   Very bad weather, the lake quite frozen over in one night –

the thermo last night nearly down to 20.

10 January   I ought to have attended the Quarter Sessions today at Retford, but it was so pinchingly cold and the roads so dangerous that I could not persuade myself to go. I am always annoyed and uneasy however, whenever I fail to perform a proper or public duty.

17 January   Charles arrived this evening from London ...

19 January   To my infinite dismay and grief, I learn today that Lord Powis is dead – He was one of my oldest and most valued friends ...

25 January   Georgiana is much indisposed with cold, the prevailing influenza. I have confined her to her room, as she has much fever and other derangements. She is very sorry, unselfish[*ly*], as she is not to be able to make herself useful as we have a house full of company.

1848

26 January   ... I had to attend at Worksop today, the others went out shooting – they killed, among other things, 14 woodcock ...

28 January   Out shooting with a large party ...

29 January   A letter from William dated the 3rd of this month from Constantinople ...

A cold dull day and was devoted to duck shooting ...

30 January   ... Georgiana is now recovering, thank God, she sat up for some hours yesterday, had a good night and passed this day in her sitting room from 12 o'clock. She is very weak and has a cough ...

31 January   Out shooting today, in all 6 guns – Bevercotes was our beat and afforded us very little sport indeed.

1 February   Again shooting for the last time ... I wished to take some notice of two Sons of Ibrahim Pasha who school at Worksop [*possibly at Dr. Heldenmaier's 'Pestalozzian School'*] and they accompanied me all day to see the sport. They are fine boys and speak English very well ... the name of the eldest Hassan, the youngest Mustapha – they dined and slept here ...

16 February   ... took leave of my 4 dear daughters and Charles – left Clumber at 11 – Nottingham at 2 and arrived here in Portman Square at 10m past 8 ...

17 February   [*Attended the House of Lords – spoke in opposition to the proposed Bill on intercommunication between the Church of England and the Church of Rome.*]

23 February   [*Returned to Clumber*] ... greatly grieved to find dear Georgiana very ill again ... She has an incipient giddyiness and constant sickness, and can keep nothing on her stomach.

26 February   By some accident, the Worksop bag has not arrived today and we are in darkness as to all news ...

Charles left us this morning ... Georgiana is better today ... the giddyness of her head has not left her and the nausea comes on occasionally ...

5 March   [*Recorded that Louis Philippe and his Queen had arrived in England.*]

6 March   ... I am told that Robert is gone to Ireland ...[*to stand for election at Kinsale*] ... As a son he is behaving shockingly ill, God forgive him ... I have little idea of his prospering in any way.

8 March   [*Recorded that Louis Philippe had moved into Claremont –home of the 1st Duke of Newcastle-under-Lyme, Thomas Pelham-Holles.*]

10 March   ... I have written to London, to offer Nottm. Castle for an armed Depot of Arms and Stores – as well as barracks ...

1848

11 March	... received the melancholy intelligence of the death of my old friend and brother in law General [*Godfrey*] Mundy ...
13 March	Georgiana is now fairly convalescent, has discarded the garden chair and now takes her walks regularly ...
15 March	... Robert, it seems, has failed at Kinsale ...
19 March	... pretty well settled that Charles' marriage with Miss Grant will take place. But these Scotch people – not Miss Grant – are so shockingly mercenary that they will screw every sixpence out of one's pocket if they can ...
20 March	[*Charles arrived – with news that he had been asked to stand for election at Bewdley*] – we concluded that it might be better to decline the honor, as it might look as if a Clinton was to be first turn for any vacancy that might occur ... besides which we have no more money to throw away upon elections ...
21 March	...Charles left for London tonight ... his character and conduct delight me more every time I have any communication with him.
26 March	... I had a letter yesterday from dear William at Constantinople ...
27 March	This is the day of my wood Sale ... most made up of thinnings and the very worst trees in the Woods ... My people are all new, Steward and both foresters ... Many timber merchants have made offers of buying large lots of lime. Oak Beech for piles, and oak poles ... The amount of this day's sale (of rubbish) is £4,300. One wood merchant offers me 3s a foot for the best Oak ... I am not sure that I can part with them. They are in the Haughton grounds ...
28 March	... I have looked at the trees near the fish ponds at Haughton and some of these, say 4 or 5, are magnificent – I shall not sell them for any consideration ... I have also had a hard task ... to take out ... a line of fence in the rough piece outside this Park, to be turned in cultivation and annexed to March's farm – I had no one there and had to carry the stakes and put them down myself ...
29 March	... Came to Thoresby for a few nights – only a few Notts. people here.
1 April	[*Returned to Clumber.*]
5 April	... I have a letter from Charles today, which is dated from Sir A. Campbell's place in Scotland where Mrs and Miss Grant are now staying – he seems to be more pleased than ever with Miss Grant, and thinks that she will prove to be every thing to him as a wife ...
8 April	[*Received news that Charles had been ordered back to his Regiment in London.*]

1848

10 April   *[Recording concern at the Chartist's demonstrations, the Duke wrote that he was prepared to march at the head of his tenantry if necessary.]*

26 April   I am here at Markham Clinton (Dawkins) for a night, meaning to do much upon the Estates at Tuxford and elsewhere tomorrow ...

2 May   Went to Newark today ... They require a chairman of the Red Committee and I mean to propose Mr Thorpe to be that Chairman.

[Noted that Thorpe lived at the Mill and that his partner was Mr Bullen]

[Whilst in Newark, the Duke looked at the railway lines, expressing approval of the one slightly nearer to Clumber.]

4 May   ... I have had a tough day of business with Mr Heming today ...

6 May   ... I had to ride all over the Worksop estate with Mr Heming ... for the repairs, alterations and erections of farm buildings etc. ...

9/11 May   *[Mentions that he had woken early, said his morning prayers and had then been fully occupied with business matters.]*

12 May   ... here we are in London ... safe, thank God, but after a most jolting journey – the *[rail]* roads being excessively uneven – very hot and very dusty.

14 May   This being Sunday – by way of combining exercise with amusement, I went to lionise the new buildings in the Parks – I went first to see Mr Hope's new house in Piccadilly ... I then went to the new front of Buckingham Palace – but what a thing! One felt quite humbled and downhearted to see anything so wretched and contemptible ...

15 May   ... By the by, that wise but most unsuccessful meddler in Italian affairs has yesterday returned to England ...

19 May   We went to a State Ball at Buckingham Palace this night – a very great assemblage – The Queen is a great deal altered in appearance, looking very matronly ... It is obvious to me that most people have a thoughtfulness about them, which clouds the hilarity of a Ball ... *[He noted that neither the Queen nor Prince Albert joined in the dancing.]*

23 May   ... I made the acquaintance of Prince Louis Bonaparte this evening – He appeared to be a quiet gentlemanlike man and not the sort of person I expected to find him. He is middle sized, thick set, not good looking, but disguised with a strong and large moustache.

[At this time, the Duke's entries recorded many of the 'Chartists' demonstrations.]

1848

5 June	Sat for a small portrait to Mr O'Neil ...
10 June	[*Recorded that many of his servants had been sworn in as Special Constables. Noted that he had offered to do so himself 'if occasion requires.'.*]
19 June	... I have received proposals from Mr Foljambe, for the purchase of the land at Kilton and Manton, north of the line of railway and adjacent to his property – he offers £30,000 – I must obtain double that sum, or he will not become the owner of it.
22 June	... At the Opera tonight ... Jenny Lind sang delightfully ... and acted with her accustomed excellence. She is perfect as a woman, a singer and an actress – it is a feast to contemplate her upon the stage, her cleverness and nature are truly great and admirable.
26 June	[*Returned to Clumber.*]
4 July	... Lady de Grey I see is dead – It grieves me to read it – She and Lord de Grey were formerly our very intimate friends.
13 July	I called at Welbeck today and set some time with the Duke of Portland – he was not very well, but no gout ...
25 July	A letter from Charles announces that he may be married on Saturday the 29th – this is quick work indeed ... his operations have been very eccentric ...
31 July	I began my corn harvest the day before yesterday by cutting some oats ... Charles tells me that he believes his wedding day will be on the 10th August.
9 August	[*Travelled to London by train.*]
10 August	This day my dear and worthy son Charles was married to Miss Grant [*at St. George's Church*] ... there, for the first time, my daughters made the acquaintance of their future sister in law – went to a breakfast at Mrs Grant's ... honeymoon at Beaulieu ...
11 August	... I went to O'Neil to have my figure drawn ... went to the Opera tonight with my daughters to hear and see Jenny Lind ... Nothing can be more exquisite – her acting is the prettiest thing I ever saw, it contains every thing and is nature itself, it has no appearance of acting – Her singing was truly delightful, and she fascinated us all even more than ever – She is a wonderful, as well as an admirable creature. Her [*loveliness?*] and excellence, vie and go hand in hand with her talent and genius.
15 August	I had a letter from Charles today from Beaulieu. A beautiful letter ... he is evidently delighted with his wife ... I believe that she will prove to be a real acquisition in the family ...
	We were at the Opera again last night – Jenny Lind ... she was delightful as she must be in anything – with her genius, her delicate and sensitive feeling and her [*unerring?*] judgement, she must shine in any thing ...

1848

| 18 August | [*Returned to Clumber.*] |

23 August   The rumours respecting Lady Lincoln are I fear but too true, it has been a miserable business for a long time.

26 August   This evening Charles and his bride arrived here.

28 August   Fishing etc. today, Lady Charles is evidently no counterfeit ... The opinion which I have formed of her is that she will prove worthy of him.

30 August   Yesterday was fair, and today beautifully fine and we passed a very pleasant day indeed on the banks of the rivers fishing – we had a pick nick dinner in a grass field opposite to Bothamsall – all very happy and very gay – we had tolerable sport and took about 8 trouts, several perches, daces etc. ...

6 September   We all went tonight to a concert at Worksop – a small house, brim full, very hot, the music much improved in execution.

7 September   ... being invited to the Cutlers' Feast at Sheffield, I was obliged to go there ... Charles was invited and accompanied [*me*] ... it was the first time, altho' frequently invited that I have dined in the Cutlers' Hall [*there were 230 people present*] ... I was greeted enthusiastically when my health was given and they warmly applauded my speech in return ... We did not reach home untill 2 o'clock –

On entering the drawing room, we found dear William seated reading the newspaper – it may be supposed that our salutations were not very cool ...

9 September   Out shooting today ... the poor Turk [*William*] did not make so good a go of it, as he was used to do ... [*although he*] shot 3 woodcocks ...

13 September   Charles and his wife left us this morning, they stop at Doncaster to see the races and will sleep at York ...

15 September   I am buying some things at the Stowe Sale by commission – Portraits are what I shall most probably obtain, as the good pictures will be too high for my purse.

19 September   Mr Blandford rector of Kirton is dead. I have given the living to Mr Thompson who now has the living of Elkesley.

20 September   Portraits only have been bought for me at the Stowe Sale.

Lord Clinton by Sir A. More is one of them. I do not think that my commissioner has done his duty fairly by me. Many valuable pictures have gone at a very low price – and within my range.

1848

22 September	This morning I have been shocked beyond all description by an account of the death of Lord George Bentinck ... I immediately sent over to Welbeck and found to my sorrow and dismay that this was but too true ... I rode to Welbeck with William to enquire after the poor Duke of Portland who is now in his 81st year ...

Thus has the country lost the most valuable public man in it. The only honest, fearless and unconquerable politician in public life ... few such men have been seen before him ...

25 September   William left us today for London ...

27 September   At Worksop today, we had every Magistrate on the bench – a good deal of business and some very amusing scenes ...

29 September   [*Heard from William that Thomas was ill, also that he was probably not eating sufficient due to his low income.*]

1 October   ... To my unspeakable surprise, the Duke of Portland called here today, I did not see him and am glad of it, for I should not have known what to say or do. He is a singular man, he is always delighted in making people stare, but he is carrying the joke of Stoicism too far in my opinion.

4 October   I have written both to London and to Nottingham about promoting seriously a testification of the public sense of Lord George Bentinck's merits ...

The County Memorial I propose to be a Statue within an open circular Temple supporting a dome with a figure of Fame on the top ...

5 October   ... Thomas is better ... relieved from the fever fit but not [*negus?*]

9 October   ... I called upon Lord Manvers today to consult with him [*regarding the Memorial plans*] ... I fortunately hit all the right nails on the head and all differences were smoothed.

[*On this day, he recorded that Lady Manvers was the sister of Mrs Gally Knight.*]

10 October   [*Joseph*] Browne came today from London, to assist me in doing up my hall and several other things about the house, on the terrace etc ...

11 October   Browne went today, he has been very busy and so have I with him – and I think that he has been completely successful in his works – I shall commence upon them in a few days.

16 October   [*Travelled to Nottingham.*]

17 October   [*Attended the Quarter Sessions in Nottingham. Afterwards he met his son, William. They dined and then returned to Clumber.*]

20 October   [*With reference to the Bentinck Memorial plans*] – All the work and labor lies upon me – people are very well disposed and most willing to join me, but they will not work or take any trouble.

1848

23 October   Retford Sessions which I attended – not many Justices in Court. The Chairman, Granville Vernon has been very ill and remains unwell ... his place ... filled by G.Mason ...

On the 21ˢᵗ I called at Welbeck to speak to the Duke of Portland ... he was not at home – In riding home I inspected the spot on which [*Lord George Bentinck*] fell dead – as well as the most eligible spot for creating a Memorial – I yesterday wrote to the Duke, and today I have his reply ...

24 October   The principal event of today was the anniversary of the Worksop Agricultural Labourer's Friend Society, of which I am President and was in the Chair – I was surprised to find so large a party – everything was exceedingly well done and the dinner was very well served up and really very handsome for such and occasion. I sent them fruit for the dessert, which was ample and remarkably fine – Nothing could go off better than the meeting from beginning to end ... They invited William and he went with me ...

25 October   I have taken much pains with my preparations for tomorrow's meeting and in that respect I am successful. I am stupid and [*inert?*] and my head will not answer my will – I am much afraid that my oration will be a miserable affair – I go to bed with considerable misgiving.

26 October   [*To Mansfield*] ... I was greatly disappointed ... when I went into the room and saw it but sparingly filled – my spirit dropped and my heart was depressed ... I do not think there could have been more than 300 on the floor of the Hall ... I had once before, some 35 years ago to address a meeting in the Old Hall at Mansfield which was crowded to suffocation ... but we were then excited, it was in riotous and turbulent times, and a great deal of noise and disturbance in the room ... on this occasion all was different – a large new room that I had never before seen ... I had expected at least 2,000 people ... [*expressed deep disappointment at his own performance in addressing the meeting today*] ... The meeting went off exceedingly well. A Committee was formed ... we are to meet at Nottingham on this day week ...

27 October   [*Attended Southwell Quarter Sessions*] ... one very important motion was made to consolidate the three Quarter Sessions – at Newark, Nottingham and Retford into one only ... the question was finally staved off to this time next year ...

28 October   Out shooting for a few hours today ... found plenty of partridges on [*Gyles?*] farm, but exceedingly wild ...

29 October   More wet this morning but cleared after Chapel.

31 October   I am very uncomfortable just now and have been so for above a fortnight, painting and decorating the hall here, which was a

1848

miserable thing and quite an eye sore of the house – the smell and dirt and scaffolding etc. renders the house almost uninhabitable – in ten days or so I am told it may now be completed ...

1 November   We all left Clumber today. Caroline and Henrietta went with me to Col. Rolleston's (*Watnall*) and Georgiana, Charlotte and William to Nottingham – where they will occupy the Judge's lodgings.

2 November   ... we all went to Church in the morning ... In the evening we went to the Ball, and did not break up before 3 to 4 o'clock.

3 November   Returned home today, having all visited Miss Spencer [*exgoverness at Clumber, now aged 57*] on the way, at her cottage at Nuthall ...

4 November   I find today that the marbling in the Hall has made considerable progress ... I shall be able to make the painter (Foster) accomplish his work very successfully, he is very painstaking, intelligent and clever and receives criticism and instruction wisely.

6 November   [*Recorded that the weather was very cold, with snow*] –

              ... with dahlias and other flowers all destroyed and black as charcoal.

8 November   [*Attended the Court at Worksop.*]

11 November   [*Charles 'and his bride' arrived.*]

17 November   ... Lord Henry Bentinck arrived here this morning and sat with me a long while ... He is most anxious that Mr Disraeli should be our leader in the H.of Commons ...

18 November   ... Last night a most magnificent Aurora Borealis ... it lasted all night, it's illumination was lighter than twilight – There were perpetually renewed streams of light, emanating from a centre overhead which assembled an immense canopy.

22 November   [*Recorded the death of Ibrahim Pasha – see 1 February above.*]

26 November   [*Recorded the death of Lord Melbourne*] – He was Captain of the House (Dr Longford) when I first went to Eton, and was then and ever after excessively kind to me ...

27 November   Out shooting but poor sport ...

1848

28 November   Attended the Committee meeting at Mansfield ... the Subscription is but small as yet, only a little above £400 ... it seemed to be decided that the market place at Mansfield is the most eligible place for the building.

Fig. 78 *The 'Bentinck Memorial' in Mansfield's Market Place.*

4 December   ... I have now a statement from my Steward (Mr Heming) of the result of the collection of the rents in the last month – it is very favourable to me more so than I have ever known it, and proves to me that he has been a good Steward – and also proves that others have been very bad Stewards. I believe that for the first time, I shall be able to pay all my bills, country and London, up to the coming Christmas – perhaps I may be a little short in the payment of the London bills, but probably not much – and this is a happy prospect. If I accomplish it in future, I will pay every 6 months. The remittances to Coutts by him are above £14,000.

7 December   ... I was in the Chair today at a rather numerous meeting at Worksop, to receive the Report of the Committee on the building of a Corn Exchange and Market ... carried unanimously.

11 December   Left Clumber today with two of my daughters, Charlotte and Caroline to sleep at Derby ... in the railway hotel we find excellent accommodation ..

12 December   [*Train to Birmingham, then by road to Stoke Edith, via Worcester and Malvern*] – to attend a Ball at Hereford, of which Lady Emily Foley is patroness ... [*Lady Emily had been widowed in 1846*].

14 December   Shooting in the morning – the Ball in the evening ... Through Lady Emily's kindness my Daughters found partners for every dance – other wise we knew scarcely any one in the room ...

17 December   ... I have taken leave of Lady Emily Foley tonight, and leave tomorrow with deep regret – She is as charming as she is amiable.

18 December   Left Stoke Edith with a heavy heart ... did not reach Clumber till between 10 and 11 – a very tiresome day's journey.

1848

21 December ... Lord Aberdeen, who is staying at Ossington, came here this afternoon with Mr Denison to see this place, he seemed very much taken with it, and evidently surprised and greatly pleased with what he saw in and out of doors.

24 December ... recd. a letter which has given me infinite consolation and eased my mind of almost insupportable anxiety – God be praised for it – my heart overflows with gratitude.

25 December Another Christmas day passed with my family and, thank God, with more of them surrounding me than of late years I have been able to count –

My Daughter in law, Lady Charles is a great addition and acquisition, she is most amiable and I believe thoroughly good – and gains upon one every day –

We all received the Sacrament – but the day has not been favorable to doing anything out of the house, it has rained all day.

27 December At Worksop, no serious cases ...

29 December Out shooting today at Bevercotes – very bad day, thick fog with icicles on the trees and grasses, saw but few pheasant altho' more than last year, 4 guns killed only 15 and 3 woodcocks, with hares and rabbits.

31 December A letter from Lady. E. Foley today which extinguishes all my sanguine hopes and expectations – It is a grievous and bitter disappointment to me, the gravest that I ever experienced, and I fear that I may not easily get over it –

I entertain the strongest possible attachment to her – for she is admirable and good and agreeable, amiable, virtuous, manners perfect every external and internal gift but beauty – she is not handsome, but so pleasing that no one can be in her company without delighting in it beyond all powers of description. It pleases God that it should be so – I have prayed fervently most fervently to Him to make it otherwise but His will be done – I must endeavour not to [*reprise*?] and to bear my calamity with fortitude and resignation – but He knows that this is not an easy task to me – I am ever, apparently to myself, unfortunate and unsuccessful in every undertaking and expectation of life – This is the greatest of all – But I am grateful I hope, humble and submissive, and I shall try to sustain myself by making a cheerful sacrifice of myself and of the comfort and happiness which I anticipated, and which might have been too great a bliss, to be good for me in this world.

Here ends the most extraordinary and eventful year that has occurred since the coming of our Saviour. The rapid fulfilment of prophesy is most marked and indisputable – and is but a small beginning of immense events yet to come – For these may God in his infinite mercy prepare us individually and nationally.

Fig. 79 *A sample of the terrace decorations at Clumber (circa 1900). It has not been established whether any of these were part of the consignment mentioned in the Duke's diary (on 20th August 1833). It is probable that some of the vases, urns, etc. were moved to Clumber from Worksop Manor in 1838, following the Duke's purchase of that estate.*

1 January   I have commenced my journal of a new year – If I could but have commenced with a record that I was about to begin with a new life, united to the only woman who would be perfectly calculated to make me what I am not, who would supply all my wants and administer in every way to my comfort and happiness ... cheering me through the remainder of my life, I should have been instead of the most dejected, the happiest and most elated of mortals, which but a short time ago, I was by expectation. The miserable disappointment is bitter in the extreme and is near to breaking my heart ...

I am most wretched today and feel as if the world is a blank to me ... I feel as if I could never be tranquil again or survive the calamity ...

4 January   I shot a Bittern today at the Decoy – a very fine bird I never saw one on wing before. These birds are now extremely rare in England.

5 January   We all went to Newark today to attend a Ball there. We went to the Inn there – The ball was the best I ever saw there – we did not return to the Inn untill between 4 and 5.

6 January   Returned to Clumber today to receive several persons who are come to us – among them Lord Henry Bentinck ... I shall write to Lord Stanley tomorrow, signifying that I consider Mr D. [*Disraeli*]as the fittest and only man [*to be leader of their party in the Commons*].

8 January   [*Left Clumber for Bloxholme – 40 miles – through Leadenham.*]

9 January   [*His host, Mr Christopher, persuaded him to join the hunt with the Duke of Rutland's hounds.*] In the evening we attended a Ball [*at Aswarby or Asgarby?*] – bed at nearly 7am ... the country about here ... is quite new to me ...

10 January   Returned to Clumber today, as I had left some company here and expect more tomorrow ...

14 January   [*Sir James and Lady Graham left Clumber for London.*]

1849

22 January   ... Poor Foljambe and Lady Milton are here – it is the first time that he has come here since his blindness ... it is a melancholy thing to see him in such a state ...

23 January   Went to Newark this morning ... to attend a general sessional meeting of Magistrates, for the purpose of considering a report on the state of Kelham bridge and it seemed to be the unanimous opinion that a new bridge must be built ...
My excellent friend Winchilsea arrived this evening.

24 January   Lord H.Bentinck was here today [*regarding Disraeli's appointment*] ... tells me that all Peel's followers – including Lincoln – profess to be in favor of the extension of the suffrage and reform of all kinds ... Who could have supposed that my deluded Son could ever have permitted himself to be drawn into the kind of advocacy of principles, the very opposite of all that he formerly professed, and in which he was carefully and anxiously educated – Peel has done this and has ruined him and disgraced his family ...

25 January   Attended the Committee meeting at Mansfield today ...
the Subscriptions amount to about £1,130 ...

27 January   We have a clear house today ... Charles and his wife are gone to Serlby ... only my daughters and William remain.

30 January   This is my natal day ... I have been able to spend the day in packing and arranging ... I go off this evening to sleep at Nottingham ...

31 January   [*Nottingham to London by train*] – in good time for Lord Stanley's dinner ...

3 February   [*Went to the Carlton Club*]
I omitted to mention yesterday, that I commissioned my bookseller to bid for the 4th Volume of Prynne's Records, the only one in existence saved, it is presumed, in some manner not known from the great fire of London, this volume was discovered in the Stowe Library ... my bookseller took up the bidding at £180 and continued them to 335£ when he thought it useless to contend further ...

6 February   ... Mr Disraeli called upon me today and remained a long time with me, it is the first confidential interview that I have had with him ... I am sure that he is to be relied upon ... Called upon Lord Stanley ... Charles and I dined at 3 and left London by the 4 o'clk train and we reached Watnall about 9 1/2 where we found our host and hostess and all my daughters collected and Lady Charles happy to see her husband back again.

1849

7 February   This is the day for Sir Thomas and Lady White's ball ... the Ball was given in the Exchange rooms ... 300 present ... This is the 5th Ball that I have been to this season, and I am very glad that it is the last.

8 February   [*Returned to Clumber.*]

9 February   Attended the Committee of the Bentinck Memorial today at Mansfield [*he arrived late*] ... to my infinite surprise, I found that it had been decided to adopt the market cross instead of the statue – A Market cross has about as much to do with the subject as the Archbishop of Canterbury in a ballroom – Market crosses were erected for pious purposes in popish times ...

10 February   Charles has been very unwell, with violent cold ...

20 February   Two days ago, one of my tenants, (Fox) of Elkesley, had his whole stackyard (11 stacks) destroyed by fire ... Fox is unpopular, having been the first man to lower the laborers' wages.

26 February   Tomorrow my wood Sale will take place – in riding about today I have seen several parties engaged in surveying.

27 February   To my infinite disappointment, I have learnt this evening that my wood sale has been the worst ever known – I expected an amount of about £5,000 – instead of which very few lots are sold, in all amounting to little more than £900 –

It seems that a close combination had been effected among the wood buyers and there was no competition, altho' the room was full of people ... I have fortunately sold my wool (2 years clip) just in good time, it was sold at 30s a tod ...

28 February   [*Mentions that the Great Northern Railway Company was*] – making a difficulty of giving me £250 per acre for ruining my estate at Manton.

[*Also mentions that 87-year-old Doctor Staunton, who he had not seen for more than thirty years, made an appearance in Worksop Court today.*]

3 March   ... I today received a letter from Miss Wilmot, who was directed by her mother Lady Wilmot to inform me that her brother Edward Mundy had died ... He was an excellent man ... William Mundy of Markeaton will probably succeed him in the representation of Derbyshire.

8 March   ... with my Steward Mr Heming to Maplebeck, to examine and consider what can best be done to provide for a resident clergyman there – It is the first time (strange to say) that I ever was there, except when formerly I was hunting in that quarter – I was ashamed and annoyed to see the wretched condition of the Village and all around it – it would take 5 or 6,000£ to put it in proper order – Flawborough is now the only Estate belonging to me that I have not seen.

331

1849

9 March   ... Charles had a serious accident this afternoon ... drove over to Osberton in the pony phaeton ... on their return at the bottom of Ash Tree Hill, by some sudden turn, the bottom of the carriage broke and separated the hind from the four wheels – Lady Charles was fetched out on her head and Charles fell upon his shoulder – She was not in the least hurt, but he hurt his shoulder very much ... [*Doctor*] Dethick has seen Charles and pronounces that there is nothing broken or out of its place.

13 March   ... Charles and his lady left us this morning ...

14 March   Petty Sessions at Worksop ...

15 March   [*He notes that Jenny Lind is to be married. – Surprisingly, he does not mention that she had appeared at a concert in the Mechanics Hall, Nottingham, just six days ago.*]

22 March   A long conference this morning with my newly appointed clergyman at Maplebeck – He tells me that the house I mentioned will not suit him, being small with no accommodation, and some parts in a ruinous state – I dare say I shall have to build him a house – which will certainly be very inconvenient at this time, but I require him to reside and I engaged to give him a resident [*sic*] and must therefore fulfil my engagement however inconvenient. – I shall be doing a good act, and I feel sure that the means will be found without distressing me.

Fig. 80 *Maplebeck Church – in 1999.*

24 March   Mr Sherbrooke called here this morning ... [*regarding a replacement for Colonel Rolleston, who was resigning his seat for the County.*]

26 March   Mr Milward called here this morning ... [*on the same subject as Mr Sherbrooke – see 24 March above.*]

1 April   The lambing at Hardwick is nearly over – it has been very prosperous ... about 750 lambs from 600 ewes ...

4 April   ... Visited Egmanton and Markham E. [*East?*] Churches and parsonages – both Church and parsonage at Egmanton required the first most extensive repairs, being shamefully out of order, the other a new house building.

       The Church may be made excessively pretty. The Church at E. Markham is one of the finest in the county and in good repair.

1849

9 April   Attended the last meeting of the Committee for the Bentinck Memorial ... a very handsome Gothic erection, with an inscription on it ...

11 April   The fair at Worksop – I sent some beasts and sheep there – which were acknowledged to be the best in the fair – 2 of the beasts were Ayrshires and beautiful animals, and greatly admired for their symmetry and quality, people were astonished that Ayrshires could be brought to so great perfection – their fame is established by this manifest fact, as well as the reputation of my sheep, which were really as exceptional and as fine as any I ever saw – 3 were better than others, and sold for £3.10 a piece, being 3 year old wethers and sold to the butcher – [I] never saw a duller fair, my animals were almost the only things which sold, scarcely any biddings were made for others – The depreciation of stock and corn is deplorable – my bailiff tells me that by the present state of the market he loses 6 or 7£ a head on the beasts which he sells – and wheat is selling at 48 and 50 a quarter.

14 April   ... William left us yesterday for London ...

15 April   ... Chaloner of Bristol is desirous of buying Firbeck, for the purposes of erecting a large Popish establishment upon it.

21 April   As a proof probable of the extraordinary cold and inclemency of the season, no swallows have as yet appeared here. Commenced a survey of the Worksop property to see what had been done – there has been much done, much more is required but it is beginning to wear an improved appearance.

23 April   I have today settled with the architect Mr Hine, to build a Parsonage at Maplebeck – and he thinks that he may be able to complete it before the end of the autumn – I shall then have the satisfaction of thinking that I have afforded the means of residence to every clergyman who holds a living in my gift – and no village certainly, more requires a resident clergyman than Maplebeck ...

24 April   The swallows still refuse to visit us. They are right, they would find it very cold here.

1 May   [*Again mentions the cold weather and notes that*] – the lilacs still show no colour.

5 May   [*Travelled by train to London.*]

9 May   ... We all dined with Charles tonight ... in a nice new house of his own ... made comfortable and happy by an amiable and good wife.

28 May   My French horses, which I have long been anxious to inspect, are at last arrived. They arrived this morning. Lord Normanby, our Ambassador at Paris, has been so good as to select, buy and send them over to me. The stallion is a chestnut horse, very

handsome strong and with remarkably good action, he is about 4 years old – The three mares are all greys, 2 of them 5, one 6 years old – extraordinarily resembling each other in form, altho' bought at different farms in the neighbourhood of Havre – They were shipped on board a steamer at Havre yesterday and came over in 24 or 25 hours – they are all perfectly well and have not a blemish about them – I consider them very valuable prizes and will form the basis for the best breed of draught horses for England – in this if I have success, I shall have done a good deal for England.

2 June   I learn today that my horses have arrived safely at Clumber and are highly thought of.

5 June   Too unwell with bad sore throat and chest and cold to pay attention to any thing.

7 June   I am so unwell – principally from severe cold ...

9 June   ... today I am a great deal better ...

13 June   A great Ball at the Queen's which we attended.

16 June   Arrived here (Clumber) ... my cough very troublesome all the way. A great deal of rain here ...

17 June   Sunday – A very small congregation in my Chapel today.

Mr Rawlinson complains of being by no means well – and that such has been the case for some months past. Everything is looking well here – Vegetation of every description is pre-eminently promising and beautiful – Change of air has certainly done me good – I am better today and my cough much less troublesome.

18 June   ... my cough was very troublesome last night and impeded my sleep.

20 June   [*Travelled to London*] – very unwell and unfit for a dinner.

22 June   I cannot boast of being better today – but indeed how can I be so – every thing is against, I have not a comfort or a consolation in the world nor anything to look forward to. Day after day the same miseries occur ...

23 June   Altho' much better but not well, I dined today with the Lord Mayor at the Mansion House ... every male guest seated by his wife, if he had one, which alas I have not ...

25 June   ... I have taken a house at Ramsgate where I propose to go on Saturday next (30th) for 10 days or a fortnight ...

I was at the H. of Lords this afternoon ...

2 July   Left London this afternoon with my Daughters and arrived safely at Ramsgate ...

3 July   Bathed this morning and really feel better for the warm bath and change of air and sea breezes.

1849

18 July [*Hired a special train to travel to Sandgate – to see Mr and Mrs Dawkins*] – She is wretchedly altered poor thing and in a miserable state but her mental faculties are as fresh and strong as ever – Theirs is a beautiful little place and surprisingly grown since I saw it long years ago ... arrived in London at 10½ –

Poor Caroline had her pocket picked at the Terminus, of her purse and £11.

22 July ... I was told today that I was going to be married, so I suppose the old story is revived – and it will be made a certainty of in the course of a week I suppose as the Lady is coming to visit us at Clumber – But she will not wed, I wish she would, for I believe her to be capable of making the happiness of any husband who can appreciate her worth and merits.

23 July [*Presented a petition in the Lords*] – I gave the Noble Lords opposite a little bit of my mind on this occasion.

24 July [*Returned to Clumber*] – The terrace here is looking in her best beauty – William accompanied us here, we six filled a carriage very comfortably.

25 July Looking about things near the house. The trees and shrubs have grown so much that there appears no space – we have been cutting away a good deal today in the pleasure ground very much to its advantage – every branch that goes aides the effect from the walks – and of course improves the air ...

27 July I saw my French mares today and was delighted with them ...

30 July We drove to Worksop Manor today and afterwards went round by Shire Oaks on our way home by Worksop crossed the railroad for the first time since it has been made – I find many buildings made since I was last there in the beginning of Spring.

14 August [*Mentions Lord Dartmouth*] – an old school fellow and friend of mine ...

16 August ... we went a large party ... to see Chatsworth – which is 30 miles off and a very hilly road ... many things have been perfected ... extraordinary beauty and magnificence. Nothing in my opinion equals this place ... not even Versailles ... The great wonder to me was the new jet – which is probably the largest in the world. Lord [?] and I were on the box of the landau and were not so well pleased with the wetting, which we experienced from the pelting and pitiless rain.

22 August On going to the stackyard this afternoon I found 8 oat stacks up and the oats cleared off the ground. The barley is all down a good deal of the [rape?], and the same of the wheat – The crops are so large there will not [be] room for it in the stackyard ...

335

1849

26 August   We learn by this day's post, that Lincoln's yacht, the 'Victoria', has been wrecked at Ryde on her passage from Portsmouth to Cowes ... a merciful dispensation that Lincoln had not sailed in her ... Lincoln's loss will be considerable – He gave £1,700 for the yacht – William tells me – All their things and stores were on board [*Lincoln and his brother Robert were due to sail to the Mediterranean*] ...

29 August   Today I believe will finish my harvest, it never has been more prosperous. – May others be as fortunate as I have been – and may they all be thankful to God ...

30 August   A letter from Mr Henderson, this morning, informs me that Mr Parkinson had called upon him, thinking it right that I should be made acquainted with Lady Lincoln's present state. She left England ... in the beginning of August last year ... became acquainted with Lord Walpole ... she went to Rome, and Lord W. followed her there by a different route – Lady L. afterwards took a villa on the Lake of Como – There Ld. W. was always in her society – He passed under a foreign name – She became pregnant, and it is understood that she is to lie in at the end of this month of August – I have written at some length to Henderson with particulars of how he should advise Mr Parkinson to proceed, so that Lady L's infamy shall be completely proved and exposed and that this little bastard shall not be palmed upon my family as a legitimate child and a Clinton. [*At this stage, he did not know that Lady Susan had given birth to a son on the 2nd August*]
It is a most scandalous and horrible affair, but it is no more than I expected and foretold of Lady L., when Lincoln so weakly and so inconceivably took her back ...

1 September   Charles and his wife arrived this afternoon. She is very well notwithstanding that she is much increased in size ... Went out shooting for a few hours – I walked and shot better than I expected ... troubles and anxieties and disappointments weigh me down and oppress my mind.
This post brings me a letter cutting off all hope of future happiness, and my heart is really almost ready to break – In fact – I had so much reason to hope for a successful issue, and I looked forward so sanguinely and so intently, to this haven of tranquillity and healing of so much sorrow and misery that I have nothing now to look forward to, and the future view in this world is cheerless indeed. Lady Emily Foley is every thing, the most desirable for a wife and to lose her, is a blow too heavy to sustain.

2 September   No particular news – except that every thing has been done to bring Lady Lincoln's filthy wickedness to light – and possibly a divorce may follow as well as illegitimatising the bastard.

1849

3 September   William returned today.

6 September   ... I am going to the Cutler's Feast at Sheffield this afternoon. Charles and William are also invited ...

7 September   The dinner went off very well yesterday ... I had a special train to take us back to Worksop – we reached Clumber about 11 o'clock ...

8 September   Rode about, a long ride, to show the country to one of my guests ...

17 September   This day Lincoln was to sail for the Mediterranean ... it is impossible not to fear for him ... his children, who I believe are to be at Harwarden Castle, in the care of I know not who – and his infamous wife in the predicament previously described ... I cannot conceive any man undertaking such an expedition ...

21 September   My chief occupation yesterday and today has been cutting out trees whilst the leaves are on, so as to open views, to let in the air and to increase the apparent extent both in the pleasure ground and in the home grounds. Trees grow so fast, that one is constantly obliged to repeat the operation.

1 October   Dear Charlotte's birth day – but too wet for shooting pheasants.

[On two occasions at this stage in his diary, the Duke (apparently inadvertently) turned over two pages when continuing his entries, leaving the missed pages blank. His handwriting had also become less controlled.]

3 October   Soon after going to bed last night I had a seizure of the most alarming kind – I have had indications of it lately, but wheezing and impediment of breathing came on and increased to such an degree that I could scarcely inspire or expire, and I thought that death was coming on – it was I suppose an asthmatic affection of the most distressing kind and for some time it became worse and worse until we hit upon a remedy, in salvolatile and hot water. Our Doctor (Dethick) was sent for ... I did not wish to disturb any body but my servants – but Caroline and Henrietta heard of it, and came into my room and I sent for William, to give him some messages in case I was carried away by the attack – their conduct was admirable. Head and heart were at work to do their utmost, and no fear of what might after likely to happen put them off their guard or show the slightest weakness, altho' their love and affection were tried to the full and they were all of the greatest use and comfort to me.

4 October   I am better today thank God and passed a comfortable night ...

5 October   Most of the family have colds – Georgiana has a bad attack and Mrs Grant is laid up in her room.

6 October   William has received a letter from Robert dated Lisbon 27th ...

1849

7 October ... I never saw so small a congregation in Chapel.

9 October Poor Lady Charles left this morning ... They had a beautiful day for their journey.

10 October I rode out today, and liked my ride, a beautiful day ...

13 October ... I am unexpectedly better – this, after entirely from drinking a little brandy and water at dinner, which has had, as it always has upon me, a wonderful effect.

14 October [Records that during the night he had suffered] a choking paroxysm and icy coldness ...

15 October ... almost well again today – Georgiana is nearly well again ...

21 October A letter from Charles announces to me the birth of a good daughter at about 6 o'clock yesterday morning ...

23 October Charles writes that all is going on as well as possible.

25 October [Presided at the Worksop "Labourers Friend Society"] –

Lord Galway was there and did very well ... [I] was tired before dinner was over, the carving alone always is a great fatigue ... reached home ... "dead knocked up" ...

There were no further diary entries until

13 December On the 28th of October, illness came on rapidly and I was obliged to take to my bed, to which I was closely confined for above a month. Doctors from London came down to see me and others from the country ... I was a skeleton ... could only drink a little and that broth and milk, the latter being the favorite. Eating was impossible ... Doctor Packman fortunately came down and insisted upon my leaving my bed and sitting up out of it ... I resolved to exert every energy to accomplish the result which he held out to me ...

On the 25th or 26th November I was forced out of my bed, and in about a fortnight after, I was fit to leave my rooms upstairs and was carried to my room at the bottom of the backstairs, which I have inhabited ever since.

30 December About the 18th or 19th I took my first drive in the close carriage, having previously hobbled a little about the lower front of the house with the assistance of sticks ...

Poor Mrs Dawkins has died ... The Queen Dowager Adelaide has died ...

On Christmas day I had the happiness of dining with my family and I also was able to attend Chapel and receive the Sacrament ...

1 January	... I dined with my family today and passed the day as cheerfully as circumstances would permit.
4 January	[*Took a train from Mansfield to Nottingham and then on to London*]
5 January	Went to see Charles' little child – little Emily is a very nice baby ...
8 January	... to St.Leonards ... Charlotte and William have accompanied me ...
9 January	... as cold as Clumber or any other place in winter.
13 January	[*Records that they are staying at the Victoria Hotel*] – we are to have some rooms occupied by Louis Philippe and his family ... I have sent for all my daughters from Clumber.
18 January	My Daughters arrived today ...
28 January	... I have unfortunately taken cold ...
29 January	... ill today. I have been obliged to send for the Doctor.
30 January	... This is my birth day and my companions have all greeted me upon it and wished me many happy returns – I am confined to the house.
26 February	I have been almost perpetually attacked every night with the breathless seizures which are so indescribably distressing ... I have gone off to London and here I shall remain for some days, for full examination and medicine advice.
1 March	... I went for a short time, when the sun was out a little, to see Charles' child ... a very nice little girl, perhaps rather delicate ... Today I have returned to St Leonards ...
8 March	Went to see Battle Abbey ...
14 March	Combermere and Lady Combermere kindly came from London to pay us a visit for a day ... I and my two eldest daughters went to see Herstmonceaux and they each took sketches of the ruins of the Castle. This was formerly a magnificent residence of the Fienneses ...

1850

April   ... There have been several mischievous burnings lately at Clumber – how caused has not yet been discovered.

25 April   William left us and went to London today.

4 May   ... I was taken ill last night ...

10 May   I am receiving petitions from some of my parishes, praying that I will give them some relief, lower the rent, postpone payment to a future day or something. I also learn from Newark that my shop keepers are failing, leaving their shops etc.

14 May   [*Having returned to London*] – my Doctor ... thinks me thin and of bad colour ...

15 May   Better today ... less palpitations, legs less swollen.

25 May   I go on from day to day much in the same manner of living, taking my medicines, my meals and my exercise very much by rule.   I see a good many people in my own home but I do nothing else, I am forbidden the H. of Lords.

27 May   ... Lincoln's divorce bill has passed the second reading [*in*] the H. of Lords – His vile and [*abandoned?*] wife offered no defence.

30 May   I went with my daughters to see the Hippopotamus just arrived at the Zoological Gardens, and was resting myself near the houses, when one of my daughters came up and told me that we had just passed two of Lincoln's children, Edward the second boy and the daughter, Susan. – She said that they were close by and that the boy in the blue jacket was Edward, I looked at him with wonder for I could not recognise a feature of his countenance or see any likeness to his family – the girl I afterwards found, I had even touched as I passed her on the walk, and heard her voice but did not know her tho' she is less altered than the boy – I subsequently came upon them near where the hippopotamus is kept and renewed my acquaintance with them – they were very civil and well behaved as to a stranger, and stared at me very much, but shewed no emotion – They were with Mrs Gladstone.

The Diary entries ended at this point.

The Duke died on the 12th January 1851.
[*He died at Clumber, reportedly 'to the sounds of Radcliffe the violinist playing in an adjourning room'.*]

The 'Illustrated London News' [*25 January 1851*]
carried the following report on the funeral of the Duke:

The remains of the late duke of Newcastle were conveyed to the family burial-place at Markham-Clinton about ten miles from Clumber, on Tuesday morning last. The nobility and gentry of the neighbourhood had sent communication to the bereaved family, requesting permission to pay a last mark of respect to his Grace's memory, by their attendance; but, in consequence of the late duke having expressed a wish that the funeral should be conducted as unostentatiously as possible, all applications were declined. From ten in the morning until two P.M., the bells of the neighbouring village's churches were tolled. At half-past eleven o'clock, the funeral left Clumber, en route for Markham-Clinton, where a small church, in the Grecian-Doric style, was created a few years since by order of the late duke, from designs by Sir Robert Smirke. The procession consisted of 300 of the late duke's tenantry on horseback; the Rev.E.H.Dawkins, Vicar of Markham-Clinton, in his carriage; and the chaplains and officers of the late duke's household, in mourning coaches; the eight pall-bearers, on horseback; the late duke's chariot, containing the coronet, borne by the house steward; the stud-groom, undertakers, and the clerk of the works, on horseback; the hearse (with escutcheon), drawn by six horses, and containing the coffin; a mourning coach, containing the Earl of Lincoln (now duke of Newcastle), and the Lords Charles; Thomas and Robert Pelham Clinton, sons of the late duke. Among: the other mourners in attendance were Viscount Combermere; the Lord Clinton, now Earl of Lincoln; and the Lords Edward and Arthur Pelham Clinton, grandsons of the late duke; H.Fyne Clinton Esq.; E.W. Mundy, Esq.; and Col. Dawkins. The procession was closed by the head keepers and foresters on horseback, and tenants in carriages. At Markham-Clinton, the Rev.E.H.Dawkins, who read the funeral service in a most impressive manner, met the cortege at the church gates. All the Ladies Clinton were present at the interment in the church, whither they had proceeded privately. As soon as the coffin had been placed upon the platform appointed to receive it, the undertaker removed the pall, when the coronet was set upon it, and the mourners withdrew. The pallbearers were selected from the principal class of the late duke's tenants; some of whom and their families had held farms for upwards of 300 years. The under-bearers were selected from the class of cottage farming tenants, some of whom and their families had held for upwards of 250 years. The body was first placed in a shell of Spanish mahogany, covered with crimson Genoa velvet, having eight massive handles, with a coronet over each: the lid studded with gilt stars, and having upon it the breast-plate, with the noble duke's arms heading, the inscription.

 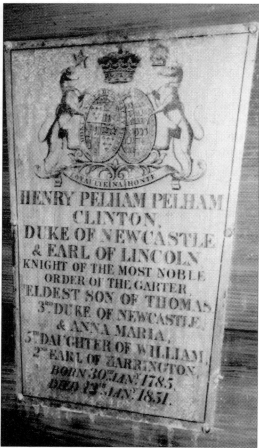

HENRY PELHAM PELHAM
CLINTON,
DUKE OF NEWCASTLE
& EARL OF LINCOLN
KNIGHT OF THE MOST NOBLE
ORDER OF THE GARTER
ELDEST SON OF THOMAS
3ᵈ DUKE OF NEWCASTLE
& ANNA MARIA,
5ᵗ DAUGHTER OF WILLIAM
2ᵈ EARL OF HARRINGTON,
BORN 30ᵗ JANᵞ 1785,
DIED 12ᵗ JANᵞ 1851.

Figs. 81/82 *These memorials to the fourth Duke were placed in the Markham-Clinton Church, Nottinghamshire. It is possible that the piece shown on the left may be the one referred to in the Diary extracts dated 3 December 1825 and 23 June 1827. The duke had intended such a monument, to his own father, to be placed in St. George's Chapel, Windsor but (according to the archivists at Windsor) no such memorial is recorded as having been erected there.*

Lord Lincoln's divorce was finalised on the 14ᵗʰ August 1850.

Lady Susan re-married in 1862 – she died on the 28ᵗʰ November 1889.

Lord William died on the 4ᵗʰ September 1850.

Lady Caroline married in January 1852.

Lady Emily Foley died on the 1ˢᵗ January 1900.

ACKNOWLEDGEMENTS & REFERENCES

The main reference documents are, of course, the Diaries. Held in the Manuscripts and Special Collections Department of the University of Nottingham, they are to be found under 'Newcastle Manuscripts' reference 'Ne F2'. My grateful thanks go to the Keeper, Dr Dorothy Johnston and her staff (especially Jayne Amat, John Briggs and Nick Davies) for their valuable assistance.

To better understand the period of British history during the period covered by the Diaries, many and varied resources were used. In addition to biographical encyclopaedias and peerage records, published and unpublished books and papers were obtained from the University of Nottingham Hallward Library; Nottinghamshire Records Office and the Nottinghamshire Libraries Service. The National Library of Wales; Aberystwyth Archives Office; 'Hafod Trust' and 'Friends of Hafod' assisted with research on the period of the Hafod Estate purchase. The staff of the Bassetlaw Museum, together with those of the library at Retford, provided valuable assistance on the electoral machinations in that town at the time of the early years of the diaries. Understanding of the period of Worksop Manor ownership was greatly enhanced by the assistance of the staff of the Worksop library.

The following list represents a very small portion of the published material that has a bearing on the Diary Extracts:

Bassett, A.T. (Ed.) (1936). Gladstone to his wife.:Methuen.

Bradbury, D.J. (1988). Clumber.:Wheel Publications.

Chambers, M.B. (c1980). 4th Duke of Newcastle.:Private Publication.

Contencin, J. & Smith T. (1860). Steetley church – illustrations of English architecture.:Robert White.

Eddison, Edwin. (1854). History of Worksop; with historical, descriptive and discursive sketches of Sherwood Forest and the neighbourhood.: Longman and Co. London.

Gilpin, W.S. (1832). Practical Hints upon landscape gardening: with some remarks on domestic architecture as connected with scenery.: T. Cadell, Strand.

Holland, J. (1826). History of Worksop, in the County of Nottingham.:Blackwell, Sheffield.

Inglis-Jones, E. (1950). Peacocks in Paradise: Faber and Faber.

Jackson, A. (1971). History of Retford.:Eaton Hall.

Jackson, M.J. (1992), Victorian Worksop.:Worksop Archaeological and Local Historical Society.

Martineau, J. (1908). Henry Pelham Clinton, 5th Duke of Newcastle.:John Murray.

Munsell, F.D. (1985). Unfortunate Duke. Henry Pelham, 5th Duke of Newcastle, 1811-1864.:University of Missouri Press. Columbia.

Roberts, J. (2000). Georgiana, 4th Duchess of Newcastle.:Country Books.

Surtees, V. (1977). Beckford Inheritance – Lady Lincoln scandal.: Michael Russell.

Thomis, M.I. (Ed.). (1967). Thoroton Society Record Series Vol. XXVI. Luddism in Nottinghamshire. :Phillimore.

Grateful acknowledgement is made to the following, by whose courtesy illustrative material has been used to enhance the text:
- John & Ruth Alcock, also Margo Lovegrove, for many postcard depictions of Clumber Park (Figs. 11, 17, 28, 49, 52, 53, 71, & 79)
- John R. E. Borron; also Linda & Roger Hallett of the 'Friends of Hafod' (Fig. 45)
- Christie's, King St., London (Fig. 7)
- Eric R. Coddington (Fig. 64)
- W.E. Cowell, custodian of Brodick Castle (Fig. 35)
- Malcolm Dolby, curator of the Bassetlaw Museum, Grove Street, Retford (Figs. 57, 73 & 77)
- Provost and Fellows of Eton College (Fig. 44)
- Robin Fryer, Ashlow, Warwickshire (Figs. 59, 62 & 63)
- Janet L. Green, Hafod Arms Hotel (Fig. 54)
- Ken Jeary, Pontrhydygroes, Ceridigion (Fig. 60)
- South Lanarkshire County Council (Fig. 36)
- Manuscripts and Special Collections Department, University of Nottingham (Figs. 4, 16, 24, 29, 33, 39, 69 & 74)
- National Portrait Gallery, London (Figs. 23, 26 & 75)
- National Trust, East Midland Regional Office, which has a large collection of Clumber photographs, including "Cecil Brown's Collection" (Figs. 1, 25, 27, 31, 32 & 51)
- Newcastle Trustees (Fig. 2)
- Nottingham City: Leisure and Community Services: Local Studies Libraries (Figs. 12, 15, 18, 22, 30, 42, 50, 56, 58, 65, & 76)

- Nottinghamshire County Council: Libraries, Archives and Information:
  Mansfield Library (Fig. 78): Retford Library (Fig. 42)
- Charles J. Stableforth (Figs 3, 21,34, 37, 38, & 55)
- Weindenfeld & Nicolson Archives (Fig. 20)
- Wordsworth Editions Limited (Fig. 9)
- Worksop Guardian Newspaper (Cover picture & Fig. 47)

The source of some items (e.g. newspaper cuttings from the early nineteenth century), have proved impossible to identify from the content. All other depictions are from the Editor's own collection. If the names of any owners of rights to the pictures have been omitted, or if any have been incorrectly attributed, I apologise unreservedly. Any aggrieved owner should contact the Editor for amendments to be made in future editions.

I most gratefully acknowledge the financial assistance of the National Trust in sponsoring this publication. My hope is that that the Trust will benefit from its sales for many years.

Two members of the Trust's East Midland office merit special mention. David Wilson, Area Manager, has been a great support throughout the past four years, particularly in covering many of the travelling costs involved in the research. Andrew Barber, Historic Buildings Representative, has always shown a keen interest in the project and continues to be a well-informed 'sounding board' for my efforts.

Many other individuals have encouraged the work and it is probably unwise to list them for fear of omitting someone. However, with advance apologies for any such oversight, my grateful thanks go to: Bernadette Ayton, John & June Bower, David Bradbury, Garry Cox, Malcolm Dolby, Patsy Fletcher, Richard Gaunt, the late Don Gilbert, Janet Green (Hafod Arms Hotel), Roger & Linda Hallett (Friends of Hafod), Claire Herring, Neville Hoskins, Philip Lynd-Evans, Hilary Lynskey, Jennifer Macve (Hafod Trust), Janet Robb, Charles Stableforth, Edward & Pat Tansey, also to Philip & Dinah Webster. Finally, and very specially, thanks go to Sandra, my long-suffering wife, who knows only too well that this is not even the mid-point in my attempts to produce a social history of Clumber Park and the families who influenced its development.   J.F.

APPENDIX I

THE DUCAL TITLE:

'Newcastle-under-Line'; 'under-Lyne'; 'under-Lyme'?

The award of this contrived ducal title has caused considerable confusion, ever since it was awarded to Thomas Pelham-Holles in 1756.

Already holding the title as 'Duke of Newcastle-upon-Tyne' – from 1715 and in its third creation – Thomas knew that on his death, as he had no son, that particular title would again be extinct. However, he wished to pass a senior title to his favoured nephew, Henry Fiennes Clinton, who had been in his care since the death of Henry's parents. Henry already held the title of Earl of Lincoln.

November 1756 was an opportune time to request a favour of King George II. At that time, Thomas had been forced to stand down from his post as First Lord of the Treasury. As a reward for political services, his wish for a ducal title to pass on to his nephew was granted.

It was agreed that a new title would be created and that Thomas Pelham-Holles should hold both titles. The new title would contain a 'special remainder' ensuring that, on the death of Thomas, it could be passed to nephew, Henry. In the event, this dual title-holding lasted until Thomas's death in 1768. The 'new' title went on until 1988, passed down a line of nine 'Clintons'.

In drafting the petition for the new title, the clerks of the Attorney General's office entered the words:

'Duke of Newcastle-under-Line, in the County of Stafford' (1)

This same title was then used on the list of expenses involved in preparing the necessary documentation for the award. (2)

Certain publications relating to the peerage have changed their ground over the years, and 'Newcastle-under-Lyme' has become a regularly used option by some but not others.

The University of Nottingham, Manuscripts and Special Collections Department, which houses the bulk of the 'Newcastle Manuscripts', has (after seeking advice from the College of Arms) opted to use the 'Newcastle-under-Lyne' version.

For the purposes of this current work, and after much consideration, a decision was made to use the modern usage, following the example of 'Burke's Peerage' and also that of the 'Newcastle Trustees'.

(1) Reference NeC 4,399 University of Nottingham, Manuscripts and Special Collections.
(2) Reference NeC 4,457 ditto.

APPENDIX II

BRIEF OUTLINE
OF THE DIARY EXTRACTS

1822

Georgiana, Duchess of Newcastle, died as a result of her twelfth confinement. Her newly-born twins also died. Their eldest daughter had died just five months before this tragedy.

1823

Duty bound, by the presence of his young and large family of six boys and four girls (the eldest child being twelve years old and the youngest only two), the Duke busied himself with family and estate matters.

His mother, the Dowager Duchess, living close by at Ranby Hall, became a thorn in his side, by strenuously attempting to influence the upbringing of his children.

In May, he took all ten children with him to London. There, he rented a house on the banks of the Thames at Chiswick. Whilst there, he spent large amounts at the sales.

He met Robert Smirke, and began planning a new family church/mausoleum.

On meeting Richard Westmacott, he commissioned a monument to the late Duchess.

The year ended with him attempting to consolidate all his financial matters.

1824
William Sawrey Gilpin and Robert Smirke assisted with 'outdoor work'.
Substantial construction work began at Clumber – e.g. roads and terraces.
The Duke continued his plans for a new church/mausoleum – selected the site at Markham and the building work commenced.
His son and heir, Lord Lincoln, began his education at Eton.
Plans were made to build houses on the Duke's land at Nottingham Park.
The Duke was in London from April to August.
A poor speaker, the Duke chose to have his 'Anti-Reform' thoughts published.

1825
Involved himself in politics, both in and out of the House of Lords.
He was greatly concerned by daughter Charlotte's ill health.
Terrace and other construction work continued – Library alterations begun.
More timber was sold, to pay for the new works.

1826
Construction work continued – waterpower was increased to supply the new fountains.
Design plans for Markham Clinton Church were altered.
Clumber Library extension building works were commenced.
Visited Southwell House of Correction and the 'associated Poor House'.
Began regular Bible reading.

1827
Had an audience with King George IV.
The first houses were built at his Nottingham Park Estate.
Terrace ballustrading and fountains were installed at Clumber.
Financial problems intensified – Sold the leasehold of his Walkeringham properties.

1828
He was given a leopard, and had it kennelled at Hardwick.
Sponsored an Eton scholarship prize.
Eldest daughter, Georgiana (aged 18), was presented at Court.
The family went on holiday to the Ramsgate area.
The Duke's portrait, by Lawrence, was completed (after 21 years!).
Continued with his anti-electoral reform convictions.

1829
Had another audience with King George IV – became annoyed by the King's attitude over voting arrangements on the Reform plans.
Complained of the high levels of election costs at Newark.
Issued Notices to Quit to his Newark tenants who had voted against his wishes.
As last year, he went on holiday to Ramsgate.
Ended the year with stated intentions to do more for the poor of his Estates.

1830

Rearranged his finances to provide for his children.

Terrace, Garden and Library work continued at Clumber.

Lord Lincoln began his studies at Oxford.

Lord Edward (aged 14) joined the navy.

The Duke had an audience with King William IV. He also spoke in the Lords on the matter of his right to 'do as I please with mine own'.

More heavy spending on the Newark and Retford elections.

1831

Borrowed money.

Lord Charles (aged 17) joined the army.

Had the frigate 'Lincoln' rebuilt.

Dined with the Duchess of Kent and her daughter, Victoria.

Lady Charlotte was presented at Court.

Lord Thomas obtained his army commission.

Reform Act riots led to an attack on his London home.

Handbills were published, calling for his dismissal as Lord Lieutenant.

Declined an invitation to attend William IV's coronation.

Reform Act riots – Nottingham Castle set on fire.

Clumber House defences were strengthened.

1832

Improvements continued at Clumber. Graffiti appeared on the Greek Temple and the Bridge.

The Reform Acts led to a reduction in potential monies for the Duke. His Yorkshire properties and Retford lost their parliamentary representatives.

Lord Lincoln was elected to the South Notts constituency.

William Ewart Gladstone was elected to represent the Duke's interest at Newark.

Lord Lincoln was married to Lady Susan Hamilton, at Hamilton Palace.

1833

Celebratory parties were held at Clumber, for the newly-weds.

The Duke bought the Hafod Estate, near Aberystwyth for £62,000 – hoped to benefit from mining prospects -later, he bought even more Welsh land.

A new avenue was completed from the Great North Road to Clumber.

He sponsored a second prize to his Eton Scholarship foundation.

Lady Lincoln was presented at Court.

New vases were purchased for the Clumber Terraces.

The Duke and his heir had a disagreement.

The new Church/Mausoleum was consecrated at Markham Clinton.

1834
Lady Lincoln's first son was born.
The Duke bought a Park Lane house for Lord and Lady Lincoln.
He spoke in the House of Lords on Church matters.
His (twice-widowed) mother died.

1835
Had an audience with King William IV.
Attended the Lords, spoke on the Municipal Corporation Act.
Upset by his Thoresby neighbour, Lord Manvers.
Purchased more land at Cromwell – £6,600
Purchased the Cwmelan Estate for £23,200.
Discovered many art treasures at Hafod, had them cleaned and sent to Clumber.
Agreed 20% rent rebates to his tenants.
Work continued on his Cascade, Library and Drawing Room at Clumber.
Upset by his heir, he altered his will.

1836
Made an attempt at reconciliation with his heir, Lord Lincoln.
Attended House of Lords debates, involved himself in Reform Act aspects.
Met the young Princess Victoria again
Spent around £67,000 on land at Newark.
Added more 'ornaments' to the Clumber Terrace.
Railway plans were put to him for approval.
Buried remains of his family were moved from Bothamsall to Markham Clinton.
Refused consent for Lord Charles to marry Lady Lincoln's cousin.

1837
Lord William sent a love letter to his sister-in-law, Lady Lincoln.
Lady Caroline was presented at Court.
The Duke met the new Queen – Victoria.
Made his first attempts to buy the Worksop Manor Estate.

1838
At Clumber, financed the planting of the Lime Tree Avenue and also a new Icehouse.
Launched the newly built 'Lincoln' boat – to replace the original.
Agreed to purchase the Worksop Manor Estate for £370,000. Offered 550 acres of it for sale at £73,000.
Unsuccessfully bid for the Rossington Estate – offered £90,000.
Completed his purchases in Newark – spent over £71,000.
His Nottingham 'town' properties were put up for sale.
Sold his properties at Aldborough and Boroughbridge, Yorkshire.
Did not attend the Queen's coronation.
Invited Sir Robert Peel to address a meeting at Clumber.
Learnt more of Lady Lincoln's 'indiscretions'.

1839

About 1,500 trees were felled during a storm – much timber was sold to Hull shipbuilders.

The large marble basin for the central fountain was delivered.

Sorted the books from the library at Hafod – to add them to his Clumber Library.

Settled queries over his purchase of the Worksop Manor Estate.

Paid £3,600 for Worksop Manor furniture – Worksop land sales began.

Sold stone from his Steetley quarries, to be used in building the new Houses of Parliament.

Attended the House of Lords.

He was dismissed as Lord Lieutenant of Nottinghamshire.

Travelled by train, for the first time.

The Westmacott Monument was placed in Markham Clinton Church.

1840

Began to attend the Quarter Sessions regularly.

Promoted a play at the Worksop theatre, to mark the Queen's marriage.

Became optimistic about the coal boring on the Worksop Manor Estate.

Made plans to sell the Worksop Manor House.

Met Queen Victoria.

Purchased Westmacott's statue of Euphrosyne.

Arranged for a monument to the Johnes family at Hafod Church.

Approved Lord Lincoln's farming arrangements at Ranby.

Valuable paintings (e.g. by Costigliona and Van Dyke) were cleaned.

1841

Completed the construction of his 'grand avenue and road thro' the Park'.

Attended an agricultural show on Retford Common.

Worksop Manor House and timber sales were held.

Made plans to rebuild Elkesley Church.

Visited the Chatsworth estate – saw Paxton's 'new Conservatory'.

Regretted that Sir Robert Peel had not appointed him as Minister for Ireland.

Lady Lincoln was suspected of drug addiction.

1842

Timber prices were so low that his income from this source was heavily reduced.

Borrowed money from his children to clear a large debt.

Made drastic reductions in Estate expenditure – and decided to sell more land.

Calculated his debts at £116,000 (approaching 6 million pounds, at year 2000 levels).

Hired a financial adviser to advise on his money problems.

Visited Steetley Chapel.

Lord and Lady Lincoln separated.

Son, Edward (aged 26), died of fever whilst at sea off China.

His family shunned him at Christmas.

1843
Moved temporarily to Worksop Manor, following a smallpox scare at Clumber.
Explosives were used to demolish a 'back wall' at Worksop Manor.
Sales of Worksop Manor land continued.
Decided to sell his Hafod Estate.
Reduced his South Down breeding flocks at Clumber to around 560 ewes.
His son, Thomas (aged 30), married in secret.
Queen Victoria visited Nottingham – the Duke did not attend.
His family continued to shun him.

1844
His family softened their behaviour towards him.
Lady Lincoln (dressed as a man), attempted to visit her children at Ranby.
New building work was begun at Bothamsall, Elkesley and Manton Farm.
New brickworks opened at Bothamsall.
Refused to support a Newark to Sheffield (via Mansfield) railway plan.
Sold his 'railroad shares'.
Sold the Cwmelan Estate for £25,000.
Planned to sell his Basford Estate.
Nottingham Park developments continued.
Attended and spoke in the Lords on ecclesiastical matters.
Removed chimneypieces and other items from Hafod for Clumber.
Lord and Lady Lincoln were (temporarily) reconciled.

1845
Timber prices improved.
Completed the sale of his 'Nottingham Town' property.
Hafod Estate sold for £105,000.
His debts had been reduced to around £8,000.
Twenty five of his sheep were stolen.
Attended and spoke in the Lords.
Wrote two 'letters' to 'My Countrymen' – provoking considerable reaction.
Took his daughters on holiday to France.
Planned a change of walks in the Clumber Pleasure Ground, and began the
'Lincoln Terrace' construction.
Resisted further railway plans, in and around Clumber Park.
Lord Lincoln became a member of the Sir Robert Peel's Cabinet.

1846
The rift with his son and heir widened – he opposed Lord Lincoln's re-election.
Completed the 'Lincoln Terrace' at Clumber.
Began widening the lake opposite House.
Visited France again.

1847

Hosted a 'Protectionist's' meeting at Clumber.

Met Benjamin Disraeli.

Dismissed his Agent/Steward.

Opposed further plans to construct a railway near the borders of Clumber Park.

Completed his alterations to the Clumber Lake.

Became more than a little attracted to the singer, Jenny Lind.

Had his photograph taken.

Went to Filey for a holiday.

1848

Sponsored local musicians.

Met Louis Bonapart and the sons of Ibrahim Pasha.

Offered Nottingham Castle as an Arms Depot.

Refused to sell his best oak trees.

Improved the Entrance Hall at Clumber House – bought paintings from Stowe Sale.

Charles, twin brother of Thomas, married.

Supported efforts to erect a Memorial to Lord George Bentinck.

Supported efforts to appoint Disraeli as his leader in the Commons.

Proposed marriage to Lady Emily Foley – and was rejected.

1849

Provided a resident clergyman and a parsonage for Maplebeck village.

Purchased horses from France.

Took a holiday at Ramsgate.

Visited Chatsworth again.

Became broken-hearted on receiving another rejection from Lady Emily Foley.

Improved the views from the Clumber Pleasure Ground.

Lord Lincoln (with his brother Robert) sailed his yacht to the Mediterranean.

Lady Lincoln bore an illegitimate child.

The Duke's state of health became very poor.

1850

Went to St. Leonards on a winter holiday.

Moved to London for medical care.

Unexpectedly met some of his grandchildren.

Lord Lincoln's divorce case was heard in the House of Lords.

The final diary entry was dated 30 May 1850

APPENDIX III

DOCTOR DETHICK'S DIARY

During the Duke's final illness, 'Surgeon' John Dethick of Bridge Street, Worksop, Nottinghamshire, kept a daily diary of his patient's progress. This diary was deposited in the Library of the Royal College of Physicians of Edinburgh, and it is with the kind permission of that body that the following details are entered here.

The diary entries – which cover the period from 11th November 1850 to 12th January 1851 – give a fascinating insight into the atmosphere that surrounded the Duke's home at Clumber House during the last two months of his life. The doctor attended the Duke everyday, sometimes being 'called up' eight times in one day (and throughout the night).

It is clear that, by early November 1850, the Duke was known to be terminally ill. His mobility was almost gone, he had severe breathing problems and was incontinent. His mental state was poor and he was a very difficult patient, frequently losing his temper with family and servants.

With family members, all his resentment of the times when they had ignored him came to the surface and he became very abusive towards them, even to his daughters, whose praises he had so freely sung in better days. To his son and heir, Lord Lincoln, he was particularly cool and unfeeling, demanding that he remove his children from Clumber, despite the knowledge that Lincoln (recently divorced) had nowhere else to take them and had little money of his own.

The Duke showed no emotion when Doctor Dethick, at the request of the family, informed the Duke that his fourth son, Lord William, had died three months earlier.

Servants were directly in his 'firing line' and, in spite of their best efforts, came in for hard treatment from His Grace. The Valet, Frederick Latham (always described by Doctor Dethick as 'poor Latham'), was much abused and insulted by the Duke, although his caring attention to his master was without question. The nurse and also the cook, Mrs McVay, suffered the Duke's anger, the latter having been seven minutes late in providing one of his meals! The diet enjoyed by His Grace (despite his doctor's advice) makes fascinating reading – *Tea, Cocoa & Coffee (all at the .same meal); Asses Milk, Sandwiches, Eggs; Toast & Bread & Butter; Chicken Broth; Turtle Soup (fresh & mock); Giblet Soup; Pheasant Puree; Partridges; Leg of Mutton; Apple Pudding; Cheese Cakes; Jelly; Rum & Milk; Ale; Wine & Water; Punch; White Wine; Brandy; Sherry and a Pint of Claret each day.*

His lifelong habit of rashly spending money on large expensive projects had not abated, and (even in these dying days) Heads of Departments were regularly called in to discuss yet another 'Improvement Plan' with him. These plans (described by Lord Lincoln and Doctor Dethick as *'insane projects'*) included one to have a new avenue of ornamental trees planted at Clumber, to link the 'Truman's Gate' entrance to the Worksop Road. Another was to have the central roof of Clumber House removed, the height raised and a 'Colonnade' erected thereon, with Turrets built on the four wings of the House. On a smaller scale, he promised the gift of clock for the new Corn Exchange at Worksop [*an undertaking that was honoured after his death*].

Without question, the Duke's last days were distressing for him and everyone about him. Some relief was obtained from the enjoyment of violin music, played (on most days of his final illness) in the corridor outside his room, by his local favourite, William Radcliffe, of Worksop. During his calmer moments, the Duke had told his Head Gardener, Thomas Moffatt, that his greatest grief was to be leaving so beautiful a place as Clumber. He also indicated how aware he was of the kindly attention of everyone during his illness.

His life had been full of pain and mental distress, with so many of his family and friends having died, the domestic turmoil in Lord Lincoln's life, and also his own failure to find another spouse. His 'outsider' position in politics and his difficulty in public speaking had caused much loneliness. There had also been the apparent inability (despite brave attempts) to restore some firm financial basis for his operations. His volatile personality must have put a huge strain on his constitution and the events indicated in this careful record of his final days come as little surprise.

R.I.P.

INDEXES

Index One – *NAMES / TITLES* (excluding immediate family)
Index Two – *PLACES* (excluding Nottinghamshire)
Index Three – *PLACES IN NOTTINGHAMSHIRE* (excluding Clumber Park)
Index Four – *PLACES IN CLUMBER PARK*

N

Nash. (architect) – 26.6.1825, 6.4.1827
Neal. Colonel – 26.2.1839
Neale. Mr – 10.5.1828
Nesfield. Willam A. – 15.8.1837, 3.8.1846
Neville. Mr – 29.10.1827
Newark. Lord – 29.1.1827
Newling. Rev – 24.12.1831
Nichols. (sculptor) – 23.6.1827
Norfolk. Duke of – 1.8.1823, 19.6.1824,
 22.6.1824, 30.1.1825, 30.4.1825,
 2.9.1831, 9.1.1833, 16.8.1834,
 17.6.1837, 9.2.1838, 15.3.1838,
 16.3.1838, 4.4.1838, 16.4.1838,
 24.5.1839, 27.5.1839, 12.6.1839,
 17.3.1842
Normanby. Lord – 28.5.1849
Norrison. Mr – 3.11.1837, 24.10.1839
Northumberland. Duke and/or Duchess of –
 8.2.1824, 2.5.1826, 6.6.1827,
 11.7.1838, 12.2.1847
Norton. Mr – 11.12.1832, 30.8.1846

O

Oastler. Mr – 28.3.1839
O'Connell. [Daniel] – 8.10.1828
O'Donnell. Major Sir C. – 22.3.1839
O'Neil (artist) – 5.6.1848, 11.8.1848
Orde. Madge – 7.6.1835, 19.11.1836
Otway. Sir Loftus – 22.2.1844
Owen. Edward Pryce – 9.3.1833

P

Packman. Doctor – 13.12.1849
Paganini. Niccolo – 13.6.1831
Parke. (artist) – 22.1.1835, 1.2.1835
Parkinson. Mr – 26.3.1823, 7.10.1826,
 8.3.1834, 28.10.1835, 30.8.1849
Parkinson. John (steward) – 10.8.1838
Parr Samuel – 14.10.1826
Pasha. Hassan – 1.2.1848
Pasha. Ibrahim – 1.2.1848, 22.11.1848
Pasha. Mustapha – 1.2.1848
Patterson. Mr – 21.6.1827
Payne. (auctioneer) – 18.4.1839, 16.3.1840
Paxton. Joseph – 15.6.1841
Peel. Sir Robert – 23.4.1824, 8.3.1825,
 1.5.1827, 13.5.1827, 13.6.1827,
 8.5.1829, 12.5.1832, 7.7.1833,
 21.12.1834, 31.1.1835, 9.3.1835,
 8.4.1835, 30.12.1835, 19.4.1838,
 16.6.1838, 30.10.1838, 1.11.1838,
 2.11.1838, 4.11.1838, 14.1.1839,
 1.5.1839, 11.5.1839, 19.11.1839,
 31.8.1841, 2.9.1841, 28.9.1841,
 19.5.1842, 19.7.1842, 25.3.1843,
 9.1.1845, 31.1.1845, 21.2.1845,
 18.4.1845, 20.12.1845, 23.12.1845,
 19.7.1846

Pelham-Clinton. Lord John – 27.12.1838
Penrose. (tutor) – 16.1.1837
Plymouth . Earl of – 11.12.1843
Pocklington. Mr (Cromwell) – 27.11.1835
Pocklington. Rev (Walesby) – 19.7.1847
Portland. Duke and/or Duchess of –
 21.2.1823, 22.2.1823, 7.8.1823,
 13.9.1824, 3.10.1825, 5.8.1826,
 27.11.1826, 10.1.1827, 4.2.1827,
 8.8.1830, 23.3.1835, 26.3.1835,
 17.6.1837, 4.8.1837, 9.2.1838,
 19.2.1838, 21.2.1838, 25.3.1838,
 4.4.1838, 23.4.1838, 2.1.1839,
 20.2.1839, 25.2.1839, 7.3.1839,
 11.3.1839, 18.3.1839, 14.5.1839,
 14.8.1839, 28.12.1839, 29.12.1839,
 9.1.1840, 20.1.1840, 22.1.1840,
 11.11.1840, 30.11.1842, 27.12.1843,
 2.5.1844, 29.5.1844, 31.5.1844,
 27.11.1844, 1.1.1845, 26.12.1845,
 30.12.1845, 22.2.1846, 7.3.1846,
 2.4.1846, 14.7.1846, 29.3.1847,
 26.6.1847,13.7.1848, 22.9.1848,
 1.10.1848, 23.10.1848
Powis. Lord – 2.7.1844, 19.1.1848
Pugh. Mr L – 8.9.1837, 30.10.1839
Pusey. Doctor – 25.11.1841

R

Radcliffe. (musician) – 22.12.1847
Ramsden. Mr – 2.11.1838
Ratsey. (shipbuilder) – 12.11.1838
Rawlinson. Mr – 17.6.1849
Rayner (kennels) – 3.2.1842
Reynolds. [S.W.?] – 24.7.1823, 22.8.1823,
 22.9.1823, 23.9.1823, 25.3.1825,
 22.7.1825, 19.9.1826
Richmond. Duke of – 9.3.1846, 18.7.1846
Robins (auctioneer) – 13.7.1840, 7.10.1840
Robinson. Mr – 20.11.1826, 3.9.1827,
 11.11.1828, 19.1.1829
Rolleston. Colonel – 13.1.1840, 1.11.1848,
 24.3.1849
Rolleston . Mr – 30.4.1831
Roper. (Southwell House of Correction) –
 16.11.1843, 24.10.1845
Rowlands. Griffiths (retired butler) –
 17.6.1823, 2.9.1825, 14.9.1825,
 26.10.1825, 25.12.1838, 27.12.1838
Russell. Samuel (doctor) – 24.7.1826,
 26.8.1830. 17.10.1834
Russell. Lord John – 14.3.1839, 30.4.1839,
 2.5.1839, 3 5.1839
Rutland. Duke of – 9.6.1827, 9.1.1849

S

Sadler. Mr – 22.2.1829, 7.3.1829, 8.3.1829,
 2.7.1829, 29.9.1829
Salisbury. Marquis of – 3.1.1838

Salvin. (architect) – 3.8.1846
Salvin. (butcher) – 31.10.1825
Samping. Mr – 1.2.1844
Saunders (tutor) – 11.7.1832
Savilles [various] – 10.2.1823, 18.10.1824,
    18.10.1825, 21.10.1825, 12.10.1829,
    16.5.1835
Saxe Coburg. Prince of – 21.3.1836
Saxe Weimer. Duke of – 14.10.1838
Scarbrough. Lord – 6.10.1829, 16.5.1835,
    20.2.1837, 12.3.1838, 19.7.1838,
    3.5.1839, 28.10.1840
Shaftesbury. Lord – 5.6.1827
Sherbrook. Mr – 24.3.1849
Short (farmer) – 6.10.1829
Simpson. J. (foreman of the woods) –
    26.11.1842
Sinclair. John (sailor) – 21.9.1825
Sissons. Mr – 14.3.1825
Sleigh. ('vagabond') – 12.4.1841
Smirke, Sir Robert – 9.4.1823, 17.7.1823,
    22.8.1823, 10.9.1823, 22.9.1823,
    25.2.1824, 26.2.1824, 5.8.1824,
    20.10.1824, 22.10.1824, 10.11.1824,
    10.5.1825, 11.5.1825, 12.5.1825,
    9.10.1825, 11.10.1825, 3.12.1825,
    2.3.1830, 10.11.1837
Smith. Mr – 11.11.1828
Smith. (auctioneer) – 20.9.1843
Somerset. Duke of – 25.7.1834
Sotheron. Admiral – 19.3.1823, 23.1.1825,
    26.6.1826, 30.10.1826, 21.2.1836,
    7.2.1839
Spencer. (shipbuilder) – 12.11.1838
Spencer Helen (governess) – 7.5.1823,
    4.7.1823, 21.8.1823, 20.9.1823,
    24.4.1824, 19.6.1824, 5.10.1824,
    16.6.1825, 24.6.1825, 20.12.1825,
    14.3.1826, 25.3.1826, 6.4.1827,
    19.7.1827, 28.6.1828, 13.10.1831,
    8.8.1833, 17.9.1835, 10.9.1835,
    10.10.1835, 5.7.1836, 9.8.1836,
    8.10.1836, 31.7.1837, 20.10.1838,
    3.11.1848
St. Helens. Lord – 28.5.1826
Stacye. Rev Thomas (Worksop) – 8.9.1847
Stanhope. Lincoln – 1.3.1840
Stanhope. Mrs – 26.5.1825
Stanley. [Edward G.S.] – 5.5.1833
Stanley. Lord – 4.1.1847, 23.1.1847,
    22.11.1847, 6.1.1849, 31.1.1849,
    6.2.1849
Staunton. Doctor – 28.2.1849
Surrey. Lord – 29.9.1824, 9.1.1833,
    25.9.1837, 4.4.1838, 16.4.1838
Sutherland. Duke and/or Duchess of –
    3.1.1838, 31.1.1839, 16.6.1847
Sutton. Mr & Mrs – 18.7.1822
Sutton. family (of Kelham) – 18.7.1822,

30.3.1824, 18.2.1826, 30.8.1826,
    4.7.1837, 29.4.1847

T

Tallents. (agent) – 6.4.1826, 26.4.1826,
    11.12.1832, 21.7.1837, 15.8.1837,
    24.12.1837, 12.1.1839, 21.1.1840,
    31.12.1845
Tallents. [Junior] (agent) – 7.5.1846
Taylor. (mining) – 9.10.1838
Thompson (tutors) – 9.3.1823, 7.5.1823,
    14.7.1823, 24.4.1824, 28.4.1824,
    1.5.1824, 13.9.1824, 23.5.1825,
    18.1.1827, 25.1.1827, 2.3.1827,
    7.5.1833, 6.2.1837, 5.1.1838
Thompson. [engineer?] – 3.3.1823,
    6.3.1823
Thompson. Mrs – 17.1.1837
Thompson. Rev (Elkesley/Kirton) –
    13.8.1838, 13.4.1841, 23.10.1842,
    27.8.1844, 13.4.1845, 5.10.1845,
    19.9.1848
Thorpe. (of Newark Mill) – 2.5.1848
Thumb. Tom – 6.8.1846
Todd. (house steward) – 5.12.1825,
    10.12.1825
Tomlinson. Mr – 13.10.1831
Tomlinson. Rev – 23.10.1842
Tremin. (builder) – 8.6.1844, 24.11.1845
Trimmer. (tutor) – 14.7.1823, 5.8.1823
Turner. [Joseph M.W.?] – 14.6.1829

V

Vachel. (valet) – 16.9.1836
Vernon. Mr and/or Mrs – 15.2.1842,
    2.8.1844, 7.9.1847, 23.10.1848
Vessey. Miss – 1.3.1845
Victoria, Princess – 26.4.1828, 3.5.1828,
    20.4.1831, 14.4.1832, 10.10.1835,
    7.3.1836, 21.3.1836, 15.4.1836,
    27.4.1836, 24.4.1837, 24.5.1837
Victoria. Queen – 20.6.1837, 23.6.1837,
    28.6.1837, 14.7.1837, 19.7.1837,
    11.10.1837, 18.6.1838, 20.6.1838,
    28.6.1838, 26.7.1838, 14.10.1838,
    4.5.1839, 6.5.1839, 11.5.1839,
    5.6.1839, 6.6.1839, 15.10.1839,
    19.11.1839, 16.1.1840, 10.2.1840,
    18.2.1840, 5.4.1840, 25.5.1840,
    4.6.1840, 10.6.1840, 22.6.1840,
    22.11.1840, 10.12.1841, 28.4.1842,
    19.5.1842, 30.5.1842, 1.6.1842,
    4.7.1842, 13.8.1843, 29.11.1843,
    30.11.1843, 7.8.1844, 2.10.1844,
    4.2.1845, 12.5.1847, 11.6.1847,
    16.6.1847, 19.5.1848
Vyvian. Lord – 7.7.1846

W

Wales. Prince of – 20.7.1843

Walker. Major – 25.11.1840

Walker. (mining) – 9.10.1838

Walpole. Lord – 30.8.1849

Walsh. Sir John – 1.3.1844

Watson. (of Walkeringham) – 3.4.1841

Watts. (of Brabaham, Cambs.) – 25.7.1841

Webster (butler) – 27.12.1838, 13.6.1840,
14.6.1840

Webster. Rev (chaplain) – 28.3.1843,
5.11.1843, 21.1.1844

Weightman. (of Elkesley) – 17.8.1844,
21.11.1844

Welby. Miss – 9.5.1825

Willement. T. (painted glass specialist) –
3.11.1824

Wellington. Duke of – 8.2.1825, 6.5.1827,
20.5.1827, 9.6.1827, 1.2.1828,
3.11.1828, 27.12.1828, 13.2.1829,
9.3.1829, 22.3.1829, 15.12.1829,
23.9.1830, 12.10.1831, 8.6.1834,
15.7.1835, 4.2.1836, 19.2.1836,
16.4.1836, 18.11.1837, 3.1.1838,
4.1.1838, 13.6.1838, 1.5.1839,
2.5.1839, 4.7.1839, 20.7.1839,
19.11.1839, 15.1.1840, 2.5.1840,
19.5.1842, 21.11.1842

Wells. (tenant at Holme) – 10.5.1839

Westley and Clarke. (bookbinders) –
5.7.1845

Westmacott. Richard – 28.5.1822,
22.8.1823, 22.9.1823, 30.4.1825,
24.6.1825, 30.3.1826, 28.5.1826,
8.9.1826, 10.9.1826, 12.9.1826,
27.5.1827, 23.6.1827, 5.12.1839,
3.8.1840

Westmoreland. Lord – 31.3.1825, 1.5.1826

Whall. (solicitor) – 11.8.1847

Whetham. Mrs – 30.10.1826, 7.2.1839

White. (shipbuilder) – 12.11.1838

White. Sir T – 22.5.1841, 29.11.1843,
30.11.1843, 17.2.1846, 7.2.1849

Whitling. Mr – 20.10.1839

Wilde. Sgt. – 1.3.1829, 3.3.1829, 3.6.1841

William of Orange – 30.3.1826

William IV – 6.7.1830, 19.7.1830,
23.7.1830, 24.7.1830, 23.4.1831,
28.4.1831, 28.5.1831, 20.8.1831,
2.9.1831, 8.1.1832, 27.9.1832,
24.4.1833, 12.8.1833, 3.3.1835,
14.4.1835, 28.5.1835, 3.6.1835,
23.3.1836, 23.4.1836, 24.4.1837,
17.5.1837, 20.6.1837

Williams. (Nottingham Asylum doctor) –
28.9.1843

Williams. Doctor – 4.10.1833, 25.11.1835,
17.9.1839

Wilmot. (agent) – 12.3.1838, 10.8.1838,
16.11.1838, 13.4.1839, 4.3.1840,
5.3.1840, 6.3.1840, 9.3.1840,
29.5.1843, 16.6.1843, 4.11.1843,
17.10.1845, 13.5.1846, 14.7.1846,
13.3.1847, 25.6.1847, 20.11.1847

Wilmot. Lady – 3.3.1849

Wilmot. Miss – 3.3.1849

Wilson. Sir Henry – 17.11.1825, 11.2.1826,
9.6.1826, 18.8.1826

Wilton. Lord – 3.1.1838

Winchilsea. Lord – 11.6.1824, 22.3.1829,
17.5.1829, 22.1.1836, 11.5.1836

Winter (Nottingham clerk of works) –
4.11.1843, 6.12.1843

Wombwell. (farmer) – 28.8.1831

Woodhouse. Mr – 2.6.1840

Wright. (valet) – 12.7.1823

Wright. Charles – 9.12.1824, 17.12.1824,
23.12.1824

Wyon. (artist) – 12.7.1833

Y

York. Archbishop of – 29.4.1824, 8.9.1825,
27.12.1833

York. Duke of – 22.6.1824, 25.6.1824,
21.5.1825, 29.3.1826, 1.5.1826,
2.5.1826, 4.5.1826, 27.5.1826,
7.1.1827, 11.1.1827, 20.1.1827

Younghusband. Rev – 28.3.1841

INDEX TWO
PLACES
(Excluding those in Nottinghamshire)

A

Aberystwyth – 8.11.1832, 4.10.1833,
24.10.1833, 29.9.1834, 5.9.1835,
4.9.1835, 10.10.1835, 28.10.1835
3.11.1835, 8.10.1836, 7.11.1836,
28.9.1837, 30.9.1837, 17.10.1837,
6.10.1838, 3.9.1839, 10.2.1841,
24.9.1841, 13.10.1841, 14.10.1841
Acton – 26.1.1827
Albany, South Africa – 9.10.1826
Alconbury – 17.6.1822, 1.2.1828, 9.2.1836
Aldborough – 11.6.1826, 23.5.1832,
25.2.1833, 20.12.1833, 12.3.1834,
8.4.1835, 16.9.1838
Alexandria – 17.11.1840
Alfreton – 2.11.1832, 17.11.1835,
20.10.1840
Almeira – 19.2.1836
Alnwick – 3.8.1824
America – 8.12.1832
Amiens – 22.9.1845
Antwerp – 13.7.1837, 11.8.1838, 15.8.1838
Arran – 16.9.1847
Asgarby – 9.1.1849
Ashbourne – 19.1.1831, 2.11.1832,
17.11.1835
Ashford-in-the-Water – 14.11.1832
Ashton – 4.9.1834, 27.10.1834, 18.11.1834
Aswarby – 9.1.1849

B

Babraham – 25.7.1841
Bakewell – 14.11.1832
Barmouth – 17.7.1834
Bath – 20.8.1833
Battle Abbey – 8.3.1850
Beaulieu – 10.8.1848, 15.8.1848

Beddgelert – 19.9.1839
Beirout – 17.11.1840
Belgium – 15.12.1829
Belvoir Castle – 3.1.1838, 5.1.1838
Beverley – 11.11.1844
Bewdley – 20.3.1848
Biggleswade – 2.9.1823, 16.5.1825,
8.6.1826, 28.1.1828, 20.4.1829,
7.7.1831, 14.2.1834, 28.2.1836,
2.8.1837
Birkenhead – 15.9.1844
Birmingham – 25.6.1837, 10.11.1837,
16.8.1838, 19.9.1838, 12.8.1839,
14.7.1840, 7.9.1843, 12.12.1848
Blicking – 1.8.1825
Bloxholme – 8.1.1849
Bolton – 14.10.1826
Bordeaux – 11.3.1840, 30.3.1840
Boroughbridge – 11.6.1826, 23.5.1832,
15.12.1832, 25.2.1833, 20.12.1833,
12.3.1834, 8.8.1834, 9.8.1834,
26.8.1834, 31.7.1835, 16.9.1838,
24.3.1841
Boulogne – 19.7.1837, 25.9.1845
Bradford – 19.11.1834
Brentford – 14.7.1823
Bridlington – 11.9.1844, 26.9.1844,
3.10.1847
Brighton – 23.1.1835, 30.4.1846, 16.9.1847
Bristol – 21.7.1843, 15.4.1849
Britain – 31.12.1832
Broadstairs – 21.8.1828
Buckingham House/Palace – 26.6.1825,
6.4.1827, 10.5.1838, 11.7.1839,
14.5.1847, 14.5.1848, 19.5.1848
Buxton – 14.11.1832

C

Cadiz – 1.5.1831
Calais – 19.9.1845
Callao – 2.1.1836, 4.9.1836
Canterbury – 21.8.1828, 20.7.1847, 31.7.1847

Cape of Good Hope – 9.10.1826, 6.5.1842
Carlisle – 23.11.1832
Catterick – 15.12.1832
Chapel Royal – 31.3.1831
Chatsworth – 15.6.1841, 16.8.1849
Cheadle – 2.11.1832, 22.8.1837, 23.8.1837
Chelsea – 21.11.1842
Cheltenham – 17.7.1834, 16.9.1836
Chester – 9.10.1838, 15.9.1844
Chesterfield – 13.11.1841, 7.9.1843,
    18.8.1847
China – 14.3.1840
Chiswick – 9.4.1823, 2.9.1823, 15.4.1824
Cirencester – 27.8.1842, 4.7.1843
Claremont – 8.3.1848
Combermere Abbey – 2.11.1832,
    9.11.1832, 13.11.1835, 23.8.1837,
    4.9.1843, 25.10.1845, 25.8.1847
Constantinople – 2.6.1846, 3.4.1847,
    30.11.1847, 29.1.1848, 26.3.1848
Cowes – 17.7.1836, 26.8.1849
Crewe – 4.9.1843, 7.9.1843, 25.8.1847
Cromford – 2.11.1832
Croxton Park – 5.1.1838
Cullesden – 11.9.1832
Cwmelan – 22.12.1834, 20.4.1835,
    8.9.1836, 4.9.1838, 25.5.1839,
    26.1.1844, 22.2.1844, 2.3.1844,
    27.7.1844, 11.8.1845
Cwmystwyth – 15.9.1836, 3.10.1838
Cyprus – 30.8.1831

D

Darlington – 15.12 1832
Derby – 8.2.1826, 21.10.1827, 13.11.1833,
    9.8.1836, 11.11.1837, 16.8 1838,
    20.10.1838, 13.8.1839, 20.4.1840,
    12.11.1841,13.11.1841, 1.8.1842,
    7.9.1843, 11.12.1848
Devil's Bridge – 7.11.1832, 3.11.1837,
    21.9.1839, 24.10.1839, 29.8.1840,
    11.11.1841, 3.8.1842
Dolclythis – 3.11.1835
Dolyclettwr – 25.5.1839, 22.2.1844
Doncaster – 16.6.1832, 19.11.1834,
    13.12.1838, 13.9.1848
Dover – 27.9.1845, 27.7.1846
Drayton Manor – 14.1.1839, 19.11.1839
Dublin – 17.7.1827, 24.3.1840, 7.4.1844,
    13.4.1844
Durham – 15.12.1832

E

Ealing – 2.6.1823
East Sheen – 15.5.1837
Eastnor Castle – 10.11.1837
Eaton (Cambs) – 26.1.1827, 11.7.1827,
    1.2.1828, 15.6.1829, 15.2.1830,
    14.12.1830, 3.2.1834, 11.3.1835, 5.2.1839

Eckington – 13.11.1841, 22.1.1842,
    1.2.1844, 13.11.1844, 28.9.1847
Edensor – 15.6.1841
Edinburgh – 19.12.1842, 24.12.1842
Epsom – 30.5.1838
Eton – 1.9.1823, 12.2.1824, 28.4.1824,
    15.6.1824, 14.9.1824, 20.11.1824,
    19.1.1825, 23.2.1825, 25.5.1825,
    8.6.1825, 19.1.1826, 22.9.1826,
    21.1.1827, 28.2.1827, 17.3.1827,
    5.5.1827, 30.6.1827, 21.7.1827,
    31.7.1827, 21.1.1828, 20.3.1828,
    4.5.1828, 7.6.1828, 29.9.1828,
    13.12.1828, 20.5.1829, 10.12.1829,
    22.1.1830, 31.3.1830, 29.4.1830,
    27.7.1830, 8.12.1831, 19.5.1832,
    30.5.1832, 21.1.1833, 28.2.1833,
    21.6.1833, 31.1.1834, 28.2.1834,
    21.3.1834, 24.5.1834, 14.6.1834,
    29.7.1834, 3.1.1835, 23.5.1835,
    28.9.1835, 3.12.1835, 29.2.1836,
    22.3.1836, 21.4.1836, 24.4.1836,
    21.6.1836, 26.7.1836, 16.9.1836,
    14.10.1836, 26.1.1837, 26.6.1837,
    27.6.1837, 31.7.1837, 27.9.1837,
    6.12.1837, 22.1.1838, 4.4.1838,
    4.6.1838, 21.9.1838, 5.12.1838,
    23.5.1840, 14.4.1842, 12.2.1847,
    26.11.1848

F

Falkirk – 29.4.1846, 5.5.1846
Falkland Islands – 8.11.1834
Farnham – 25.6.1837
Ferrybridge – 27.10.1834
Filey – 28.9.1847
Firbeck – 27.12.1841,14.12.1844,
    17.2.1846,
Flintshire – 31.10.1845
Fonthill – 1.9.1823, 15.10.1823,
    26.11.1823
France – 19.7.1828, 31.8.1846, 26.10.1846
Frankfurt – 12.9.1838
Frogmore – 2.6.1826, 14.9.1826
Fulham – 24.8.1823

G

Gainsborough – 16.6.1832
Genoa – 19.2.1839, 17.9.1840
Gibraltar – 11.9.1837
Glasgow – 3.9.1840
Grantham – 18.7.1822, 2.5.1823,
    10.3.1826, 1.2.1828, 3.2.1829,
    2.2.1830, 29.10.1830, 2.3.1831,
    18.3.1833, 19.5.1835, 27.2.1836,
    28.2 1836, 16.5.1836, 25.5 1836,
    27.4 1837, 2.8.1838, 23.4.1839
Greenwich – 8.7.1846
Gretna Green – 24.11.1832

H

Hafod – 19.10.1832, 8.11.1832, 25.2.1833,
26.2.1833, 19.3.1833, 22.3.1833,
23.3.1833, 20.9.1833, 19.11.1833,
14.8.1834, 9.9.1834, 31.7.1835,
13.8.1835, 2.9.1835, 8.9.1835,
9.9.1835, 17.2.1836, 20.2.1836,
9.8.1836, 30.8.1836, 16.11.1836.
30.8.1837, 19.10.1837, 7.11.1837,
8.11.1837,16.8.1838, 8.10.1838,
18.10.1838, 13.12.1838, 24.8.1839,
30.10.1839, 4.11.1839, 30.5.1840,
16.7.1840, 7.8.1840, 29.8.1840,
19.7.1841, 21.7.1841, 26.7.1841,
13.10.1841, 20.10.1841, 25.10.1841,
3.11.1841, 11.11.1841, 29.4.1842,
1.8.1842, 17.2.1843, 4.7.1843,
5.7.1843, 22.2.1844, 4.7.1844,
11.7.1844, 29.7.1844, 11.9.1844,
17.9.1844, 25.9.1844, 9.1.1845,
26.3.1845, 5.5.1845, 4.6.1845,
16.7.1845, 11.8.1845, 3.4.1846,
5.4.1846, 3.8.1846
Hamburgh – 6.10.1847
Hamilton Palace – 25.11.1832, 8.12.1832,
3.9.1840,
Hampshire – 14.10.1842, 16.10.1842
Hampton Court – 29.10.1837
Hanover – 13.11.1837
Hardwick Hall – 16.2.1842
Harlaxton – 5.1.1838
Hartford Bridge – 7.5.1833, 10.6.1833
Harwarden – 17.9.1849
Hatfield – 1.8.1825, 2.8.1825,15.3.1829,
27.8.1835
Haverholme – 15.3.1829
Havre – 28.5.1849
Hereford – 8.11.1837, 4.7.1843, 12.12.1848
Herstmonceaux – 14.3.1850
Hong Kong – 9.4.1841
House of Commons – 1.5.1827, 4.3.1828,
24.3.1828, 20.5.1828, 4.6.1833,
29.1.1837, 30.3.1843, 4.2.1845,
10.6.1847, 17.11.1848
House of Lords – 23.5.1823, 9.7.1823,
5.4.1824, 11.5.1824, 23.5.1824,
24.5.1824, 11.4.1825, 21.4.1825,
27.4.1825, 27.2.1827, 2.3.1827,
15.3.1827, 10.5.1827, 23.5.1827,
7.6.1827, 2.7.1827, 29.2.1828,
6.5.1828, 5.2.1829, 13.2.1829,
2.3.1829, 3.3.1829, 9.4.1829,
10.4.1829, 28.6.1830, 1.11.1830,
3.12.1830, 9.11.1831, 25.3.1833,
2.3.1835, 10.4.1835, 26.7.1835,
28.7.1835, 12.8.1835, 20.8.1835,
4 2.1836, 8.3.1836, 28 3.1836,
30.3.1836, 16.4.1836, 18.11.1837,
10.7.1838, 23.7.1838, 10.6.1839,

11.7.1839, 25.7.1839, 14.4.1840,
4.5.1840, 24.6.1844, 1.7.1844,
23.6.1845, 21.7.1845, 22.1.1846,
22.5.1846, 7.7.1846, 17.7.1846,
5.4.1847, 23.4.1847, 17.2.1848,
25.6.1849, 23.7.1849, 27.5.1850
Houses of Parliament – 22.10.1834,
27.11.1839, 18.3.1840, 27.4.1840
Hull – 1.4.1839, 11.11.1844

I

India – 12 3.1836
Ireland – 9.2.1846, 26.2.1847, 6.6.1847
Isle of Thanet – 13.9.1845
Isle of Wight – 12.11.1838, 22.11.1840
Italy – 26.5.1827

J

Jamaica – 8.6.1834

K

Keighley – 19.11.1834
Kensington – 3.5.1828, 21.3.1836,
20.6.1837
Kenwood – 7.4.1827, 12.3.1831
Kew – 22.5.1824, 18.5.1838, 26.5.1838,
22.7.1838, 28.7.1838
Kidderminster – 17.8.1838
Kinsale – 6.3.1848, 15.3.1848

L

Lake Como – 30.8.1849
Lambeth Palace – 11.6.1825, 11.4.1827,
28.4.1827, 19.11.1830, 3.5.1834,
21.6.1836, 12.5.1838, 9.5.1840, 23.4.1842
Langold – 17.2.1846
Lausaunne – 11.9.1837, 11.10.1837
Leadenham – 15.3.1829, 8.1.1849
Leamington – 12.7 1833, 28.3.1838
Leek – 14.11.1832
Leicester – 21.6.1829, 16.11.1832
Lichfield – 8.9.1835, 10.11.1837,
11.11.1837, 19.10.1838, 20.10.1838,
19.11.1839, 20.10.1840, 19.7.1841,
12.11.1841, 25.9.1844
Lincoln – 14.3.1823, 15.2.1836, 13.3.1844,
26.12.1844, 20.11.1847
Lincolnshire – 15.2.1836, 7.6.1846
Lindrick Common – 11.8.1847
Lisbon – 6.10.1849
Liverpool – 3.9.1840, 25.7.1841, 26.8.1843,
28.8.1843, 14.9.1844, 15.9.1844
Llangollen – 15.9.1844
London (Almacks) – 25.6.1828
London (Astleys) – 19.4.1836, 17.7.1839
London (Blackwall) – 2.7.1845
London Bridge – 20.5.1826, 27.7.1846
London (British Museum) – 11.2.1845,
18.6.1847

London (Carlton Club) – 23.1.1847,
3.2.1849
London (Charing Cross Hospital) –
15.4.1836
London Coliseum – 19.11.1830
London (Covent Garden Theatre) –
13.4.1836
London (Docks) – 20.7.1837
London (Euston Square) – 24.4.1840,
13.12.1841, 20.5.1846
London (Exeter Hail) – 15.4.1836
London (Freemasons Tavern) – 1.3.1836,
1.3.1844
London (Friars Lane) – 5.7.1845
London (Goldsmiths Hall) – 1.5.1840
London (Her Majesty's Theatre) –
4.5.1847, 17.6.1847, 22.6.1848,
11.8.1848, 15.8.1848
London (Hyde Park) – 29.6.1838, 9.7.1838
London (Kensington Gardens) – 3.7.1847
London (Mansion House) – 21.6.1834,
28.4.1836, 23.6.1849
London (Marylebone) – 10.9.1843
London (Opera House) – 13.6.1831,
1.6.1837
London (Park Lane) – 25.7.1834,
25.5.1839
London (Piccadilly) – 14.5.1848
London (Pitt Club) – 28.5.1827
London (Portman Square) – 27.4.1831,
9.10.1831, 17.11.1832, 2.8.1837,
15.1.1840, 24.6.1844, 16.6.1845,
23.4.1847, 16.9.1847, 16.2.1848
London (Royal Academy) – 30.4.1836,
4.5.1847
London (Somerset House) – 5.5.1827
London (Spital Field) – 1.6.1837
London (St Catherine's Docks) –
20.11.1830
London (St. Marylebone) – 23.3.1825,
24.3.1825
London (St Paul's) – 10.9.1823, 3.5.1825,
5.7.1845
London (Stafford House) – 16.6.1847
London (Strand) – 1.12.1837
London (Thames Tunnel) – 19.5.1825,
6.4.1826, 20.5.1826, 19.5.1827,
8.8.1842
London (Zoological Gardens) – 21.6.1828,
19.1.1830, 31.5.1836, 30.5.1850
Lords' Cricket Ground – 29.7.1825
Loughborough – 29.4.1831

M
Madeira – 1.2.1842
Maidenhead – 4.5.1823
Malaya – 18.8.1837
Malta – 30.8.1831, 11.9.1837, 12.10.1837,
3.7.1838, 27.10.1838, 5.11.1838,

11.3.1840, 7.4.1841, 10.7.1841,
3.11.1842,
Malvern – 10.11.1837, 12.12.1848
Manchester – 25.8.1847
Margate – 23.8.1845
Markeaton – 3.3.1849
Marylebone – 1.6.1822
Maynooth – 13.4.1845, 17.4.1845,
19.5.1845, 26.5.1845, 2.6.1845
Mediterranean – 20.7.1837, 26.8.1849,
17.9.1849
Minster – 29.8.1845
Mosborough – 5.11.1845
Munich – 4.10.1838, 18.7.1845

N
Naples – 30.3.1840, 11.6.1840,
Newcastle-under-Lyme – 2.11.1832,
14.11.1832
Newcastle-upon-Tyne – 15.12.1832
Newport – 12.9.1835
Newtown – 9.11.1832, 11.11.1833,
9.9.1835, 9.8.1836, 18.10.1838,
2.8.1842
Norman Cross – 28.1.1827
Normanton – 5.11.1845

O
Oban – 29.6.1842
Oxford – 29.11.1829, 7.5.1830,
15.10.1830, 19.10.1831, 15.4.1831,
25.4.1831, 29.4.1831, 8.11.1831,
2.1.1832, 19.1.1832, 23.6.1832,
11.7.1832, 13.8.1832, 16.10.1832,
21.1.1833, 20.6.1833, 3.12.1833,
16.3.1834, 18.4.1834, 24.4.1834,
8.6.1834, 23.1.1835, 2.5.1835,
18.12.1835, 28.6.1836, 26.7.1836,
9.8.1836, 31.8.1836, 1.9.1836,
27.12.1838, 12.12.1839, 10.4.1840,
1.5.1840, 2.7.1840, 15.10.1840,
22.1.1841, 23.4.1841, 25.11.1841,
7.1.1842, 1.10.1842, 22.10.1842,
20.2.1843, 11.5.1844, 22.6.1844,
5.8.1847

P
Paris – 11.2.1837, 12.3.1837, 28.4.1837,
13.7.1837, 17.7.1837, 25.7.1837,
6.8.1837, 6.11.1837, 3.3.1839,
28.7.1840, 28.5.1849
Park Place – 3.8.1826
Pleasley – 7.8.1823
Pontrhydygroes – 8.9.1837
Portsmouth – 9.4.1831, 6.7.1833,
23.12.1833, 10.2.1834, 7.8.1838,
6.7.1840, 26.8.1849
Portugal – 19.3.1836, 21.3.1836
Powis Castle – 28.8.1837

Y

York – 15.2.1836, 1.2.1844, 26.9.1844,
    28.9.1847, 1.11.1847, 13.9.1848

INDEX THREE
PLACES IN NOTTINGHAMSHIRE
(Excluding Clumber Park)

B

Basford – 5.2.1828, 4.11.1843, 27.5.1844, 26.7.1844

Bassetlaw – 8.5.1829, 8.8.1830, 22.11.1834, 1.1.1835, 29.7.1837, 4.8.1837

Bawtry – 14.9.1827, 27.11.1827, 5.10.1829, 6.10.1830

Bevercotes – 27.1.1824, 25.2.1824, 20.1.1825, 1.2.1836, 31.1.1848, 29.12.1848

Blyth – 26.8.1830, 8.10.1830, 28.1.1831, 17.10.1831

Bothamsall – 1.6.1822, 10.9.1823, 25.2.1824, 14.8.1825, 8.9.1825, 29.8.1825, 27.3.1836, 6.3.1844, 8.4.1844, 18.4.1844, 19.4.1844, 22.4.1844, 4.5.1844, 20.5.1844, 8.6.1844, 17.6.1844, 2.8.1844, 10.8.1844, 17.8 1844, 27.8.1844, 21.11.1844, 25.11.1844, 3.1.1845, 2.4.1845, 13.6.1845, 13.7.1845, 4.10.1845, 20.11.1845, 25.4 1846, 13.7.1846, 4.4.1847, 29.11.1847, 30.8.1848

Brinsley – 1.3.1823

Bulwell Common – 9.5.1839

C

Carburton – 21.2.1823, 1.3.1823, 7.8.1823, 3.10.1825, 2.4.1839, 26.11.1842

Carlton-in-Lindrick – 3.11.1840

Colwick – 12.10.1831, 15.10.1831

Cromwell – 15.11.1827, 15.11.1828, 28.10.1835, 27.11.1835

Cuckney – 7.8.1823

D

Drayton – 20.2.1831

E

East Markham – 2.3.1834, 4.4.1849

Edwinstowe – 28.8.1844

Egmanton – 26.3.1823, 2.3.1834, 28.3.1841, 4.4.1849

Elkesley – 5.2.1824, 31.10.1825, 17.11.1829, 20.2.1831, 13.8.1838, 15.5.1841, 23.10.1842, 6.3.1844, 8.4.1844, 8.6.1844, 17.8.1844, 27.8.1844, 21.11.1844, 13.4.1845, 24.11.1845, 13.7.1846, 19.9.1848, 20.2.1849

Epperstone – 15.11.1832

F

Firbeck – 30.7.1826, 27.12.1841,14.12.1844, 17.2.1846, 15.4.1849

Flawborough – 1.3.1823

Flintham – 28.11.1827, 17.12.1829

G

Gamston – 5.2.1824, 16.10.1824, 25.2.1840, 1.2.1844

Gateford – 3.12.1838, 21.12.1838, 1.3.1845

Greasley – 5.10.1839

Gringley – 1.3.1823

Grove Park – 10.5.1843

H

Haughton – 25.2.1833, 12.2.1840, 9.3.1840, 2.7.1847, 19.7.1847, 6.12.1847, 27.3.1848, 28.3.1848

Holme – 10.5.1839

K

Kelham – 30.3.1824, 18.11.1825, 18.2.1826, 30.8.1826, 30.10.1826, 4.7.1837, 11.5.1841, 29.4.1847

Kilton – 8.4.1845, 19.6.1848

Kirkby – 15.2.1842
Kirklington – 19.3.1823, 30.10.1826,
    27.9.1830, 23.1.1831, 20.2.1836,
    22.2.1836, 7.2.1839
Kirton – 26.3.1823, 19.9.1848

L
Langold – 20.9.1842, 17.2.1846
Langwith – 7.8.1823, 20.11.1827

M
Mansfield – 2.11.1832, 16.4.1834,
    20.2.1839, 25.2.1839, 16.3.1839,
    27.3.1839, 11.5.1839, 14.5.1839,
    18.5.1839, 10.12.1839, 20.10.1840,
    13.4.1841, 17.6.1841, 15.2.1842,
    26.10.1848, 28.11.1848, 25.1.1849,
    9.2.1849, 4.1.1850
Mansfield Woodhouse – 26.2.1839,
    13.4.1841
Manton – 6.3.1844, 19.6.1848
Maplebeck – 10.2.1823, 23.2.1828,
    19.7.1838, 14.12.1838, 8.3.1849,
    22.3.1849, 23.4.1849
Markham (-Clinton) – 9.4.1823, 26.2.1824,
    29.4.1824, 14.7.1824, 5.8.1824,
    22.10.1824, 15.12.1824, 15.1.1825,
    10.5.1825, 31.8.1825, 23.10.1825,
    22.11.1825, 20.2.1826, 10.3.1826,
    8.9.1826, 10.9.1826, 30.7.1827,
    22.9.1832, 12.12.1833, 27.12.1833,
    8.8.1834, 1.9.1834, 24.10.1834,
    8.12.1835, 27.3.1836, 5.12.1839,
    9.12.1839, 1.5.1841, 3.4.1841,
    30.9.1842, 4.9.1844, 5.9.1844,
    15.9.1844, 26.4.1848
Markham Moor – 24.12.1830, 27.12.1830
Martin – 14.9.1827, 5.10.1829, 6.10.1829,
    6.10.1830, 19.9.1831, 27.12.1831,
    2.1.1833
Milton – 25.2.1824
Morton – 10.2.1823, 17.12.1825, 16.9.1826,
    19.7.1838

N
Newark – 18.7.1822, 30.3.1824, 30.9.1825,
    26.4.1826, 8.6.1826, 10.6.1826,
    28.11.1827, 1.2.1828, 22.2.1829,
    7.3.1829, 15.3.1829, 17.3.1829,
    2.7.1829, 29.9.1829, 17.12.1829,
    25.2.1830, 27.7.1830, 6.8.1830,
    8.8.1830, 23.10.1830, 15.12.1830,
    7.1.1831, 30.4.1831, 13.10.1831,
    26.10.1831, 23.5.1832, 5.8.1832,
    6.8.1832, 11.12.1832, 17.12.1832,
    18.1.1833, 29.12.1834, 5.1.1835,
    4.1.1836, 11.1.1836, 12.1.1836,
    3.10.1836, 11.10.1836, 14.10.1836,

21.10.1836, 10.1.1837, 11.1.1837,
    17.1.1837, 30.6.1837, 3.5.1838,
    8.6.1838, 3.8.1838, 10.1.1839,
    24.1.1839, 9.5.1839, 10.1.1840,
    21.1.1840, 7.1.1841, 10.1.1841,
    4.5.1841, 7.5.1841, 10.5.1841,
    11.5.1841, 3.6.1841, 4.7.1841,
    11.1.1844, 1.2.1844, 26.12.1844,
    24.12.1845, 31.12.1845, 9.2.1846,
    7.5.1846, 25.7.1846, 14.1.1847,
    29.4.1847, 20.11.1847, 27.12.1847,
    2.5.1848, 27.10.1848, 5.1.1849,
    23.1.1849, 10.5.1850
Newark (Castle Wharf) – 12.1.1839
Newark (Playhouse) – 18.12.1829
Normanton Inn – 3.7.1832, 3.2.1842
North Muskham – 16.6.1829
Norton Common – 18.5.1839
Nottingham (Assizes) – 14.7.1826,
    2.8.1827, 21.7.1836, 11.3.1837,
    16.3.1839, 12.3.1841, 25.7.1844
Nottingham (Asylum) – 11.10.1825,
    1.11.1827, 12.1.1842, 28.9.1843
Nottingham (Black's Head Inn) – 21.6.1827
Nottingham (Brewhouse Yard) – 30.7.1846
Nottingham (Castle) – 1.4.1824,
    11.10.1831, 12.10.1831, 15.10.1831,
    21.10.1831, 8.1.1832, 9.1.1832,
    10.8.1832, 20.8.1837, 8.4.1842,
    10.3.1848
Nottingham (Cold Bath Fields) – 6.2.1828
Nottingham (Elections) – 26.4.1841,
    27.4.1841, 25.3.1843
Nottingham (Exchange) – 27.11.1836
Nottingham (Hospital) – 17.10.1826
Nottingham (King's Meadow) - 17.8.1837,
    28.5.1839
Nottingham (Malin Hill) – 8.8.1844
Nottingham (miscellaneous) – 22.2.1828,
    23.10.1829, 17.11.1829, 13.12.1831,
    22.12.1831, 23.1.1832, 5.8.1832,
    15.8.1833, 18.3.1834, 30.6.1837,
    19.1.1839, 22.3.1839, 8.5.1839, 9.5.1839,
    22.5.1839, 25.5.1839, 15.1.1840,
    20.1.1840, 25.3.1840, 6.12.1843,
    15.6.1845, 22.4.1847, 2.7.1847,
    4.10.1848, 16.10.1848, 30.1.1849
Nottingham (Park) – 23.9.1824, 2.4.1825,
    30.11.1825, 20.11.1826, 21.6.1827,
    2.1.1828, 21.6.1829, 23.10.1829,
    10.6.1839, 12.6.1839, 8.4.1842,
    11.4 1844, 27.5.1844, 26.7.1844,
    13.3.1847, 24.6.1847
Nottingham (parliamentary petition) –
    21.4.1825
Nottingham (property matters, excluding
    the Park) – 12.10.1825, 17.10.1826,
    5.2.1828, 8.5.1838, 21.6.1838,
    28.5.1839, 4.11.1843, 16.3.1845

Nottingham (Pelham Street) – 29.12.1844
Nottingham (Quarter Sessions) –
 30.12.1839, 17.10.1848, 27.10.1848
Nottingham (Racecourse) – 26.7.1844
Nottingham (Races) – 24.7.1827, 25.7.1827
Nottingham (railway matters) –
 10.12.1839, 20.4.1840, 24.4.1840,
 12.12.1841, 20.12.1841, 28.1.1842,
 4.6.1842, 24.6.1842, 14.12.1842,
 29.2.1844, 24.6.1844, 1.7.1844,
 26.12.1844, 21.1.1846, 9.3.1846,
 20.5.1846, 23.4.1847, 20.11.1847,
 16.2.1848, 31.1.1849
Nottingham (Regiment) – 13.5.1841
Nottingham (Ropewalk) – 12.6.1839
Nottingham (royal visit) – 29.11.1843,
 30.11.1843
Nottingham (School of Medicine and
 Anatomy) – 13.12.1831, 15.8.1833
Nottingham (Thurland Hall) – 21.6.1827,
 11.11.1828, 29.12.1844, 17.10.1848,
 1.11.1848, 4.1.1850
Nottingham (Thurland Paddock) –
 28.3.1825
Nottingham (Tunnel) – 26.4.1844
Nottinghamshire – 20.6.1825, 9.10.1826,
 21.1.1829, 30.9.1836, 4.7.1837
Nuthall - 3.11.1848

O

Ollerton – 21.2.1823, 17.11.1829,
 27.12.1836, 9.2.1838, 28.8.1844
Osberton – 9.3.1823, 4.8.1837, 9.2.1838,
 3.12.1838, 21.12.1838, 21.11.1845,
 11.7.1846, 9.3.1849
Ossington – 15.11.1843, 5.1.1846,
 21.12.1848

P

Pleasley – 7.8.1823

R

Ranby – 19.7.1822, 27.3.1823, 1.1.1824,
 27.11.1825, 5.9.1826, 10.9.1826,
 16.9.1826, 22.9 1826, 21.12.1826,
 12.1.1827, 5.12.1827, 7.2.1828,
 10.2.1828, 22.2.1828, 2.3.1828,
 30.1.1830, 19.1.1831, 19.1.1832,
 30.1.1832, 13.3.1832, 7.8.1832,
 26.9.1832, 15.11.1832, 22.11.1832,
 13.11.1833, 3.3.1834, 16.10.1834,
 22.12.1834, 2.2.1835, 30.3.1835,
 19.2.1836, 13.5.1839, 26.11.1839,
 10.4.1840, 21.10.1840, 23.10.1840,
 19.11.1840, 7.3.1841, 25.3.1841,
 27.3.1841, 30.3 1841, 17.4.1841,
 21.12.1841, 24.12.1841, 26.12.1841,
 6.1.1842, 9.1.1842, 15.1.1842,
 20.1.1842, 2.9.1842, 7.9.1842,

13.9.1842, 20.10.1842, 30.12.1842,
 9.2.1843, 18.4.1843, 23.12.1843,
 30.12.1843, 8.1.1844, 25.12.1844
Redhill – 3.12.1843
Retford – 11.11 1824, 14.4.1825, 29.9 1825,
 21.10.1825, 31.10.1825, 17.11.1825,
 11.2.1826, 9.6.1826, 31.1.1828,
 8.5.1829, 22.7.1830, 8.8.1830,
 16.8.1830, 23.5.1832, 5.8.1832,
 28.1.1834, 22.11.1834, 3.1.1835,
 4.1.1836, 15.1.1836, 28.12.1836,
 6.1.1840, 11.1.1841, 3.4.1841,
 12.4.1841, 22.5.1841, 3.6.1841,
 30.9.1842, 26.11.1842, 10.5.1843,
 6.10.1843, 23.10.1843, 1.2.1844,
 13.3.1844, 14.4.1845, 6.10,1845,
 8.10.1845, 11.4.1846, 10.1.1848,
 23.10.1848, 27.10.1848
Rufford – 18 10.1824, 16.5.1835, 20.2.1837,
 28.10.1840

S

Scratta Wood – 4.2.1841
Serlby – 8.10.1830, 27.1.1849
Shireoaks – 21.12.1838, 28.2.1840,
 7.10.1840, 13.4.1841, 19.2.1842,
 30.7.1849
Southwell – 31.10.1826, 1.11.1826,
 22.2.1836, 4.3.1839, 4.2.1840,
 21.4.1840, 29.10.1840, 13.1.1842,
 15.2.1842, 24.11.1842, 26.10.1843,
 16.11.1843, 7.12.1843, 24.10.1845,
 27.10.1848
Steetley – 24.6.1839, 27.11.1839, 3.1.1840,
 18.3.1840
Steetley Chapel – 19.2.1842
Stoke Hall – 18.1.1833, 11.1.1836,
 12.1.1836, 9.1.1839, 12.1.1839,
 7.1.1841, 10.1.1841
Sutton-in-Ashfield – 12.9.1838

T

Thoresby – 29.11 1823, 6.5.1825,
 22.10.1825, 17.1.1826, 11.11.1826,
 29.1.1827, 30.1.1827, 22.7.1827,
 23.11.1827, 12.10.1829, 8.7.1831,
 17.11.1837, 3.2.1838, 21.10.1840,
 14.12.1840, 12.1.1841, 31.12.1841,
 13.1.1842, 30.11.1843, 6.11.1846,
 29.12.1846, 29.3.1848, 9.10.1848
Thorpe – 6.11.1826
Thurgaton – 22.2.1836
Trent (River) – 10.1.1841
Tuxford – 10.2.1823, 3.8.1824, 14.9.1824,
 11.2.1826, 7.11.1827, 27 7.1830,
 11.9.1831, 12.3.1832, 23.5.1832,
 3.8.1832, 25.2.1833, 26.4.1834,
 26.8.1844, 10.6.1847, 11.6.1847,
 26.4.1848

W

Walesby – 6.3.1823, 26.3.1823, 18.10.1824, 5.8.1832, 2.7.1847, 19.7.1847

Walkeringham – 29.10.1827, 15.2.1836, 3.4.1841, 19.4.1846

Warsop – 19.1.1831

Watnall – 30.4.1831, 13.1.1840, 15.1.1840, 1.11.1848, 6.2.1849

Welbeck – 13.9.1824, 20.8.1832, 4.8.1837, 2.11.1838, 29.12.1839, 22.1.1840, 2.5.1844, 29.5.1844, 2.4.1846, 26.6.1847, 27.6.1847, 13.11.1847, 13.7.1848, 22.9.1848, 23.10.1848

Wellow – 20.1.1825, 29.5.1826, 7.11.1827, 28.8.1831, 19.7.1838, 26.3.1842

West Drayton – 22.11.1825

West Markham – 25.2.1824, 14.4.1824, 25.8.1824, 20.2.1831

Willoughby – 10.2.1823, 23.10.1826

Woodsetts – 3.11.1840

Worksop (Abbey – 'Priory') – 12.1.1841, 28.8.1844, 5.2.1846, 8.9.1847, 3.10.1847

Worksop (Agricultural Labourer's Friend Society) 24.10.1848, 25.10.1849

Worksop (Armed Association) – 14.5.1839

Worksop (boundaries) – 9.2.1838

Worksop Common – 8.4.1845

Worksop Corn Exchange – 7.12.1848

Worksop (elections) – 2.1.1835

Worksop (inhabitant's behaviour) – 20.9.1823, 14.9.1832, 15.12.1832, 11.1.1833

Worksop (magistrates) – 11.11.1840, 25.11.1840, 31.3.1841, 29.12.1841, 30.11.1842, 29.11.1843, 27.12.1843, 29.5.1844, 27.11.1844, 1.1.1845, 26.2.1845, 31.12.1845, 25.2.1846, 1.4.1846, 15.4.1846, 4.11.1846, 30.6.1847, 8.9.1847, 26.1.1848, 27.9.1848, 8.11.1848, 27.12.1848, 28.2.1849, 14.3.1849

Worksop (mail delivery) – 27.12.1836, 26.2.1848

Worksop Manor – 29.9.1824, 29.8.1832, 9.1.1833, 17.6.1837, 25.9.1837, 1.12.1837, 7.12.1837, 9.2.1838, 19.2.1838, 21.2.1838, 22.2.1838, 26.2.1838, 8.3.1838, 10.3.1838, 12.3.1838, 15.3.1838, 16.3.1838, 22.3.1838, 25.3.1838, 30.3.1838, 4.4.1838, 16.4.1838, 22.10.1838, 4.11.1838, 3.12.1838, 21.12.1838, 14.3.1839, 19.3.1839, 18.4.1839, 18.5.1839, 24.5.1839, 27.5.1839, 11.6.1839, 12.6.1839, 4.3.1840, 16.3.1840, 17.3.1840, 13.7.1840, 7.10.1840, 22.11.1840, 2.3.1841, 28.4.1841, 30.4.1841, 1.6.1841, 4.6.1841, 12.6.1841, 3.1.1843, 5.1.1843, 6.1.1843, 25.1.1843, 26.1.1843, 2.2.1843, 5.2.1843, 7.2.1843, 10.2.1843, 15.2.1843, 19.9.1843, 31.1.1844, 30.3.1844, 18.9.1844, 9.1.1847, 30.7.1849

Worksop (Manor Lodge) – 6.1.1843

Worksop (market) – 29.3.1843, 9.4.1845, 8.10.1845, 25.3.1846, 14.4.1847, 11.4.1849

Worksop (mining at Shireoaks?) – 2.6.1840

Worksop (miscellaneous) – 24.12.1830, 16.10.1831, 25.5.1839, 19.2.1842, 27.10.1843, 1.2.1844, 13.5.1846, 26.6.1847, 6.5.1848, 21.4.1849,

Worksop (musicians) – 22.12.1847, 7.1.1848, 6.9.1848

Worksop (Pestalozzian School) – 1.2.1848

Worksop (prize fighting) – 11.8.1847

Worksop (railway) – 13.3.1844, 26.12.1844, 21.10.1847, 30.7.1849, 7.9.1849

Worksop (R.C. chapel) – 21.2.1840, 10.3.1840

Worksop (schoolmaster) – 2.1.1839

Worksop (Sparken Hill) – 19.9.1842

Worksop (theatre) – 18.2.1840. 6.3.1840

Worksop (timber merchant) – 23.4.1838

Worksop (turnpike road to Ollerton) – 21.2.1823

INDEX FOUR
PLACES IN CLUMBER PARK

(a) CLUMBER HOUSE
(b) TERRACES, LAWNS &
     PLEASURE GROUNDS
(c) LAKE, BOATS AND BRIDGE
(d) PARK & FARMING

(a) **CLUMBER HOUSE**

Backstairs – 25.11.1849
Bedroom – 25.9.1832, 16.2.1843
Chapel – 25.12.1822, 9. 3.1823, 14.8.1825,
    25.12.1825, 25.12.1826, 25.12.1831,
    25.12.1838, 25.3.1842, 31.10.1844,
    25.12.1844, 10.1.1847, 24.3.1847,
    27.6.1847, 29.10.1848, 17.6.1849,
    7.10.1849, 30.12.1849
Courtyard – 7.1.1833, 9.1.1833, 12.1.1833,
    16.1.1833
Dining Room – 11.1.1833, 2.11.1838,
    16.12.1840, 7.1.1848
Drawing Room – 6.1.1832, 4.9.1833,
    12.9.1833, 9.10.1834, 30.12.1835,
    18.1.1836, 22.12.1837, 16.12.1840,
    7.9.1848
Evidence Room – 4.11.1823
Hall – 10.10.1848, 31.10.1848, 4.11.1848
Library – 1.3.1824, 9.10.1825, 15.8.1826,
    12.10.1826, 3.11.1826, 2.3.1829,
    9.10.1830, 16.10.1830, 28.10.1830,
    4.9.1833, 30.11.1835, 18.1.1836,
    28.1.1836, 2.11.1838, 12.10.1839,
    8.11.1839, 5.1.1847, 6.1.1847
Little Drawing Room – 16.12.1840
Marble Room – 9.10.1825
Museum – 6.10.1823

North Front – 20 10.1824
Nursery – 24.4.1824, 20.12.1825,
    19.7.1827
Roof – 7.1.1839
Siege preparations – 13/14.10.1831
Sitting Room – 30.1.1848
Staircase Windows – 4.11.1824
West Front – 2.1.1826

(b) **TERRACES, LAWNS & PLEASURE GROUNDS**

Colonnade – 27.3.1829, 17.8.1834
Conservatory – 22.9.1830
Fountains – 27.3.1829, 25.1.1839
Home Ground – 21.9.1849
Lawns – 19.1.1824, 25.10.1825, 17.2.1826,
    5.1.1829, 8.3.1829, 21.4.1829,
    18.3.1838, 5.4.1841, 24.3.1842,
    22.4.1844, 14.7.1847
Lincoln Terrace – 25.11.1845, 29.12.1845,
    15.1.1846, 14.3.1846, 29.11.1846
Pleasure Ground – 6.11.1823, 12.8.1825,
    29.6.1826, 29.3.1829, 30.3.1829,
    3.4.1829, 14.10.1831, 31.7.1832,
    31.12.1833, 18.3.1838, 16.3.1841,
    7.3.1842, 24.3.1842, 20.11.1843,
    16.1.1844, 23.8.1844, 25.2.1845,
    10.11.1845, 25.11.1845, 24.4.1846,
    21.4.1847, 14.7.1847, 25.7.1849,
    21.9.1849
Terraces – 19.1.1824, 28.1.1824,
    20.10.1824, 10.11.1824, 11.5.1825,
    12.9.1825, 15.8.1826, 3.11.1826,
    17.10.1827, 26.10.1827, 8.3.1830,
    19.3.1830, 27.3.1830, 29.3.1830,
    29.7.1832, 31.7.1832, 20.8.1833,
    17.8.1834, 24.7.1836, 25.1.1839,
    21.3.1842, 16.1.1844, 25.2.1845,
    10.10.1848, 24.7.1849

(c) **LAKE, BOATS & BRIDGE**

Boat House – 25.11.1845
Bridge – 14.3.1824, 10.3.1838, 2.4.1838,
    27.3.1847
Cascade – 23.10.1823, 18.12.1823,
    8.5.1835, 24.3.1837
Ferry – 25.2.1845
Lake – 12.10.1825, 12.11 1825, 2.2.1826,
    17.2.1826, 9.2 1827, 12.8.1828,
    13.10.1829, 20.2.1830, 21.2.1831,
    17.11.1831, 4.9.1832, 24.3.1837,
    6.4.1837, 16.2.1838, 28.11.1840,
    17.11.1841, 25.11.1842, 7.2.1843,
    16.1.1844, 10.6.1844, 6.12.1844,
    25.2.1845, 24.3.1845, 25.11.1845,
    6.4.1846, 6.5.1846, 16.5.1846,
    30.11.1846, 8.3.1847, 27.3.1847,
    21.4.1847, 13.7.1847, 8.1.1848
'Lincoln' frigate – 22.9.1830, 21.2.1831,
    23.2.1831, 5.8.1837, 12.11.1838,
    23.8.1844
Poulter (River) – 24.3.1845

(d) **PARK & FARMING**

Apley Head – 16.10.1824, 16.2.1838,
    18.3.1838, 2.4.1838, 20.1.1839,
    2.4.1839
Ash Tree Hill – 9.3.1849
Aviaries – [See 'Little Farm' below]
Boundaries – 5.8.1826, 7.10.1826,
    10.1.1827, 4.2.1827, 9.2.1838
Budby Corner – 31.1.1824, 26.11.1842
Budby Covan – 10.1.1827
Cabin Hill – 14.3.1824, 12.7.1826
Carburton Bridge – 2.4.1838, 2.4.1839
Carburton Fishpond – 7.3.1842
Carburton Lodge – 7.9.1826, 10.1.1827,
    10.3.1838
Clumber 'Park' Cottage – 13.10.1831
Clumber Park Lane – 15.3.1835,
    23.5.1835
Coal Supplies – 29.3.1844
Cow Pasture – 29.6.1826
Decoy – 6.3.1823, 23.1.1839, 4.1.1849
Engine House – 17.1 1825, 18.8.1825,
    25.8.1825
Farming – (arable) – 16.8.1833, 1.9.1833,
    30.4.1835, 16.8.1836, 30.9.1836,
    6.4.1837, 6.3.1838, 9.8.1838,
    14.8.1838, 15.4.1839, 20.4.1840,
    15.1.1843, 29.3.1843, 13.9.1843,
    30.7.1844, 15.8.1844, 23.8.1844,
    27.8.1844, 5.10.1845, 17.3.1846,
    25.3.1846, 12.7.1846, 7.7.1847,

12.8.1847, 16.8.1847, 19.8.1847,
    23.8.1847, 9.10.1847, 31.7.1848,
    22.8.1849, 29.8.1849
Farming – (livestock) – 15.9.1834,
    31.3.1836, 23.5.1836, 25.12.1836,
    2.1.1837, 6.1.1837, 27.3.1837,
    6.10.1837, 13.11.1840, 24.11.1840,
    30.11.1840, 25.7.1841, 8.11.1841,
    23.3.1842, 22.9.1842, 23.9.1842,
    21.3.1843, 24.3.1843, 26.2.1844,
    10.3.1844, 18.3.1844, 22.4.1844,
    15.3.1845, 16.3.1845, 9.4.1845,
    13.4.1845, 6.5.1845, 29.5.1845,
    4.5.1846, 15.3.1847, 28.3.1847,
    14.4.1847, 27.2.1849, 1.4.1849,
    11.4.1849
Flag Pole – 9.3.1844
Five Thorns Plantation – 26.11.1842
Gardens – 10.8.1833, 27.2.1834,
    20.3.1834, 27.6.1842
Grotto – 18.8.1825, 25.8.1825, 24.10.1825
Hardwick – 8.1.1825, 23.2.1828,
    24.12.1830, 21.8.1831, 2.4.1838,
    6.4.1841, 22.9.1842, 26.11.1842,
    14.4.1845, 15.4.1845, 4.5.1846,
    9.10.1847, 1.4.1849
Ice House(s) – 11.1.1838, 7.12.1846
Lady Garden – 10.3.1826, 25.8.1827,
    11.8.1837
Lime Tree Avenue – 16.2.1838, 18.3.1838,
    2.4.1838
'Little Farm' – 6.1.1825, 1.10.1827,
    5.2.1843, 6.1.1845
Paddocks – 3.11.1842
Park Lane – 20.11.1845
Roads – 25.10.1825, 28.10.1825, 6.11.1825,
    27.2.1833, 15.3.1835, 10.3.1838,
    2.4.1838, 1.3.1841
Rock Garden – 17.2.1826
Stables – 18.11.1824, 2.7.1825, 29.8.1826,
    28.6.1842, 3.11.1842, 6.10.1845,
    28.5.1849, 2.6.1849, 27.7.1849
Stone Temple – 4.3.1832, 27.3.1847
Thoresby Lodge – 14.7.1824, 12.8.1824,
    14.8.1824, 17.2.1826
Trees – 12.11.1825, 2.10.1824, 14.1.1827,
    12.7.1827, 1.5.1829, 3.4.1830,
    21.4.1830, 23.4.1830, 21.8.1831,
    14.2.1833, 2.12.1833, 31.12.1833,
    3.1.1834, 6.1.1834, 27.2.1834,
    2.3.1834, 8.3.1834, 20.5.1836,
    24.12.1836, 20.10.1838, 7.1.1839,
    20.1.1839, 1.4.1839, 15.4.1839,
    24.2.1840, 23.4.1840, 5.4.1841,
    21.4.1841, 29.5.1841, 26.6.1842,
    6.11.1842, 20.3.1843, 28.3.1843,

20.11.1843, 20.12.1843, 12.1.1845,
4.3.1845, 24.3.1845, 30.4.1845,
25.11.1845, 29.11.1846, 9.3.1847,
10.3.1847, 27.3.1848, 26.2.1849,
27.2.1849, 25.7.1849, 21.9.1849

Truman's Lodge – 7.9.1826, 10.1.1827,
  11.1.1833
Water Engine – 3.11.1826, 25.11.1842
West Fields – 14.10.1826, 2.4.1839
Young Lords' Garden – 8.1.1825,
  17.1.1825, 12.8.1828